Lecture Notes in Computer Science 14713

Founding Editors

Gerhard Goos

Juris Hartmanis

Editorial Board Members

The series Lecture Notes in Computer Science (LNCS), including its subseries Lecture Notes in Artificial Intelligence (LNAI) and Lecture Notes in Bioinformatics (LNBI), has established itself as a medium for the publication of new developments in computer science and information technology research, teaching, and education.

LNCS enjoys close cooperation with the computer science R & D community, the series counts many renowned academics among its volume editors and paper authors, and collaborates with prestigious societies. Its mission is to serve this international community by providing an invaluable service, mainly focused on the publication of conference and workshop proceedings and postproceedings. LNCS commenced publication in 1973.

Aaron Marcus · Elizabeth Rosenzweig ·
Marcelo M. Soares
Editors

Design, User Experience, and Usability

13th International Conference, DUXU 2024
Held as Part of the 26th HCI International Conference, HCII 2024
Washington, DC, USA, June 29 – July 4, 2024
Proceedings, Part II

 Springer

Editors
Aaron Marcus
Principal
Aaron Marcus and Associates
Berkeley, CA, USA

Elizabeth Rosenzweig
World Usability Day and Bubble Mountain
Newton Center, MA, USA

Marcelo M. Soares
Federal University of Pernambuco
Recife, Pernambuco, Brazil

ISSN 0302-9743   ISSN 1611-3349 (electronic)
Lecture Notes in Computer Science
ISBN 978-3-031-61352-4   ISBN 978-3-031-61353-1 (eBook)
https://doi.org/10.1007/978-3-031-61353-1

This Springer imprint is published by the registered company Springer Nature Switzerland AG
The registered company address is: Gewerbestrasse 11, 6330 Cham, Switzerland

If disposing of this product, please recycle the paper.

Foreword

This year we celebrate 40 years since the establishment of the HCI International (HCII) Conference, which has been a hub for presenting groundbreaking research and novel ideas and collaboration for people from all over the world.

The HCII conference was founded in 1984 by Prof. Gavriel Salvendy (Purdue University, USA, Tsinghua University, P.R. China, and University of Central Florida, USA) and the first event of the series, "1st USA-Japan Conference on Human-Computer Interaction", was held in Honolulu, Hawaii, USA, 18–20 August. Since then, HCI International is held jointly with several Thematic Areas and Affiliated Conferences, with each one under the auspices of a distinguished international Program Board and under one management and one registration. Twenty-six HCI International Conferences have been organized so far (every two years until 2013, and annually thereafter).

Over the years, this conference has served as a platform for scholars, researchers, industry experts and students to exchange ideas, connect, and address challenges in the ever-evolving HCI field. Throughout these 40 years, the conference has evolved itself, adapting to new technologies and emerging trends, while staying committed to its core mission of advancing knowledge and driving change.

As we celebrate this milestone anniversary, we reflect on the contributions of its founding members and appreciate the commitment of its current and past Affiliated Conference Program Board Chairs and members. We are also thankful to all past conference attendees who have shaped this community into what it is today.

The 26th International Conference on Human-Computer Interaction, HCI International 2024 (HCII 2024), was held as a 'hybrid' event at the Washington Hilton Hotel, Washington, DC, USA, during 29 June – 4 July 2024. It incorporated the 21 thematic areas and affiliated conferences listed below.

A total of 5108 individuals from academia, research institutes, industry, and government agencies from 85 countries submitted contributions, and 1271 papers and 309 posters were included in the volumes of the proceedings that were published just before the start of the conference, these are listed below. The contributions thoroughly cover the entire field of human-computer interaction, addressing major advances in knowledge and effective use of computers in a variety of application areas. These papers provide academics, researchers, engineers, scientists, practitioners and students with state-of-the-art information on the most recent advances in HCI.

The HCI International (HCII) conference also offers the option of presenting 'Late Breaking Work', and this applies both for papers and posters, with corresponding volumes of proceedings that will be published after the conference. Full papers will be included in the 'HCII 2024 - Late Breaking Papers' volumes of the proceedings to be published in the Springer LNCS series, while 'Poster Extended Abstracts' will be included as short research papers in the 'HCII 2024 - Late Breaking Posters' volumes to be published in the Springer CCIS series.

I would like to thank the Program Board Chairs and the members of the Program Boards of all thematic areas and affiliated conferences for their contribution towards the high scientific quality and overall success of the HCI International 2024 conference. Their manifold support in terms of paper reviewing (single-blind review process, with a minimum of two reviews per submission), session organization and their willingness to act as goodwill ambassadors for the conference is most highly appreciated.

This conference would not have been possible without the continuous and unwavering support and advice of Gavriel Salvendy, founder, General Chair Emeritus, and Scientific Advisor. For his outstanding efforts, I would like to express my sincere appreciation to Abbas Moallem, Communications Chair and Editor of HCI International News.

July 2024   Constantine Stephanidis

HCI International 2024 Thematic Areas
and Affiliated Conferences

- HCI: Human-Computer Interaction Thematic Area
- HIMI: Human Interface and the Management of Information Thematic Area
- EPCE: 21st International Conference on Engineering Psychology and Cognitive Ergonomics
- AC: 18th International Conference on Augmented Cognition
- UAHCI: 18th International Conference on Universal Access in Human-Computer Interaction
- CCD: 16th International Conference on Cross-Cultural Design
- SCSM: 16th International Conference on Social Computing and Social Media
- VAMR: 16th International Conference on Virtual, Augmented and Mixed Reality
- DHM: 15th International Conference on Digital Human Modeling & Applications in Health, Safety, Ergonomics & Risk Management
- DUXU: 13th International Conference on Design, User Experience and Usability
- C&C: 12th International Conference on Culture and Computing
- DAPI: 12th International Conference on Distributed, Ambient and Pervasive Interactions
- HCIBGO: 11th International Conference on HCI in Business, Government and Organizations
- LCT: 11th International Conference on Learning and Collaboration Technologies
- ITAP: 10th International Conference on Human Aspects of IT for the Aged Population
- AIS: 6th International Conference on Adaptive Instructional Systems
- HCI-CPT: 6th International Conference on HCI for Cybersecurity, Privacy and Trust
- HCI-Games: 6th International Conference on HCI in Games
- MobiTAS: 6th International Conference on HCI in Mobility, Transport and Automotive Systems
- AI-HCI: 5th International Conference on Artificial Intelligence in HCI
- MOBILE: 5th International Conference on Human-Centered Design, Operation and Evaluation of Mobile Communications

List of Conference Proceedings Volumes Appearing Before the Conference

1. LNCS 14684, Human-Computer Interaction: Part I, edited by Masaaki Kurosu and Ayako Hashizume
2. LNCS 14685, Human-Computer Interaction: Part II, edited by Masaaki Kurosu and Ayako Hashizume
3. LNCS 14686, Human-Computer Interaction: Part III, edited by Masaaki Kurosu and Ayako Hashizume
4. LNCS 14687, Human-Computer Interaction: Part IV, edited by Masaaki Kurosu and Ayako Hashizume
5. LNCS 14688, Human-Computer Interaction: Part V, edited by Masaaki Kurosu and Ayako Hashizume
6. LNCS 14689, Human Interface and the Management of Information: Part I, edited by Hirohiko Mori and Yumi Asahi
7. LNCS 14690, Human Interface and the Management of Information: Part II, edited by Hirohiko Mori and Yumi Asahi
8. LNCS 14691, Human Interface and the Management of Information: Part III, edited by Hirohiko Mori and Yumi Asahi
9. LNAI 14692, Engineering Psychology and Cognitive Ergonomics: Part I, edited by Don Harris and Wen-Chin Li
10. LNAI 14693, Engineering Psychology and Cognitive Ergonomics: Part II, edited by Don Harris and Wen-Chin Li
11. LNAI 14694, Augmented Cognition, Part I, edited by Dylan D. Schmorrow and Cali M. Fidopiastis
12. LNAI 14695, Augmented Cognition, Part II, edited by Dylan D. Schmorrow and Cali M. Fidopiastis
13. LNCS 14696, Universal Access in Human-Computer Interaction: Part I, edited by Margherita Antona and Constantine Stephanidis
14. LNCS 14697, Universal Access in Human-Computer Interaction: Part II, edited by Margherita Antona and Constantine Stephanidis
15. LNCS 14698, Universal Access in Human-Computer Interaction: Part III, edited by Margherita Antona and Constantine Stephanidis
16. LNCS 14699, Cross-Cultural Design: Part I, edited by Pei-Luen Patrick Rau
17. LNCS 14700, Cross-Cultural Design: Part II, edited by Pei-Luen Patrick Rau
18. LNCS 14701, Cross-Cultural Design: Part III, edited by Pei-Luen Patrick Rau
19. LNCS 14702, Cross-Cultural Design: Part IV, edited by Pei-Luen Patrick Rau
20. LNCS 14703, Social Computing and Social Media: Part I, edited by Adela Coman and Simona Vasilache
21. LNCS 14704, Social Computing and Social Media: Part II, edited by Adela Coman and Simona Vasilache
22. LNCS 14705, Social Computing and Social Media: Part III, edited by Adela Coman and Simona Vasilache

47. LNCS 14730, HCI in Games: Part I, edited by Xiaowen Fang
48. LNCS 14731, HCI in Games: Part II, edited by Xiaowen Fang
49. LNCS 14732, HCI in Mobility, Transport and Automotive Systems: Part I, edited by Heidi Krömker
50. LNCS 14733, HCI in Mobility, Transport and Automotive Systems: Part II, edited by Heidi Krömker
51. LNAI 14734, Artificial Intelligence in HCI: Part I, edited by Helmut Degen and Stavroula Ntoa
52. LNAI 14735, Artificial Intelligence in HCI: Part II, edited by Helmut Degen and Stavroula Ntoa
53. LNAI 14736, Artificial Intelligence in HCI: Part III, edited by Helmut Degen and Stavroula Ntoa
54. LNCS 14737, Design, Operation and Evaluation of Mobile Communications: Part I, edited by June Wei and George Margetis
55. LNCS 14738, Design, Operation and Evaluation of Mobile Communications: Part II, edited by June Wei and George Margetis
56. CCIS 2114, HCI International 2024 Posters - Part I, edited by Constantine Stephanidis, Margherita Antona, Stavroula Ntoa and Gavriel Salvendy
57. CCIS 2115, HCI International 2024 Posters - Part II, edited by Constantine Stephanidis, Margherita Antona, Stavroula Ntoa and Gavriel Salvendy
58. CCIS 2116, HCI International 2024 Posters - Part III, edited by Constantine Stephanidis, Margherita Antona, Stavroula Ntoa and Gavriel Salvendy
59. CCIS 2117, HCI International 2024 Posters - Part IV, edited by Constantine Stephanidis, Margherita Antona, Stavroula Ntoa and Gavriel Salvendy
60. CCIS 2118, HCI International 2024 Posters - Part V, edited by Constantine Stephanidis, Margherita Antona, Stavroula Ntoa and Gavriel Salvendy
61. CCIS 2119, HCI International 2024 Posters - Part VI, edited by Constantine Stephanidis, Margherita Antona, Stavroula Ntoa and Gavriel Salvendy
62. CCIS 2120, HCI International 2024 Posters - Part VII, edited by Constantine Stephanidis, Margherita Antona, Stavroula Ntoa and Gavriel Salvendy

https://2024.hci.international/proceedings

Preface

User experience (UX) refers to a person's thoughts, feelings, and behavior when using interactive systems. UX design becomes fundamentally important for new and emerging mobile, ubiquitous, and omnipresent computer-based contexts. The scope of design, user experience, and usability (DUXU) extends to all aspects of the user's interaction with a product or service, how it is perceived, learned, and used. DUXU also addresses design knowledge, methods, and practices, with a focus on deeply human-centered processes. Usability, usefulness, and appeal are fundamental requirements for effective user-experience design.

The 13th Design, User Experience, and Usability Conference (DUXU 2024), an affiliated conference of the HCI International conference, encouraged papers from professionals, academics, and researchers that report results and cover a broad range of research and development activities on a variety of related topics. Professionals include designers, software engineers, scientists, marketers, business leaders, and practitioners in fields such as AI, architecture, financial and wealth management, game design, graphic design, finance, healthcare, industrial design, mobile, psychology, travel, and vehicles.

This year's submissions covered a wide range of content across the spectrum of design, user-experience, and usability. The latest trends and technologies are represented, as well as contributions from professionals, academics, and researchers across the globe. The breadth of their work is indicated in the following topics covered in the proceedings, encompassing theoretical work, applied research across diverse application domains, UX studies, as well as discussions on contemporary technologies that reshape our interactions with computational products and services.

Five volumes of the HCII 2024 proceedings are dedicated to this year's edition of the DUXU Conference, covering topics related to:

- Information Visualization and Interaction Design, as well as Usability Testing and User Experience Evaluation;
- Designing Interactions for Intelligent Environments; Automotive Interactions and Smart Mobility Solutions; Speculative Design and Creativity;
- User Experience Design for Inclusion and Diversity; Human-Centered Design for Social Impact.
- Designing Immersive Experiences Across Contexts; Technology, Design, and Learner Engagement; User Experience in Tangible and Intangible Cultural Heritage;
- Innovative Design for Enhanced User Experience; Innovations in Product and Service Design.

The papers in these volumes were accepted for publication after a minimum of two single-blind reviews from the members of the DUXU Program Board or, in some cases, from Preface members of the Program Boards of other affiliated conferences. We would like to thank all of them for their invaluable contribution, support, and efforts.

July 2024

Aaron Marcus
Elizabeth Rosenzweig
Marcelo M. Soares

13th International Conference on Design, User Experience and Usability (DUXU 2024)

Program Board Chairs: **Aaron Marcus,** *Aaron Marcus and Associates, USA,* **Elizabeth Rosenzweig,** *World Usability Day and Bubble Mountain Consulting, USA* and **Marcelo M. Soares,** *Federal University of Pernambuco, Brazil*

- Sisira Adikari, *University of Canberra, Australia*
- Ahmad Alhuwwari, *Orange Jordan, Jordan*
- Claire Ancient, *University of Winchester, UK*
- Eric Brangier, *Université de Lorraine, France*
- Lorenzo Cantoni, *USI - Università della Svizzera italiana, Switzerland*
- Silvia De los Rios, *Indra, Spain*
- Romi Dey, *Solved by Design, India*
- Marc Fabri, *Leeds Beckett University, UK*
- Michael R. Gibson, *The University of North Texas, USA*
- Zaiyan Gong, *Tongji University, P.R. China*
- Hao He, *Central Academy of Fine Arts, P.R. China*
- Ao Jiang, *Nanjing University of Aeronautics and Astronautics, P.R. China*
- Hannu Karvonen, *VTT Technical Research Centre of Finland Ltd., Finland*
- Zhen Liu, *South China University of Technology, P.R. China*
- Wei Liu, *Beijing Normal University, P.R. China*
- Ricardo Gregorio Lugo, *Tallinn University of Technology, Estonia*
- Keith Owens, *University of North Texas, USA*
- Francisco Rebelo, *University of Lisbon, Portugal*
- Christine Riedmann-Streitz, *MarkenFactory GmbH, Germany*
- Patricia Search, *Rensselaer Polytechnic Institute, USA*
- Dorothy Shamonsky, *Brandeis University, USA*
- Qi Tan, *Central Academy of Fine Arts, P.R. China*
- Ana Velhinho, *University of Aveiro - Digimedia, Portugal*
- Elisangela Vilar, *University of Lisbon, Portugal*
- Wei Wang, *Hunan University, P.R. China*

The full list with the Program Board Chairs and the members of the Program Boards of all thematic areas and affiliated conferences of HCII 2024 is available online at:

http://www.hci.international/board-members-2024.php

HCI International 2025 Conference

The 27th International Conference on Human-Computer Interaction, HCI International 2025, will be held jointly with the affiliated conferences at the Swedish Exhibition & Congress Centre and Gothia Towers Hotel, Gothenburg, Sweden, June 22–27, 2025. It will cover a broad spectrum of themes related to Human-Computer Interaction, including theoretical issues, methods, tools, processes, and case studies in HCI design, as well as novel interaction techniques, interfaces, and applications. The proceedings will be published by Springer. More information will become available on the conference website: https://2025.hci.international/.

General Chair
Prof. Constantine Stephanidis
University of Crete and ICS-FORTH
Heraklion, Crete, Greece
Email: general_chair@2025.hci.international

https://2025.hci.international/

Contents – Part II

Speculative Design and Creativity

Designing Interactions for Intelligent Environments

Exploring a Behavioral Model of "Positive Friction" in Human-AI Interaction

Zeya Chen(✉)⬛ and Ruth Schmidt⬛

Institute of Design, Illinois Institute of Technology, Chicago, IL 60616, USA
zchen103@id.iit.edu

Abstract. Designing seamless, frictionless user experiences has long been a dominant trend in both applied behavioral science and artificial intelligence (AI), in which the goal of making desirable actions easy and efficient informs efforts to minimize friction in user experiences. However, in some settings, friction can be genuinely beneficial, such as the insertion of deliberate delays to increase reflection, preventing individuals from resorting to automatic or biased behaviors, and enhancing opportunities for unexpected discoveries. More recently, the popularization and availability of AI on a widespread scale has only increased the need to examine how friction can help or hinder users of AI; it also suggests a need to consider how positive friction can benefit AI practitioners, both during development processes (e.g., working with diverse teams) and to inform how AI is designed into offerings. This paper first proposes a 'positive friction' model that can help characterize how friction is currently beneficial in user and developer experiences with AI, diagnose the potential need for friction where it may not yet exist in these contexts, and inform how positive friction can be used to generate solutions, especially as advances in AI continue to be progress and new opportunities emerge. It then explores this model in the context of AI users and developers by proposing the value of taking a hybrid 'AI+human' lens, and concludes by suggesting questions for further exploration.

Keywords: Friction · Behavioral design · Artificial intelligence · Behavioral Science · Human-AI interaction

1 Introduction

There is often an underlying presumption when designing for behavioral change that friction is bad, reinforced by advice to 'make it easy' or otherwise reduce behavioral barriers as a relatively low-cost, minimally intrusive way to help people act in their own best interests [63]. However, seeing friction as uniformly undesirable is too simple. While many applications of 'make it easy' remain useful and valid, too much ease can escalate issues of self-control or impulsive behavior [10]. Further still, judicious and intentional addition of friction can productively slow down behaviors in a variety of ways, whether by interrupting autopilot behaviors, "cooling off" hot-state decisions through tactics such as waiting periods, or building confidence or rapport by prioritizing interactions over automated efficiency [53].

A. Marcus et al. (Eds.): HCII 2024, LNCS 14713, pp. 3–22, 2024.
https://doi.org/10.1007/978-3-031-61353-1_1

Purely from a behavioral perspective, therefore, systematically examining how and when friction can yield positive benefits can be useful in situations when speed or convenience tend to dominate problem-solving attention. This is especially pertinent for generative AI and machine learning (ML) platforms and tools, whose recent proliferation has surfaced a new set of tensions between efficiency and reflection both for users and developers of these offerings. This paper first positions the use of friction in a broader behavioral context and presents a behavioral framework that breaks positive friction into various forms. It then applies this framework to real-world examples to illustrate how friction can play a role in AI-informed systems and human-AI interactions (HAI) through characterization, diagnostic, and generative modes, and concludes by proposing future directions.

2   Behavioral Design in Human-AI Interaction

The field of behavioral science is often underrepresented in HAI studies, particularly compared to the focus on persuasive technologies in Human-Computer Interaction (HCI) research [13,30]. Where persuasive technologies primarily aim to alter or influence human behavior through technological and design principles [18], behavioral science encompasses a broader spectrum of disciplines that pulls from psychology, sociology, and economics to understand human decision-making and behavior, and use these insights to design intervention environments [66]. This concept of "behavioral design" merges behavioral science with design research to address complex challenges, emphasizing problem framing before solution development to transcend traditional product-centric design and envision broader interaction experiences, choice environments, and cultural contexts [51].

However, behavioral research is increasingly seen as supplying a valuable perspective on understanding and designing for the dynamics of AI within broader socio-technical systems in Human-AI Interaction contexts. Where behavioral science historically has concerned itself exclusively with human behavior, contemporary HAI perspectives that emphasize viewing AI as interactive agents rather than mere technological artifacts underscore the importance of applying a behavioral lens to study their behavioral patterns [40]. Recent HCI scholarly debates regarding AI anthropomorphism also advocate for a balanced behavioral understanding in AI development that bridges ethical responsibility and the synergies between human and non-human intelligence [59]. This more systemic and behaviorally-informed approach to AI/human hybrid activities positions it as a promising direction for addressing the increasingly complex, adaptive nature of human-AI interactions within structures, challenging researchers to ensure AI is integrated thoughtfully into these systems.

Therefore, this research positions AI as interactive intelligent agents within socio-technical systems, going beyond traditional computing roles to emphasize its dynamic role in reshaping interactions and solving problems, echoing scholars like Mills [40] and Shneiderman [54]. By embracing a behavioral design perspective, we aim to ensure AI's ethical integration into society, fostering responsible interactions between humans and AI.

3   A Model for Positive Friction

Friction-reducing strategies and 'nudges' include examples such as the Save More Tomorrow (SMarT) program, which leverages human tendencies toward effort aversion by requiring a user to deliberately opt out of auto-enrollment and uses default settings to remove the need to explicitly make a choice [62]. Similarly, studies have found that healthcare behaviors such as getting flu shots or vaccinations can also benefit from reducing behavioral friction in the form of just-in-time targeted information through text messages [9]. But making hard things too easy can result in an inability to exercise self-control. Amazon's unquestionably convenient One-Click feature removes useful pause points from online shopping, which can easily result in impulsive purchases [23]. Similarly, waiting periods serve the useful purpose of forcing us to reflect, even if briefly, before committing to a path of action [36]. At a systems scale, an absence of friction can have significant negative effects when individual actions aggregate into critical mass movements, such as when easy access to credit and mortgage loans resulted in 2009's real estate market crash and spate of underwater mortgages, in which property owners found themselves saddled with properties that were worth less than the mortgage they owed [53].

However, positive friction is not a one-size-fits-all proposition. Introducing behavioral speed bumps can provide a stalling mechanism for impulsive behavior, but it can also interrupt auto-pilot behaviors, highlight opportunities or information that might otherwise be overlooked, and provide important feedback [38]. Looking beyond efficiency can also reveal alternative forms of value, as when the comparatively inefficient mode of train travel reframes getting from Point A to Point B into an experiential benefit compared to traveling by air [11].

Breaking down the forces behind positive behavioral friction into two opposing axes—inhibiting vs. stimulating actions and goal-based, intentional motivations vs. expanding to see new possibilities—can help differentiate these various forms (Fig. 1). Below, we briefly explain each quadrant and provide examples before exploring how positive friction manifests in a generative AI context.

3.1   Saving Me from Myself: Increasing Self-control to Achieve Goals

Self-control is a well-known behavioral challenge across a wide variety of settings, including healthcare, purchasing, and social interactions, in which individuals struggle to overcome "hot state" temptations if even their more reticent "cold state" selves fully know the downsides of impulsive behaviors [34]. As a result, 'save me from myself' interventions that intentionally insert logistical, physical, or temporal friction can curtail impulsive tendencies and interrupt undesirable behaviors. These cases of self-control are characterized by clear goals and concrete motivation to change, which can be strategically leveraged by behavioral designers to help individuals avoid temptation. Tactics to help people resist doing things they know they should not may include limiting access to content

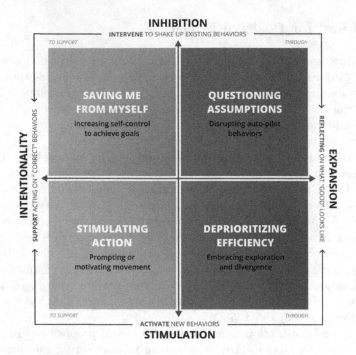

Fig. 1. Mapping dimensions of positive friction as activities in service of inhibition vs. stimulation against resultant intentionality vs. expansion of purpose.

or engagement, such as reducing product features; imposing timeouts or waiting periods to dampen impulsive actions; adding layers of social accountability or oversight; or introducing self-imposed de-escalation techniques to modulate behavior.

3.2   Questioning Assumptions: Disrupting Auto-pilot Behaviors

A second form of positive friction is less concerned with promoting self-control over impulsive behavior than overcoming personal 'cruise control' that numbs, rather than heightens, impulses in the form of subconscious or autopilot behaviors. While autopilot behaviors can helpfully reduce cognitive effort, they can lead to tuning out important environmental signals or overlooking opportunities to deviate from the norm even in instances where this may be beneficial. In this case, positive friction may be less oriented toward eliciting a specific preferred outcome, and more toward introducing a greater openness and attention to a full range of options. Behavioral tactics to broaden individuals' active attention and receptivity to inputs include examples such as modal dialog boxes that prompt reflection before quitting applications, strategies for 'inoculating' individuals against disinformation by pre-empting their exposure to false news [50] or disfluency techniques that employ intentionally malformed fonts to slow the pace of information processing [3].

3.3 Stimulating Action: Prompting or Motivating Movement

In addition to dampening tendencies toward impulsive or autopilot behaviors, positive friction can also be used to stimulate or encourage new behaviors by providing prompts that energize individuals to take action. This can be especially helpful in cases where adopting good behaviors is challenging due to effort aversion or where an abstract promise of logical gains (e.g., "good health," "sustainability") does not supply sufficient motivation. In this case, strategies that employ social norms—such as commitment contracts—can serve as forcing mechanisms to stimulate behaviors by increasing external sources of accountability [17]. Behavioral activation can also occur through increasing the concreteness of both actions and potential benefits; for example, where novel or highly experiential activities can increase engagement by motivating action, focusing on specific stories or individuals, known as the identifiable victim (or actor) effect, can help us overcome the malaise of generic data [20, 31].

3.4 Deprioritizing Efficiency: Embracing Exploration and Divergence

Finally, broad societal tendencies to valorize efficiency often encourage solutions that generate maximal value for minimal effort. However, this can lead to over-indexing on speed and precision over other valuable outcomes and overlook possibilities to create or recognize new forms of value [53]. Positive friction that disrupts efficiency in productive ways can play an important role in reframing the value of experiences and heightening opportunities to capture these benefits. Behavioral theorists have suggested that amplifying alternative and qualitative aspects of an experience, rather than relying only on quantifiable indicators, can help surface new forms of value and overcome default tendencies toward efficiency. These can include instances of 'stealth health' seen in Pokemon Go, in which the motivation to exercise is subsumed into gameplay [29], or in activities that intentionally cater to alternative values, such as slow lanes in grocery stores that convert transactional activities into social opportunities [42].

4   Positive Friction and AI

Despite the widespread application of positive friction in digital environments to tackle specific behavioral challenges—e.g., "save me from myself" interventions in the case of self-control or impulsive behavior—none of these forms of friction are correlated with or constrained by delivery mechanism; in other words, positive friction is technology-agnostic. However, the specific attributes and complexity of AI technologies' development, problem-solving settings, and opportunities for application make it an especially important area of inquiry. Having laid out the general behavioral positive friction model above, below we suggest how it can inform the design and deployment of AI-informed technology.

4.1   Current Research on Friction in AI

Many companies now rely on AI as a key component of solutions to craft seamless, personalized experiences and reduce barriers that impede customer journey efficiency [14]. For instance, Facebook's recent launch of AI-powered "smart glasses" provides an example of "ultra-low-friction input" that enables users to remain effortlessly connected [27]. Retail giants like Amazon, Aldi, and Hudson have also embraced frictionless shopping models, allowing customers to bypass traditional checkout lines [35]; similarly, in the transportation sector, Hitachi and Genfare have experimented with frictionless mobility with AI-based traffic management to optimize traffic flow, reduce congestion, and expedite travel times [22,64].

While the trend of "frictionless" AI and machine learning solutions brings certain advantages, it also introduces significant risks, related to privacy concerns, potential amplification of algorithmic biases, intellectual property issues, and ethical challenges. Tendencies such as algorithm appreciation bias, which reveals a preference for algorithmic advice over human input in certain situations, regardless of the transparency of the algorithm [35,48] can lead to overreliance on AI, and underscore the potential pitfalls of excessive appreciation of AI advice in the absence of critical safeguards. These tendencies may be particularly important to consider in light of findings from fields concerned with human cognition that integrate neural and symbolic methods to distinguish between quick, instinctive 'System 1' human processing of information and the slower, more thoughtful 'System 2' [21]. While current trends in AI development show a preference for the rapid responses characteristic of 'System 1', favoring technologies that offer immediate, effortless solutions, recent proposals have reintroduced interest in specific types of friction to encourage reflection, conflict, and care in AI systems, essentially integrating slower and more reflective 'System 2'-oriented thinking [49].

Research into algorithm appreciation, cognitive ease, and strain has informed investigations into the intentional use and design of positive friction across various AI-informed domains and challenges. These include examining computational friction on XAI's interface to calibrate users' trust in the AI system [43]; the use of friction as a cognitive tool to foster the civility of online discourse against false algorithmic information [25]; how friction can inform 'micro-moments' of human-computer interaction in impulsive and reflective behavioral perspectives [8]; and the value of positive friction by Contestational Design for civic engagement [24]. Expanding on these experiments and findings from the perspective of strategic behavioral design can help inform and enrich the design of future AI-empowered products and service systems.

4.2   Exploring the Beneficiaries of Positive Friction in AI

While designers and developers can build on a long tradition of removing and employing friction in products and services, the widespread and embedded nature of AI in consumer offerings has increased both the need and the stakes to consider the role—and intentional incorporation—of friction in AI solutions. Just as instances of positive friction designed into offerings can target end-user or consumer behaviors to encourage self-regulatory behaviors and cultivate beneficial habits [47], AI practitioners can also benefit from behavioral speed bumps during the design and development of AI-enabled solutions by productively slowing down or interrupting design processes or inserting opportunities to identify and rectify biases that algorithms may perpetuate (Table 1). However, the specific application of positive friction for both users and developers of AI may differ, depending on the nature of the situation or the intended goal.

In addition, different stakeholders may have diverse interactions, values, and contexts of use that require different strategies and considerations for when, why, and for whom positive friction is used. This parallels findings in the recent AI-related socio-technical research highlighting the significance of clearly defining and considering not only multiple stakeholder groups, including those who contribute to, develop, deploy, and consume or are otherwise affected by AI, but by development stages—such as data collection, training, model evaluation and analysis, and system deployment—when developing AI regulatory oversight [41].

Considering positive friction at multiple levels can yield improved products and experiences, as illustrated through two examples of 'X' (formerly known as Twitter). The "Read before you post" feature [58] applies positive friction as a social media safeguard to deter impulsive sharing of misinformation or harmful content. While this feature effectively shields some participants from harmful or deceptive information, its impact is limited to resharing and replying by users. As a result, the use of friction is reactive rather than preventive given that it does not extend to the creators of harmful content or the biased algorithms that promote such content.

In contrast, 'X's' Algorithmic Bias Bounty Challenge [7] represents an example of employing positive friction more proactively by managing misinformation closer to its origination by targeting AI developers [7]. In this case, the Challenge founders shared 'X's' saliency algorithm (also known as Twiitter's image cropping algorithm), making their code available for participants in order to reproduce and examine bias issues in the algorithms at DEFCON, a prominent hacker conference [7]. The results of this challenge showed that participating hackers succeeded in revealing several hidden biases inside 'X's' AI systems for future debugs, including but not limited to encoded stereotypical beauty standards, algorithmic preferences for certain race features, and linguistic biases [70].

Unlike the purely user-focused "Read before you post" feature, the Bounty Challenge introduced friction within the platform itself; this not only prompted AI developers to reassess and refine machine functions, but also proactively addressed AI algorithmic issues in advance rather than designing positive friction features that users would need to use reactively. While both examples share the objective of fostering a less biased and more inclusive online environment, their differences illustrate how effective use of positive friction in an AI context not only can affect different stakeholders in varying contexts but highlight that different forms of positive friction serve distinct roles. Identifying relevant stakeholder groups can help designers better understand the benefits, harms, and risks presented by different

Table 1. Illustrative examples of positive friction in AI end-user and practitioner contexts

	Positive Friction for AI Users	Positive Friction for AI Practitioners
Saving me from myself: Increasing self-control to achieve goals	– ChatGPT's cautionary message under its input box encourages users to verify information, reducing over-reliance on AI [45]. – X (formerly Twitter)'s "Read before you post" feature aims to prevent impulsive sharing of misinformation or harmful content [58].	– Adobe's diverse design team acts as a safeguard, testing Adobe Firefly's outputs to prevent stereotypical imagery and enhance data diversity [1].
Questioning assumptions: Disrupting auto-pilot behaviors	– Grammarly's feature that highlights gender pronouns in AI-assisted writing helps prevent unconscious misuse of "he/she/they" [69]. – Studies show that news recommendation AI with 'opposing views' features can break echo chambers by suggesting diverse viewpoints [19].	– X's algorithmic bias bounty challenges invite public scrutiny to uncover hidden biases in machine behavior [7].
Stimulating action: Prompting or motivating movement	– Tesla's Autosteer mode requires drivers to hold the steering wheel, enhancing attentiveness and safe driving [61]. – Google's Jigsaw Perspective API prompts users to reconsider potentially harmful comments before posting [46].	– Microsoft's Fairlearn [4] and IBM's AI Fairness 360 [2] are toolkits that help mitigate bias in machine learning models, promoting responsible AI development.
Deprioritizing efficiency: Embracing exploration and divergence	– Academic authors are increasingly required to clarify AI's contribution in research [56], fostering exploration of AI's potential and ethical use. – The "6-month pause on giant AI experiments" open letter [32] may delay AI development and allow time for human reflection and reaction.	– Google's decision to end third-party cookies shifts focus from efficient data tracking to protecting user privacy and responsible AI marketing strategies [6].

AI applications, thus guiding the development of more effective and precise positive friction strategies and avoiding a one-size-fits-all approach that is inadequate for complex issues surfaced by advances in AI.

4.3 Collaborative Dynamics of Positive Friction in AI+Human Hybrids

Recognizing the stakeholders involved also underscores the interconnectedness between AI technology, AI practitioners and users. Frequently, efforts to integrate AI into society foster a "competitive, human-machine opposition mindset," either through technical approaches to improve the algorithms themselves outside of human oversight or through governance and oversight that create regulations around algorithms, both of which isolate AI technology from human operators (AI practitioners), and collaborators (AI users) [16]. By introducing behavioral speed bumps into AI development, however, developers can more easily surface hidden issues in algorithms that can subsequently enhance user experiences and promote healthier human-AI interaction behaviors. This positions positive friction less as a choice between "assisting developers for AI" or "improving AI for users" or reinforcing a divide between AI developers and end users, than fostering a collaborative "practitioner-AI-user" dynamic flow through responsible integration of technology and human experience (Fig. 2). In short, incorporating positive friction into both the design and deployment of AI can reframe the antagonistic dynamic between human agents and algorithms into a collaborative one, with the potential for human-machine hybrid intelligence.

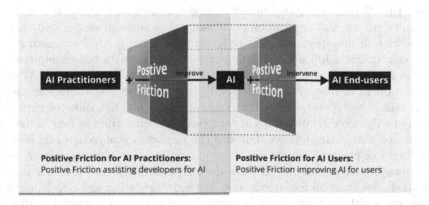

Fig. 2. Grammarly's mutual supportive "practitioner-AI-user" relationship with Positive Friction Model.

Grammarly's recent research on gender-inclusive grammatical error correction in natural language processing (NLP) systems [37] presents an example of this kind of multi-faceted, multi-stakeholder mutual support problem-solving. For AI users, Grammarly's AI-driven spell-checker and autocorrection function serves as positive friction through pop-up messages questioning personal pronoun usage ('he', 'she', or 'they') or suggestions to replace 'mankind' with 'humankind,' which disrupt writers' unconscious typing behaviors but encourage them to reconsider pronoun biases, or prompt reflections on gender-neutral language. For AI practitioners, flagging corrections' biases made by the Autocorrection represents positive friction in the form of a trigger during the evaluation of AI, as when Autocorrections suggest changing "Charlie's earnrings" into "his earnings" or "her earrings" [69]. Although time-consuming, this use of positive friction to conduct internal checks and 'mine clearance' is not only vital for debugging and improving the AI systems, but also reinforces organizational values in support of LGBTQIA+ inclusivity and a diverse workforce [15,69]. Grammarly's commitment to positive friction not just as a device to improve technology but to bolster social and cultural values can be seen in their engineering team's Counterfactual Data Augmentation (CDA)-supported model for internal Grammatical Error Correction (GEC) systems testing and training, and its subsequent open-source release to the public [37]. This initiative not only enhances self-control to mitigate gender bias in Grammarly's AI systems, but also encourages the inclusive development of linguistic AI on a broader scale.

The increased prevalence and use of AI requires considering how a diverse range of stakeholders and situations can benefit from positive friction across AI development and end-user engagement. Recognizing that AI/human hybrid behavior as a complex multi-stakeholder unit underscores that identifying the need for positive friction, selecting strategies to address it, and incorporating it into AI, developer, and user dynamics is not a 'one-size-fits-all' solution. The case of Grammarly, for example, illustrates how different forms of positive friction, sourced from various quadrants in the model, can benefit different stakeholders to improve the offering as a whole. In addition, given the wide range of stakeholders, community values, and application environments, a singular design approach to positive friction may resonate differently across various groups, suggesting that AI design requires a full understanding of relevant contexts before implementation, and further that designing friction solely with specific groups like AI users or practitioners in mind can inadvertently overlook the needs and responsibilities of still other stakeholders. This suggests not only the value of exploring the model's dynamic relationships in combination rather than as four individual strategies or a singular audience, but also the importance of recognizing how different forms of positive friction might be naturally intertwined. However, more is not always better, and the effective use of positive friction does not require using strategies from all four quadrants. Instead, the design and development of AI requires a rich understanding of context, the nature of potential challenges that might benefit from positive friction, and a sense of which strategies are best suited to the task.

4.4   Positive Friction Model as Lens

Seeing positive friction in an AI context as a complex design challenge that requires solving for multiple people and problems simultaneously suggests that employing the Positive Friction Model can take three different forms: 1) as a characterizing lens to systematically identify the nature of existing friction, 2) as a diagnostic lens to analyze how situations within complex challenges that would benefit from positive friction, and 3) as a generative lens to craft targeted positive friction that effectively address these challenges.

Characterizing Lens: When used to characterize existing forms of friction, the Positive Friction Model can help designers better understand where strategies are already in use, who is benefitting from them, and how they might be analyzed to see how they are creating impact. Below, we examine three cases—the Future of Life Institute (FLI)'s Open Letter proposing a pause on AI system training [32], Tesla's auto-driving features [60, 61], and Grammarly, as introduced above—by capturing and characterizing positive friction features employed in each.

On March 22nd, 2023, FLI published an Open Letter calling for a six-month pause on "the training of AI systems more powerful than GPT-4," warning of "an out-of-control race to develop and deploy ever more powerful digital minds that no one—not even their creator—can understand, predict, or reliably control", and asking the world to bask in a "long AI summer, not rush unprepared into a fall" [32]. The short but highly publicized statement garnered over 30,000 signatures in a few short months [32]. Characterizing this instance according to the Positive Friction Model provides several immediate insights. First, it can help us break down which various friction-based strategies are in use; for example, the letter simultaneously applies a self-imposed waiting period in the form of an explicit and lengthy pause, as a kind of self-control mechanism, to slow down AI progression (Save me from myself); introduces skepticism and critical thinking as mechanisms to questioning the tempting convenience of AI (Question assumptions); uses social norms and concreteness in the form of signatories as prompts for reflection, accompanied by an urgent tone that raises the stakes for AI regulators to take actions (Stimulating actions); and suggests friction in the form diversity by encouraging more inclusive discussions (Deprioritizing efficiency). Second, taking a categorizing lens also allows us to identify not just what strategies are used, but to whom these interventions are directed; in this case, across three distinct groups, including developers, regulators, and the public [57]. Finally, identifying the range of strategies in use and their intended targets allows us to see patterns to identify where and for whom friction is currently being used, and just importantly where it is not.

Tesla's auto-driving mode offers another example of the value of categorizing existing friction, in the form of Autosteer alerts [61] and behavioral-score-driven insurance [60]. The use of friction in autosteer mode requires drivers to maintain contact with the steering wheel during auto-steering, triggering visual and auditory alerts if compliance is not detected, using direct feedback to encourage safe driving behavior by stimulating responsiveness and evasive actions as necessary. In contrast, Tesla's insurance scheme bases premiums on real-time driving safety scores rather than conventional factors like gender and age. This more subtle form of friction encourages drivers to avoid risky behaviors like hard braking, aggressive turning, or phoning while driving, due to the knowledge that overly aggressive behaviors risk incurring penalties in the form of higher insurance rates. While these instances of friction differ in their design—the former explicitly prevents drivers from engaging in dangerous activities where the latter employs implicit punishment for 'bad' behaviors, both target AI users and both share the same underlying purpose of increasing drivers' attentiveness and promoting safer driving behaviors during auto-driving. Positioning these instances within the Model also allows us to recognize the additional insight that both strategies appear on the "intentionality" side of the model, which is perhaps not surprising given they are both highly goal-driven to support specific 'correct' behaviors, but which also can spur new thinking about how expanding perceptions might be employed to encourage driver safety.

Combining these instances and insights with the previous example of Grammarly allows us to observe how different cases exhibit unique combinations of positive friction in types, purposes, and target audiences (Fig. 3). It also reinforces that more or more types of friction do not automatically lead to better outcomes if the specific context does not require them or if they are designed to solve different things. For instance, although all four quadrants of positive friction strategies can be seen in the Open Letter case, they address different groups with varied objectives. In contrast, the Tesla case employs only two types of positive friction, but in sharing an intended purpose for a specific user-stakeholder they are able to play a useful reinforcing role. This highlights the important point that merely increasing the quantity of friction is not inherently beneficial and that effective use of friction requires focusing on context-specific designs that enhance the effectiveness of solutions.

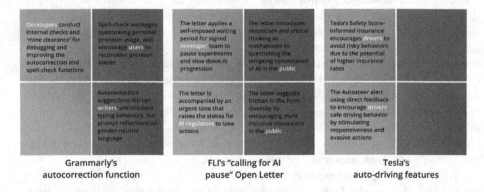

| Grammarly's autocorrection function | FLI's "calling for AI pause" Open Letter | Tesla's auto-driving features |

Fig. 3. Three cases as characterized according to the Positive Friction Model

Diagnostic Lens: The Positive Friction Model can also be used diagnostically to help identify when situations might benefit from positive friction and how to apply it. Where an emphasis on characterization enables us to analyze existing friction, taking a diagnostic lens can help us identify why, when, and where positive friction should be introduced in new problem contexts, or to augment where the existing use of friction may not go far enough.

Consider the FLI's Open Letter; where characterizing current forms of friction identified a wide range of strategies, a diagnostic lens might enable more insight into whether all instances of positive friction were equally effective, and where they might need to be complemented by other interventions. For example, even signatories who doubted the feasibility of a six-month pause valued the letter's public awareness of AI's rapid advancements [57]. This suggests that while the letter supplied a useful form of friction in the form of a conversation starter, additional and more explicit brakes on the system might be necessary to more forcefully stall and reflect on AI development. Similarly, adding friction does not ensure that system participants and stakeholders will respond as expected; this can lead to reactant behaviors that achieve the opposite effect of interventions' intent, as seen in instances of individuals who perceived the letter as a stimulus accelerating AI development rather than pausing it [28] or concerns about the letter's potential to increase public AI anxiety or inadvertently promote AI hype for commercial gains [65]. Similarly, while Tesla's initial use of positive friction measures to enhance driver attention saw early success, users soon devised ways to trick them, such as using 'wheel weights/knobs' or even oranges to mimic hand pressure on the steering wheel to such an extent that 'wheel weights' were still among the top sellers in Amazon's "automotive steering wheels" category in 2023 [55]. These unintended consequences highlight the importance of testing friction-based behavioral interventions in a rapidly evolving AI landscape.

In these cases, using the Positive Friction Model diagnostically helps us identify new situations and appropriate ways in which to employ positive friction to improve AI design. In the Open Letter case, for example, a diagnostic lens can signal the need to adopt more inhibitory strategies; in Tesla's scenario, developers might redesign how friction is built into offerings, to avoid situations where the temptation for some users to exhibit control over driving is strong enough that they deliberately game the system. But a diagnostic lens can only do so much, and in some cases the need for positive friction may not reveal itself until after negative consequences have already occurred. For example, despite ChatGPT's cautionary message ("ChatGPT can make mistakes. Consider checking important information") [45], an insufficient degree of friction combined with plausible-looking results and the temptation of efficiency have led individuals to believe AI's "hallucinated" references and citations [68]. Tesla also was forced to institute recalls when auto-drive features flouted local driving laws, such as inappropriate lane changes or traveling through yellow lights before the driver had the opportunity to intervene [33]. These cases reinforce the need to not just solve problems as they occur but learn how to identify where adaptations to friction can fill gaps in current preventative measures and where new approaches—such as regulatory oversight—may be necessary to address new and emerging situations more proactively.

Generative Lens: Finally, the Positive Friction Model can be used generatively to help create structured, multifaceted interventions that target diverse stakeholders both effectively and ethically. While there is no one-size-fits-all approach to generating positive friction solutions, the specific characteristics of AI offerings and capabilities suggest several key considerations:

Expanding the Scope of Stakeholder Analysis - While focusing on AI users and practitioners will continue to be at the core of any positive friction strategy to address AI-related behaviors, exploring a broader array of relevant stakeholders can surface other important challenges that might otherwise go overlooked. In the Tesla scenario, for example, addressing the 'wheel weight [55]' workaround that overcame initial driver-based-friction interventions might require new approaches that encourage AI developers to decrease machine intelligence and encourage manual control in certain situations to buy time for AI upgrades. Even more dramatically, new positive friction interventions could extend beyond the immediate AI+human (i.e., vehicle+driver) hybrid unit to focus on 'wheel weight' manufacturers and retailers by imposing stricter regulations or penalties for selling harmful devices, or on traffic police to incentivize noting the use of wheel weights at traffic stops.

Embracing Expansive, Reflective Friction - Beyond goal-driven interventions, there's value in embracing expansive, reflective friction. For example, Tesla's Autosteer alerts and behavioral-scored insurance may not achieve their intended goals in part due to limitations of interventions solely focused on modifying behavior without enhancing users' willingness to comply. This may suggest the value in exploring additional forms of friction represented in the model, less as a quest for comprehensiveness or more-is-better attempt to force-fit additional forms than an effort to more holistically gauge the constellation of challenges that various stakeholders may represent. For example, James Bridle's 'Autonomous Trap 001' project [5] cleverly used a salt circle on the ground to deceive an autonomous vehicle's vision system; this not only sparked debates on AV safety and limitations, but also challenged the overconfidence and overreliance of AV users.

Integrating Hard and Soft Friction - While the Positive Friction Model introduces four specific types of positive friction strategies, it is less specific about the material or form factor that friction might take in practice. Similar to system design's characterization of hard (e.g., physical, technological) and soft (e.g., cultural, social) system features, instances of friction can also be positioned as hard or soft [44]. Hard applications of positive friction usually influence behavior more directly either through physical barriers or technological infrastructures, often employing more top-down or paternalistic strategies leading to specific actions. Examples of this may include Tesla's Autosteer alerts [61], 'X's' "read before you post" feature [58], governance policies, and fine punishments, all of which are structurally embedded in system infrastructures. Conversely, soft friction influences behavior more indirectly by affecting mental attitudes or social norms to encourage user actions. These might include Tesla's behavioral-scored insurance [60], FLI's celebrity-endorsed Open Letter [32], and Bridle's AV trap project [5], which apply principles like 'mental avoidance of harm', 'social norms', and behavioral 'nudges.' Integrating both hard and soft friction can enhance the overall impact of positive friction.

4.5   Implications and Questions for Further Exploration

While integrating behavioral science and design research approaches like the Positive Friction Model more deeply into HAI practice may enhance HCI approaches to socio-technical studies, merging disciplines faces challenges of methodological and definitional alignment. In addition, advances in AI's capabilities and use continue to evolve nearly on a daily basis. On the one hand, this research heightened the potential value and urgency of employing a behavioral design lens; on the other, key questions about situations of use and potential applications of behavioral tools, such as positive friction, have yet to be defined or even understood. However, despite this uncertainty, there are several potential research questions and further exploratory directions for positive friction in AI worth considering even at this early stage.

First, the Positive Friction Model should be seen not as a stand-alone tool but as a complementary approach that can be used in conjunction with established design frameworks (e.g., journey maps, POEMS [26]) and behavioral tools (e.g., the COM-B framework [39], the Choice Triad [52]), combining familiar methods in novel ways that can potentially reveal insights not previously considered. Employing mixed methods can balance the reliance on a single discipline, merging data-driven confidence with openness to a broader range of solutions; for instance, the use of journey maps that demonstrate forms of multi-stakeholder involvement may yield insight into postures and attitudes involved in various AI-related activities, providing an experiential perspective that the Positive Friction Model currently lacks. This also suggests the potential value of exploring how HCI frameworks or tools can integrate with the Positive Friction Model, whether using HCI approaches to enhance the implementation of positive friction from strategic principles to practical experiments or how targeted use of positive friction can benefit HCI solutions.

In addition, no methodology is entirely neutral [67]; every designer, framework, and solution inherently carries biases, and even methodologies that are scientific and objective (such as behavioral science), openly participatory (as design strives to be), or data-driven and evidence-based (as HCI studies) are influenced by underlying ideologies that dictate disciplinary norms, what qualifies as evidence, and what constitutes a successful solution. Diversity is itself a form of friction, suggesting that successful collaborations across disciplines can benefit from the insertion of deliberate pause points or stimulations that prompt seeing old ideas in new ways. The Positive Friction Model, therefore, can play a significant role within the design process, in which it can inform and support cross-disciplinary exchange as a dialogic tool that helps transdisciplinary teams to identify tensions or blind spots, foster continual conversation,

encourage engagement with diverse viewpoints, and position design as an iterative exchange rather than a final decision-making point.

Finally, effective use of the Positive Friction Model and positive friction strategies may change over time as AI itself evolves. Just as the widespread use of
LLMs such as chatGPT and visual engines such as DALL-E and Midjourney
in the Fall of 2023 introduced both fascination (of their 'automagical' abilities
to conjure convincing and well-structured content and media) and fear (of AI
taking over jobs or concerns about cheating in educational settings), new and
emergent forms of AI will also arise. In addition, the distinction between users
and practitioners may blur as AI evolves, requiring new or adaptable design
strategies to accommodate new use cases that may be difficult to identify in
advance. Given that designers are likely to have a front seat as these new technologies are ushered in, designers will also have the ability to influence how AI is
seen and adopted by people and more broadly by society [12]. With this ability
comes the responsibility of proficiently employing positive friction across the arc
of AI development, implementation, and use; minimizing its potential to create
unintended consequences, and updating why, when, and how strategies are used
in future contexts or to address future challenges in ethical and equitable ways.

5   Conclusion

Despite the fact that friction is traditionally seen as a negative when designing for behavior, positive friction can be used in situations requiring greater
self-control, higher reflexivity, and contexts in which efficiency and autopilot
behaviors may dominate. The application of positive friction may be increasingly useful in the case of both AI development, in which frictionless processes
can too easily increase the likelihood of algorithmic bias or misuse, and for AI
users, who may lack the knowledge or ability to adequately question AI outputs. This may be particularly necessary given the recent theory that positions
'human+AI' not merely as users and tools, but as hybrid agents that complement and supplement each others' strengths in a wide range of personal and
professional settings [16].

However, successful use of positive friction requires the ability to characterize
when it is already being used in offerings and products, how to diagnose its effectiveness or identify challenges that would benefit from additional attention, and
a generative lens that can integrate positive friction into structures, processes,
and offerings as necessary. In the case of AI, this means being both reactive to
emergent issues—such as algorithmic biases that cause harm or human behaviors in need of adjusting—as well as an openness to proactively identifying new
opportunities where friction may be beneficial, especially as technology continues to advances in as yet undetermined ways. This also requires recognizing
that positive friction is not a one-size-fits-all approach, but a systematic way to
design for multiple stakeholders, values, and complex systemic contexts of AI,
ensuring that AI systems are not just efficient and technologically sound but
also mindful of societal values and user welfare. While AI technology and its use

will assuredly continue to evolve, it is equally likely that positive friction will continue to demonstrate adaptability and relevance in an evolving technological landscape. As AI continues to evolve, we believe the concept of positive friction can help steer this progression toward beneficial and equitable outcomes as well.

References

1. Bardlavens, T.: How adobe's product equity team is setting new standards for our experiences — adobe blog (2023). https://blog.adobe.com/en/publish/2023/09/20/how-adobes-product-equity-team-setting-new-standards-for-our-experiences
2. Bellamy, R.K., et al.: AI fairness 360: an extensible toolkit for detecting, understanding, and mitigating unwanted algorithmic bias. arXiv preprint arXiv:1810.01943 (2018)
3. Benartzi, S.: The Smarter Screen. Penguin (2015)
4. Bird, S., et al.: Fairlearn: a toolkit for assessing and improving fairness in AI. Microsoft, Technical report, MSR-TR-2020-32 (2020)
5. Bridle, J.: Autonomous trap 001. NTT Inter Communication Center [ICC] (2017). https://www.ntticc.or.jp/en/archive/works/autonomous-trap-001/
6. Chavez, A.: The next step toward phasing out third-party cookies in chrome. Google (2023). https://blog.google/products/chrome/privacy-sandbox-tracking-protection/
7. Chowdhury, R., Williams, J.: Introducing twitter's first algorithmic bias bounty challenge (2021). https://blog.twitter.com/engineering/en_us/topics/insights/2021/algorithmic-bias-bounty-challenge
8. Cox, A.L., Gould, S.J., Cecchinato, M.E., Iacovides, I., Renfree, I.: Design frictions for mindful interactions: the case for microboundaries. In: Proceedings of the 2016 CHI Conference Extended Abstracts on Human Factors in Computing Systems, pp. 1389–1397 (2016)
9. Cutrona, S.L., et al.: Improving rates of outpatient influenza vaccination through EHR portal messages and interactive automated calls: a randomized controlled trial. J. Gen. Intern. Med. 33(5), 659–667 (2018). https://doi.org/10.1007/s11606-017-4266-9
10. Duckworth, A., Milkman, K.L., Laibson, D.: Beyond willpower: strategies for reducing failures of self-control. Psychol. Sci. Public Interest 19(3), 102–129 (2018). https://doi.org/10.1177/1529100618821893
11. Dyson, P., Sutherland, R.: Transport for humans: are we nearly there yet? London Publishing Partner, S.L. (2021)
12. Eggink, W., van der Heijden, K., Dorrestijn, S., Ouwens, I., et al.: Tool-based ethics education for engineers; wonderberries and wisdom tiles. In: DS 117: Proceedings of the 24th International Conference on Engineering and Product Design Education (E&PDE 2022), London South Bank University in London, UK, 8th–9th September 2022 (2022)
13. Faiola, A.: The design enterprise: rethinking the HCI education paradigm. Des. Issues 23(3), 30–45 (2007). https://doi.org/10.1162/desi.2007.23.3.30
14. Gosline, R.R.: Why AI customer journeys need more friction (2022). https://hbr.org/2022/06/why-ai-customer-journeys-need-more-friction
15. Grammarly: Circles at grammarly: How we foster an inclusive culture (2023). https://www.grammarly.com/blog/fostering-inclusive-culture/#:~:text=At%20Grammarly%2C%20Circles%20are%20employee

16. Guszcza, J., et al.: Hybrid intelligence: a paradigm for more responsible practice. Available at SSRN (2022)
17. Halpern, S.D., Asch, D.A., Volpp, K.G.: Commitment contracts as a way to health. BMJ **344**(jan30 1), e522 (2012). https://doi.org/10.1136/bmj.e522
18. Harris, A., Islam, S.U., Qadir, J., Khan, U.A.: Persuasive technology for human development: review and case study. EAI Endorsed Trans. Game-Based Learn. **4**(12), 153401 (2017). https://doi.org/10.4108/eai.8-12-2017.153401
19. Heitz, L., et al.: Benefits of diverse news recommendations for democracy: a user study. Digit. J. **10**(10), 1710–1730 (2022)
20. Jenni, K., Loewenstein, G.: Explaining the identifiable victim effect. J. Risk Uncertain. **14**(3), 235–257 (1997). https://doi.org/10.1023/a:1007740225484
21. Kahneman, D.: Thinking, Fast and Slow. Macmillan (2011)
22. Kaled, E.: Public transit is driving toward frictionless travel — genfare (2019). https://genfare.com/archive/public-transit-driving-toward-frictionless-travel/
23. Kim, S.: The psychology behind why you spend so much money on amazon prime (2021). https://www.cnbc.com/2021/10/29/hooked-psychology-explains-why-you-spend-money-on-amazon-prime.html
24. Korn, M., Voida, A.: Creating friction: infrastructuring civic engagement in everyday life. In: Proceedings of the Fifth Decennial Aarhus Conference on Critical Alternatives, pp. 145–156 (2015)
25. Kozyreva, A., Lewandowsky, S., Hertwig, R.: Citizens versus the internet: confronting digital challenges with cognitive tools. Psychol. Sci. Public Interest **21**(3), 103–156 (2020)
26. Kumar, V.: 101 Design Methods: A Structured Approach for Driving Innovation in Your Organization. Wiley, Hoboken (2012)
27. Facebook Reality Labs: Inside Facebook reality labs: the next era of human-computer interaction (2021). https://tech.facebook.com/reality-labs/2021/3/inside-facebook-reality-labs-the-next-era-of-human-computer-interaction/
28. Leaver, T., Srdarov, S.: Chatgpt isn't magic: the hype and hypocrisy of generative artificial intelligence (AI) rhetoric. M/C J. **26**(5) (2023)
29. Lee, J.E., Zeng, N., Oh, Y., Lee, D., Gao, Z.: Effects of pokémon go on physical activity and psychological and social outcomes: a systematic review. J. Clin. Med. **10**(9), 1860 (2021). https://doi.org/10.3390/jcm10091860
30. Lee, M.K., Kiesler, S., Forlizzi, J.: Mining behavioral economics to design persuasive technology for healthy choices. In: Proceedings of the SIGCHI Conference on Human Factors in Computing Systems (2011). https://doi.org/10.1145/1978942.1978989
31. Lee, S., Feeley, T.H.: The identifiable victim effect: a meta-analytic review. Soc. Influ. **11**(3), 199–215 (2016). https://doi.org/10.1080/15534510.2016.1216891
32. Future of Life Institute: Pause giant AI experiments: an open letter - future of life institute (2023). https://futureoflife.org/open-letter/pause-giant-ai-experiments/
33. Linkov, J.: Tesla recalls models with full self-driving due to software-related crash risk (2023). https://www.consumerreports.org/cars/car-recalls-defects/tesla-recalls-models-due-to-software-related-crash-risk-a1156985481/
34. Loewenstein, G.: Hot-cold empathy gaps and medical decision making. Health Psychol. **24**(4S), S49 (2005)
35. Logg, J.M., Minson, J.A., Moore, D.A.: Algorithm appreciation: people prefer algorithmic to human judgment. Organ. Behav. Hum. Decis. Process. **151**, 90–103 (2019)

36. Luca, M., Malhotra, D., Poliquin, C.: Handgun waiting periods reduce gun deaths. Proc. Natl. Acad. Sci. **114**(46), 12162–12165 (2017). https://doi.org/10.1073/pnas. 1619896114
37. Lund, G., Omelianchuk, K., Samokhin, I.: Gender-inclusive grammatical error correction through augmentation. arXiv preprint arXiv:2306.07415 (2023)
38. Luo, X., Ge, Y., Qu, W.: The association between the big five personality traits and driving behaviors: a systematic review and meta-analysis. Accid. Anal. Prev. **183**, 106968 (2023)
39. Michie, S., Atkins, L., West, R., et al.: The Behaviour Change Wheel. A Guide to Designing Interventions, 1st edn, vol. 1003, p. 1010. Silverback Publishing, Great Britain (2014)
40. Mills, S.: AI for Behavioural Science. CRC Press, Boca Raton (2022)
41. Mitchell, M.: The pillars of a rights-based approach to AI development (2023). https://www.techpolicy.press/the-pillars-of-a-rightsbased-approach-to-ai-development/
42. Moran, C.D.: Aisles abroad: Dutch grocer jumbo embraces a slower checkout option (2023). https://www.grocerydive.com/news/aisles-abroad-dutch-grocer-jumbo-slow-chat-checkouts/645702/
43. Naiseh, M., Al-Mansoori, R.S., Al-Thani, D., Jiang, N., Ali, R.: Nudging through friction: an approach for calibrating trust in explainable AI. In: 2021 8th International Conference on Behavioral and Social Computing (BESC), pp. 1–5. IEEE (2021)
44. Nold, C.: Towards a sociomaterial framework for systems in design (2021)
45. OpenAI: Introducing chatgpt (2022). https://openai.com/blog/chatgpt
46. Perspective API: How it works. Perspective API (2023). https://perspectiveapi.com/how-it-works/. Accessed Feb 2023
47. Piras, M.: Using friction as a feature in machine learning algorithms (2023). https://www.smashingmagazine.com/2023/08/friction-feature-machine-learning-algorithms/
48. Poursabzi-Sangdeh, F., Goldstein, D.G., Hofman, J.M., Wortman Vaughan, J.W., Wallach, H.: Manipulating and measuring model interpretability. In: Proceedings of the 2021 CHI Conference on Human Factors in Computing Systems, pp. 1–52 (2021)
49. Rakova, B.: The importance of friction in AI systems (2023). https://foundation. mozilla.org/en/blog/the-importance-of-friction-in-ai-systems/
50. Roozenbeek, J., Van Der Linden, S., Goldberg, B., Rathje, S., Lewandowsky, S.: Psychological inoculation improves resilience against misinformation on social media. Sci. Adv. **8**(34), eabo6254 (2022)
51. Schmidt, R.: Strange bedfellows: Design research and behavioral design. In: Boess, S., Cheung, M., Cain, R. (eds.) Synergy–DRS International Conference 2020, pp. 1443–1457. 11–14 August 2020 (2020). https://doi.org/10.21606/drs.2020.252
52. Schmidt, R., Chen, Z., Soldan, V.P.: Choice posture, architecture, and infrastructure: systemic behavioral design for public health policy. She Ji J. Des. Econ. Innov. **8**(4), 504–525 (2022)
53. Schwartz, B.: Security: tradeoffs between efficiency and friction, freedom and constraint. J. Positive Psychol. **17**(2), 171–176 (2022). https://doi.org/10.1080/17439760.2021.2016908
54. Shneiderman, B.: Human-Centered AI. Oxford University Press, Oxford (2022)
55. Siddiqui, F.: Tesla owners are using steering-wheel weights to drive hands-free. Washington Post (2023). https://www.washingtonpost.com/technology/2023/07/07/tesla-fsd-autopilot-wheel-weights/

56. Stokel-Walker, C.: Chatgpt listed as author on research papers: many scientists disapprove. Nature **613**(7945), 620–621 (2023)
57. Struckman, I., Kupiec, S.: Why they're worried: examining experts' motivations for signing the 'pause letter'. arXiv preprint arXiv:2306.00891 (2023)
58. Twitter Support@Support: Read before you tweet: Twitter's latest feature to promote informed discussion. Twitter (2020). https://twitter.com/Support/status/1270783537667551233
59. Tan, C.: On AI anthropomorphism (2023). https://medium.com/human-centered-ai/on-ai-anthropomorphism-abff4cecc5ae#bb4b
60. Tesla: Tesla insurance using real-time driving behavior (2021). https://www.tesla.com/support/insurance/real-time-insurance
61. Tesla, Inc.: Tesla Model 3 Owner's Manual: Using Autopilot (2023). https://www.tesla.com/ownersmanual/model3/en_us/GUID-20F2262F-CDF6-408E-A752-2AD9B0CC2FD6.html#GUID-A64D9025-E8AE-4661-9528-80A188DFA2BB. Accessed Feb 2023
62. Thaler, R.H., Benartzi, S.: Save more tomorrowtm: using behavioral economics to increase employee saving. J. Polit. Econ. **112**(S1), S164–S187 (2004). https://doi.org/10.1086/380085
63. The Behavioural Insights Team (BIT): East: Four simple ways to apply behavioural insights (2014). https://www.bi.team/publications/east-four-simple-ways-to-apply-behavioural-insights/
64. Vennelakanti, R.: Frictionless multimodal mobility for public transportation (2021). https://social-innovation.hitachi/en-us/think-ahead/transportation/frictionless-multimodal-mobility-for-public-transportation/#:~:text=With%20a%20frictionless%20public%20transportation,to%20realizing%20true%20multimodal%20mobility
65. Weiss-Blatt, N.: Tweet on [insert topic or first few words of the tweet here]. Twitter post (2023). https://twitter.com/DrTechlash/status/1675155157880016898
66. Wiese, L., Pohlmeyer, A.E., Hekkert, P.: Design for sustained wellbeing through positive activities-a multi-stage framework. Multimodal Technol. Interact. **4**(4), 71 (2020). https://doi.org/10.3390/mti4040071
67. Winner, L.: Do artifacts have politics? In: Computer Ethics, pp. 177–192. Routledge (2017)
68. Wise, J.: Lawyer's AI blunder shows perils of chatgpt in "early days" (2023). https://news.bloomberglaw.com/business-and-practice/lawyers-ai-blunder-shows-perils-of-chatgpt-in-early-days
69. Yavnyi, S.: Earnings for earrings: mitigating gender bias in autocorrect (2020). https://www.grammarly.com/blog/engineering/mitigating-gender-bias-in-autocorrect/
70. Yee, K., Peradejordi, I.: Sharing learnings from the first algorithmic bias bounty challenge (2021). https://blog.twitter.com/engineering/en_us/topics/insights/2021/learnings-from-the-first-algorithmic-bias-bounty-challenge

A Study on Enhancing the Influence of Intelligent Investment Advisors on Users Through Experience Design

Beilei Feng[✉] and Yichen Wu

School of Industrial Design, China Academy of Art, Hangzhou, People's Republic of China
2231351460@caa.edu.cn

Abstract. With the advent of the Internet finance era, intelligent investment advisors have become a trend in the current investment and financial management landscape and have also become a hot topic of interest in various circles. This article will elucidate how applying experience design to the current market of intelligent investment advisory can provide users with a better service experience, allowing more users to understand and trust the intelligent investment advisory service industry. For users, intelligent investment advisory represents a relatively low entry point into investment. However, research has shown that the factors influencing users' choice of intelligent investment advisory are the learning curve and the high financial literacy threshold, which deter many young and inexperienced individuals from opting for intelligent investment advisory. Based on research findings, the vast population of young and inexperienced individuals presents a potential target for the intelligent investment advisory market. Moreover, this demographic's financial awareness is not yet fixed and can be molded, making it an opportunity for design. This article will focus on explaining how to expand the influence of intelligent investment advisory through experience design, thereby fostering positive financial awareness among users. This, in turn, will cultivate healthy financial habits among young and inexperienced individuals, making them the primary users of the intelligent investment advisory market.

Keywords: Intelligent investment advisors · Experience Design · Internet Finance

1 Introduction

1.1 Research Background and Current Situation

In the current era of rapid artificial intelligence development, intelligent investment advisors are gradually entering the public eye. Public opinions on intelligent investment advisors have become polarized, with some believing that the future market for these services has positive development prospects, while others view the algorithmic black box of intelligent investment advisors as a massive scam. The reasons for this polarization are diverse and may be influenced by factors such as users' financial literacy, understanding of intelligent investment advisory services, and trust in financial platforms. The intelligent investment advisory industry is developing positively with reasonable scientific and technological means, but still faces some challenges.

To understand the logic behind the intelligent investment advisory industry, it is important to note that intelligent investment advisors use specific algorithmic models to manage accounts. They combine investor risk preferences, financial status, and financial goals to provide users with automated asset allocation and investment advice. Intelligent investment advisors offer low-threshold professional services to users, primarily catering to those who need assistance with financial planning or lack the time for it. They conduct risk assessments and match strategies to achieve automated investments, aiming to generate returns for users.

However, the term "challenges" implies that the intelligent investment advisory market is known and understood by only a few people and has not yet entered the mainstream public view. How to achieve inclusive finance and bring the intelligent investment advisory services into the public eye while gaining trust is a topic worthy of exploration.

1.2 Research Significance and Objectives

Making the intelligent investment advisors market more visible to the public holds certain value. Firstly, intelligent investment advisory services cater to a broad user base. Secondly, intelligent investment advisors can create financial services tailored to individual users. Thirdly, intelligent investment advisors align with the vision of inclusive finance.

With the rapid development of the internet information era, there is a high demand for the popularization of financial management on major platforms. As a result, the number of people attempting financial management is positively correlated. However, a significant portion of people still harbor a cautious mentality, rejecting various financial information. This bias is widespread and can be attributed to factors such as cognitive biases, others' experiences, and negative public opinion. Intelligent investment advisors are suitable for various user types and can customize investment strategies. Therefore, they hold value for inexperienced users.

For the aforementioned user groups, intelligent investment advisors are a suitable investment solution. However, they often struggle to actively engage with intelligent investment advisors, preventing them from realizing their true inclusive value. Currently, the majority of users in the intelligent investment advisors market are from the high-net-worth group. The low-net-worth group has potential value for the intelligent investment advisors market, making the popularization of intelligent investment advisors meaningful.

2 Research and Analysis on Influencing Factors of Financial Management

2.1 Qualitative Analysis of Influencing Factors in Financial Management

The Objective of Qualitative Research. Utilizing a semi-structured interview research methodology, the study conducts a preliminary exploration of existing financial management issues to understand user needs. This method is employed to determine the research direction and identify the factors influencing financial management, thereby delving into the relationship between users and financial management.

Before the interviews, a logical framework for semi-structured interviews was established (Fig. 1). Initially, basic information about users is collected, categorizing them based on their engagement in financial management. Subsequently, open-ended questions are posed to gather information about their purchasing patterns, reasons for purchases, and their tolerance for potential losses. Finally, in-depth interviews are conducted to explore whether users are willing to embrace intelligent investment advisors.

In the end, the study conducts qualitative interviews with 16 participants, including students around the age of 20, young professionals, stay-at-home homemakers, and middle-aged to elderly individuals facing retirement.

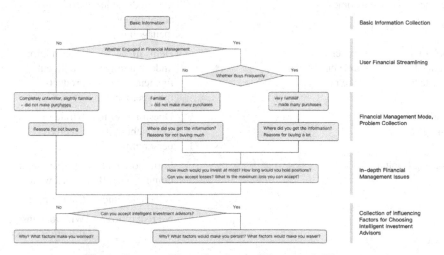

Fig. 1. Structured Interview Logical Framework Diagram

Identifying the Factors Influencing Financial Management. Based on the semi-structured interviews, the research participants were categorized into five groups: Non-Financial Management Group, Low-Risk Financial Management Group, High-Risk Financial Management Group, Intelligent Investment Advisors Acceptance Group, and Intelligent Investment Advisors Non-Acceptance Group. Through in-depth interviews, insights were gathered on the reasons for their purchasing decisions. Statistical analysis was conducted based on the responses of the interviewees, resulting in the following findings (Table 1).

Based on the results obtained from semi-structured interviews, an analysis and summary of the identified factors were conducted. Two major influencing factors were categorized: factors affecting the choice of traditional financial management and factors affecting the choice of intelligent investment advisors.

Factors influencing the choice of traditional financial management include risk perception (user's ability to perceive risks), learning costs (user's learning and time costs

Table 1. Semi-Structured Interview Results Summary Table

Investment in Finance: Low	Investment in Finance: High	Not involved in financial management	Will choose intelligent investment advisors	Will not choose intelligent investment advisors
Fear of risk	Knows the financial industry	Not familiar with financial management	High level of public trust	Only trust myself
Cannot afford losses	No pressure	No disposable income	Safe and effective	Fear of data leakage
No disposable income	Has disposable income	Feels complicated	Not knowledgeable about financial management	Low security level
Lack of financial knowledge	Financial management can make money		Helps in understanding financial management	Does not trust intelligent products
Unwilling to manage money			Doesn't have to worry about it personally	Afraid of being deceived
Working Capital			Earn more than doing it oneself	Chooses are not what I want
			Adequate funds	Cannot operate
			No risk of loss	Will not consider if there is a loss

associated with financial management), income and expenditure awareness (levels of income, expenditure, and financial awareness), and environmental influences (including family, friends, region, etc.).

Factors influencing the choice of intelligent investment advisors include risk perception, learning costs, level of trust (user's trust in the platform and intelligent investment advisors), user experience (user's experience when using intelligent investment advisors), privacy concerns (issues related to personal information and privacy), and profitability (returns on intelligent investment advisors).

2.2 Quantitative Analysis of Financial Management Influencing Factors

The Goal of the Quantitative Questionnaire. After subjectively summarizing the interview results and objectively analyzing the data, a quantitative questionnaire research method was employed to delve deeper. Based on the summarized impact factors, a logic for the quantitative questionnaire was established. This questionnaire primarily utilized situational questions to quantify the influence of different factors on the research users, aiming to derive the most significant impact factor based on the objectively obtained data (Fig. 2).

First, users are divided into two groups: those who do not engage in financial management and those who do. The financial management group is further divided into those willing to purchase high-risk products and low-risk products. Before entering the situational questions, there is a preliminary assessment of the user's likelihood of making a purchase. By comparing this with the purchase likelihood from the situational questions through controlled variable methods, a scored numerical value is obtained. Finally, basic demographic research is conducted to analyze the impact of the environment on financial management.

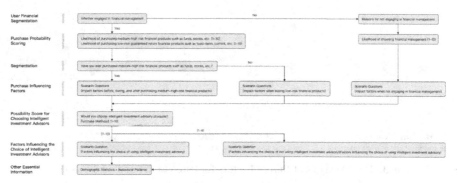

Fig. 2. Quantitative Questionnaire Logic

Analysis of Quantitative Questionnaire Results. The quantitative questionnaire targeted individuals aged 20 and above, with the majority falling within the 20 to 30 age range. A total of 316 questionnaires were collected, with 295 deemed valid for analysis. Demographic analysis revealed a predominant presence of young participants spanning various age groups. Occupationally, respondents were primarily students and employed individuals, with a minority being entrepreneurs or freelancers, and very few retirees. Regarding education, the majority held a bachelor's degree or higher, constituting 60% of the sample.

Cross-analysis indicated that individuals aged 35 and above were the primary purchasers of high-risk financial products such as funds and stocks. Additionally, the demographic of those who had purchased funds and stocks included young adults aged 21 to 25, suggesting an increasing financial awareness among the younger population. This group, characterized by strong information dissemination capabilities, holds potential value for future research.

Distinct differences were observed in the financial behavior patterns of the participants. Those who invested in current or fixed-term products tended to have a low tolerance for losses, with the maximum acceptable loss typically being less than 10% of the total investment. Conversely, individuals who had experience with high-risk products like funds and stocks demonstrated a higher acceptance of potential losses. This indicates a correlation between risk awareness and financial literacy among the participants.

In the questionnaire scenario, a comparative analysis was employed by setting up contrasting groups to accurately calculate the inclination of the impact. In the following charts, the higher the absolute value on the y-axis, the greater the impact of the influencing factor on the users.

For the analysis of impact factors on purchasing high-risk investments such as funds and stocks, it is divided into pre-investment, mid-investment, and post-investment based on the investment timeline. As seen in Fig. 3, "Financial Awareness" has the greatest impact on users before investment, while "Risk Perception" has the greatest impact on users during and after the investment.

Fig. 3. Data Analysis of Impact Factors for Purchasing Funds and Stocks

From Fig. 4, it can be observed that for individuals who do not engage in financial management, "financial awareness" has the greatest impact on them. They lack proper financial knowledge, which is one of the significant reasons influencing their reluctance to participate in financial activities. For individuals purchasing low-risk financial products, "learning cost" has the most substantial impact on them. Lack of understanding of financial knowledge becomes a hurdle on their investment journey.

From Fig. 5, it can be observed that the most significant factor affecting both the choice and non-choice of intelligent investment advisors is "learning cost." Users who choose not to use intelligent investment advisors do so because of a lack of understanding of financial knowledge, making the learning cost of financial management too high for this group. On the other hand, users opt for intelligent investment advisors if these platforms can reduce the learning cost associated with financial management, making them a viable investment channel.

In conclusion (Table 2), "financial awareness," "risk perception," and "learning cost" emerge as the three most significant factors in the financial decision-making process and the selection of intelligent investment advisors. Consequently, addressing how to instill positive financial awareness in users, cultivate healthy financial habits, and scientifically disseminate knowledge about finance and intelligent investment advisors becomes a challenging aspect of this research topic.

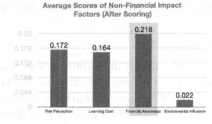

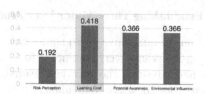

"Financial Awareness" Scenario Question:
If a platform recommends a risk-free financial product to you, but you currently don't have any spare money.

"Learning Cost" Scenario Question:
If a platform recommends highly profitable low-risk financial products to you, but you have limited knowledge of financial matters

"Financial Awareness"
has the greatest impact on users.

"Learning Cost"
has the greatest impact on users.

Fig. 4. Analysis of Impact Factors for Non-Financial Planning and Purchase of Low-Risk Financial Products

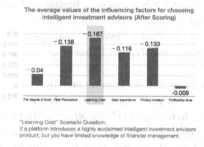

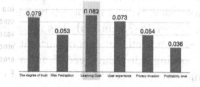

"Learning Cost" Scenario Question:
If a platform introduces a highly acclaimed intelligent investment advisors product, but you have limited knowledge of financial management.

"Learning Cost" Scenario Question:
If a platform introduces an intelligent investment advisors product that allows individuals unfamiliar with financial management to easily get started.

"Learning Cost"
has the greatest impact on users.

"Learning Cost"
has the greatest impact on users.

Fig. 5. The impact factor data analysis of whether to choose intelligent investment advisors is as follows

Table 2. Summary Table of Maximum Impact Factors

Investment Situation	Maximum Impact Factor
Not engaging in financial management	Financial Awareness
Before purchasing medium to high-risk financial investments	
During and after purchasing medium to high-risk financial investments	Risk Perception
Purchasing low-risk financial investments	Learning Cost
Choosing not to use intelligent investment advisors	
Choosing to use intelligent investment advisors	

3   Exploration of User Demand for Intelligent Investment Advisors

3.1   Establishing Three Major User Profiles

Based on the qualitative and quantitative research and analysis in the previous stages, in-depth interviews were conducted for different types of people regarding intelligent investment advisory. The interview results can be broadly categorized into three groups: the first group consists of individuals who understand finance but lack time for managing it, the second group includes those with limited knowledge about finance and weak awareness of income and expenses, and the third group comprises complete novices with no understanding of finance.

3.2   Identifying the Target Users

The final decision is to target individuals aged 25 and above who are working and have limited knowledge in financial management, specifically young novices in finance. Based on the earlier quantitative research, this age group tends to show a higher inclination toward purchasing medium to high-risk financial products, indicating a relatively strong risk tolerance. When categorized by whether they engage in financial management, the age group of 26–35 currently has fewer individuals involved in financial management, suggesting potential market opportunities.

Choosing individuals aged 25 and above in the workforce is motivated by their stable income, existing asset base, and the fact that they already possess some level of financial awareness influenced by their professional environment. However, selecting young finance novices is based on the idea that they have a blank slate in terms of financial knowledge and awareness of income and expenditure. This group is highly malleable, and targeting them aligns with the goal of intelligent investment advisors, which is to assist individuals who lack financial knowledge or time for financial management. Engaging finance novices and convincing them to understand and use intelligent investment advisory products remains a current challenge.

3.3   Explore Opportunities for Intelligent Investment Advisors in the Young Novice Demographic

The young novice demographic holds potential value in the intelligent investment advisors market. Based on the cross-analysis of financial willingness and willingness to choose intelligent investment advisors in the previous quantitative analysis, it can be concluded that among the group willing to choose intelligent investment advisors, the majority prefer to invest in medium to high-risk financial products, constituting 48.6% of the total surveyed population. "Trust level" has the most significant impact on this group. On the other hand, among those unwilling to choose intelligent investment advisors, the majority are individuals who do not engage in financial management, accounting for 81.3% of the total surveyed population. "Risk perception" has the most significant impact on this group.

At the current stage, individuals with experience in investment and financial management are more likely to choose intelligent investment advisors. However, young novices who do not engage in financial management are hesitant to enter the field of intelligent investment advisors due to their lack of experience. Therefore, the barrier to entry for novices in the intelligent investment advisory domain has not decreased but rather increased, and this barrier refers to experience.

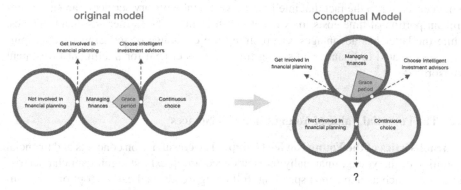

Fig. 6. Derivation of Preliminary Conceptual Model

Based on the current analysis, explore the opportunities for intelligent investment advisors in the young novice financial group, and conduct a preliminary analysis of the future connection between novice financial groups and intelligent investment advisors (Fig. 6). Is it possible to break the existing state, reduce the threshold of intelligent investment advisors for financial novices, allowing them to bypass financial experience and directly engage with intelligent investment advisors? This can achieve incremental market growth for intelligent investment advisors in the young novice market, and it holds certain significance.

4   The Incremental Market for Intelligent Investment Advisors in the Young Novice Financial Group

4.1   Cognitive Level and Learning Costs of Young Financial Novices Regarding Intelligent Investment Advisors

The Cognitive Level of Young Financial Beginners Regarding Intelligent Investment Advisors. Based on the preliminary qualitative and quantitative research, it is evident that novice financial beginners have certain cognitive biases towards financial matters. These biases are primarily manifested in misconceptions about disposable income, misunderstandings about internet products, and misconceptions about asset management. The mentioned cognitive biases have an impact on the decision to choose intelligent investment advisors. The current cognitive level of young novice financial individuals needs improvement, and fostering a solid financial awareness is crucial to breaking into the incremental market for intelligent investment advisors.

The Learning Cost of Young Financial Beginners for Intelligent Investment Advisors. From the results of the quantitative study, research subjects' learning costs for intelligent investment advisors mainly manifest in cognitive costs and time costs. These two factors interact inversely—complex cognitive costs hinder users, while saving time costs can help them. Cognitive costs refer to users' understanding of financial knowledge. Novice users often perceive finance as complex and high threshold, leading to resistance to financial-related matters, which greatly hinders a potential user base. Time costs refer to the fact that intelligent investment advisory services can save a significant portion of time costs for low-net-worth clients. The former has disadvantages, while the latter has advantages. Overcoming the challenge of reducing users' cognitive costs related to finance and saving time costs is crucial for intelligent investment advisors.

4.2   The Potential Value of Young Financial Novices

Characteristics of the Young Novice Group. The consumption concepts and financial cognition of the young, financially inexperienced group exhibit significant characteristics. Traits such as unplanned spending, following trends, and early adoption are common among the young demographic. Despite this, there are opportunities and latent value within this group. They are easily influenced by their environment, and with the rapid spread of information, internet products tend to proliferate within their social circles. Additionally, this demographic has quick asset liquidity, engages in frequent internet consumption, and is more likely to allocate a portion of their funds for financial purposes. As a result, they can potentially become an incremental market for intelligent investment advisory services. Given their immature financial mindset, nurturing a solid financial understanding is crucial for this novice group.

Psychological Characteristics of the Young Novice Group. The young novice group also possesses certain psychological characteristics, including group thinking, herd mentality, and suggestibility. This group is susceptible to the influence of surrounding factors; for instance, if there are many individuals engaging in financial activities in their environment, those who initially had no interest in finance may be influenced to consider financial management. Leveraging these psychological traits, intelligent investment advisory services need to gain recognition from a portion of the group to impact more individuals and encourage them to try intelligent investment advisory platforms. This underscores the importance of building trust in intelligent investment advisory products and platforms within this demographic.

Beliefs of the Young Novice Group. The young demographic exhibits a strong sense of belief in most things, curiosity, and a pursuit of goals. In the realm of finance, individuals with good financial knowledge aim for high returns, accumulating sufficient assets, and surpassing average levels. For novices, even a small profit can evoke a sense of self-satisfaction, motivating them to take an interest in finance, thus forming a positive cycle that transforms into actively learning financial knowledge. The strong belief system of the young demographic is a distinctive characteristic during this age period.

5   Overview of Experience Design

5.1   Definition of User Experience Design

Experience is a dynamic process in which the emotions of the experiencer change with the variations in experiential behaviors. Experience involves the establishment and maintenance of relationships between cognition, behavior, and emotion. Therefore, experiences can be categorized into cognitive experience, behavioral experience, and emotional experience. Experience significantly impacts users' perceptions of a product, influencing their attitudes and opinions toward it. User experience is a dynamic and continuous process with various touchpoints along the experience journey. Addressing pain points at each stage and enhancing user experience are critical factors for the sustainable development of a product.

5.2   The Necessity of Experience Design in Intelligent Investment Advisors

Analyzing the necessity of experience design in intelligent investment advisors based on the three experiences mentioned above.

From the perspective of cognitive experience, intelligent investment advisors need to capture the public's attention and require users to approach them with a rational mindset. However, cognitive biases result in mixed opinions among the public about intelligent investment advisors, leading to information asymmetry. Therefore, it is necessary to address how to effectively use cognitive experiences to enable the public to form a rational understanding of intelligent investment advisors.

From the perspective of behavioral experience, user investment behavior is a linear process. However, a poor user experience can prevent this linear process from forming a closed loop, affecting the sustainability of a product. Additionally, intelligent investment advisors require users to have a good understanding, and achieving long-term holding is essential to highlight the product's advantages. However, in reality, most users, especially financial novices, find it challenging to achieve long-term holding. Improving the user experience in financial behavior, including various stages such as pre-investment, during investment, and post-investment, is essential for intelligent investment advisors.

From the perspective of emotional experience, investment may seem rational and cold, but for users, it involves investing assets and emotions. Users have expectations for their investments, and long-term investment can stabilize their mindset. There are certain emotional factors at play. Additionally, a stable mindset can lead users to achieve long-term holding, and this is based on both cognitive and behavioral experiences.

In conclusion, cognitive experience, behavioral experience, and emotional experience are all essential. There is a necessity for the development of intelligent investment advisors to encompass all these aspects.

5.3   The Advantages of Applying Experience Design in the Market of Intelligent Investment Advisors

The majority of internet financial products operate in an online mode, which has certain limitations in terms of user experience. Firstly, users are often passively receiving information. Secondly, there is a potential for cognitive biases in online information retrieval. Thirdly, users can easily be distracted by other information, leading to a short experience cycle. Considering these three issues, it is challenging to make significant breakthroughs in experience design based solely on online applications.

Therefore, the offline experience of intelligent investment advisory services might serve as a breakthrough. Applying cognitive, behavioral, and emotional experiences in an offline setting could address the limitations of online experiences. By leveraging experience design, it is possible to enhance the impact of intelligent investment advisory services, help users develop a solid financial understanding, and cultivate positive financial habits.

Transforming the user investment process into a closed loop of positive feedback is beneficial for the development of the intelligent investment advisory market and contributes to the overall advancement of the financial market.

6   The Practical Application of Experience Design in the Intelligent Investment Advisory Market

6.1   Ideas for Offline Experience Design

The final established design involves telling the story of intelligent investment advising through offline experience stores. The aim is to provide users with a tangible financial experience, expanding the financial experience beyond the online realm.

The design comprises three main sections: the testing section, the interaction section, and the trading section.

The testing section is designed in a tangible user interface (TUI) format to conduct tests. Based on users' judgments of market fluctuations, an analysis of their financial personalities is performed. Users engage in buying and selling transactions based on their judgments, avoiding the probabilistic cognition of a gambler's mentality. Ultimately, a paper-based user financial personality card can be printed as a keepsake. In the stage where users input the amount, a tangible interaction method is employed. Users can directly operate using provided physical coins, distinguishing it from online tests where users may freely drag numerical sliders. This ensures that users are more cautious, intuitive, and aligned with their psychological tendencies during the investment process.

In the interaction section, users can control the content on the interactive wall (Fig. 7) using a sensor-equipped bracelet. This section includes popular science information about financial knowledge and explanations of intelligent investment advising. After users perform operations, the wall generates projected animations and text, allowing users to gain a deeper understanding of financial knowledge. The interactive wall uses a comparative narrative to illustrate the differences between intelligent investment advising and individual financial management, metaphorically representing weather as market conditions and plants as investment amounts. Through interactive projections and sound interactions, users can vividly experience the information conveyed by the interactive wall, enhancing their understanding of intelligent investment advising and financial management.

The trading section follows the characterization obtained from the testing section to recommend strategies that match the user's financial personality. When consumers

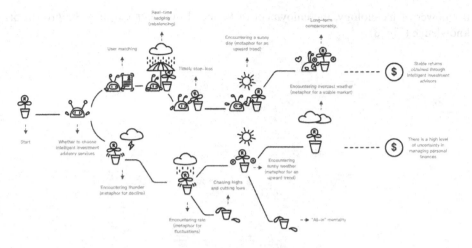

Fig. 7. The content on the interactive wall includes projections, animations, and textual information

purchase funds, they receive a financial card containing information about the purchased funds. In the offline experience store, users can scan the QR code on the card to access fund information. Users can set reminders to sell when reaching a certain profit within a specific time, encouraging long-term holding. This trading method differs from the original online financial management, introducing a certain level of passivity. This helps prevent users from frequently checking returns and encourages them to achieve long-term holdings.

Based on the above introduction, the testing section aims to help users establish a good financial understanding, the interactive section aims to expand the influence of intelligent investment advisory through experience, and the trading section aims to cultivate users' positive financial habits. This simultaneously addresses the "income and expenditure awareness," "risk perception," and "learning costs" mentioned in the earlier qualitative results. It also corresponds to the behavioral experience, cognitive experience, and emotional experience mentioned in the experience design. The three major sections connect the experience of intelligent investment advisory into an inseparable chain, from the pre-investment financial knowledge input and self-awareness, to the cautious investment and long-term holding during the investment, and then to the repeated investment after the investment returns. It forms a positive loop, holding significant meaning for the future development of the young and inexperienced demographic in the financial market.

6.2 Design Plan

The offline experience center of intelligent investment advisory aims to provide visitors with the enjoyment of financial management and encourage them to invest wisely to create wealth. The design is presented in the form of an exhibition hall, with the overall emotional theme being technology, fun, and growth. The goal is for visitors to perceive the power of technology, the enjoyment of financial management, and the growth of knowledge (Fig. 8).

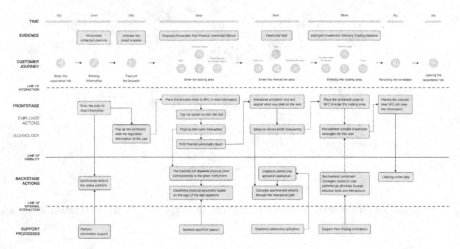

Fig. 8. Service Blueprint

7 Summary and Outlook

7.1 Conceptual Design Summary

The offline experience hall is dedicated to reducing users' learning costs in financial management and expanding a brand-new financial experience. Research indicates that the willingness of young people to engage in financial management is relatively low. One reason for this is that, despite the accelerated flow of information, the financial management community is relatively closed, with a high entry barrier. Users on online platforms need to actively seek financial information, and due to the inherently counter-intuitive nature of financial management, users often hope to achieve high returns with low investment in a short period.

The goal of the offline experience hall is to fill the gap in young users' experience with tangible financial activities. Through passive, simple, and enjoyable means, users can acquire relevant information about financial management and intelligent investment advisory. The aim is to transform the financial and consumption habits of the younger demographic and enhance their awareness of income and expenses. By providing information in a direct and engaging manner, the offline experience hall allows intelligent investment advisory to enter the field of view of young novices, offering them suitable choices for investment and financial management.

7.2 For the Outlook of Intelligent Investment Advisory in the Future

For intelligent investment advisory itself, with the rapid advancement of global AI technology, there remains significant potential for the intelligence enhancement of intelligent investment advisory. As time progresses, the market's acceptance of intelligent investment advisory is expected to increase gradually compared to the traditional advisory industry. Correspondingly, the development of the industry should expand on a sustainable basis within reasonable and legal frameworks. It is hoped that more individuals will continuously optimize products in the intelligent investment advisory industry, providing the general public with higher-quality and inclusive financial products.

References

1. Day, M.Y., Lin, J.T., Chen, Y.C.: Artificial intelligence for conversational robo-advisor. Springer, Heidelberg (2016)
2. Li, R.: Study on the governance issues of intelligent investment advisors algorithm under technological ethics. J. Dalian Univ. Technol. (Soc. Sci. Ed.) **5**, 88–95 (2020)
3. Zhang, L.: Enormous potential in china's intelligent investment advisory market. Tsinghua Financ. Rev. **10**, 93–97 (2016)
4. Back, C., Morana, S., Spann, M.: When do robo-advisors make us better investors? The impact of social design elements on investor behavior. J. Behav. Exp. Econ. **103**, 101984 (2023)
5. Yang, Y.: Research on the risks and market development of intelligent investment advisors in China. Era Finance **27**, 93–94 (2019)
6. Tang, S.: Research on characteristics and issues of contemporary college students' consumption behavior. Mod. Bus. Trade Ind. **16**, 218–219 (2009)
7. Atwal, G., Bryson, D.: Antecedents of intention to adopt artificial intelligence services by consumers in personal financial investing. Strateg. Chang. **30**(3), 293–298 (2021)
8. Qin, R., Chen, X.: Research on user experience design methods in mobile finance. Design **13**, 138–140 (2018)
9. Gray, W.R., Carlisle, T.E.: Quantitative Value: A Practitioner's Guide to Automating Intelligent Investment and Eliminating Behavioral Errors, 2nd edn. Wiley, Hoboken (2012)
10. Sun, X.: Research on design methods of internet inclusive finance based on user experience paths. Design **13**, 55–57 (2019)
11. Lewis, M., Perry, M.: Follow the money: managing personal finance digitally. Springer, Heidelberg (2019)
12. Lu, C.: Enhanced user experience in managing personal finance. In: Jacko, J.A. (ed.) HCI 2011. LNCS, vol. 6764, pp. 375–383. Springer, Heidelberg (2011). https://doi.org/10.1007/978-3-642-21619-0_47
13. Krombholz, K., Judmayer, A., Gusenbauer, M., Weippl, E.: The other side of the coin: User experiences with bitcoin security and privacy. In: Grossklags, J., Preneel, B. (eds.) FC 2016. LNCS, vol. 9603, pp. 555–580. Springer, Heidelberg (2017). https://doi.org/10.1007/978-3-662-54970-4_33

Psychological Perspectives on the Influence of Robotic Emotional Cues on Human User Interaction Intention

Haoran Feng[1] and Yi Liu[2(✉)]

[1] Guangzhou Academy of Fine Arts, No.257 Changgang Road, Guangzhou, People's Republic of China
[2] Province Key Lab of Innovation and Applied Research on Industry Design, No.257 Changgang Road, Guangzhou, People's Republic of China
liuyi@gzarts.edu.cn

Abstract. Intelligent robots are a highly visible development in the field of science and technology, and have been undergoing a technological revolution in the last decade, driven by Industry 4.0, the Internet of Things, and emerging technologies. Influence on the design strategy and even the production method of the update iteration, which makes the intelligent robot designers and intelligent robot users, the concept of intelligent robots and the way of use has changed; at the same time, the influence of the robot has been more than the robot product itself, which is a clear indication of the importance of intelligent robots for the improvement of human society's productivity and the progress of social civilization. In the industrial field, the use of intelligent robots has become very common in the production line, they can perform repetitive and dangerous tasks, freeing up human resources, reducing the risk of accidents and improving productivity. In the medical field, intelligent robots are used in surgery and rehabilitation, making medical treatment more precise and efficient. In the field of agriculture, the application of drones and automated farm machinery has helped increase the productivity of agricultural products. In the field of education, intelligent robots can be used as educational assistants to interact with students and provide a personalized learning experience; however, in order to realize the full potential of intelligent robots, not only advanced technology is needed, but also an in-depth understanding of the psychological factors of human-robot interaction. Effective interaction between intelligent robots and human users is the key to realizing their potential. This involves not only the external design and functionality of the robot, but also many aspects of the user's attitudes, emotions, and habits. Most of the current research around intelligent robots has been devoted to defining what factors affect human users' willingness to interact, but few systematic studies have analyzed how the factors affecting willingness to interact work from a multidisciplinary perspective. Therefore, the purpose of this paper is to explore the integration of intelligent robots with the causes of interaction willingness in psychology, to examine the literature on related topics using a combination of scoping reviews, scientific mapping, and bibliometrics, to reveal the current state of research and hotspots in the field, to identify the developmental and emerging areas in the field, and to point out the trends and directions for future research. The findings emphasize the psychological disciplinary perspective to analyze the significance

A. Marcus et al. (Eds.): HCII 2024, LNCS 14713, pp. 38–60, 2024.
https://doi.org/10.1007/978-3-031-61353-1_3

and necessity of human-robot interaction, and the specific influencing factors on the willingness of intelligent robots to interact with human users. Providing tools and frameworks for in-depth understanding of user needs and feedback from a psychological perspective helps to refine the theoretical and practical approaches based on user experience in intelligent robot applications, providing references for future research, as well as potential themes for future research.

Keywords: Human-robot interaction · interaction willingness · design psychology · robotic emotional cues

1 Introduction

Currently, in the scenario of popularization of intelligent robots [1], people are frequently interacting and associating with them in the production environment as well as in the daily life environment [2]. Intelligent robots are important intelligent facilities that replace human productive labor and have great potential for development in the field of service and production industries. In addition to assisting service industry personnel to provide intelligent services (e.g., robots in shopping malls, restaurants, or other public guides), these systems can be used as a tool to replace repetitive labor in industrial assembly line production; the "willingness of human-robot interaction" is a worthwhile research topic for the design and development of intelligent robotic systems. The study of human-robot interaction willingness can help to understand users' needs and preferences for robots [3], which can lead to the design of more user-friendly interfaces and functions to improve the user experience, help to optimize the operation of robots, reduce unnecessary complexity, and improve the efficiency of human-robot collaboration [4], and help to identify factors that may lead to misunderstandings, reduce communication barriers, and improve the accuracy and reliability of task execution. As well as human-robot interaction willingness research provides guidance to the R&D team and promotes technology development by understanding the user's acceptance and expectations of new technologies.

The research proposition on the interaction willingness of intelligent robots integrates the disciplines of medicine, psychology, artificial intelligence, engineering, and design, enabling the influencing factors of human-robot interaction willingness to be systematically explained from a disciplinary perspective. When analyzing human-robot interaction willingness from a psychological perspective, it is clear that the user's first psychological impression [5] of an intelligent robot is given by the form factor consisting of emotional cues [6] such as the robot's body movements and facial expressions. Whether the impression formed is biased or effective, it will affect the human user's willingness to interact with the current intelligent robot; in the field of researching the influence of intelligent robots on the human user's willingness to interact with them, the past literature has focused on the study of the two factors of "intelligent robots" and "human users", due to the technology, and the fact that the human user's willingness to interact with intelligent robots is not the same as the human user's willingness. In the field of researching the influence of intelligent robots on human users' willingness to interact, the past literature has focused on the study of "intelligent robots" and "human users", and due to the limitations of the technical level, the lack of immature technologies such as simulated neurons and haptic feedback systems, it is not possible to study the specific mechanisms affecting the human users' willingness to interact. In the decade approaching 2023, along with technological progress, there are mature technologies and theories, and research hotspots focus on intelligent robots for natural language processing and speech recognition [7], emotion recognition and expression [8], user personalization and customizability [9], social robots and cooperative robots [10], and trust and privacy [11].

Most of the existing research focuses on the active interaction between human users and intelligent robots, and some robots can perceive the active participation intention of human users and carry out training accordingly. However, this is based on the perception of the user's "functional activity ability", ignoring the high or low willingness of the user to interact; willingness to interact refers to the degree to which the human user actively interacts with the intelligent robot, and the factors that influence it include schema [12], first impression [13], emotional cues of the robot [14], and individual variability. In the process of using the robot, the user will perceive and evaluate the intelligent robot based on the robot's initial evaluation, strength, mobility, and the robot's corresponding character schema, script, and nonverbal cues consisting of facial expressions and body movements, and the user's own self-schema and changes in immediate emotions will also affect the willingness to interact. In addition to providing basic functions, it is important to understand the psychological experience of the user, so it is very important to make the experience of the user as the focus of intelligent robot product design.

Based on the experience of human users in using robots, this study attempts to analyze the research themes and key research elements to provide a reference for future research directions in the field of human-robot interaction willingness. It also clarifies why the important influencing factors affecting the willingness of human-robot interaction are important, improves the interaction between humans, intelligent robots and the use environment, and uses this to develop intelligent robot design strategies. Secondly, the multidisciplinary approach adopted in this paper can provide theoretical and methodological references for future research and help researchers understand the theoretical and terminological differences in interdisciplinary research.

2 Materials and Methods

2.1 Selection of Literature Databases and Research Methods

Due to the interdisciplinary integration of intelligent robotics with interaction willingness and psychology, and the unclear thematic directions and trends, quantitative research methods were used in this investigation. In this study, bibliometric analysis was used to review current research findings and to analyze the literature for performance and scientific mapping. Data from 914 articles retrieved from three high-impact journals in Web of Science, SSCI, SCI, and A&HCI, were examined and the research areas were visualized using CiteSpace. The purpose of the article scope review section was to examine the current state of research, collaborative networks and research trends, and to identify the scope of the study.

Through statistical correlation maps based on keywords, emerging terms, timelines, and trending themes from previously aggregated literature data, bibliometrics enables quantitative analysis of specific published literature, allowing researchers to objectively and directly analyze the structural characteristics and patterns of development of the current research field. This study presents, through, bibliometrics, the complex evolution of this research field in a knowledge graph and automatically identifies the frontiers indicated by citation nodes and clusters of co-citations. The research steps of this work, include performance analysis and scientific maps. They are specified below:

1. Performance analysis: macro quantitative analysis of publication time, authors, keywords and research content based on literature on specific topics.
2. Scientific mapping: Through the keywords of the statistical literature, we can derive keyword clustering mapping, timeline mapping and burst word mapping, etc., so as to gain insights into the current research hotspots and disciplinary structure, as well as to sort out the past research development trends and cooperation networks in the field.
3. Micro-qualitative analysis: analyze the factors that affect the interaction willingness of human users when interacting with robots from the perspective of psychology, and clarify the role and importance of the user's emotional experience in evaluating the robot; then analyze the application fields and future development trends of psychology in guiding the design strategies of intelligent robots.

In order to provide theoretical and methodological research in the area of providing good interaction willingness for future intelligent robots, the practical approach of combining the discipline of psychology with research on the willingness of human-robot interaction is further discussed by analyzing specific research cases in influential literature journals.

2.2 Literature Search, Selection and Collection

For the purpose of searching the literature in the field of human-computer interaction, the search terms were categorized into TS = ("Intelligent Robot" AND "Interaction willingness") OR TS = ("Intelligent Robot" AND "Human-computer interaction" AND "Willingness") OR TS = ("Human-computer interaction" AND "Emotion"), And representative charts and graphs were produced with literature analysis methods.

The research field has always been highly cutting edge and current. From the search results of Web of Science, the research has been developing at a relatively steady growth rate since the first literature in the field was published in 1993, and diffused to other fields. Therefore, English literature published between January 1, 1993 and June 1, 2023 was selected for this study. The titles, abstracts, authors, and keywords of the literature were analyzed; moreover, the intersection of research on intelligent robotics and psychology was identified from the literature study. The connection lies in the fact that psychology provides important insights about human cognitive load [15], task completion efficiency, and emotional experience [16], which are crucial for designing, evaluating, and improving user-friendly robotic systems and interfaces, creating a more effective and satisfying human-robot interaction experience. From 2009 onwards, two papers examining the positive psychology of research based on human cognition set a precedent for studying human-robot interaction from a psychological perspective. Therefore, in the subsequent phase of analyzing interaction willingness from a psychological perspective, literature published between January 1, 2009 and June 1, 2023 was selected for qualitative analysis with the same information described above.

Duplicate and irrelevant literature was also manually and automatically screened out using CiteSpace software. Then the screened literature data were bibliometric analyzed. Keyword emergence chronological analysis charts, keyword clustering charts, and research hotspot categorization charts were made to illustrate the findings in the research intersection of intelligent robots' willingness to interact with human users. The following insights can be gained from them: (1) Robot body movements and facial expressions are important factors affecting human users' interaction willingness; (2) Psychological perspective can provide insights into the specific influencing factors of human-robot interaction willingness, and the design strategy of intelligent robots can be explored according to the influence weights of the influencing factors.

3 Result

3.1 Multidisciplinary Perspectives on Analyzing Intelligent Robot Emotional Cues as a Trend in Human-Robot Interaction Willingness Research

The analysis of WoS produced 914 records, of which 819 had valid data. The following is an analysis of articles published on the topics of "Intelligent Robots" and "Willingness to Interact". Selected papers were analyzed based on keywords, subject, year of publication, chronological trend, and publication analysis by journal, author, and citation relationship (Table 1).

Table 1. Web of Science Process and results of core ensemble data collection.

Source	Web of Science Core Collection
Citation	SCI-EXPANDED, SSCI, A&HCI
Search Steps	#1 = TS = ("Intelligent Robot" AND "Interaction willingness") #2 = TS = ("Intelligent Robot" AND "Human-computer interaction" AND "Willingness") #3 = TS = ("Human-computer interaction" AND "Emotion") #4 = #1 OR #2 OR #3
Timespan	1993.1.1—2023.1.1
Document Type	Article and Review
Qualified records	819

Publications and Citations Throughout Years. The number of papers on related topics reflects the academic interest in the field, and the higher the number of papers, the more active the research in the field. Figure 1 depicts a total of 819 publications and 24,933 citations in the related field during the three decades from 1993 to 2023, indicating that the combination of intelligent robots and the willingness of human users to inter-act has a solid research foundation and shows a growing trend year by year. Figure 1 depicts that the first re-search in this field was born in 1993 [17]. Although the concept of intelligent robots had already been conceptualized in movies and books at that time, the limitations of the technological level of producing intelligent robots in the context of the era made the research in this field lack prominence. It was not until the rise of intelligent robot chip technology [18, 19] and the accumulation of research bases in 2001 that it gradually gained academic attention. There were 10 relevant publications in 2002, about three times as many as in 2001, while there were 37 relevant publications in 2014, about three times as many as in 2009; the number of publications peaked in 2014, then declined slightly in 2015, followed by a steady increase and an overall upward trend. In addition, the number of citations in related disciplines shows a general upward trend from 2016 to 2022, with inflection points in 2016, 2018, and 2020 showing growth. The rise of experience design has encouraged academics to consider issues from the user's perspective and to incorporate user experience, emotions, perceptions, and willingness to use into design strategies. The sharp decline in publications and citations in 2023 is attributed to the late and incomplete inclusion of literature data in that year, rather than to a decline in research enthusiasm in the related disciplines. The trend of research growth in this field is likely to continue in the future;

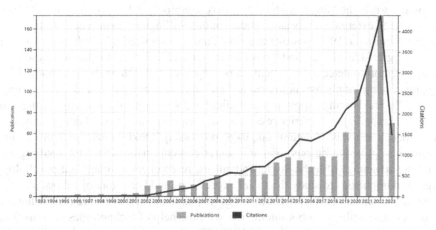

Fig. 1. Number of Publications and Citations per Year (1993–2023) via WoS.

Keywords Co-occurrence Analysis and Cluster Analysis, Research Hotspots. The keywords of articles on related topics were clustered to produce nine clusters. The clusters refer to the application of knowledge from several disciplines such as human behavior, feature capture, affective computing, mechanical usability disciplines, information perception disciplines, psychology, and linguistics.

Based on the results of the keyword co-occurrence analysis, Fig. 2 shows the knowledge graph of the clustering of the studied high-frequency keywords, with a Q-value of 0.4262 (>0.3), which indicates that the obtained structure of the class clusters is significant. The clusters are designated according to their size, starting from 0 for the largest clusters, 1 for the second largest, and so on. As shown in Fig. 7, the top 10 clusters formed by the high-frequency keywords in the related studies are as follows: #0 Emotion Recognition (Cluster 0), #1 Structural Design (Cluster 1), #2 Emotion Recognition (Cluster 2), #3 Human-Computer Intelligent Interaction (Cluster 3), #4 Affective Computing (Cluster 4), #5 Usability (Cluster 5), #6 Facial Expression Generation (Cluster 6), #7 Situational expression (Cluster 7), #8 Non-realism (Cluster 8). Among them, cluster #1 and cluster #7 have low relevance to the current study and were thus excluded.

Citespace's keyword co-occurrence graph describes each node as a keyword, and the node size represents the frequency of that keyword. The keyword co-occurrence analysis was performed on 819 data with Citespace's "keyword" function, and the resulting keyword co-occurrence graph is shown in Fig. 2, where "perception", "emotion recognition", and "affective computing" are high-frequency keywords, and "emotion", "attention", "expression", "emotional cognition", "Attention", "Expression", and "Emotional Cognition" all emphasize the human user's experience during the use of the robot, while "Robot Behavior", "Facial Expression Recognition", "Emotional Computing", and "Environment" are high-frequency keywords, and "environment" focus more on the influence of intelligent robots on the willingness to interact and external factors such as the usage scenario; Of which "emotion recognition", the "emotion recognition", "affective computing" and "transfer learning" apply the knowledge of signaling physiology, while the "brain model", "positive emotion" and "socialization" are more focused on the external factors such as the robot's willingness to interact and the usage scenarios. "brain model", "positive emotion", and "social sharing" apply psychological and sociological knowledge, and "experiential arousal", "emotion detection experience arousal", "emotion detection", "attention perception", "speech analysis", "natural language processing" apply psychological and sociological knowledge, and "positive emotion" and "social sharing" apply psychological and sociological knowledge. Linguistic knowledge is applied to "experience evocation", "emotion detection", "attention perception", "speech analysis", "natural language processing"; and knowledge from various disciplines is applied in various popular research contents in the field of HCI willingness.

Taking advantage of technological advances, researchers have applied psychology, design, and linguistics to study the facial expressions and behaviors of robots.

During the last 20 years, psychology has helped to understand more deeply the process of human-intelligent robot interaction with the help of technologies such as functional magnetic resonance imaging (fMRI) [20], electroencephalography (EEG) [21], brain imaging techniques (PET, TMS) [22], virtual reality (VR) [23], and augmented reality (AR) [24]. And in this research topic, the researchers applied these technologies to specifically analyze the possibility of robot facial expressions and behaviors to have an impact on human users through a psychological perspective.

Keyword Mutation and Timeline Mapping Analysis--Research Frontiers and Trends. "Human robot interaction" is an important factor that influences the willingness of intelligent robots to interact with human users. In recent years, human robot interaction research is closely related to "behavior" and "facial expression" (collectively referred to as "affective cue" [4]). Figure 3 shows that another research hot emotion in this field is also related to facial expression and behavior; therefore, facial expression and behavior of intelligent robots is an important part of "human robot interaction". Therefore, facial expression and behavior of intelligent robots is an important research

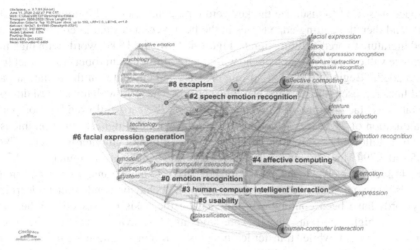

Fig. 2. Keyword Co-occurrence Network for Interaction willingness in Intelligent Robot Literature.

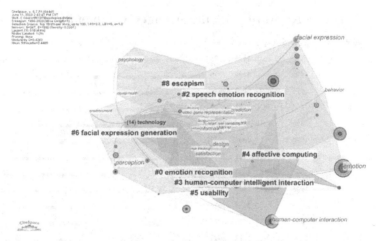

Fig. 3. Keyword Co-occurrence Clustering Network for Interaction willingness in Intelligent Robot Literature (Focus on the influencing factors of human-computer interaction).

content in "human robot interaction", so it can be seen that the robot body movement and facial expression have an effect on the willingness to interact.

The research frontier specifically refers to the topic characterized by the literature frequently cited by researchers in a particular field, and is the most active part of the research field, reflecting the future research direction and development trend of the subject area, and promoting the theoretical improvement of academic research.

Keyword emergence refers to the change in the level of interest in a topic in a research field over a specific time period, while keyword emergence rate reflects the rate of increase in the number of occurrences of a keyword over a time period. In this study,

CiteSpace was used to visualize the keyword emergence rate of bibliometric research results, and then the cutting-edge topics in the field were analyzed in conjunction with related literature to predict future trends. Figure 4 shows the 18 keywords with high final occurrence values in the research on the willingness of intelligent robots to interact from 1996 to 2023. "Beginning" and "End" are the start and end dates of the mutations, and the red lines represent the start and end time periods. The term with the longest duration of mutation is "facial expression" with a duration of 28 years, followed by "computer" with a duration of 21 years. "Emotion" is the term with the highest mutation intensity of 21.6941, followed by "affective computing" and "human-computer interaction" with 9.7505 and 7.7941 mutation intensities, respectively. The intensity of mutation is 9.7505 and 7.8442 respectively. "facial expression", "behavior" and "transfer learning" are the keywords in the previous study. "facial expression", "behavior", and "transfer learning" as keywords have been continuously mutated on the basis of previous studies until now, and are highly current. "facial expression" and "behavior" constitute the core of research in this field, while "transfer learning" is a current cutting-edge topic. It shows that researchers are using a multidisciplinary approach to study the hot, cutting-edge content in the field of HCI willingness.

Top 18 Keywords with the Strongest Citation Bursts

Keywords	Year	Strength	Begin	End	1996 - 2023
facial expression	1996	3.3685	1996	2023	
computer	1996	4.2277	1996	2016	
emotion	1996	21.6941	2002	2018	
affect recognition	1996	3.5426	2003	2014	
user	1996	3.6286	2004	2016	
affective computing	1996	9.7505	2006	2015	
human-computer interaction	1996	7.8442	2006	2018	
design	1996	7.7188	2007	2018	
usability	1996	3.618	2009	2016	
recognition	1996	3.852	2010	2016	
expression	1996	4.8734	2010	2015	
emotion recognition	1996	3.402	2012	2013	
system	1996	4.4301	2013	2016	
music	1996	4.2003	2014	2015	
speech	1996	4.764	2014	2017	
information	1996	3.93	2016	2019	
behavior	1996	4.4172	2017	2023	
transfer learning	1996	4.0107	2021	2023	

Fig. 4. Mapping of Keyword Mutations in Interaction willingness in Intelligent Robot Literature.

As shown in Fig. 5, the research field is divided into the following two main evolutionary paths: (1) the research perspectives of the field have become enriched over time; and (2) the content of the research in the field, from macro to specific, has been continuously refined; In 2009, six literature studies based on the optimistic psychology perspective were born, and the subsequent research shifted to the study of mental health as well as brain modeling. Fraune et al. [25], in 2019, after analyzing from a sociological perspective, argued that social behaviors among robots increased the anthropomorphism and solidity of robots, as well as the positive perception or willingness to interact with human users. Zhang et al. [26] explored the specific factors influencing the willingness to interact by assessing people's willingness to interact from a social psychology disciplinary perspective in 2021. Demonstrating the potential of an interdisciplinary research approach when studying interaction willingness in human-robot interaction. Pande et al. [27], in 2022, explained customers' willingness to use a service robot in a specific restaurant service environment by modifying the Artificial Intelligence (AI) Device Use Acceptance Model (AIDUA). Dang et al. [28], by synthesizing the results of five experiments from a human cognitive perspective After synthesizing the results of five experiments, Dang et al. found that "people's responses to robots are to some extent rooted in human thinking differences". Specifically, it is divided into the difference between the "fixed mindset" and the "growth mindset"; In the past decade, the research on intelligent robots affecting human user's willingness to interact has been increasingly analyzed from different disciplinary perspectives, which not only enriches the research perspectives in this field, but also generates more and more research results. This not only enriches the research perspectives in this field, but also generates systematic theories to be used to analyze the influencing factors in the process of human-robot interaction, which also provides reference value for future interaction research between this field and other disciplines.

Bruce et al. [29], back in 2002, argued that the lack of information feedback in intelligent robots makes it difficult for users to operate them. Therefore, the ability of people to perceive information was utilized as a feedback mechanism to test the ability of intelligent robots to convey expressions on their faces, as well as to investigate how robotic body orientation gains user attention. It is confirmed that robot facial expressions and behaviors can produce a superimposed relationship of increased willingness to interact for human users. The empirical study, with a robot as the object of study, is a precedent in the field of human-robot interaction willingness research that combines robot facial expressions and body movements. Even though it has not yet been defined, the expressions and movements of robots mentioned in this paper are the prototype concepts of today's "emotional cues". By 2011, due to the boom of specialized hardware for simulating neurons in the discipline of neurodynamics [30, 31], Bray et al. [32] used virtual neural real-time simulation of neurons in 2012 to combine the discipline of human-computer interaction with other disciplines. By analyzing the virtual neuron changes of human users, it reveals the effects of robot emotion cues on human users during human-computer interaction. Then in 2016, the application of robot emotion cues was shown to promote user satisfaction [33]. It used specific movie content matched with robot emotion cues to argue the point in conjunction with content objects in real-life scenarios. With the solidification of the basic research, the discussion about the specific information conveyed by robot emotion cues is refined. Inbar et al. [34] in 2019 further refined to explore the interaction between robot identity, application scenarios, and emotion cues. The study was specifically about "whether the terminological politeness of intelligent robots has an impact on users' perceptions of their use." Subsequently, Pocius et al. [35] also pinpointed the study to the haptic feedback provided by intelligent robots when generating body movements. From the emergence of the first empirical study in this field, subsequent literature has detailed the research content to specific scenarios, specific functions, and even specific interaction objects, showing a trend of increasingly detailed research content.

Figure 5 depicts the evolution of keywords in the study of factors influencing the willingness of intelligent robots to interact over three decades, as well as the evolution of keywords in relation to each time zone, from which the following three conclusions can be drawn: First, synthesizing the findings reveals multiple threads in the evolution of this field of research, with strong multidisciplinary integration and portability. All clusters in the figure are interconnected, and research has evolved in three main directions: functional deficits, emerging technologies, and embodied experience. Over time, the scope of research has expanded and become more in-depth; second, there is already a mature theoretical and research base, and the analytical approach of studying and analyzing emotional cues in intelligent robots from a psychological perspective has value for use; third, since the birth of the field in 2002, the "3D Intelligent Interfaces (#3 Human-Computer Intelligent Interaction)" and "Emotional Cues (#4 Emotional Computing)", after 22 years of disciplinary evolution, are still highly current research areas today.

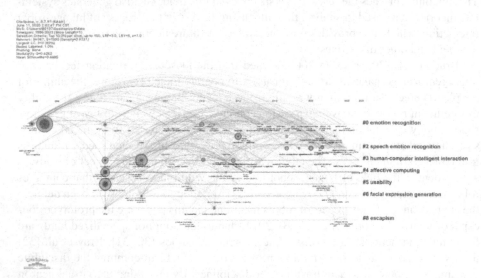

Fig. 5. Timeline Mapping in Embodied Experience in Interaction willingness in Intelligent Robot Literature.

3.2 Psychological Perspectives Provide a Clear Insight into the Weighting of Factors Affecting Willingness to Interact

Keyword Co-occurrence Analysis. Using interdisciplinary and respective domain knowledge, researchers have been able to generate scientific knowledge about the factors influencing human users' willingness to interact.

In this field, the basis for the creation of the psychological component of the research were two studies on positive psychology in 2008. Technological developments in the medical field have made it possible to measure internal body data corresponding to psychological manifestations and to quantitatively analyze psychological factors. The specific application is to be able to analyze the psychological changes and explain the mechanism of action of the human user when receiving information about the robot's body and expression from a psychological perspective. Because in the psychological perspective, the research content covers a wide range and is closely linked. As shown in Fig. 6, the research on "psychology" involves "positive psychology", "mental health", "social health", and "psychological behavior". Mollahosseini et al. [36] in their study of "speech-enabled communication", "speech-enabled communication", "speech-enabled communication", and "mobile technology". Mollahosseini et al. [36] studied "speech perception" together with "embodiment" and "social robot". The study of "social robot" has been done together with "embodiment". In 2019, Gallimore et al. [39] directly verified the methodological feasibility of combining psychology with robotics, and Cross et al. [40] indicated that the contribution of intelligent robots is a combination of sociology and cognitive neuroscience. Synthesizing findings from different but complementary research fields such as sociology and cognitive neuroscience, psychology, artificial intelligence and robotics suggests that research in the biological sciences, social sciences and technological disciplines deepens our understanding of the potential and limitations of robotic agents in human social life.

In the research field of psychology, there are precedents of mature applications to cross-disciplinary perspective research with a theoretical basis for incorporating new research elements.

Qualitative Analysis of Key Literature. The influencing factors of human-computer interaction willingness contain first impression, schema, emotional cues, and individual differences in the social cognitive model. The influence mechanism of each factor follows the psychological conceptual model, and there are differences in the magnitude of influence weights among the factors.

Of the 819 collected documents, 16 were analyzed with the keyword of psychology, and it was found that "behavior" and "facial expression" were high-frequency keywords, which appeared for the first time in 2016 and 2017, respectively. The first appearance of the 16 literatures. As the research in this field had accumulated the foundation of psychology on the interaction behavior and perception of intelligent robots before 2016, the keywords "behavior" and "facial expression" were found to be high-frequency keywords.

In the psychological perspective, the appearance of the robot is the first and continuously perceived factor in the process of information reception by the human user, i.e., when the robot user interacts with the intelligent robot. The user's first psychological impression of the intelligent robot is composed of people's immediate evaluation, power

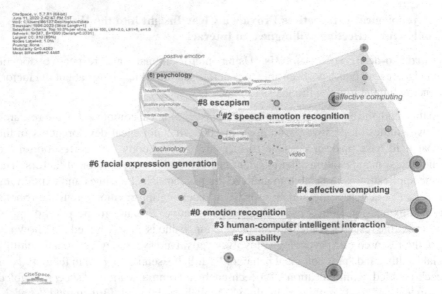

Fig. 6. Keyword Co-occurrence Clustering Network for Interaction willingness in Intelligent Robot Literature (Focus on the psychology).

and activity [41] due to the appearance and utility of the intelligent robot. Moreover, human users' knowledge and experience background [42, 43], cultural background [44], mental age and physical age [45] have individual variability, all of which affect the first impression that human users have of the robot; for example, users who have had knowledge related to the information conveyed by the robot are more likely to understand the behavioral intent of the intelligent robot, and similarly, human users who have extensive life experience Similarly, human users with rich life experience are more likely to understand the information conveyed by robots than those who lack life experience. The physiological age of human users determines the minimum degree of information acceptance, as if the ability of young children to understand external information is different from the ability of adults to understand external information [46]. The psychological age of human users is a reflection of the psychological maturity of human users, and people with different levels of psychological maturity have greater differences in the cognition of the same thing and greater differences in the interpretation of the same information [47].

In the process of social cognition of human beings, the first thing that is carried out is the categorization of affairs, and the basis of categorization is schema. Containing self-schema, role schema, and script; self-schema (self-schema) has a high individual variability, is a cognitive structure that people form about themselves, and has a close structure with the self-concept. Due to the individual variability of self-concept, self-schema is a biased factor in this study. However, the specific applicable population and usage environment can reduce the uncontrollable influence of this factor; Role schema refers to the organized cognitive structure that people have towards the special role players (intelligent robots), and people should generate role schema in order to predict the possible interaction behaviors before contacting the intelligent robots and to improve the efficiency of the interaction behaviors when interaction occurs; "script" is a term used in social psychology to describe the role schema that people form towards themselves. It's a category of schema in social psychology, which refers to a series of sequential schemas of events or events, especially a series of behaviors with a standard process over a period of time. It is used for human users to predict a series of event processes that may occur in a particular situation, and the higher the degree of match between the overall interaction process and the script, the higher the willingness of human-computer interaction. However, the mismatch between the overall process and the script does not completely mean that the willingness to interact is low, and the conflict with the script may arouse the user's curiosity, which in turn improves the willingness to interact. However, there is less literature centered on related research content, and this type of field has a greater research potential.

Also due to the rise of experience design encouraging academics to think from the user's perspective and incorporate user-specific experiences, emotions and perceptions into design practice. This led to the rise of intelligent robot emotional cues as an important research component in the field of psychology around 2016. At that time, Rosenberg et al. [48] argued that robotic nonverbal cues (facial expressions, body movements) can influence human users' behavior, action choices, and play an influential role in human-robot interaction in the perspective of psychology discipline. And Zabala et al. [49], after doing research on robot facial expressions, concluded that robots are artificially programmed to express emotions have an impact on human interaction willingness. And users are more willing to interact with robots when they are able to respond to their emotional needs with appropriate verbal expressions [50].

Individual variability includes age, intellectual and experiential background, and cultural background, e.g., people raised in rural areas are likely to have a mental model that emphasizes self-sufficiency, hard work, and traditional gender roles, whereas people raised in urban environments may have a mental model that prioritizes individualism, creativity, and diversity [51]. Those working in healthcare may have a mental model that emphasizes empathy, compassion, and evidence-based decision making, while those working in finance may have a mental model that emphasizes risk management, strategic thinking, and financial analysis [52]. In addition, there are also relatively uncertain factors such as people's personal relationships, political affiliations, or more volatile immediate moods, encounters, and immediate needs; the degree of variability of the volatile factors is high, and therefore the factors within the individual differences in the proposed social cognitive model are not fixed, and will vary with the actual application.

After qualitatively analyzing the clustering results in Fig. 6 and the popular research themes, the factors affecting willingness to interact were grouped into two main categories: "personal factors" and "situational factors". Individual factors refer to influences that are internal to the research subject in the social cognitive model. On the other hand, situational factors are external influences that are outside the object of study. Personal factors play a decisive role in determining the level of willingness to interact, while situational factors also have an impact on human users' willingness to interact, and some situational factors can directly constitute personal factors, which have an indirect impact on the final willingness to interact.

The above types of influencing factors constitute influencing factors affecting inter-action willingness and follow the weighted average rule [53], which finally form the evaluation of intelligent robots. Such influencing factors as script, character schema, emotional cues and other influencing factors have industry paradigm and small uncer-tainty, but the role of influencing the interaction willingness is significant, and high level weight value is given; such as instant mood emotions, instant needs, encounters, and other unstable factors are the main variables affecting the evaluation of human user's perception of the robot, but the role of influence is small. Therefore, low level weight values are given in the model.

From this, it can be analyzed by psychology that people form their first psychological impression of the robot through immediate evaluation, activity, and power after inter-acting with the intelligent robot, as well as taking into account the role of the robot's emotional cues, schema, and the influence of individual differences. With the social cognitive model, the role of factors with different weights in the process of human-robot interaction is analyzed in order to develop design strategies.

4 Discussion

4.1 Analyzing Human-Computer Interaction Willingness by Social Cognitive Modeling

Inappropriate human-computer interaction behavior creates barriers at the psychological level, negatively affecting human users' experience and perception, and further weak-ening their willingness to interact. From the above bibliometric analysis, it can be seen that in the past decade, research has shifted from "perception" to "positive psychology", from "positive psychology" to "psychology" and "emotion". "Psychology" to "affective computing", a process of gradual refinement of the research content. The more specific research content has clarified the influencing factors of human-robot interaction, so that designers know what factors to pay attention to when designing intelligent robots. The social cognitive model is able to list the current influences based on other studies and assign different weighting ratios to differentiate the degree of importance.

The social cognitive model understands and speculates on the thoughts, feelings, and intentions of others in people's social interactions, including, but not limited to, observing signals such as behaviors, words, and expressions of others. This model has been widely used in many real-world scenarios, such as psychological diagnosis; since the behavior of intelligent robots often differs from that of humans, traditional social rules and habits may not be fully applicable to interactions with robots. Therefore, by applying the social cognitive model can help human users better understand the inter-action process with intelligent robots, including how to perceive the robot's expression, voice, and behavior, and infer the robot's intention and purpose, and analyze what con-stitutes a person's emotional will; the paradigm underlying the social cognitive model has "self-perceived efficacy", The underlying paradigm of the social cognitive model has three processes: "self-perceived efficacy", "subjective norms", and "attitudes", and the current research has derived a variety of models applicable to different real-world scenarios based on the general paradigm of the existing results; the literature has pro-posed a theoretical framework based on the modification of the existing social cognitive model to guide the development of cognitive functioning under adversity [1]. A theoretical framework has been proposed to guide the development of cognitive functions in adversity [54]. It describes in graphic form that when people are in a specific adversity situation, information processing is affected by the feedback effects of "appropriate feedback" and "inappropriate feedback", as well as "positive cognition" and "information processing base". The interaction between "positive cognition" and "information processing base" affects the final information processing output. Or we can construct mental models of different service domains based on the user's mental model [55], and transform them into new cognitive models based on Ingwerson's holistic cognitive theory [56], which include "motivation", "emotion", "internal and external environments", and "positive cognition", "internal and external environment" and "needs", and the factors in the model interact with each other and have an impact.

The interaction between intelligent robots and human users is regarded as a psychological "social interaction", a social-cognitive process, which is a thinking strategy and cognitive mechanism used by people in receiving, processing and utilizing information. The social cognitive process is divided into four processes: perception, inference, prediction, and attribution. "Perception" corresponds to "self-perceived efficacy", "inference and prediction" correspond to "subjective paradigm", "Attribution" corresponds to "attitude"; the contextual and personal factors mentioned above constitute the content of the perceptual process, while inference and prediction are based on the processing of perceptual information in the perceptual process, and finally the attribution process generates the willingness to interact and the attribution style that influences the subsequent treatment of the same Finally, the attribution process generates the willingness to interact and influences the subsequent attribution style towards the same thing. The "Social Cognitive Model" is suitable for studying the factors influencing the willingness to interact with human-robot interaction; the model is based on cognitive psychology and social psychology, and the research involves how to process information from others, how to interpret their behavior and how to predict their behavior, which can be applied to the interaction between robots and users in the research. Research. The social cognitive model has several components, the most important of which is the perceptual process, which involves influences on the content of the information processing that directly determines the existence of the social cognitive process. In the field of human user interaction willingness, researchers have paid high attention to the emotional cues of robots, and it has been proved that robotic emotional cues affect interaction willingness significantly, and should be given a high level of weight to robotic emotional cues.

4.2 Psychological Perspectives on Robot Emotional Cues as the Most Important Factors Influencing Interaction Intention

Robot emotional cues are contextual factors, which are outside the user's own, and are not affected by individual variability. Emotional cues are composed of robot facial expressions, action behaviors, and language expressions, which are more direct than the information conveyed to human users by character schemas, scripts, and evaluations, and have a higher perceptual impact on human users, so it is necessary to increase the weight ratio of this factor in the social cognitive model.

The change of emotional cues of intelligent robots applied in the production and service industries is socially normative, and the functional requirements of the actual scene make it necessary to match the robot's set behavior with it. If the robot's emotional cues are contrary to the functional requirements of the scene, it will reduce the task completion efficiency or even fail to complete the task, losing the meaning of replacing the original manual labor, and secondly, it will affect the user's psychological expectations, and will not produce a good willingness to interact. In addition, the design of emotional cues of intelligent robots must comply with industry standards, industrial robots need to comply with ISO 10218 standards, medical robots need to follow the ISO 13485 standards; intelligent robots emotional cues of variables with predictable norms, the range of change is small, but the impact on the willingness of human users to interact with a large.

The information conveyed by the robot's emotional cues is intuitive; the information can be captured by the human user's vision or hearing, and the subsequent information processing and handling process is simple and direct, and the perceptual impact on the human user is rapid. For example, when the facial expression of the robot is consistent with the emotion of the task content, it will make the user feel that the robot has solidity, and if the expression is inconsistent with the emotion of the robot's task content, it will produce the Valley of Terror effect, which will reduce the user's willingness to interact; when the human user observes that the robot produces action interaction behavior among robots, it can also make the user think that the robot has solidity, which will increase the willingness to interact; the movement rate of the limbs of the intelligent robot is close to the rate of the human limbs movement. The rate of body movement of intelligent robots is considered to increase willingness to interact when it is close to the rate of human body movement; and the accuracy of information conveyed by robotic gesture symbols should also be considered. Including the social contractual nature of hand communication symbols, the same semantic meaning may be expressed differently in different scenarios or environments; the OK gesture means "no problem", "I agree", and so on. In France, the OK sign means "zero" or "of no value", indicating that something is not important or that one is against something. The same gesture can have opposite meanings in different countries; and robot verbal expressions provide emotional feedback, which, when appropriate, can be perceived as emotionally resonant by the user, thus increasing willingness to interact; the above intelligent robot emotional cues are an overview of existing research that has influenced the human user's perception of the robot as an object. The high or low willingness to interact stems from whether the emotional cues are designed to efficiently accomplish tasks and solve needs with human cognitive habits.

The cognitive model of the intelligent robot's emotional cues on the human user's willingness to interact is shown in Fig. 7. It is chronologically divided into four processes: "Perception", "Inference", "Prediction", and "Attribution". External or internal perception directly affects the purpose of the human user of the intelligent robot. "Perception" is the orientation of the mind to the behavior that is going to happen in the present moment, reflecting the needs, desires, and values of the individual [57]. The perceptual orientation in the mind motivates human users to make plans for interacting with the robot and inevitably generate expectations about the usage experience and interaction style based on individual experiential knowledge. The combined effect of the established plan and prediction affects the robot user's behavior and produces real use experiences while the interaction behavior occurs, and these real use experiences, when compared with the previous expectations, eventually form a cognitive evaluation of an intelligent robot.

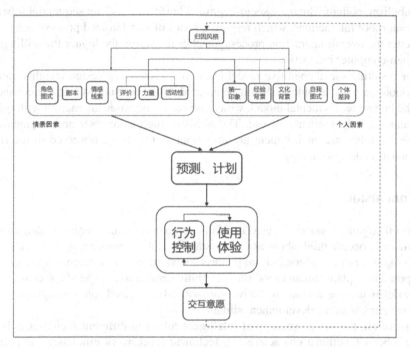

Fig. 7. A model for influencing human users' willingness to interact

The needs of different robot users have a direct impact on the users' purpose of using the robot, which in turn affects the production of plans and predictions. That is, different users' needs have an indirect effect on behavioral plans and predictions, which ultimately affects human users' cognitive evaluation of the robot. It can be seen that meeting the user's needs is an effective way to improve the cognitive evaluation. The differentiation of user needs is the fundamental reason for differentiated design, and thus the purpose of differentiated robot design is to meet a variety of needs, and the differentiated design of robots oriented to specific needs in order to meet the various needs of today's social development. Among the contextual factors, the "environment" factor not only affects the user's purpose, but also the environment in which the user is placed directly affects the user's expectation. The specific scene environment can also confirm whether the user's purpose is correct or not, such as a person with the purpose of going to the amusement hall to play into a solemn environment, will soon be able to notice the difference; and in a specific scene, the user's expectations are related to the nature of the scene characteristics, core values. For example, the core value conveyed by a high-speed rail passenger terminal is "fast and efficient", so the robot in the high-speed rail passenger terminal should be designed as a product that meets this expectation.

Schemas are established mental models used by human users to make sense of things. Self-schemas, role schemas, and scripts all influence whether or not a human user is willing to interact positively; the human user's self-schema influences the perception of the robot. Role schemas require the use of scenarios that match, characters that fit, and functions that make sense, and follow the basic proportionality information and the law of symbolism, both of which are socio-cognitive laws; "scripts" are sequential schemas of human-robot interactions, which require a series of standardized process behaviors. The better the overall interaction process matches the script, the higher the willingness of human-computer interaction.

The resulting social cognitive model leads to the following design insights: intelligent robots, as a social object, should be aligned with expectations that are consistent with the human user's mental model, which indirectly increases interaction willingness by enhancing the experience of use. The needs of the human user and the nature of the specific robot use environment are important factors to be observed in the robot differentiation design strategy.

5   Conclusion

The social cognition model selected in this paper, based on the mental model, emphasizes the way people think about and understand social phenomena, and describes and explains how humans understand and process social information. Accordingly, a model is proposed to explain human users' robot cognitive evaluation of specific scenarios, and this model is used as a guide to derive scenario-differentiated robot design strategies under the current social development situation.

First of all, the design strategy of intelligent robots in different scenarios is based on the robot's functional characteristics, technical level, work efficiency, etc., and is oriented to user needs. Therefore, when designing robots, it is necessary to determine their functions and expressions according to the needs of different scenarios and the characteristics of users and the nature of the scenarios, so as to enhance the positive impact of robots on the user's experience; and personal factors, although unconscious, the user's own experience, knowledge, perception, and age of the composition of the self-schema, the first impression, the immediate emotions also influence the actual human-robot interaction willingness.

Limitations of this paper: First, in terms of research methodology, this paper mainly adopts analytical techniques such as scope review, knowledge mapping, and bibliometric analysis. The scope of sample selection is limited to the Web of Science database, and the sample size is insufficient; second, from the research perspective, this paper examines the interaction status and experience research with intelligent robots from the perspective of human users, and the references tend to be service robots, lacking references about industrial production robots, and not including the experience of industrial production personnel and mechanics.

Based on the findings of this paper, the influence of human users' psychological level factors on human-robot interaction willingness is an increasingly hot topic for future research in this field, but its mode of action and practical applications need further study, such as the role of the influence on interaction willingness and its relationship when the actual human-robot interaction process does not match the script. These findings are of great significance to the study of effective human-robot interaction between human users and intelligent robots and the environment in which they are used. Future research will focus on the empirical study of human users' willingness to interact and psychological factors, as well as the application of cross-disciplinary and emerging technologies to capture, recognize, process, and feed back the users' physical and emotional states, in order to achieve a natural and effective human-robot interaction between human users and intelligent robots and the environment in which they are used, thus enhancing human-robot interaction and improving the effectiveness of human-robot interaction. Human-robot interaction, thus enhancing the willingness of human-robot interaction.

References

1. Gonzalez-Aguirre, J.A., et al.: Service robots: trends and technology. Appl. Sci. **11**(22), 10702 (2021)
2. Laudante, E.: Industry 4.0, innovation and design. In: A New Approach for Ergonomic Analysis in Manufacturing System, pp. S2724–S2734. (2017)
3. Faibish, T., et al.: Human preferences for robot eye gaze in human-to-robot handovers. Int. J. Soc. Robot. **14**(4), 995–1012 (2022)
4. Himmelsbach, U.B., et al.: Human–machine differentiation in speed and separation monitoring for improved efficiency in human–robot collaboration. Sensors **21**(21), 1744 (2021)
5. Swider, B.W., Harris, T.B., Gong, Q.: First impression effects in organizational psychology. J. Appl. Psychol. **107**(3), 346–369 (2022)
6. Aly, A., Tapus, A.: On designing expressive robot behavior: the effect of affective cues on interaction. SN Comput. Sci. **1**, 1–17 (2020)
7. Hameed, I.A.: Using natural language processing (NLP) for designing socially intelligent robots. In: 2016 Joint IEEE International Conference on Development and Learning and Epigenetic Robotics (ICDL-EpiRob), pp. 268–269. IEEE (2016)
8. Spezialetti, M., Placidi, G., Rossi, S.: Emotion recognition for human-robot interaction: recent advances and future perspectives. Front. Rob. AI **7**, 532279 (2020)
9. Rückert, P., et al.: Calibration of a modular assembly system for personalized and adaptive human robot collaboration. Procedia CIRP **76**, 199–204 (2018)
10. Moro, C., et al.: Social robots and seniors: a comparative study on the influence of dynamic social features on human–robot interaction. Int. J. Soc. Robot. **11**, 5–24 (2019)
11. Rossi, S., Rossi, A., Dautenhahn, K.: The secret life of robots: perspectives and challenges for robot's behaviours during non-interactive tasks. Int. J. Soc. Robot. **12**, 1265–1278 (2020)
12. Phan, H.P., Ngu, B.H., White, M.O.: Introducing 'holistic psychology' for life qualities: a theoretical model for consideration. Heliyon **7**(1), e05843 (2021)
13. Xu, J., Howard, A.: The impact of first impressions on human-robot trust during problem-solving scenarios. In: 2018 27th IEEE International Symposium on Robot and Human Interactive Communication (RO-MAN), pp. 435–441. IEEE (2018)
14. Boccanfuso, L., et al.: Autonomously detecting interaction with an affective robot to explore connection to developmental ability. In: 2015 International Conference on Affective Computing and Intelligent Interaction (ACII), pp. 1–7. IEEE (2015)
15. Paas, F., Sweller, J.: An evolutionary upgrade of cognitive load theory: using the human motor system and collaboration to support the learning of complex cognitive tasks. Educ. Psychol. Rev. **24**(1), 27–45 (2012)
16. Moscoso, J.: Emotional experiences. Hist. Psychol. **24**(2), 136 (2021)

17. Beaudouin-Lafon, M.: An overview of human-computer interaction. Biochimie **75**(5), 321–329 (1993)
18. Adati, N., Taheri, J.: Genetic algorithm in robot path planning problem in crisp and fuzzified environments. In: 2002 IEEE International Conference on Industrial Technology, IEEE ICIT 2002, vol. 1, pp. 175–180. IEEE (2002)
19. Dai, Y., Yan, J., Tang, G.: Research on enterprise modeling architecture and supporting tool for agile manufacturing. In: Proceedings of the 4th World Congress on Intelligent Control and Automation (Cat. No. 02EX527), vol. 4, pp. 2575–2579. IEEE (2002)
20. Cohen, O., et al.: fMRI robotic embodiment: a pilot study. In: 2012 4th IEEE RAS & EMBS International Conference on Biomedical Robotics and Biomechatronics (BioRob), pp. 314–319. IEEE (2012)
21. Hu, J., Hou, Z.G., Chen, Y.X., Kasabov, N., Scott, N.: EEG-based classification of upper-limb ADL using SNN for active robotic rehabilitation. In: 5th IEEE RAS/EMBS International Conference on Biomedical Robotics and Biomechatronics, pp. 409–414. IEEE (2014)
22. Fox, P.: Robotic, image-guided TMS: methods, validations and applications. In: Proceedings of the Second Joint 24th Annual Conference and the Annual Fall Meeting of the Biomedical Engineering Society. Engineering in Medicine and Biology, vol. 2, pp. 984–vol. IEEE (2002)
23. Adami, P., et al.: Effectiveness of VR-based training on improving construction workers' knowledge, skills, and safety behavior in robotic teleoperation. Adv. Eng. Inf. **50**, 101431 (2021)
24. Suzuki, R., Karim, A., Xia, T., Hedayati, H., Marquardt, N.: augmented reality and robotics: a survey and taxonomy for AR-enhanced human-robot interaction and robotic interfaces. In: Proceedings of the 2022 CHI Conference on Human Factors in Computing Systems, pp. 1–33 (2022)
25. Fraune, M.R., et al.: Effects of robot-human versus robot-robot behavior and entitativity on anthropomorphism and willingness to interact. Comput. Hum. Behav. **105**, 1–13 (2020)
26. Zhang, Z., Zheng, J., Thalmann, N. M.: Engagement intention estimation in multiparty human-robot interaction. In: 2021 30th IEEE International Conference on Robot & Human Interactive Communication (RO-MAN), pp. 117–122. IEEE (2021)
27. Pande, S., Gupta, K. P.: Indian customers' acceptance of service robots in restaurant services. Behaviour & Information Technology, 1–22 (2022)
28. Dang, J., Liu, L.: A growth mindset about human minds promotes positive responses to intelligent technology. Cognition **220**, 104985 (2022)
29. Bruce, A., Nourbakhsh, I., Simmons, R.: The role of expressiveness and attention in human-robot interaction. In: Proceedings 2002 IEEE International Conference on Robotics and Automation (Cat. No. 02CH37292), vol. 4, pp. 4138–4142. IEEE (2002)
30. De, S., Deo, D., Sankaranarayanan, G., Arikatla, V.S.: A physics-driven neural networks-based simulation system (phynness) for multimodal interactive virtual environments involving nonlinear deformable objects. Presence **20**(4), 289–308 (2011)
31. Rast, A., et al.: Concurrent heterogeneous neural model simulation on real-time neuromimetic hardware. Neural Netw. **24**(9), 961–978 (2011)
32. Bray, L.C.J., et al.: Real-time human–robot interaction underlying neurorobotic trust and intent recognition. Neural Netw. **32**, 130–137 (2012)
33. Staffa, M., Rossi, S.: Recommender interfaces: the more human-like, the more humans like. In: Agah, A., Cabibihan, J.-J., Howard, A.M., Salichs, M.A., He, H. (eds.) ICSR 2016. LNCS (LNAI), vol. 9979, pp. 200–210. Springer, Cham (2016). https://doi.org/10.1007/978-3-319-47437-3_20
34. Inbar, O., Meyer, J.: Politeness counts: perceptions of peacekeeping robots. IEEE Trans. Hum.-Mach. Syst. **49**(3), 232–240 (2019)

35. Pocius, R., Zamani, N., Culbertson, H., Nikolaidis, S.: Communicating robot goals via haptic feedback in manipulation tasks. In: Companion of the 2020 ACM/IEEE International Conference on Human-Robot Interaction, pp. 591–593 (2020)
36. Mollahosseini, A., et al.: Role of embodiment and presence in human perception of robots' facial cues. Int. J. Hum. Comput. Stud. **116**, 25–39 (2018)
37. Kabir, R.S., Sponseller, A.C.: Interacting with competence: a validation study of the self-efficacy in intercultural communication scale-short form. Front. Psychol. **11**, 2086 (2020)
38. Schiphof-Godart, L., Roelands, B., Hettinga, F. J.: Drive in sports: How mental fatigue affects endurance performance. Front. Psychol. 1383 (2018)
39. Gallimore, D., Lyons, J.B., Vo, T., Mahoney, S., Wynne, K.T.: Trusting robocop: gender-based effects on trust of an autonomous robot. Front. Psychol. **10**, 482 (2019)
40. Cross, E.S., Hortensius, R., Wykowska, A.: From social brains to social robots: applying neurocognitive insights to human–robot interaction. Phil. Trans. Roy. Soc. B **374**, 20180024 (2019)
41. Osgood, R.: First impressions of the opportunity for orthopaedic work at the american ambulance (1915)
42. McLean, K.C., Riggs, A.E.: No age differences? no problem. Infant Child Dev. **31**(1), e2261 (2022)
43. Wang, S., Hong, Z., Xiaomei, Z.: Effects of human–machine interaction on employee's learning: a contingent perspective. Front. Psychol. **13**, 876933 (2022)
44. Hu, Y.: Impact of rural-to-urban migration on family and gender values in China. Asian Popul. Stud. **12**(3), 251–272 (2016)
45. Copeland, D.E., Radvansky, G.A.: Aging and integrating spatial mental models. Psychol. Aging **22**(3), 569–579 (2007)
46. Dixon, R.A., Cohen, A.: The psychology of aging: Canadian research in an international context. Can. J. Aging/La Revue canadienne du vieillissement **20**, 125–148 (2001)
47. Göthe, K., Esser, G., Gendt, A., Kliegl, R.: Working memory in children: tracing age differences and special educational needs to parameters of a formal model. Dev. Psychol. **48**(2), 459–476 (2012)
48. Chopik, W.J., Bremner, R.H., Johnson, D.J., Giasson, H.L.: Age differences in age perceptions and developmental transitions. Front. Psychol. **9** (2018)
49. Rosenberg, M., et al.: Expressive cognitive architecture for a curious social robot. ACM Trans. Interact. Intell. Syst. (TiiS) **11**, 1–25 (2021)
50. Zabala, U., Rodriguez, I.R., Martínez-Otzeta, J.M., Lazkano, E.: Expressing robot personality through talking body language. Appl. Sci. **11**, 4639 (2021)
51. Bonarini, A.: Can my robotic home cleaner be happy? issues about emotional expression in non-bio-inspired robots. Adapt. Behav. **24**(5), 335–349 (2016)
52. Aspinall, P., Mavros, P., Coyne, R., et al.: The urban brain: analysing outdoor physical activity with mobile EEG. Br. J. Sports Med. **49**(4), 272–276 (2015)
53. Anderson, C., Keltner, D.: The role of empathy in the formation and maintenance of social bonds. Behav. Brain Sci. **25**(1), 21–22 (2002)
54. Anderson, N.H., Alexander, G.R.: Choice test of the averaging hypothesis for information integration. Cogn. Psychol. **2**, 313–324 (1971)
55. Parsons, S., Kruijt, A.W., Fox, E.: A cognitive model of psychological resilience. J. Exp. Psychopathol. **7**(3), 296–310 (2016)
56. Jones, B.: Designing public services for mental models of citizens: introducing a user-centered approach to public service design and delivery. J. Public Adm. Res. Theory **28**(4), 523–534 (2018)

57. Han, Y., Li, P., Li, L., et al.: Embedded cooperative information searching and retrieval social cognitive model. Inf. Sci. **30**(03), 444–449 (2012)
58. Deci, E.L., Ryan, R.M.: The "what" and "why" of goal pursuits: human needs and the self-determination of behavior. Psychol. Inq. **11**(4), 227–268 (2000)

Modeling of Behavior and Interaction Analysis of Autonomous Robots in Smart Logistics Environment: A Case Study on iLoabot-M

Hua Li[1,4], Laxmisha Rai[2(✉)], Xiang Liu[3], and Lianfu Wei[4]

[1] SENAD Inc., No.599, East Huiwang Road, District Jiading, Shanghai, China
[2] College of Electronic and Information Engineering, Shandong University of Science and Technology, Qingdao 266590, China
laxmisha@ieee.org
[3] School of Automotive Studies, Tongji University, Shanghai 200092, China
liuxiang@tongji.edu.cn
[4] College of Information Science and Technology, Southwest Jiaotong University, Chengdu 610031, China
lihua@my.swjtu.edu.cn, lfwei@swjtu.edu.cn

Abstract. In recent years using autonomous robots for the purposes of loading and unloading objects is highly ubiquitous, especially in the fields of smart-manufacturing and logistics industry. The main purpose of these robots is to increase the efficiency of product management and thereby increase the productivity in logistics sector. However, with the rapid development of big data, artificial intelligence, machine learning, computer vision and internet of things (IoT), one of the main challenges is to evaluate how these robots interact in unpredictable and uncertain environments. In this paper, the experiments conducted on the iLoabot-M (developed by SENAD Inc, Shanghai, China) autonomous and loading and unloading robot is described, and how the user interaction is minimized by understanding the behavior analysis over a period of time are evaluated. Initially, system's prototyping model with the required components such as sensors, actuators, cameras, and other communication and navigation systems is considered for behavior analysis, and then the interaction capabilities are evaluated by assigning specific tasks. The perception system, decision making system, and execution system form the core system components, and results show that they are directly influence the performance in terms of behavior generation, interaction, and task allocation. The behavior analysis is conducted based on different patterns of movements, task-allocation and number of software, hardware, and communication components involved. With this way, users could able to analyze the behavior of the prototype by evaluating the system incrementally within a short time-frame.

Keywords: Mobile Robot · Interaction · Evaluation · Behavior · Logistics

A. Marcus et al. (Eds.): HCII 2024, LNCS 14713, pp. 61–75, 2024.
https://doi.org/10.1007/978-3-031-61353-1_4

1 Introduction

In logistics industry, with the integration with cutting-edge technologies has undergone a transformative evolution, especially when it comes to loading and unloading capabilities. These robots increased the efficiency of overall industry operations by streamlining them, and played pivotal role in overall growth. The key features of robots used in these kinds of environments include self-loading, autonomous navigation, intelligent loading, and other delivery methods. The use of robots in logistics and manufacturing domain is not a new concept. There are several studies earlier on their applications in shop-floor logistics [1], and warehouse logistics [2], modular palletizing systems [3] and smart factories [4]. However, many operations still need manual effort, because there are rigorous requirements when it comes to the movement of goods, loading and unloading of items as well as interactions with different systems. Moreover, there are also issues of ensuring safety, and reliability requirements while dealing with human-computer/human-robot interactions. So, generally, the robots which are used in logistics applications also pose new challenges along with the recent developments in the field of artificial intelligence (AI), big data, and internet of things (IoT). These kinds of robots are widely applicable in tobacco industries, cold supply chains, import and export of commodities, industries related to medicine, milk, wine, food, clothing and in other loading and unloading scenarios.

In this paper, we have proposed how the intricate features of loading, and unloading robots along with their interaction with surrounding environment can able to generate new behaviors. Key features, such as self-loading, autonomous navigation, intelligent loading, and various supported incoming delivery methods, contribute to the overall capability of these robots. Our main objective is to evaluate the performance of iLoabot-M (developed by SENAD Inc, Shanghai, China) targeting the application of loading and unloading operations in smart logistics environment. In summary, we are considering analysis of performance in three domains. They are behavior analysis, interaction analysis, and task allocation analysis.

This paper is organized as follows. The Sect. 2 introduces the related studies in this area. The basic details of iLoabot-M robot, core components, behavior generation, interaction analysis are presented in Sect. 3. The details of performance evaluation, and testing results are provided in Sect. 4. Finally, the concluding remarks are presented in Sect. 5.

2 Related Work

When it comes to using robots in manufacturing or logistics environments, there are many factors such as flexibility, safety, interaction, and engagement of operating environment need to be considered. Most of the robots used in these kinds of environments required to have capabilities of interaction with other robots, as well as with humans for achieving the assigned tasks. To achieve totally unmanned system, some researchers developed vision-sensor based autonomous loading, and unloading unmanned forklift system [5]. Here, the system components are connected to a shared CAN (Controller Area Network). Similarly, the performance of an unloading system is presented in [6], and the performance is evaluated in a laboratory testbed with a container and different sized parcels. Moreover, the individual task times of the system as well as the acceleration of the parcels are recorded. The improvement of efficiency in smart logistics systems with heuristic planning and scheduling was discussed in [7]. Here, proposed method is targeted on multiple automatic guided vehicles (AGV) logistics system.

Smart manufacturing driven the successful implementation of human-robot collaboration (HRC) [8]; and flexibility, efficiency, collaboration, consistency, and sustainability are some of the key industrial requirements. Most of the autonomous systems focus on reducing human intervention, and react to outside actions appropriately. For example, there are studies, where different levels of autonomy of on the user experience (UX) is conducted on a case study involving autonomous flying drones [9]. Considering the interaction, many earlier studies focused on the collaborative interactions to achieve individual, and collective goals, as well as loading, and unloading operations while minimizing interference [10]. Similarly, in mobile robots which are interacting with humans, the safety, legibility, and efficiency are the essential parameters [11]. For example, it is encouraging when the robots actively choose safer paths, and reduces shortest distance during an encounter. Moreover, there are several studies about logistics warehousing and the sorting capacity to express delivery in China, where importance of human assistance is stressed during identification, sorting, and transportation of express parcels [12].

In [13], capabilities of safe operation of human-robot interaction are explored by demonstrating an architecture of a robot system for logistic applications. The main purpose of this robot is to use in automated depalletizing applications. Similarly, in [14], the safe interaction and engagement between the autonomous forklifts are discussed. The purpose of forklifts is to manage the containers for stacking and unstacking operations. Interaction between humans, and AGVs in a hospital environment is discussed in [15]. The main purpose of robots used in such environments is autonomously carrying or delivering objects such as devices, and medicines. Interaction involving, humans, and autonomous transport vehicles (ATV) for intra-logistics is discussed in [16].

In [17], a novel task description language for human-robot interaction in warehouse logistics is introduced. The main objective is to let the human workers to interact with robots in natural way. Here, both the capabilities of human, and robots are used efficiently to improve the overall performance through human-robot collaboration. In [18], the concept of "Digital Product Memory" (DPM), a data storage, and how the robots interact with such a memory is described. The DPM is a data storage which contains the data related to all kinds of product information such as complete product history or handling information which are obtained through RFID (Radio Frequency Identification) technology. The main idea is handling each product individually including in automated logistic processes. Using mental commands to evaluate user experience (UX) in a logistic scenario is discussed in [19]. Here the mental commands are sent through an EEG headset, and application of brain-computer interface (BCI) is discussed.

Considering behavior modelling in robots, a framework is developed in [20], where system behavior can be predicted during system operation. The system responses during unpredictable situations are managed dynamically based on sensor responses. The focus of this study is to model the non-deterministic behaviors to reduce the uncertainty during system operation. Similarly, generating different gestures, and behaviors of a robot using rule-based system is discussed in [21].

3   iLoabot-M Autonomous Loading and Unloading Robot

3.1   Basic Details of iLoabot-M

As shown on the Fig. 1, the robot is developed by SENAD Inc. Consisting of multiple components such as robot arm, conveyor, mobile base, control units, cameras, lights, and batteries. The control units are responsible for central management and control operations of the entire robot. Firstly, it can autonomously use cameras to determine the package status, plan the optimal route, and then freely schedule palletizing and depalletizing operations. Finally, robot can optimize the optimal route by moving in real-time through autonomous navigation. The robot arm can be replaced by multiple fixtures (suction cups), suitable for gripping cardboard boxes, cylinders, and paper bags. The arm has multiple movable joints that can rotate at any angle, suitable for grasping packages at different angles. The foot adopts a tracked chassis to ensure stability during autonomous driving. It can pass through a gap of 400 mm, support climbing with a tilt angle of 45°, and achieve obstacle crossing at a height of 80 mm. The robot's vision system is formed by the fusion of multiple 2D cameras and depth cameras, which can capture two-dimensional images and three-dimensional depth maps of packages. This is the basis for robots to freely schedule walking and achieve fast loading and unloading work. The power system of the entire robot adopts a rechargeable mobile power supply, abandoning the traditional plug-in working mode. Its advantages are higher flexibility and better environmental adaptability. The fill-light mechanism provides real-time supply while working in low light environments, as well this reduces the impact of other light refraction and reflection, ultimately improving the accuracy of object recognition. The conveyor belt facilitates fast loading and unloading of packages during operation.

The dimension, and features of SENAD iLoabot-M robot are summarized in Table 1. Table 2 described the dimension and features of parcels, or packages used during loading, and unloading. Firstly, the robot is designed for logistics applications, where it can perform both loading, and unloading of cargo items based on capabilities provided by 3D machine vision, and radar navigation. The robot is able to accomplish assigned tasks intelligently, and load and unload boxed and bagged items.

Some of the features of this robot make it unique while compared to other robots. For example, the crawler truck chassis, is suitable for loading and unloading mixed goods in platform, outdoor, vehicle and other complex conditions. The self-guided navigation is supported by integration of multiple transceivers and AI decision engines. The robot arm is with 7-DOF and has provided with flexibility for replacement of actuators and compatible with cartons and bags. The logistic companies existing systems such as Warehouse Control Systems (WCS), and Warehouse Management Systems (WMS) can be easily and seamlessly integrated.

The robot is basically composed of hardware, software, and operating environment. The sensors are used to detect environmental information such as temperature, humidity, light, etc. There are actuators such as motors are responsible for robot actions, movements of robotic arms, wheels, and conveyor belts. The camera is used to obtain the

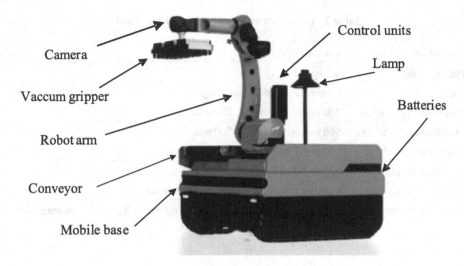

Camera

Vaccum gripper

Robot arm

Conveyor

Mobile base

Control units

Lamp

Batteries

Fig. 1. SENAD iLoabot-M

Table 1. Dimension and features of iLoabot-M

Parameters	Dimension/Features
Minimum package size	200 mm × 200 mm × 200 mm
Maximum package size	500 mm × 960 mm × 1000 mm
Gripping weight	2 kg–100 kg, support bag and box packing
Gripping method	Special actuators, suction cups, grippers
Overall dimensions	1600 mm × 1400 mm × 1550 mm
Operating voltage	DC 48 V
Operating temperature	−20 °C–60 °C
Conveying speed	1 m/s
Drive mode	Tracked differential
Charging power source	AC 220 V–240 V

images, and for the purposes of object recognition. There is other communication, and navigation systems such as GPS, LiDAR (Light Detection and Ranging) which are used for communication between different robot components, and for navigation and control capabilities. Considering the object recognition, and path planning, different machine learning algorithms are used. These algorithms are significant when it comes to decision making such as path planning, and task scheduling. The robot in the smart logistics systems can operate in various environments, including indoor, outdoor, warehouse, factory, etc. However, the characteristics and requirements of these environments are different, so it is necessary to design and optimize for different environments.

Table 2. Dimension and features of packages used

Parameters	Dimension/Features
Package load	0.2 kg–32 kg
Package Type	Cartons, cylinders, paper bags
Minimum cartons size	200 mm × 200 mm × 200 mm
Maximum cartons size	960 mm × 500 mm × 500 mm
Conveying speed	0.1 m/s–1.0 m/s
Container height	2.2 m–3.3 m
Container width	Comply with the width of the vehicle body
Container length	Supports containers of different lengths, with a maximum length of 17.5 m

3.2   Core System Components

The equipment is an autonomous loading and unloading robot based on 3D machine vision guidance and radar navigation. It features autonomous navigation, self-reliant cargo loading and unloading, pallet movement and disassembly, and intelligent handling. The robot is designed for loading and unloading tasks in scenarios such as containers, container trucks, and flatbed trucks. It can handle cargo in both boxed and bagged forms. Additionally, it supports heavy-duty cargo trucks, and no structural modifications to the cargo truck or unloading platform are required.

When the cargo compartment reaches the designated position, a signal is required. The loading and unloading robot, guided by the signal provided by the system, autonomously navigates to the specified location. Through 3D visual detection, it determines the parcel's position and guides the robotic arm for grasping. After grabbing, the parcel is placed on the conveyor line for transport to the rear end for unloading. Visual detection is also employed to determine the parcel's location on the conveyor, guiding the robotic arm for grasping and stacking cargo.

This type of automated loading and unloading robot finds extensive applications in scenarios involving handling of goods in industries such as tobacco, cold chain, import/export commodities, pharmaceuticals, dairy, beverages, food, and apparel. In summary, the system is composed of three core sub-systems. They are (a) perception system, (b) decision making system, and (c) execution system. The schematic and relevance of these three sub components are described in Fig. 2.

The Perception System. Robots perceive the position, size, shape, and other information of goods through sensors and cameras, as well as the stacking status of goods and the status of loading and unloading equipment. In the perception system, the various lighting technologies such as laser, and radar technologies are utilized. These systems are responsible for generating 2D images, RGBD maps, 3D point clouds, and radar data.

The Decision-Making System. Robots utilize artificial intelligence algorithms and optimization techniques to make autonomous decisions based on perceived information

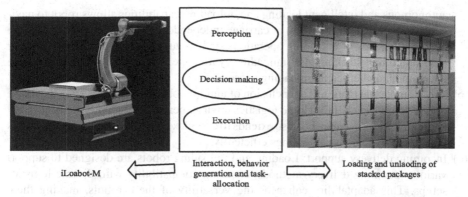

Fig. 2. Schematic of the core-system components and their relevance

and develop the optimal loading and unloading plan. This includes determining the optimal loading and unloading sequence, handling path, cargo placement position, etc. The decision-making system is driven by the recognition algorithms for object identification. These algorithms are responsible for creating grasping strategies, generating path plans, and implementing control algorithms.

The Execution System. The robot completes loading and unloading operations of goods through actuators based on decision results. This includes actions such as grabbing, moving, stacking, and unloading goods. The moving of crawler mobile platform is realized by controlling a motor, and the grabbing is realized by a vacuum system, an executing mechanism and a conveying mechanism. The execution system enables the tracked platform movement through motor control. It also supports facilitating grasping through vacuum systems, actuation mechanisms, and conveying systems.

3.3 Behavior Generation

As mentioned in the [20, 21], the different tasks organized in a specific, and predetermined sequence able to generate specific behaviors. Moreover, such behaviors directly able to reduce the human intervention, and make the robot to operate autonomously. After careful understanding of the robot, the following behaviors of robots are identified. They are (a) intelligent autonomous-loading and unloading, (b) autonomous navigation, (c) incoming delivery support, (d) conveyor belt picking, (e) intelligent unstacking for direct loading, and (f) intelligent sorting and palletizing. These behaviors are briefly described as follows.

(a) Intelligent autonomous loading, and unloading: Loading and unloading robots are equipped with the capability to autonomously load goods onto their platform, eliminating the need for manual intervention. This feature not only reduces labor costs but also enhances operational efficiency by optimizing the loading process. Intelligent loading features enable these robots to strategically load goods, considering factors such as weight distribution, fragility, and stacking optimization. This ensures that the goods are securely loaded, minimizing the risk of damage during transportation. The autonomous and intelligent loading and unloading capabilities allows robot to navigate to the designated platform or carriage independently. This feature enhances the overall efficiency of unloading operations such as automatic unloading to conveyor belts and direct stacking after unloading (yard cage). These capabilities contribute to a smooth and efficient unloading process.

(b) Autonomous navigation: The inclusion of autonomous navigation ensures that these robots can navigate through the logistics environment independently. This not only includes basic movement but also extends to complex maneuvers, allowing the robots to adapt to dynamic surroundings efficiently.

(c) Incoming delivery support: Loading and unloading robots are designed to support various incoming delivery methods, ensuring compatibility with diverse logistics setups. This adaptability enhances the versatility of these robots, making them suitable for a wide range of applications.

(d) Conveyor belt picking: The ability to pick-up items directly from a conveyor belt further streamlines the loading process, allowing for a seamless transfer of goods from one stage of the logistics chain to another. Robot support unloading methods including automatic unloading to conveyor belts, direct stacking after unloading (yard cage), mixed stacking and unstacking (cage), and further operations such as box moving, and autonomous package cage dismantling.

(e) Intelligent unstacking for direct loading: The robots demonstrate intelligent unstacking capabilities, including cage dismantling, facilitating direct loading of goods. The robots showcase the ability to automatically unstack goods from cages, ensuring a constant and uninterrupted supply of items within the logistics environment. This behavior optimizes the loading process and contributes to time and space efficiency.

(f) Intelligent sorting and palletizing: The other important features that robots can exhibit is the automatic unstacking (cage), and facility for supply sorting center compartmentalization. In this operation, the robot can automatically identify and remove boxes from their packing or containers enabling a seamless supply chain operation. The robot can intelligently sort and organize materials on pallets, ensuring that they are arranged in a structured and efficient manner. This operation helps in improving the efficiency of subsequent handling and transportation operations. Loading and unloading robots can intelligently sort and palletize items within mobile cages, further optimizing the logistics workflow. The integration of sorting center compartments enhances the robots' organizational capabilities, allowing for efficient categorization and distribution of goods. Loading and unloading robots play a pivotal role in replacing manual labor for automatic picking and palletizing tasks, reducing the risk of human errors and increases overall efficiency.

3.4 Interaction Analysis

The Fig. 3 and Fig. 4 shows the robot in operation such as loading, and loading/unloading respectively. An important operation is to consider depalletizing, where the main operation involved is to remove the products from a pallet. The depalletizing operation involves the process where products or boxes which were stacked on the pallet were taken and placed into the individual truck containers. This operation is performed by the iLoabot-M robot efficiently so that, the robot is suitable in manufacturing, and logistics applications.

The autonomous nature of the robot makes the intervention of manual effort to the minimum. The Fig. 5 shows the diagram of depalletizing workstation operation. The Fig. 6 shows the real-time operation of 3D depalletizing workstation, where the equipment is automatically performing tasks such as volume measurement, weighing, and scanning codes for parcels.

Fig. 3. Robot in operation, during unloading mode.

Fig. 4. Robot in operation, during loading and unloading modes.

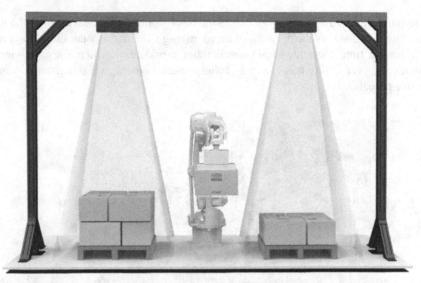

Fig. 5. 3D depalletizing workstation operation.

Fig. 6. The real-time operation of the 3D depalletizing workstation, where the equipment is automatically performing tasks such as volume measurement, weighing, and scanning codes for parcels.

4   Performance Evaluation

We are considering evaluation of performance of the robot in three parameters. Firstly, the evaluation is considered in terms of behavior modeling. The main question is how to define a behavior, and modeling in robots used in logistics management. The behavior of the robot is judged by synchronizing the decision-making tasks organized in a way as expected by the operating environment. Considering this, it is significant to understand whether the robot could able to understand the environment before performing any tasks such as unloading and loading, and able to achieve real-time performance in unpredictable environments. For this, there are several factors are considered. For example, if the environment lighting is dark, how the robot could able to identify the object, and able to achieve the task without failure? To achieve such behavior there is strong need of coordination between the sensors/actuators within the robot, and the sensors/actuators placed within the environment. As the robot itself is designed to behave without much of external assistance even in the unpredictable environments, the main goal of behavior modelling phase is to increase the efficiency with real-time performance, and to have efficient operation with minimum external support. The details of behavior generation are discussed in Sect. 3.3.

The second performance parameter is regarding the interaction analysis as described in Sect. 3.4. One of the main objectives, as mentioned is to minimize the interaction, and maximize the robot operation efficiency. The interaction is either with humans/operators, or external environment plays a major role, when it comes to number of hardware components or software modules required. So, parameters of interaction are fundamentally related to reducing the system hardware components so that high efficiency is achieved using minimum usage of hardware. In most of the general robot systems, number of sensors and actuators added incrementally to achieve higher and meaningful interactions. The interaction with surrounding can be generally achieved using beep sounds, or through vision sensors, and touch sensors etc. Similarly, robot also able to visualize the surrounding, and able to sense the surrounding environment so that, it interacts in a more flexible and friendly way. However, as embedding many sensors and actuators in a logistics robot is not only incur higher costs and also increases the complexity. Moreover, placing sensors or actuators surrounding the robot, and within the smart logistics environment also pose numerous challenges. For example, as the robot is constantly moving, and in some short-range communication systems require line-of-sight, which is difficult to achieve. Considering this, in this phase, irrespective of these bottlenecks, we aim to model the interaction in such a way that, with minimum number of sensors and actuators, the expected results are achieved. The Table 3 summarizes the comparison of different studies regarding the interaction capabilities along with iLoabot-M. Table 4 summarizes the impact test of unloading performance using different parameters.

The third phase of analysis is conducted in terms of task allocation. In general, the robot tasks are programmed in a such a way that each task is accomplished one by one in a serial style. There are several factors need to be considered when we allocate the tasks, as well as how these tasks are able to achieve a meaningful behavior. In the past several researchers have identified the modeling of tasks, and its relevance while generating meaningful behavior. For example, to accomplish a particular set of operation, there are several tasks are involved in the entire step. For an example, an operation may start with task t_1, and then progressed with several intermediate tasks towards final task t_f. However, as the code is flexible, it is possible to have as many tasks as possible, but the question is how to make intelligent decisions in selecting minimum number of tasks out of several existing tasks. Moreover, in some situations, we may need several micro-operations involving multiple tasks need to synchronized or need to be executed

Table 3. Comparison of interaction capabilities in different studies.

Interaction mode	Objective	Application(s)
Human-robot interaction [13]	Safe operation	Logistics
Human-robot interaction [17]	Natural interaction using task description language	Warehouse logistics
Human-robot interaction [19]	Evaluate user experience (UX) using mental commands	Logistics
Humans and AGVs [15]	Autonomous carry and delivery of devices/objects	Hospital environment
Humans and ATVs [16]	Interaction	Intra-logistics
Between autonomous forklifts [14]	Safe interaction, and engagement	Stacking/unstacking operations
Human-memory interaction [18]	Product information handling	Logistic processes
Human signal-robot interaction (iLoabot-M)	Autonomous loading and unloading, and minimization of human intervention	Logistics, transportation, and manufacturing

Table 4. Impact test unloading performance parameter T.

T	Parameters	Objective	Length considered in experiments
1	Package detection	Carton size (carton length, carton height, carton width), speed (luminance, grayscale), refraction, reflection (container surface)	
2	Mobile base movement	Distance (carton depth), resistance (ground tilt angle)	$l_x, 1$
3	Arm movement	Distance (carton height), resistance (carton mass)	l_z
4	Hand movement	Resistance (carton mass, arm tilt angle)	$l_x, 3$
5	Suction control	Resistance (carton surface, porosity, carton mass, arm tilt angle)	
6	Conveyor movement	Distance resistance (carton mass)	$l_y, 1, l_y, 2, l_y, 3$ $l_x, 2, l_x, 3$

in parallel. So, in our work, we evaluated these scenarios, so that minimum number of tasks are selected to achieve an expected operation; also achieving energy consumption by utilizing minimum of sensors and actuators. The Table 5 summarizes the unloading performance of cartons of different sizes.

Table 5. Unloading performance of cartons of different sizes

Scenario	Size	Unloading quantity (Unit per hour)	Capture success rate
Large Carton	≤300 mm × 300 mm × 300 mm	1500	95%
Small Carton	300 mm × 300 mm × 300 mm–960 mm × 300 mm × 300 mm	600–800	98%

Key benefits of this robot can be highlighted as follows. Firstly, the robot includes the tracked load-bearing chassis, which is suitable for loading and unloading of mixed cargo in complex environments such as platforms, outdoors, and vehicle interiors. Secondly, integration of multiple sensors and AI decision engine enables the system to perceive its surroundings and achieve autonomous navigation. Thirdly, the integrated all-in-one design is adaptable for operations within containers, high-platform vehicles, and box trucks. Fourthly, the heavy-duty 7-axis robotic arm allows the flexible interchangeability of execution mechanisms compatible with both containerized and bagged cargo. Finally, the system can be integrated seamlessly WCS and WMS of different logistics companies, ensuring compatibility and smooth integration with existing systems.

5 Conclusion

The iLoabot-M robot described in this paper, has the ability to improve their loading and unloading abilities through continuous learning and optimization. This includes learning and adapting to goods of different sizes, shapes, and weights, as well as learning and optimizing different loading and unloading environments and conditions. In addition, robot can ensure the reliability and safety of loading and unloading work. This includes ensuring the integrity of the goods and avoiding injuries to personnel. Overall, iLoabot-M integrated with multiple sub-components for perception, decision-making, execution, and learning to achieve efficient, accurate, and reliable loading and unloading tasks.

In conclusion, the features of loading and unloading robots are crucial in revolutionizing logistics operations. In this study, the ability of iLoabot-M to interact intelligently with the surrounding environment, coupled with the innovative methods for generating new behaviors is explored. We have analyzed the robot performance based on three domains. They are behavior generation, interaction analysis, and task allocation. Results shows that, it is of significant importance to focus on interaction capabilities, when a robot is operating autonomously. Considering this we have compared interaction modes, capabilities, features, and their applications in different studies. Testing results shows that, the unloading performance of large and small cartons, the capture success rate of iLoabot-M is 95% and 98% respectively. In summary, the abilities of loading and unloading robots such as iLoabot-M form basis for understanding the developments in modern logistics landscape. As technology continues to advance along with new developments in the artificial intelligence, and artificial general intelligence, robots such as iLoabot-M are expected to play an increasingly significant role in shaping the future of logistics industry.

Disclosure of Interests. The authors have no competing interests to declare that are relevant to the content of this article.

References

1. Guo, D., Zhong, R.Y., Rong, Y., Huang, G.G.Q.: Synchronization of shop-floor logistics and manufacturing under IIoT and digital twin-enabled graduation intelligent manufacturing system. IEEE Trans. Cybern. **53**(3), 2005–2016 (2023). https://doi.org/10.1109/TCYB.2021.3108546
2. Gabellieri, C., et al.: Towards an autonomous unwrapping system for intralogistics. IEEE Rob. Autom. Lett. **4**(4), 4603–4610 (2019). https://doi.org/10.1109/LRA.2019.2934710
3. Blumenstein, M., Henkel, V., Fay, A., Stutz, A., Scheuren, S., Austermann, N.: Integration of flexible transport systems into modular production-related logistics areas. In: Proceedings of the IEEE 21st International Conference on Industrial Informatics (INDIN), Lemgo, Germany, pp. 1–8 (2023). https://doi.org/10.1109/INDIN51400.2023.10218262
4. Kalempa, V.C., Piardi, L., Limeira, M., de Oliveira, A.S.: Multi-robot preemptive task scheduling with fault recovery: a novel approach to automatic logistics of smart factories. Sensors **21**(19), 6536 (2021). https://doi.org/10.3390/s21196536
5. Park, J.H., Kim, M.H., Lee, S., Lee, K.C.: Development of autonomous loading and unloading for network-based unmanned forklift. J. Inst. Control Rob. Syst. **17**, 1051–1058 (2011). https://doi.org/10.5302/J.ICROS.2011.17.10.1051(inKorean)
6. Wilhelm, J., Hoppe, N.H., Petzoldt, C., Rolfs, L., Freitag, M.: Evaluation of performance and cargo-shock of an autonomous handling system for container unloading. Logist. Res. 15(1), 10 (2022). https://doi.org/10.23773/2022_10
7. Lian, Y., Yang, Q., Xie, W., Zhang, L.: Cyber-physical system-based heuristic planning and scheduling method for multiple automatic guided vehicles in logistics systems. IEEE Trans. Ind. Inf. **17**(11), 7882–7893 (2021). https://doi.org/10.1109/TII.2020.3034280
8. Othman, U., Yang, E.: Human-robot collaborations in smart manufacturing environments: review and outlook. Sensors **23**(12), 5663 (2023). https://doi.org/10.3390/s23125663
9. Christ, P.F., Lachner, F., Hösl, A., Menze, B., Diepold, K., Butz, A.: Human-drone-interaction: a case study to investigate the relation between autonomy and user experience. In: Hua, G., Jégou, H. (eds.) Computer Vision – ECCV 2016 Workshops: Amsterdam, The Netherlands, October 8-10 and 15-16, 2016, Proceedings, Part II, pp. 238–253. Springer, Cham (2016). https://doi.org/10.1007/978-3-319-48881-3_17
10. Farinelli, A., Boscolo, N., Zanotto, E., Pagello, E.: Advanced approaches for multi-robot coordination in logistic scenarios. Robot. Auton. Syst. **90**, 34–44 (2017). https://doi.org/10.1016/j.robot.2016.08.010
11. Chadalavada, R.T., Andreasson, H., Schindler, M., Palm, R., Lilienthal, A.J.: Bi-directional navigation intent communication using spatial augmented reality and eye-tracking glasses for improved safety in human–robot interaction. Rob. Comput.-Integrat. Manuf. **61**, 101830 (2020). https://doi.org/10.1016/j.rcim.2019.101830

12. Zhang, L., Hu, X., Song, T.: Design and optimization of AGV scheduling algorithm in logistics system based on convolutional neural network. In: Proceedings of the 2023 2nd International Conference on Artificial Intelligence and Autonomous Robot Systems (AIARS). Bristol, UK, 29–31, pp. 167–171 (2023). https://doi.org/10.1109/AIARS59518.2023.00040

13. Baldassarri, A., Innero, G., Di Leva, R., Palli, G., Carricato, M.: Development of a mobile robotized system for palletizing applications. In: Proceedings of the 2020 25th IEEE International Conference on Emerging Technologies and Factory Automation (ETFA), Vienna, Austria, pp. 395–401 (2020). https://doi.org/10.1109/ETFA46521.2020.9212124

14. Haanpaa, D., Beach, G., Cohen, C.J.: Machine vision algorithms for robust pallet engagement and stacking. In: Proceedings of the 2016 IEEE Applied Imagery Pattern Recognition Workshop (AIPR), Washington, DC, USA, pp. 1–8 (2016). https://doi.org/10.1109/AIPR2016.8010590.

15. Caccavale, R., Finzi, A.: An automated guided vehicle for flexible and interactive task execution in hospital scenarios. In: Proceedings of AIRO@AI*IA (2019). https://ceur-ws.org/Vol-2594/short8.pdf

16. Kirks, T., Jost, J., Uhlott, T., Jakobs, M.: Towards complex adaptive control systems for human-robot-interaction in intralogistics. In: Proceedings of the 2018 21st International Conference on Intelligent Transportation Systems (ITSC), Maui, HI, USA, pp. 2968–2973 (2018). https://doi.org/10.1109/ITSC.2018.8569949

17. Detzner, P., Kirks, T., Jost, J.: A novel task language for natural interaction in human-robot systems for warehouse logistics. In: 2019 14th International Conference on Computer Science & Education (ICCSE), pp. 725–730 (2019). https://doi.org/10.1109/ICCSE.2019.8845336

18. Vogt, A., Eich, M., Samperio, R., Kirchner, F.: A practical interaction between robots and RFID-based Digital Product Memories in a logistic scenario. In: Proceedings of the 2009 IEEE International Conference on Technologies for Practical Robot Applications, pp. 95–100 (2009). https://doi.org/10.1109/TEPRA.2009.5339636

19. Fiolka, M., Jost, J., Kirks, T.: Explorative study of a brain-computer interface for order picking tasks in logistics. In: Proceedings of the 2020 12th International Conference on Intelligent Human-Machine Systems and Cybernetics (IHMSC), pp. 253–256 (2020). https://doi.org/10.1109/IHMSC49165.2020.10135

20. Rai, L., Kook, J., Hong, J., Hahn, H.: Behavior modelling of embedded real-time systems operating in uncertain environments. In: Proceedings of the 2008 IEEE International Symposium on Knowledge Acquisition and Modeling Workshop, Wuhan, China, pp. 367–370 (2008). https://doi.org/10.1109/KAMW.2008.4810499

21. Rai, L., Hong, J.: Conceptual framework for knowledge based decision migration in multi-component robot. Int. J. Adv. Rob. Syst. **10**(5), 237–249 (2013). https://doi.org/10.5772/56103

Application of Participatory Design in the Development of a Front-End for an AI-Based Decision Support System with Two Companies

Antonia Markus[(✉)] [iD], Kristien Klaka, Johanna M. Werz[iD], Esther Borowski[iD], and Ingrid Isenhardt[iD]

Chair of Production Metrology, Quality Management, and Information Management in Mechanical Engineering – Laboratory for Machine Tools and Production Engineering (WZL) of RWTH Aachen University, 52074 Aachen, Germany
antonia.markus@wzl-iqs.rwth-aachen.de

Abstract. This study explores the application of Participatory Design (PD) in the development of a frontend system, involving collaboration between designers and end-users. The methodology emphasizes user involvement throughout the design process, encompassing requirement analysis, evaluation, and active participation in design creation. This is realized by the steps of an information event, a GUI-Workshop, and a survey ensuring the involvement of the user in the design process. While feedback from two participating companies indicates a positive reception of the approach, the lack of a comparative study restricts definitive conclusions regarding its impact on user attitudes and system usage. Consequently, to validate our findings, we therefore recommend further comparable studies.

Keywords: Participatory Design · AI-based Decision Support · Human Centered Design

1 Introduction/Motivation

In recent years, work environments have undergone a paradigm shift, characterized by digital transformation. This shift spans various sectors and includes many professional occupations (Morkovkin et al. 2020; Parviainen et al. 2022). This rapid digitalization drives the integration of advanced technologies, particularly artificial intelligence (AI) systems, which increasingly augment workforce capabilities. However, various challenges accompany this synergy between technological advancement and human engagement within a human-AI collaboration (Kelly et al. 2023).

The effectiveness of AI in enhancing workplace productivity and augmenting decision-making heavily depends on user acceptance and utilization. The optimal functionality of state-of-the-art AI systems requires seamless adoption by the human workforce (Aung et al. 2021). Moreover, the prevalent distrust directed at AI systems still poses an obstacle on the way to cooperation between humans and AI. This skepticism often

A. Marcus et al. (Eds.): HCII 2024, LNCS 14713, pp. 76–85, 2024.
https://doi.org/10.1007/978-3-031-61353-1_5

creates misconceptions and unfounded apprehensions, most prominently exemplified by the fear of AI replacing humans (Aung et al. 2021).

An approach that considers this adoption and therefore has perceived increasing attention is human-centered design. It aims at cultivating trust, and perceived utility, and, subsequently, enhances users' willingness to interact with the new technologies (Kelly et al, 2023). Several projects have shown the success of applying human-centered design in the working world (Zysk et al. in press; Büttner and Röcker 2016).

The participatory design approach takes one step further in integrating the user. At its essence, participatory design advocates for the active involvement of end-users in the developmental processes of AI interfaces, integrating stakeholders to be co-authors and be empowered (Bratteig and Verne 2018). Despite several examples from the design domain, the applications of a participatory approach for AI integration in the workforce are rare. The question arises of how such a participatory approach to introduce AI in the workforce can look and to what end this approach is suitable for AI-based systems.

In the following case study, we present a comprehensive methodological procedure of participatory design within the context of AI interface development. This procedure builds on the principles of engaging prospective users in the phases of ideation, optimization, concretization, and evaluation (Bratteig and Verne 2018). The study seeks to discuss the benefits and limitations of this approach in the context of front-end design for AI-based decision support systems.

2 Theoretical Background

Human-Centered Design. The ISO standard 9241-110 details the principles and guidelines for implementing this human-centered design, also called user-centered design. It provides a framework for tailoring system design to align with users' cognitive processes, tasks, and environmental contexts. This standard underscores the importance of adaptability and responsiveness to the user's understanding and needs (National Institute of Standards and Technology 2021). Initially, Don Norman introduced this approach as user-centered design in the 1980s. Since then, it turned into a fundamental approach that aims at fostering positive user experiences and preventing user disengagement (Saffer 2009). User-centered design represents a departure from the traditional engineering-centric approach that focuses on technical aspects of systems. On the contrary, user-centered design places importance on understanding and addressing the unique characteristics and needs of the end-users (Chammas et al. 2015). It shifts the development focus from a purely technical standpoint to prioritizing the target audience's perspective and requirements. A user-centered design process is inherently iterative, encompassing the complete user experience journey. Therefore, it requires the collaboration of a multidisciplinary team, comprising individuals with diverse expertise. They follow the goal of comprehensively addressing various facets of design and usability (National Institute of Standards and Technology 2021). This inclusive approach ensures that user feedback, perspectives, and insights are integral to the design evolution, leading to solutions that align with the end-user's expectations and requirements (National Institute of Standards and Technology 2021).

Several researchers have recently expressed the need for AI systems to be human-centered. A Human-Centered AI allows high levels of control for both computers and the people interacting with it and has the ultimate goal of being reliable, safe, and trustworthy (Shneiderman 2020). The rather general idea of the human-centeredness of AI systems is complemented by guidelines for Human AI Interaction targeting the user interface (Amershi et al. 2019).

Participatory Design. Participatory design, a concept rooted in democratic principles, emerged in the 1970s with the fundamental idea of empowering workers to actively shape their work experiences, particularly in the context of implementing new technologies (Bjerknes et al. 1987; Bjerknes and Bratteteig 1995). the approach serves as a bridge between researchers and end-users who are no longer passive subjects observed by the expert but as active partners co-creating their technological support systems (Sanders and Stappers 2008). It aims to foster their collaboration and to define how technologies can be implemented to meet the diverse needs and expectations of the workforce (Spinuzzi 2005). The concept of participatory design has found its way into modern work environments for several purposes:

- Skill and knowledge adaptation: One central aim is to tailor technology and work processes to employees' skills, knowledge, and other individual characteristics (Gregory 2003). By aligning technology with the workforce's capabilities, this approach enhances usability and efficiency.
- Realistic expectations and willingness to use: Participatory design also helps the involved employees to create realistic expectations and increase their willingness to utilize new technologies (Gregory 2003). Involving end-users in the design process builds a sense of ownership and familiarity with the technology, reducing resistance to change.
- Enhancing collaboration and worker appreciation: Furthermore, participatory design seeks to convey appreciation for the contributions of workers by involving them in decision-making and design processes, ultimately improving collaboration and job satisfaction (Kang et al. 2015). This collaborative approach not only empowers employees but also fosters a sense of shared responsibility for the success of technology implementation.

While Human-Centered Design also includes the first aspect, the latter two are additional aspects of Participatory Design. Especially the sense of ownership and familiarity with technology as well as the worker appreciation provide the opportunity to overcome the fear people are having toward AI-based systems. Therefore, adding Participatory Design to the Human-Centered Design approach seems specifically promising in the development project of AI systems.

As the relevance of Human-Centered AI increases, the principles of participatory design, rooted in a theory that is over 50 years old, may become just as valuable in the face of the rising number of AI systems. In this context, participatory design offers a framework for addressing AI-specific challenges and complexities. Therefore, we used it for the digitalization of work, aligning technology with human needs, and fostering a harmonious and productive working environment.

Recent research shows that participatory design has been gaining relevance in AI contexts, for instance in decision-support tools. However, the specific methodology of participatory design differs heavily between the studies. For example, an empirical study on AI design in legal decision-making workflows used participatory design. In this approach, an interactive simulation and a role-play helped to evaluate a review system to select one of several existing technologies (Delgado et al. 2022). The participatory design was therefore used within the context of an interactive simulation methodology. Thus, the participants had only a minor connection to their real working environment.

Two other studies focused on the involvement of potential users in the evaluation of their application. One of them explored the evaluation of the functionality of the algorithm, where the researchers conducted scenario workshops to explore the acceptance of algorithms supporting child welfare services decisions (Brown et al. 2019). Here, the participatory approach focused on the participation of various stakeholders in evaluating an existing system. In the other example, the users evaluated the designed interface, and indicators like usability and cognitive workload were measured (Gkonos et al. 2019).

A contrary understanding emerged in a study in which stakeholders designed an algorithm themselves. In addition, the participatory approach was used to measure if the developed system reflected the beliefs of the stakeholders. The study showed that applying the framework raised users' algorithmic awareness and confidence in use. However, the system was not implemented and evaluated on a performance level (Lee et al. 2019).

The presented studies show a broad interpretation of the participatory design approach. Based on these inconsistent applications, the following research question emerges: How can Participatory Design be applied throughout the entire process of developing interfaces of AI-based decision support systems? Based on the previous work, we hypothesize that a participatory design approach is especially suitable for the design processes of AI systems as those systems in particular require an active involvement of the prospective end-users.

3   Use Case

The research project "AIXPERIMENTATIONLAB" aims to address the challenges of employees in the domain of customer service and sales operations. The employees are confronted with a growing amount of accompanying data and increasing customer expectations regarding response times. The main goal of the project is therefore to develop human-centered AI applications for decision support to improve the employees' work situation during task completion through complexity reduction, stress reduction, and eventually efficiency gains. One of the main research interests within the project is thus to develop an optimal interface design between the AI system and humans. The project's research took place by exploring the use cases of two partner companies.

Use Case A from the First Company. The first enterprise is a direct sales company for exclusive building elements such as awnings, windows, and doors. The family-owned company is one of the largest manufacturers of its kind on the German market with over 1.4 million customers. The individual in-house production of the offered elements accounts for the company's core business competence. For on-site assembly at the customer's premises, the company commissions independent assembly partners, most of whom have collaborated with the company for many years.

The company's major operational challenge is the daily balancing and coordination between, first, built-to-order production, second distribution warehouses, and third the service provided by third-party suppliers. This situation requires a constant striving for an optimal distribution of resources across the three business fronts. In addition, efficient warehouse utilization by third-party suppliers and timely fulfillment of customer orders in the face of globally fluctuating supply chains represent highly complex planning tasks.

The envisioned digital solution for this use case involved the development of a sorting algorithm to assist the assembly coordination department in prioritizing customer orders. Although the company's database contains all relevant key figures in a well-structured manner, the information overflow resulting from the increase and volatility of orders poses a challenge for the assembly coordination department. Within the project, we developed a decision support system that automatically prioritizes customer orders taking into account all the different figures and delays within the three business fronts. The system was supposed to support the workers of the assembly coordination department so that they could better plan their activities, use resources to ensure the delivery of orders, and communicate with the different stakeholders.

Use Case B from the Second Company. For more than 25 years, the second company has been providing after-sales support and service for manufacturers in the IT, communications, and electronics industries. A technical hotline provides support for questions, advisory, complaint, and return handling in seven languages. In addition, the company repairs electronic devices and overhauls in a self-managed repair center.

A large volume of incoming customer inquiries characterizes the daily business of the company. Fast response times by mail and telephone are key for an efficient day-to-day operation, and the number of processed orders is a determinant of customer satisfaction. Due to a growing customer base and product portfolio, the content of customer inquiries has been increasing in variance, which poses a major challenge for steady response and processing times. Consequently, employees are faced with more complex tasks. This is a major challenge, especially for new team members who are still in the onboarding phase.

To address this problem, we enhanced the internal knowledge management system of the company with text classification algorithms. Text classification enables the creation of clear, well-structured problem formulations. These formulations are then linked with the internal knowledge management system to provide the employee with a fast-matching answer to the problem in question (Münker 2023). In this way, searching and problem-solving times are significantly reduced, and customer support inquiries can be answered more quickly and in a more targeted manner, resulting in greater efficiency. Moreover, the matching system works as a guide tool for accelerating the onboarding of new employees.

4 Approach

Within the research project, we used the process model of the ISO standard 9241-110 as a guide. Therefore, besides the classical process recordings we included observations of and interviews with the future users. We classically derived the users' requirements from these methods for the technical development of the backend. What is more, we aimed to involve the employees during the development phase. The central goal was to include them not only in the final evaluation process but also in the development of the system itself. While developers took care of the technical development after the identification of the required functions, the design of the front end offered easier access to active design for the users who did not require any prior and in-depth technical knowledge.

Together with the companies, we developed a multi-stage process to allow employees to participate both directly and indirectly as well as openly and anonymously in the design of the front end. In total, 16 future users took part in the design workshops, which were divided up by companies and held on-site at the companies. With the subsequent questionnaires, twenty-one employees contributed anonymously to the final Graphical User Interface (GUI).

In the context of the described research project, we applied the approaches of user-centered design and participatory design using the following methods, also depicted in Fig. 1:

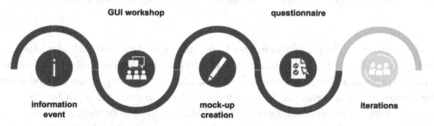

Fig. 1. Human-centered design process to enable employee participation in the GUI development of the AI-based decision support system

Information Event. At the beginning of the process, the employees had to be enabled to play an active role as designers of their future GUI. Therefore, a remote information session provided basic knowledge about interfaces, respectively a GUI. Furthermore, the participants got to know a variety of design elements to open their minds to the creation of individual ideas. Finally, the technical solution including the input and output parameters was presented in a simplified manner, so that the employees could directly think about how they would like to design those parameters.

GUI Workshop. Afterward, a GUI workshop took place on-site. For each company, two groups of three to six employees created at least two different versions of mock-ups. The workshop consisted of a brainstorming session, an individual sketching part, and a collaborative sketching part.

First, the employees thought about which information and functions would be essential to integrate into the GUI and what design principles are important for their specific use case. With the guidance of the project team, they created an overview of which features they expect from the user interface. Subsequently, each workshop participant sketched their vision of the future GUI on paper. A selection of templates helped them jump-start this task without already imposing design aspects on them. Figure 2 provides an overview of selected results. This procedure allowed the participants to create a variety of sketches without influencing each other. Each participant presented their idea to the group and received feedback. The group analyzed each proposal. The goal was to reconsider individual functions and presentation methods and to identify strengths and weaknesses. This evaluation finally served as the basis for the joint development of a definitive version in each group.

Fig. 2. Drafts of the paper mock-ups developed during the GUI workshop.

Mock-Up Creation. The project team transferred the paper sketches that had evolved due to the GUI workshops into digital mock-ups. In addition, they elaborated on the variation of different proposed design elements. This procedure helped to gain an understanding of the employees' requirements. Based on these requirements, the team builds visual blueprints of which features the system should include to best support employees. We adopted functions, information, positions, colors, sizes, and other design aspects from the employees' versions.

Questionnaire. To allow employees to actively participate in deciding on one of the design variations for a mock-up, an online survey was conducted. The survey was spread among the employees. The sample included employees who could not participate in the workshops, which led to a greater involvement of different workers. In the end, 21 participants participated. The last step of the design process was the evaluation of the survey and compilation of the employees' favored design elements into the final mockup.

Iterations. The companies themselves took over the front-end implications within their software solutions. Nevertheless, their first realization was not the final GUI but several feedback loops took part to maintain the iterative nature of the development process. These iterations are still running. The users started to interact with the AI solution via the self-designed GUI and further changes and adaptions were made based on their feedback from their daily experience.

5   Evaluation and Discussion

In this paper, we present an approach to applying Participatory Design in the human-centered development of interfaces for AI-based decision support systems. Our initial hypothesis assumed that this approach is particularly well-suited for AI systems. Several aspects are speaking in favor of this hypothesis:

One notable advantage of our participatory approach lies in its success in managing user expectations. The use of AI often elicits diverse and sometimes extreme expectations, ranging from overly optimistic to overly pessimistic views (Lichtenthaler 2019). Our approach effectively navigated the balance of addressing misleading expectations by involving the users every step of the way and keeping them updated about developments within the process.

On a higher level, the involvement of users can also play a key role in preventing digital transformation projects from failing altogether. This effect has been a large problem of such projects (Westenberger et al. 2022). One reason for this preventive effect might be that integrating users into the development process can prevent the construction of inaccurate conceptions by developers or executives. In the presented use cases, involving the users helped to build a more realistic understanding of their perspectives and needs, which resulted in a good fit between the requirements of the users and the final system.

Despite the observed success, some challenges emerged and might affect other projects replicating our procedure. It became apparent that the participatory approach as we applied it can face difficulties in projects with high system complexity. Too many features and dependencies might overwhelm users and deteriorate their involvement and motivation. In our case, the introduction of a separate program as an add-on to an existing infrastructure facilitated the workers' comprehension of the system. For larger projects, applying user-centered design to a dedicated portion of a large system might be an option. Adopting a stepwise approach, particularly in more complex cases, could mitigate these challenges.

Additionally, despite having many benefits user involvement might not always lead to highly innovative solutions. Users tend to develop what is familiar, making it difficult to generate novel design ideas. To address this limitation, combining user-generated ideas with the expertise of design professionals could offer a more balanced and innovative design process.

Finally, we recognized the importance of expectation management for the AI solution and the project's overall success. Users, when actively involved, might feel an increased responsibility for the success of a project. However, it is crucial to emphasize that success is not guaranteed, and users should not bear the burden of failure. Highlighting these aspects can contribute to a more realistic understanding of project outcomes. Such expectation management is critical in projects implementing AI-based systems (Buschmeyer et al. 2022).

In conclusion, our exploration of the Participatory Design approach in the context of AI-based decision support systems reveals both its strengths and challenges. By carefully addressing these considerations, a Participatory Design approach along a User-Centered Design process provides the possibility to enhance the effectiveness of both approaches in creating usable and successful AI interfaces.

6   Conclusion and Outlook

In this case study we presented an example for applying a human-centered approach in combination with Participatory Design to develop a frontend together with its future users. The advantage of the procedure is that the users were not only involved in the requirement analysis and evaluation but also took an active role in creating the designs. The approach received positive feedback from the two participating companies. To further evaluate these positive study results, comparative studies should be conducted, as well as studies examining performance and long-term effects. These investigations should also consider the findings of this study regarding the advantages and disadvantages of the method.

Summarizing, we experienced several benefits of applying a Participatory Design approach to the given use cases. Other companies and research projects might also profit by proceeding similarly. However, there is still a lack of quantitative proof of the effect of participatory procedure. We are looking forward to seeing additional applications and evaluations of similar procedures. Such tests are especially valuable as effective and convenient Human-Centered approaches face an increasing relevance due to the rise of AI-based systems that start shaping our work contexts.

Acknowledgments. AIXPERIMENTATIONLAB stands for Augmented Intelligence Experimentation Laboratory — the research project runs until the end of 2023 and is funded by the Federal Ministry of Labour and Social Affairs (BMAS) as part of the funding program "Future-oriented companies and administrations in the digital transformation (room for learning and experimental AI)" — EXP.01.00016.20.

Disclosure of Interests. The authors have no competing interests to declare that are relevant to the content of this article.

References

Amershi, S., et al.: Guidelines for human-AI interaction. In: Proceedings of the 2019 CHI Conference on Human Factors in Computing Systems, pp. 1–13 (2019). https://doi.org/10.1145/3290605.3300233

Aung, Y.Y.M., Wong, D.C.S., Ting, D.S.W.: The promise of artificial intelligence: a review of the opportunities and challenges of artificial intelligence in healthcare. Br. Med. Bull. **139**(1), 4–15 (2021). https://doi.org/10.1093/bmb/ldab016

Bjerknes, G., Bratteteig, T.: User participation and democracy: a discussion of scandinavian research on system development. Scand. J. Inf. Syst. **7**, 1 (1995)

Bjerknes, G., Ehn, P., Kyng, M.: Computers and democracy—a scandinavian challenge. Aldershot (1987)

Bratteteig, T., Verne, G.: Does AI make PD obsolete? Exploring challenges from artificial intelligence to participatory design. In: Proceedings of the 15th Participatory Design Conference: Short Papers, Situated Actions, Workshops and Tutorial, vol. 2, pp. 1–5 (2018). https://doi.org/10.1145/3210604.3210646

Brown, A., Chouldechova, A., Putnam-Hornstein, E., Tobin, A., Vaithianathan, R.: Toward algorithmic accountability in public services: a qualitative study of affected community perspectives on algorithmic decision-making in child welfare services. In: Proceedings of the 2019 CHI Conference on Human Factors in Computing Systems, pp. 1–12 (2019). https://doi.org/10.1145/3290605.3300271

Buschmeyer, K., Hatfield, S., Heine, I., Jahn, S., Markus, A.L.: Expectation management in AI implementation projects: a case study. EuroMed J. Bus. **18**(3), 441–451 (2022). https://doi.org/10.1108/EMJB-10-2021-0161

Büttner, S., Röcker, C.: Applying human-centered design methods in industry–a field report. Hum.-Comput. Interact.-Perspect. Ind. **4** (2016)

Chammas, A., Quaresma, M., Mont'Alvão, C.: A closer look on the user centred design. Procedia Manuf. **3**, 5397–5404 (2015). https://doi.org/10.1016/j.promfg.2015.07.656

Delgado, F., Barocas, S., Levy, K.: An uncommon task: participatory design in legal AI. Proc. ACM Hum.-Comput. Interact. **6**(CSCW1), 1–23 (2022). https://doi.org/10.1145/3512898

Gkonos, C., Iosifescu Enescu, I., Hurni, L.: Spinning the wheel of design: evaluating geoportal graphical user interface adaptations in terms of human-centred design. Int. J. Cartogr. **5**(1), 23–43 (2019). https://doi.org/10.1080/23729333.2018.1468726

Gregory, J.: Scandinavian approaches to participatory design. Int. J. Eng. Educ. **19**(1), 62–74 (2003). https://www.ijee.ie/articles/Vol19-1/IJEE1353.pdf

Kang, M., Choo, P., Watters, C.E.: Design for experiencing: participatory design approach with multidisciplinary perspectives. Procedia. Soc. Behav. Sci. **174**, 830–833 (2015). https://doi.org/10.1016/j.sbspro.2015.01.676

Kelly, S., Kaye, S.-A., Oviedo-Trespalacios, O.: What factors contribute to the acceptance of artificial intelligence? a systematic review. Telemat. Inf. **77**, 101925 (2023). https://doi.org/10.1016/j.tele.2022.101925

Lee, M.K., et al.: WeBuildAI: participatory framework for algorithmic governance. In: Proceedings of the ACM on Human-Computer Interaction, vol. 3(CSCW), pp. 1–35 (2019). https://doi.org/10.1145/3359283

Lichtenthaler, U.: Extremes of acceptance: employee attitudes toward artificial intelligence. J. Bus. Strateg. **41**(5), 39–45 (2019)

Münker, S., et al.: A human-centered decision support system in customer support. In: Proceedings CAIP (2023)

Morkovkin, D.E., Gibadullin, A., Kolosova, E., Semkina, N.V., Fasehzoda, I.S.: Modern transformation of the production base in the conditions of Industry 4.0: problems and prospects. J. Phys. Conf. Ser. **1515**(3), 032014 (2020). https://doi.org/10.1088/1742-6596/1515/3/032014

National Institute of Standards and Technology. Human Centered Design (HCD) (2021)

Sanders, E.B.-N., Stappers, P.J.: Co-creation and the new landscapes of design. CoDesign **4**(1), 5–18 (2008). https://doi.org/10.1080/15710880701875068

Parviainen, P., Tihinen, M., Kääriäinen, J., Teppola, S.: Tackling the digitalization challenge: how to benefit from digitalization in practice. Int. J. Inf. Syst. Proj. Manag. **5**(1), 63–77 (2022). https://doi.org/10.12821/ijispm050104

Saffer, D.: Designing for interaction: Creating innovative applications and devices. New Riders (2009). http://ci.nii.ac.jp/ncid/BB0254736X

Shneiderman, B.: Human-centered artificial intelligence: reliable, safe & trustworthy. Int. J. Hum.-Comput. Interact. **36**(6), 495–504 (2020). https://doi.org/10.1080/10447318.2020.1741118

Spinuzzi, C.: The methodology of participatory design. Tech. Commun. **52**(2), 163–174 (2005)

Westenberger, J., Schuler, K., Schlegel, D.: Failure of AI projects: understanding the critical factors. Procedia Comput. Sci. **196**, 69–76 (2022). https://doi.org/10.1016/j.procs.2021.11.074

Zysk, J., et al.: Towards operator empowerment in assembly lines with human-centered design: a concept with application in the automotive industry. Procedia CIRP. (in press)

squad.ai: A Multi-agent System Built on LLMs, Incorporating Specialized Embeddings and Sociocultural Diversity

André Neves[1]([⊠]) [iD], Silvio Meira[2,3] [iD], Filipe Calegário[1] [iD], Rui Belfort[2] [iD], and Marcello Bressan[3] [iD]

[1] UFPE - Universidade Federal de Pernambuco, Recife, PE 50670-901, Brazil
Andre.neves@ufpe.br
[2] TDS Company, Recife, PE 50030210, Brazil
[3] CESAR - Centro de Estudos e Sistemas Avançados do Recife, Recife, PE 50030-390, Brazil

Abstract. The squad.ai system emerges as an innovative proposition in the landscape of multi-agent systems, building upon the robustness of Large Language Models (LLMs). Recognizing the potentialities and limitations of LLMs, the system integrates specialized embeddings, allowing for a deepening and specialization of agent knowledge in specific domains. A distinctive feature of squad.ai is the incorporation of rich identity and educational attributes, reflecting sociocultural diversity. This diversity, coupled with behavioral archetypes, aims to facilitate more contextualized and humanized interactions, both among agents and between agents and humans. Squad.ai, therefore, represents a stride forward in the pursuit of multi-agent systems that combine vast knowledge, deep specialization, and meaningful sociocultural representation.

Keywords: Multi-Agent System · Large Language Models (LLMs) · Specialized Embeddings · Sociocultural Diversity · Collaborative AI · Real-time Adaptability · Personalized Learning · Decision-making Support · Contextualized Collaboration · squad.ai · Agent-Human Interaction · Knowledge Enhancement · Dynamic Generation · AI in Healthcare · Legal Applications of AI

1 Introduction

The rapid pace of technological evolution over the past few decades has brought to the forefront an array of computational solutions designed to mimic, enhance, and even surpass human capabilities in various domains. Among these, multi-agent systems have garnered significant attention due to their inherent ability to model and manage complex tasks by breaking them down into smaller, more manageable sub-tasks handled by individual agents. These agents, capable of autonomous operation and interaction, jointly work towards achieving overarching system goals, often emulating the collective intelligence found in natural systems.

A. Marcus et al. (Eds.): HCII 2024, LNCS 14713, pp. 86–96, 2024.
https://doi.org/10.1007/978-3-031-61353-1_6

Historically, multi-agent systems have been rooted in decentralized problem-solving. From coordinating tasks in industrial settings to optimizing traffic flows in smart cities, these systems have proven to be versatile tools. Their strength lies in the premise that many hands (or in this case, agents) make light work. By distributing tasks among multiple agents, the system can achieve parallelism, fault tolerance, and often enhanced efficiency, especially in scenarios where centralized systems are inadequate or impractical (Wooldridge, 2009).

However, as multi-agent systems found applications in increasingly diverse domains, a pertinent question arose: How does one ensure that these agents possess the depth of knowledge and expertise required to handle specialized tasks? Enter Large Language Models (LLMs). With their ability to understand, generate, and interact using human-like language, LLMs opened avenues for creating agents with vast general knowledge. Platforms such as GPT-3 and its successors demonstrated a prowess in linguistic tasks that was, until recently, considered the exclusive domain of human cognition (Brown et al., 2020). Integrating LLMs into multi-agent systems seemed like a natural progression, offering the promise of agents capable of sophisticated linguistic interactions and knowledge processing.

Yet, while LLMs brought breadth of knowledge, the challenge of depth in specific domains persisted. LLMs, despite their impressive capabilities, are not inherently specialized for every niche domain. For instance, an LLM might know about quantum mechanics, but might it possess the deep expertise of a quantum physicist? This limitation underscores the need for specialization mechanisms that allow agents to delve deep into specific knowledge areas, ensuring they are not just jack-of-all-trades, but also masters of some.

This is where the squad.ai innovation comes into play. Recognizing the potential of LLMs and understanding their limitations, squad.ai introduces a framework where agents, based on LLMs, are enhanced with specialized embeddings. These embeddings, tailored for specific domains, allow agents to possess deep expertise, extending the capabilities of the foundational LLM. In essence, while the LLM provides a wide canvas of general knowledge, the embeddings paint detailed strokes on this canvas, bringing forth intricate patterns of specialized knowledge.

But squad.ai's innovation does not stop at knowledge enhancement. Realizing that effective multi-agent interaction is not just about knowledge but also about relatability and context, the system incorporates rich attributes of identity and education in its agents. These attributes, spanning aspects such as age, gender, nationality, and educational background, introduce a sociocultural layer to the agents. In doing so, they ensure that interactions, whether agent-agent or agent-human, are more contextual, relatable, and humanized. This addition, rooted in behavioral science and sociology, transforms the agents from mere knowledge processors to entities with simulated backgrounds, enhancing the richness of interactions within the multi-agent system.

In conclusion, as we stand on the cusp of a new era in artificial intelligence, the need for systems that are both broad in knowledge and deep in expertise becomes ever more apparent. Systems that not only compute but also relate; systems that do not just know but understand. The squad.ai, with its innovative approach, seeks to bridge these requirements, proposing a multi-agent framework that promises vast knowledge, deep specialization, and a touch of humanity. In the ensuing sections, we will delve deeper into the theoretical foundations of this system, exploring the technologies and concepts that make squad.ai a beacon in the realm of advanced multi-agent systems.

2 Theoretical Foundation

2.1 Large Language Models (LLMs): Their Role in AI and Application in squad.ai

The emergence of Large Language Models (LLMs) like GPT-3 and its successors brought a notable transformation to the domain of Artificial Intelligence (AI). These models are trained on vast datasets, enabling them to process, understand, and generate language in a remarkably human-like manner. The capability of these LLMs to respond to a wide variety of prompts with relevant and often creative information suggests a comprehensive depth and breadth of knowledge (Brown et al., 2020).

Within the context of squad.ai, LLMs serve as a backbone, granting agents a vast base of knowledge. However, while LLMs excel in covering a broad spectrum of topics, their efficacy may be limited in specific niches or questions that require deep specialization. Thus, the need to supplement and enhance these models becomes evident. **Sample Heading (Third Level).** Only two levels of headings should be numbered. Lower level headings remain unnumbered; they are formatted as run-in headings.

2.2 Specialized Embeddings: Introduction, Benefits, and Their Integration with LLMs

Embeddings, in the realm of machine learning, refer to vector representations of data. These representations capture semantics and relationships between data, making them powerful instruments for knowledge representation. Specialized embeddings, on the other hand, are fine-tuned or designed specifically for certain domains or topics (Mikolov et al., 2013).

By integrating specialized embeddings with LLMs, squad.ai seeks to overcome the inherent limitations of LLMs in terms of specialization. These embeddings, when integrated, serve to enhance, and specialize the knowledge of agents in specific areas, offering a depth the foundational LLM might not achieve on its own.

Sample Heading (Third Level). Only two levels of headings should be numbered. Lower level headings remain unnumbered; they are formatted as run-in headings.

2.3 Jungian Archetypes: Foundation and Their Relevance in Modeling Agent Behaviors

Jungian archetypes are concepts derived from Carl Gustav Jung's analytical psychology and refer to innate images or universal patterns that reside in the collective unconscious. These archetypes, such as the Hero, the Wise Old Man, or the Mother, play a pivotal role in shaping human behavior and perceptions (Jung, 1964).

In modelling the behavior of agents in multi-agent systems like squad.ai, Jungian archetypes can provide a foundation for developing agents that exhibit behavior patterns more aligned with human perceptions and expectations. By incorporating these archetypes, agents not only process information but do so in a manner that is perceived as more natural or relatable to human users.

2.4 Identity and Educational Attributes: Amplifying the Sociocultural Diversity of Agents

For agents in multi-agent systems to be genuinely effective and relatable, it is crucial that they mirror the rich tapestry of identities and backgrounds found in human society. Identity, encompassing characteristics like age, gender, nationality, and social class, bestows upon each agent a unique nuance that can be used to enhance relatability and efficacy of interactions. Education, on the other hand, refers to the agent's domain expertise and level of proficiency, which might include academic qualifications, technical training, or any other specialized learning.

By incorporating these attributes in squad.ai, agents can be modelled to mirror a sociocultural diversity. This diversity, when adeptly applied, has the potential to significantly enhance the collaboration and efficacy of a multi-agent network.

2.5 Prompt Engineering: Its Significance in Agent Specialization and Interactivity

Prompt Engineering refers to the art and science of formulating prompts or instructions in such a way that they guide a language model's output in a specific direction. Given the malleable nature of LLMs, careful formulation of prompts can steer, specialize, or even refine the responses provided by the model (Gao et al., 2020).

Within squad.ai, prompt engineering plays a critical role in ensuring that agents, grounded in LLMs, respond, and interact in ways that align with the system's and users' expectations. In addition to guiding the model's output, prompts can also be used to access and mobilize the specialized embeddings, ensuring agents deliver specialized responses when needed.

3 Methodology

3.1 squad.ai's LLM Base: Discussion on the Underlying Language Model

At the core of any language-based system lies its proficiency to process, understand, and generate language. For squad.ai, this linguistic prowess is provided by a Large Language Model (LLM). Trained extensively on expansive datasets, these models form the foundational generalized knowledge and linguistic capability.

What sets squad.ai apart is its ability to shape this underlying model adaptively and dynamically. Rather than relying on a pre-set agent, the system generates agents on-demand, dynamically adjusting to the user's needs and specifications.

3.2 Integration of Specialized Embeddings: Real-Time Process and Technique

Within the squad.ai realm, knowledge specialization is taken to a new echelon, courtesy of the dynamic incorporation of specialized embeddings. Unlike traditional systems that rely on pre-trained embeddings, squad.ai constructs embeddings in real-time based on user-provided data.

Through advanced machine learning techniques and semantic analysis, the system processes, scrutinizes, and translates user data into vector embeddings. These embeddings are then integrated into the LLM, granting the generated agent specialized and contextualized knowledge. This on-the-fly approach allows users to craft agents perfectly tailored to specific situations, ensuring relevance and accuracy in interactions.

3.3 Definition of Identity and Training: Real-Time Construction with Diversity and Depth

One of the pillars of squad.ai is its ability to humanize agents, making them relatable and contextualized. However, rather than relying on static or predefined identities, the system adopts a groundbreaking approach, allowing dynamic definition of identity and training.

Users can specify various dimensions of identity such as age, gender, nationality, and social class. Alongside this, users have the freedom to define the agent's training, choosing from various knowledge domains and levels of expertise. This user-supplied information is then processed in real-time, spawning an agent that mirrors the desired identity and training perfectly.

3.4 Behavior Modelling: Dynamic Generation Using Jungian Archetypes and Prompt Engineering

An agent's behavior is not just a function of its knowledge but also its personality and interaction style. In squad.ai, behavioral modeling is dynamically tailored based on user inputs and contextual necessities.

Using Jungian archetypes as a foundation, the system generates behavior patterns that align with user expectations and requirements. Whether it is the contemplative behavior of the "Wise Old Man" or the determination of the "Hero", squad.ai can model a spectrum of archetype-based behaviors.

Moreover, real-time prompt engineering plays a pivotal role. Through the meticulous formulation of prompts, the underlying LLM is steered, ensuring responses that align with the desired behavior and the situation at hand.

3.5 On the Responsibility Ascription and Ethical Concerns of Artificial Agents

Knowing that the training of LLMs and application of AI is not impervious to bias, the social and human intelligence contribution becomes paramount.

Regarding the LLMs as Artificial Moral Agents (Allen et al. 2000) allows us to ponder upon the demarcation of responsibility and involvement of such agents in co-creative processes and decision-making.

The debate on whether AI and LLMs should be regarded as AMAs is still far from maturity, however the responsibility gap should not be overlooked, and a normative ethical stance must be adopted on this matter (Behdadi and Munthe 2020).

This means that, from a practical standpoint, squad.ai's human agents systematically scrutinize all content generated by the Artificial Agents, may it be by rigorous curatorship (human intelligence) or through meticulous debate with stakeholders of the project (social intelligence).

Methodology Conclusion. Squad.ai redefines the traditional approach to multi-agent systems, emphasizing flexibility, customization, and adaptability. Through its novel methodology, the system not only spawns agents and specialized knowledge in real-time but also ensures these agents are perfectly aligned with user needs and contexts. This user-centric and dynamic approach establishes squad.ai as a disruptive force in the realm of artificial intelligence and multi-agent systems.

4   Operation of squad.ai

4.1   Formation and Interactivity of Squads: Mechanism of Grouping and Collaboration

The innovative essence of squad.ai is embedded in its dynamic and adaptive creation of 'squads' - clusters of artificial agents poised to work in tandem. When a user interacts with squad.ai, they do not merely engage with a singular, static agent but can invoke a multitude of agents, each tailored to specific tasks and domains.

Upon a user's request, the system swiftly evaluates the contextual requirements. Leveraging the underlying LLM, coupled with real-time embeddings derived from user-provided data, squad.ai dynamically assembles a squad. This assemblage ensures a diverse range of skills and knowledge, closely mirroring the user's contextual needs.

The interactivity within these squads is orchestrated meticulously. Agents within a squad are interconnected, enabling seamless data exchange and collaborative decision-making. Each agent, built with specific expertise and behavior, plays its role - from analyzing complex data to drafting responses or making predictions. The collective intelligence of the squad, therefore, is greater than the sum of its parts.

4.2   Agent-Agent Collaboration: Protocols and Collaboration Mechanisms

The bedrock of squad.ai's efficacy lies in its ability to foster seamless collaboration between agents. Such Agent-Agent collaboration is crucial for the holistic and efficient operation of the system.

At the onset of a task, protocols define the hierarchy and sequence of operations among agents. While one agent might specialize in initial data processing, another could focus on in-depth analysis, and yet another might be responsible for synthesizing a comprehensible output.

The communication protocol adopted by squad.ai ensures low latency and high accuracy. When one agent completes its segment of the task, it dispatches the results to the next agent in the sequence, often with meta-information or suggestions for further processing. This iterative and collaborative approach ensures optimal outputs.

Furthermore, agents within a squad possess the capability to seek assistance or validation from their peers. If an agent encounters an anomaly or uncertainty, it can request peer agents for insights or alternate perspectives, ensuring that the squad's final output is refined and accurate.

4.3 Agent-Human Collaboration: Interfaces, Protocols, and Feedback

Squad.ai is not just designed to foster collaboration among agents but is equally adept at facilitating Agent-Human interactions. This symbiotic relationship augments the capabilities of both parties, ensuring superior outcomes.

The user interface is intuitive, designed to cater to a wide range of users. Upon initiating a task, users can specify their requirements, which are then interpreted by the system to select or generate the most apt squad. As agents work on the task, users can monitor progress, interact with individual agents, or adjust parameters in real-time.

The protocols governing Agent-Human interactions prioritize transparency and flexibility. Users receive updates, insights, and even suggestions from agents, ensuring they remain in the loop. In scenarios where user intervention or decision-making is required, agents proactively seek input.

A unique feature of squad.ai is its feedback mechanism. Post-task, users can provide feedback on the squad's performance. This feedback is processed and integrated, allowing the system to learn and refine its operations. Over time, this continuous feedback loop ensures that squad.ai becomes increasingly adept at tailoring its squads to users' needs.

Conclusion on squad.ai's Operation. Squad.ai stands as a testament to the evolution of AI systems, emphasizing collaboration both internally among agents and externally with human users. Its dynamic, adaptive, and user-centric approach reimagines how we perceive and interact with AI. The system's ability to amalgamate diverse agents into cohesive squads, each tailored to specific tasks, coupled with its robust collaboration protocols, sets a new benchmark for AI-driven solutions. The emphasis on continuous learning, driven by user feedback, ensures that squad.ai is not just a static tool but a constantly evolving partner, poised to meet the ever-changing demands of its user base.

5 Potential Use Cases and Applications

The inherent flexibility and adaptability of squad.ai, which generates specialized agents in real-time to form collaborative squads, positions it as a priceless tool across a broad range of contexts. Here, we will delve into four pivotal areas, shedding light on how squad.ai can revolutionize decision-making, learning, health, and the legal environment, with special emphasis on the enriching interaction between agents and humans.

Decision-Making. Today'.s corporate environments are replete with intricate challenges where decisions often intersect various vectors of information.

Real-Time Data Analysis. In a volatile corporate setting, decisions need to be swift and informed. An executive contemplating changes in the supply chain might benefit from a squad with agents specializing in logistics, global economics, market analysis, and finance. The agents' interactivity with professionals amplifies their capability to evaluate scenarios, enabling more precise and contextualized decision-making.

Strategic Simulations. When evaluating market strategies or product launches, squads can craft simulations involving various variables, always in collaboration with strategy teams, ensuring multiple perspectives are contemplated.

Learning Environments. Learning, whether formal or informal, is ever-evolving, and personalization has become crucial.

Personalized Student Support. A student grappling with a particular concept could benefit from a multifaceted squad offering theoretical, practical, and interactive approaches. Collaboration between agents and students enhances comprehension and engagement.

Multidisciplinary Content Creation: For educators and researchers, multidisciplinary squads can assist in integrating varied perspectives, always in tandem with the educators themselves, ensuring the generated content is holistic and pertinent.

Health Environments. Healthcare is an arena where timely and accurate decisions are vital.

Assisted Diagnosis. In situations where a patient presents intricate symptoms, a squad of agents specializing across various medical specialties can assist healthcare professionals, providing a holistic view and collaborating for a more accurate diagnosis.

Treatment Suggestions. Once diagnosed, a squad can work alongside doctors to explore treatment options, considering everything from current medical literature to emerging practices, ensuring the patient receives the most apt and up-to-date treatment.

Legal Environment. The intricacies of law require a multifaceted approach.

Case Analysis. When facing a complex legal case, lawyers and jurists can benefit from the assistance of a squad specialized in different branches of law, pertinent jurisprudences, and legislations. The agents, collaborating with professionals, can facilitate a more comprehensive and in-depth analysis.

Document Preparation. In the drafting of legal documents, precision is paramount. A squad can aid in the process, ensuring all legal facets are contemplated, always in collaboration with the responsible professional.

Benefits of squad.ai Across Different Contexts. The potential of squad.ai extends beyond its technical functionality, bringing tangible benefits across all scenarios:

Adaptability. The dynamic squad generation ensures relevant and contextualized solutions.

Deep Collaboration. The interaction between agents and humans amplifies individual capabilities, fostering enriching collaboration.

Amplified Engagement. In all contexts, user engagement is enhanced by personalized and contextual interaction.

Increased Efficiency. The ability of squads to bring specialized expertise accelerates processes and heightens accuracy.

Use Cases Conclusion. Squad.ai is more than just a tool; it is a partnership. Across all scenarios, it acts as an enhancer, amplifying the individual capacities of the humans it interacts with. Through its adaptive and collaborative capabilities, it redefines paradigms across a broad spectrum of areas, promising to revolutionize how we approach and tackle challenges.

6   Experimental Application

6.1   Experiment Description

An instance of squad.ai was constructed, comprising 36 agents (Fig. 1), with the aim of assisting consultants at TDS.company, a strategic transformation consultancy firm based in Digital Port, Recife, Brazil. The agents were intentionally designed with a range of diversity covering different ages, genders, races, educational backgrounds, and behavioral profiles, based on Jungian archetypes. These agents were deployed for participation both in debates among themselves and in debates involving human beings. Discussions took place within the Strateegia.digital platform (Fig. 2), and their interventions were overseen by human consultants.

Fig. 1. Interface of the experimental squad.ai application

6.2   Discussion of Results

The findings indicate that the agents maintained performance that was similar to or even superior to human beings in strategic debates. During debates among the agents, effective self-regulation was observed, which mitigated the phenomenon of hallucinations

Fig. 2. Results of the experimental squad.ai debate with human beings in strateegia.digital

commonly seen in single-agent systems. This aspect suggests a significant improvement in the quality of the responses generated.

Human consultants who interacted with the agents displayed enhanced performance compared to those who did not make use of the agents. This improvement was notable both quantitatively, in terms of the number of interventions, and qualitatively, with respect to the depth and relevance of contributions.

As consultants became familiar with the specificities of individual agents, there was a tendency to select preferred agents for subsequent debates. This choice seemed to be influenced by the agents' skills and knowledge in specific domains.

Additionally, it was found that agents with backgrounds in areas directly related to the debate topic tended to steer the discussion toward well-established pathways within that respective field. In contrast, agents with backgrounds in more distant domains provided more innovative insights that veered off traditional pathways.

6.3 Conclusion on squad.ai's Experiment

These findings underline the potential of squad.ai to enrich strategic debates by offering a diversity of perspectives and by enhancing human performance. The observed dynamics suggest that well-orchestrated collaboration between agents and humans can result in more thoroughly grounded and innovative decisions.

7 Conclusion

As the digital age unfolds, the intersection of artificial intelligence and human expertise becomes an increasingly important frontier for innovation. squad.ai stands emblematic of this confluence, illustrating the profound potential when collaborative AI is harnessed in diverse sectors, from business decision-making to the intricate corridors of healthcare and law.

The essence of squad.ai is not solely rooted in its advanced technical capabilities but rather in its pioneering approach to integrating AI agents dynamically, in real-time, to human needs. This adaptability ensures that solutions are not just computational but contextually rich, responsive, and deeply collaborative. It demonstrates the value of a system where AI does not replace, but rather enhances, human capabilities, serving as an augmentative force that empowers individuals across various professional spheres.

Furthermore, squad.ai's emphasis on real-time, user-driven configurations, combined with the application of specialized embeddings and rich socio-cultural attributes, sets a new benchmark in personalized AI solutions. This is not just automation; it is true collaboration, where AI agents and humans engage in an iterative, co-creative process, producing outcomes that neither could achieve in isolation.

The diverse use cases explored in this work attest to the system's transformative potential. Yet, it is crucial to understand that the true impact of squad.ai lies ahead, as users across the globe adapt, innovate, and uncover new applications we have yet to envision.

In conclusion, squad.ai is more than an advanced multi-agent system; it represents a paradigm shift in how we perceive AI's role in our professional and personal lives. By fostering a harmonious environment where AI and human intelligence coalesce, squad.ai is not just setting a trajectory for the future of AI but is also reshaping our collaborative future.

References

Allen, C., Varner, G., Zinser, J.: Prolegomena to any future artificial moral agent. J. Exp. Theor. Artif. Intell. **12**(3), 251–261 (2000)

Behdadi, D., Munthe, C.: A normative approach to artificial moral agency. Mind. Mach. **30**, 195–218 (2020)

Brown, T.B., et al.: Language models are few-shot learners. arXiv preprint arXiv:2005.14165 (2020)

Devlin, J., Chang, M.W., Lee, K., Toutanova, K.: BERT: pre-training of deep bidirectional transformers for language understanding. arXiv preprint arXiv:1810.04805 (2018)

Gao, L., et al.: The next generation of large-scale language models: challenges and research directions. arXiv preprint arXiv:2012.15903 (2020)

Jung, C.G., Hull, R.F.C.: Archetypes and the Collective Unconscious. Princeton University Press, Princeton (2014)

Mikolov, T., Chen, K., Corrado, G., Dean, J.: Efficient estimation of word representations in vector space. arXiv preprint arXiv:1301.3781 (2013)

OpenAI Blog: GPT-3: language models are few-shot learners (2020). https://openai.com/research/language-models-are-few-shot-learners. Accessed 15 Nov 2023

Ribeiro, M.T., Singh, S., Guestrin, C.: Why should i trust you? Explaining the predictions of any classifier. In: Proceedings of the 22nd ACM SIGKDD International Conference on Knowledge Discovery and Data Mining, pp. 1135–1144 (2016)

Russell, S.J., Norvig, P.: Artificial Intelligence: A Modern Approach. Pearson Education Limited, Berkeley (2010)

Vaswani, A., et al.: Attention is all you need. In: Advances in Neural Information Processing Systems, pp. 5998–6008 (2017)

Wooldridge, M.L.: An Introduction to MultiAgent Systems, 2nd edn. Wiley, Chichester (2009)

Designing Conversational Human-Robot Collaborations in Silence

Naoki Ohshima[✉], Hiroko Tokunaga, Ryo Fujimori, Hiroshi Kaneko, and Naoki Mukawa

School of Information Environment, Tokyo Denki University, 2-1200 Muzaigakuendai, Inzai, Japan
ohshima@eiiris.tut.ac.jp

Abstract. In this study, we developed a robot that encourages multi-party human conversations and helps participants to deal with silences. We consider three types of robot behavior, i.e., (1) encouraging talk by specific individuals (the you condition), (2) encouraging talk by all participants (the all-of-you condition), and (3) promoting talk among us (the we condition). We evaluated whether the robot elicits participant's attitudes of working together toward one purpose by both conversational analysis and a five-point scale question. In this paper, we revealed that the robot elicits participant's playful, cooperative, and pondering behaviors appropriate to different circumstance in silence and will contribute to design conversation enhance robot's behaviors that enable participants to break silence and keep conversations going.

Keywords: multi-party conversation analysis · silence · communication-enhancement robot

1 Introduction

Since some people are more talkative than others, not all participants typically engage equally in multi-party conversations, and it is therefore desirable to regulate how long each participant speaks for. It is especially important to keep the conversation going when developing a relationship with someone you have never met before or brainstorming ideas. This can be achieved using either a device to encourage equal participation by all speakers [1–12] or a communication-enhancement robot [13] that selects one of those who have had the least opportunities to speak next. However, this type of conversation facilitation may not be designed to provide a good experience for participants in all situations.

Japanese people are often more introverted than foreigners, such as Europeans and Americans [14, 15], and often participate less in international conversations [16]. This means uncomfortable silences often occur in conversations between Japanese people. In such cases, trying to encourage participants to talk can put pressure on them. To overcome such issues, we have researched to develop a new conversational promotion system that can, for instance, keep conversations going with playful and cooperatively

© The Author(s), under exclusive license to Springer Nature Switzerland AG 2024
A. Marcus et al. (Eds.): HCII 2024, LNCS 14713, pp. 97–113, 2024.
https://doi.org/10.1007/978-3-031-61353-1_7

break awkward silences during multi-party conversations and finding ways to continue multi-party conversations by designating all-participants as the next speaker.

We believe that by facilitating human conversation with robots, which have more limited abilities than humans, we can encourage conversation in a fun way and provide participants with a better experience. However, since there is still little basic knowledge about the construction of such robots, we collected and validated basic knowledge on what types of silence and behavior there are to provide a foundation for future research expansion. The purpose of this study is to investigate appropriate design conversation enhance robot's behaviors to create a communication-enhancement robot that can choose appropriate action according to the type, state and pattern of silence, and can activate communication more smoothly without stressing the participants. Here, we introduced a robot, which we refer to as Neut [17, 18], for designating appropriate robot behaviors during silence. In this paper, we use and explore three behaviors expand on previous studies [17, 18]. Specifically, we compared three types of speaker-designation behaviors in group discussions: (1) encouraging talk by specific individuals (the you condition), (2) encouraging talk by all participants (the all-of-you-condition), and (3) promoting talk among us (the we condition). The reasons for choosing these three are described in Sect. 4. Furthermore, whereas human behavior is arbitrary, robots can repeat identical behaviors as often as needed. In this experiment and the results section (Sect. 5 and Sect. 6), we revealed that the robot elicits participant's playful, cooperative, and pondering behaviors appropriate to different circumstance in silence and will contribute to design conversation enhance robot's behaviors that enable participants to break silence and keep conversations going.

2 Previous Work

There are several types of communication systems. First, we have systems that pro-mote communication skills, such as social robots that encourage social interaction among autistic children [19–21] or stimulate conversation when a group first meets [22, 23] by primarily focusing on developing relationships with those around them. Second, there are systems that facilitate communication between people from different cultures, such as agents that support non-native speakers in joining conversations between native speakers [24, 25], which focus mainly on speed and speech rate. Third, other systems focus on turn-taking [26] to regulate how long individual participants speak for during conversations. Such systems often display the speech frequency over time on a table [3, 7], tablet [1], or monitor [9], or use a haptic or mobile device [4], a spotlight [8], a wall [6, 10, 12], sound [11], or a robot [13]. Systems to support face-to-face conversations and remote communication via video chats have also been developed [2, 5].

Systems that monitor speech duration and speed should prompt talkative participants to yield the floor during multi-party conversations. Some studies have proposed methods of enabling participants to take turns during ongoing conversations [26–29], but the robot or device must elicit an attitude of problem-solving and working toward a common purpose for further enhance communality between people. In cognitive science, this need is being discussed in terms of the keywork "we-mode [47]". Similar remarks can be found in the literature [50] and in the area of primitive communication [51, 52].

Fig. 1. Participants interacting with a communication-enhancement robot (Neut).

However, a communication-enhancement robot that encourages cooperative, all-inclusive conversations has not yet been studied. Addressing this issue could be an important step toward the future development of communication promotion systems.

The we-mode has been studied in non-conversational situations such as eye gaze [48], but not within the context of conversation. As the field is still new, it should be bolstered with the results of early experiments. In the present study, we analyze this situation in a conversation experiment mediated by a robot called Neut [17, 18], which was designed for designating appropriate robot behaviors during silence (Fig. 1). This study addresses the challenge of recovering from silence in a multiparty conversation. The impacts of various methods for selecting the next speaker during silence are assessed in a conversation experiment.

We also construct a communication-enhancement robot that prompts speaking by participants who are lulled into silence by certain situations, such as questions that are difficult to answer. The robot is implemented under three new behavioral conditions expand on previous studies [17, 18]: (1) the designation of an individual (you) as the next speaker (Fig. 2, left), (2) the designation of all listeners (all of you) as the possible next speaker (Fig. 2, center), and (3) the designation of us (we) by muttering (Fig. 2, right).

Fig. 2. Triadic relationship between user and robot

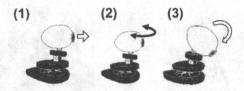

Fig. 3. Eye-gaze directions, indicating (1) one designated speaker (left), (2) several designated speakers (center), and (3) all designated speakers.

3　Behavior Design

The three types of speaker-designation behaviors implemented on the robot are described below.

3.1　You-Condition

When a conservation ceases, the robot moves the conversation forward (promotes the conservation) by designating one participant as the next speaker (Fig. 2, left), who is then obliged to speak. Although this technique breaks the silence, it may enforce a sense of responsibility in a participant who is unsure how to respond.

3.2　All-of-You-Condition

During a silence, the robot moves the conversation forward (promotes the conversation) by simultaneously designating multiple participants as the speakers (Fig. 2, center). Again, the designated participants are obliged to speak, but the conversation is reestablished by the response of one participant. Unlike the first condition, the responsibility to reply is diffused because multiple listeners are expected to respond, thus lessening the psychological load of individuals.

3.3　We-Condition

Under the we condition, everyone is obliged to speak (Fig. 2, right). Because the floor is obliged to reply, the conversation is reestablished by one participant who voluntarily converses. This condition fosters a conversational atmosphere in which the robot decides the next speaker together with the human participants rather than designating the listeners (humans).

3.4　The Conversation Promotion Robot Neut

The conversation promotion methods were developed in the Neut robot [17, 18]. Neut indicates the designated speaker(s) by changing its eye gaze direction. In previous studies, the gaze of a robot has been used to designate a speaker [31] and investigate the effects of robot gaze direction on human decision-making [32]. Based on the results of these studies, the gaze of a robot was deemed effective for selecting the next speaker under the individual (you), multiple people (all of you), and (3) us (we) conditions in the present study. The robot's head was designed with an eyeball motif that enables all participants to easily interpret the eye gaze direction (Fig. 3). As Neut lacks physical structural elements such as hands or legs, its head (i.e., gaze) becomes the focal point for the participants.

This simple and easy implementable minimal robot behavior was modified in three ways. Such a minimal design approach might also avoid over expectation of the robot by users [33, 34], increase the likeability of the robot [35], sustain interest in the robot interaction, and extract the human drive to relate to others [36, 37] owing to its low modality of communication channels. However, such a minimally designed robot might elicit unusual utterances by participants. In the conversation experiment with Neut, we thus ensured that the designated speaker received a positive impression of the robot despite the low number of conversational functions. For these reasons, standard platforms such as NAO and Pepper were not applied.

Concepts of the Three Behaviors. Neut exhibited three behaviors when intervening in multiparty conversations. The first behavior was "obligating an individual," in which the robot directly addresses a specific participant after a one-second silence (the standard maximum length of comfortable silence during a conversation [38]). For this purpose, the robot utters a phrase such as "What about you?" The second behavior was "obligating all participants," in which the robot addresses all participants with a phrase such as "What about all of you?" after a one-second silence. The third behavior was "designation of us," in which the robot does not address the participants but prompts the floor to speak with phrases such as "what should we do?" After a one-second silence. The effects of these different behaviors in eliciting appropriate conversational states were then assessed.

Implementation of the Three Behaviors. Prior to obligating a participant to speak, Neut performs two phases of actions. In phase 1, Neut listens to the designated speaker while facing the speaker and nodding. These actions are elicited at most 0.3 s (the length of comfortable transfer during a conversation [53]) after the participant begins speaking. In phase 2, Neut interjects with phrases such as "Well…" and "Yeah, I know," indicating that the robot wants to be the next speaker. The robot then utters prepared statements intended to diverge or converge the discussion. Through repeated divergence and convergence, the facilitator robot guides the discussion toward its conclusion [39, 40].

We prepared 45 utterances for Neut (listed in Table 1), including phrases that encourage participants to diverge and converge the current conversation (phrases ID1–ID8 and ID9–ID15, respectively). The designed utterances can be used in any conversational context and are supplemented with fillers such as "ummm." The robot's utterances and fillers were randomly selected under the following rules.

Phase 1 actions are implemented under all conditions.

1. After a silence lasting one second or longer under the you condition, a human experimenter directs the robot's gaze to the last-speaking participant, who is likely to resume the conversation. The robot uses the second-person personal pronoun "you" at the beginning of a sentence. A phase 2 utterance by the robot ends with a question which the listener is expected to answer (Table 1, column 2, (1) individual condition).

Table 1. Robot Utterances

ID	(1) You condition	(2) All of you condition	(3) We condition
1	Well..., why don't you try to think the opposite?	Well..., why don't you all try to think the opposite?	Well..., why don't we try to think the opposite
2	Well..., do you have any other ideas?	Well..., do any of you have any other ideas?	Well..., do we have any other ideas?
3	Well..., can you think of any specific examples?	Well..., can any of you think of any specific examples?	Well..., maybe we should try and think of some specific examples
4	Well..., can you think of anything offhand?	Well..., can any of you think of any- thing offhand?	Well..., maybe we should just try and think of something off- hand
5	I see... Do you have any experience with this?	I see... Do any of you have any experience with this?	I see... Maybe we should talk about our experiences with this
6	I see... Does anything spring to your mind?	I see... Does anything spring to mind for any of you?	I see... Maybe we should try and see if anything springs to mind
7	I see... Do you have anything else to say?	I see... Do any of you have anything else to say?	I see... Do any of us have anything else to say?
8	I see... Why don't you try looking at this from a different point of view?	I see... Why don't you all try looking at this from a different point of view?	I see... Maybe we should try looking at this from a different point of view
9	I see... Do you remember the original conversation topic?	I see... Do you all remember the original conversation topic?	I see... Do we all remember the original conversation topic?
10	I see... Can you try to put the points we've discussed together?	I see... Can you all try to put the points we've discussed together?	I see... Maybe we should try and put the points we've discussed together
11	I see... Do you think this is in line with the aim of this discussion?	I see... Do you all think this is in line with the aim of this discussion?	I see... Do we all think this is in line with the aim of this discussion?
12	I see... How do you think we can arrive at a conclusion?	I see... How do you all think we can arrive at a conclusion?	I see... Maybe we should try and arrive at a conclusion
13	Well..., can you try to put it all together?	Well..., can any of you try to put it all together?	Well..., maybe we should try and put it all together
14	Well..., can you please summarize our discussion?	Well..., can any of you please summarize our discussion?	Well..., maybe it would help to summarize our conversation
15	Well..., can you perhaps summarize everyone's opinions?	Well..., can any of you perhaps summarize everyone's opinions?	Well..., maybe it would help to summarize everyone's opinions

2. After a silence lasting one second or longer under the all-of-you condition, the human experimenter directs the robot's gaze to each participant in turn. The robot then uses the second-person personal pronoun "all of you" at the beginning of a sentence. A phase 2 utterance ends with a question which one of the listeners is expected to answer (Table 1, column 2, (2) multiple people condition).
3. After a silence of one second or longer under the we condition, the robot looks downward to clearly convey that the floor is promoted to speak. It then utters phrases associated with phase 2 actions. A phase 2 utterance concludes with a self-contained term such as "Maybe...," which is not directed at a particular participant (Table 1, column 3, (3) no-designation condition).

Selection of Robot Behaviors. When the conversation becomes silent for one second, Neut utters a sentence using one of the recorded phrases (ID1–ID15) listed in Table 1. These phrases were initially spoken by an adult male and were changed to robotic-mimetic voices using MorphVOX Junior.

Hardware Configuration of Neut. The robot is installed with servo motors, one each on the neck, stomach, and lower part. These motors generate the robot behaviors such as looking down and turning the head toward the next speaker. The servo motors are controlled by a microcomputer located on the back of the robot. The robot's head is attached with a thin plastic board modeling a large eyeball. The robot turns its head toward the intended receiver of its utterance. The voice is output by a small speaker installed on the lower-front part of the robot. The participant voices are input through a microphone and the computer detects the silent sections (lasting one second or longer) in the audio data. In future work, we will consider a method that distinguishes silences at the end of a conversation from thoughtful pauses during the conversation.

4 Experiment

We investigated which of the speaker-designation behaviors described in Subsects. 3.1, 3.2, and 3.3 increased the psychological load from that of resuming an all-human conversation. We also investigated the circumstances under which the robot's designation behavior creates a cooperative atmosphere for restarting the conversation. To assess whether the participants could distinguish among the robot's speaker-designated behaviors, the participants were asked to rate their impressions on a five-point scale. Two further impressions, "Right and obligation to speak [26]" and "pressure to speak" were also rated to estimate the psychological loads of restarting the conversation under the different behaviors.

For our multiparty conversation experiment, we designed a robot exhibiting all three behaviors and analyzed the differences among the psychological impressions of the robot with questions such as "Which participant got rights or obligation to speak?" [26] and "Who felt a pressure to speak?." The results reveal the impacts of the robot's behavior on the participants' behavior and conversation (i.e., process of repairing the silence). We will evaluate impressions of the robot behaviors in a five-point scale questionnaire. In addition to the 5-point scale evaluation, we compared differences in behavior across conditions using the method of behavioral analysis [49].

4.1 Participants

Twenty-four undergraduate students in Japan (8 females, 16 males; average age 19.6 years; SD = 0.86) participated in the experiment. All participants provided prior written informed consent. The participants were divided into eight groups (three participants per group) for multiparty conversations. All participants achieved average Japanese scores in the KiSS-18 communication skills evaluation test [42]. The participants spoke Japanese throughout the experiment. The participants were acquainted with each other. Having a conversation with a robot was the participants' first experience. We evaluated participants' first impressions of the robot. This experiment was conducted in accordance with the ethical review process of Tokyo Denki University.

4.2 Experimental Procedure

During the robot–participant interactions, the robot addressed (1) an individual participant, (2) multiple participants, or (3) no particular participant. During the conversation flow under each condition, the robot expressed its behavior approximately four times, sufficient for observing the differences among the behavior categories. Under all three conditions, the ordering effect was reduced by counterbalancing (randomly administering the robot behaviors). We wanted to eliminate regularity and observe various behaviors. In a questionnaire administered after each condition, the participants were asked to rate their impressions of the robot's behaviors and conversations.

Under each condition, the participants discussed various topics, such as the "significance of being adult" and "what friendship should be," which are considered as important conversational themes [43]. The coverage time of each topic was 15 min. The topics and robot behavior conditions were again counterbalanced against the ordering effect. In the "individual" and "multiple people" conditions, the robot's gaze was guided by a human experimenter. Each participant received instructions on how to communicate around the robot.

4.3 Experimental Setup for Video Analysis

Four cameras were arranged in the experiment room such that all participants could be observed, and the conversation could be recorded clearly (Control errors participants and clear recordings of the conversations). The participants selected their own seating at a round table with a diameter of 100 cm. The participants were free to choose their seats at the table with the robot.

5 Result

5.1 Impressions of Robot Behaviors

We first confirmed the participants' impressions of the robot's speaker-designation behaviors. The ratings of the obligation and pressure to speak were validated to estimate the psychological load of restarting the conversation under the three conditions. The statistical significances of the ratings are evaluated using the Holm–Bonferroni method

[30]. Significant differences of the ratings appeared between the "You" and "All of you" conditions and the "You" and "We" conditions ($p < 0.05$). This result demonstrates the different impacts these have on the participants' conversations. We therefore decided to conduct a detailed conversation analysis to investigate what subtle differences might exist.

Table 2. Six categories of initial utterances by participants following an utterance by Neut

ID	Label	Intention/function	Example
1	Statement of opinion	Expressing the speaker's opinion	I think... That means...
2	Accepting the speaker role (designated speaker)	Indicating that a speaker knows I am the next speaker	What am I supposed to think the opposite of? Me? A specific example?(repeated utterances)
3	Recommending other speaker(s)	Deflecting the turn to speak to another	Can you think of anything?
4	Stalling for time (no designated speaker)	Speaking simply to fill the silence	Anything else? Something specific?
5	Encouraging others to speak	Encouraging the designated speaker to speak	It's you! Come on! Yeah
6	Giving some advice to a speaker (no designated speaker)	Providing hints to the designated speaker or guiding them toward an opinion	It'stheface, right? That's surprising, isn't it?

5.2 Video-Recorded Behavior Analysis

The behavior of Neut did not largely affect the participants' behavior because the ro-bot lacks advanced functions for talking to humans. We thus focused on the first utterances of the participants in response to Neut, and on the speeches of the participants designated by Neut. In particular, we analyzed the state of the environment after Neut had appointed a speaker. The qualitative differences among the conditions are assessed in a behavioral analysis [49].

Table 2 lists the six categories of speech intentions and functions resulting from the behavioral analysis [49]. In Category 1 ("Statement of opinion"), the participants stated their own opinions, which is the desired outcome. In ("Categories the speaker role"), 3 ("Recommending other speaker(s)"), 4 ("Stalling for time"), 5 ("Encouraging others to speak"), and 6 ("Giving advice to a speaker"), the participants helped to manage the discussion guided by Neut's utterances. Focusing on Categories 2–6, we

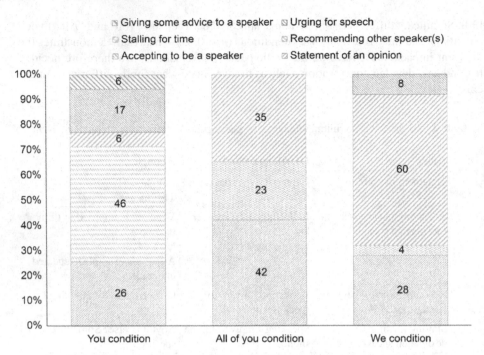

Fig. 4. Intent of the next speaker, under different designation conditions

attempted to under-stand how the participants broke the silence and thereby maintained the conversation.

5.3 Examples of the "You Condition"

The frequencies of the six categories of responses (Table 2), calculated from the results of multiple evaluators, were evaluated under each of the three designation conditions. In a Cohen's kappa [45] comparison analysis, the kappa coefficient was 0.73, indicating substantial agreement among the raters [46].

According to Fig. 4, when Neut focused on an individual, Category 2 responses ("Designating a speaker") were significantly more frequent than under any other condition. That is, participants felt that "I must say something (but I have nothing to say)." Category 2 thus indicates that the designated next speaker cannot immediately contribute to the conversation. In these cases, Neut designated a specific individual as the next speaker to break the silence, then urged them to talk.

Category 5 responses ("Encouraging others to speak") were also common, indicating that when reluctant participants were designated as the next speaker, they were encouraged by others with phrases such as "Hey, it's you!" Such urging may have exerted pressure on the designated speaker [17].

To examine the impact of being designated as the next speaker by Neut, we monitored the conversation of the participants in Group 7. As an example, Fig. 5 shows the situation recorded at 9 min 51 s. Herein, Neut addressed Participant B with "Well…, can you

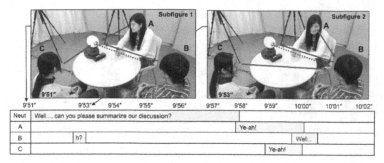

	9'51"	9'53"	9'54"	9'55"	9'56"	9'57"	9'58"	9'59"	10'00"	10'01"	10'02"
Neut	Well.... can you please summarize our discussion?										
A							Ye-ah!				
B		h?								Well...	
C								Ye-ah!			

Fig. 5. Example where the robot designated an individual and the participants urged that individual to speak

please summarize our discussion?" (subfigure 2). Participants A and C responded with "Yeah" (urging B to speak, Category 5), and smiled as they turned to Participant B. The designated speaker, B, replied "Well…" but remained hesitant.

This observation clarifies that a specific individual may feel pressured to speak despite having nothing to contribute. Participant B was expected to speak, so the other two participants smiled as their tension was relieved. Although this approach can effectively extract an opinion from an appropriately selected speaker, it may negatively affect the conversation if an inappropriate speaker is selected.

5.4 Examples of the "All-of-You Condition"

When all participants were engaged in the conversation, the commonest responses (Fig. 4) were (in descending order) Category 1 responses ("Statement of opinion"), Category 4 responses ("Stalling for time"), and Category 3 responses ("Recommending other speaker(s)").

Category 1 responses were most frequent because all participants were designated as speakers, so any participant who desired to talk could become the next speaker. In this experiment, the participants voluntarily expressed their opinions approximately 40% of the time. However, if none of the designated participants were ready to speak, the silence was not easily broken and many of the responses fell into Categories 3 and 4.

As an example, Fig. 6 shows the situation of Group 2 at 10 min 37 s when all participants were designated as speakers. When Neut addressed all participants with "I see… Does anything spring to mind for any of you?" (Subfigure 3), Participants B and C momentarily looked at each other and asked "Do you have anything to say?," attempting to assess the willingness of the other person to be the next speaker (subfigure 4). These reflex responses granted other participants the opportunity to speak. When no participant offered an opinion, more reflex utterances were made, bringing the conversation into the "stall for time" situation that did not encourage further discourse (Category 5).

5.5 Examples of the "We Condition"

During nondirected utterances by Neut, Category 4 responses ("Stalling for time") were significantly more common than the other response types (Fig. 4). In particular, Category

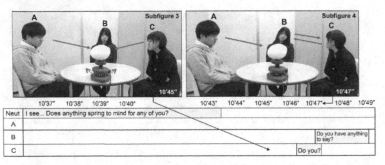

Fig. 6. Example where the robot designated all participants and the participants tried to let someone else speak

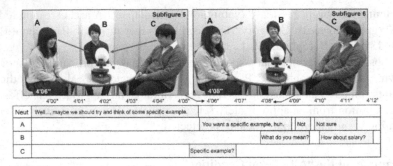

Fig. 7. Example where the robot designated every participant and the participants tried to stall for time

1 responses ("Statement of opinion") were less frequent than when all participants were designated as speakers, meaning that participants were disinclined to state their opinions.

As an example, Fig. 7 shows the situation of Group 5 recorded at 3 min 55 s. When Neut prompted the participants with "Well…, maybe we should try and think of some specific examples," (subfigure 5), Participant C responded with "specific example" while Participant A responded with "You want a specific example, huh." These simultaneous responses were followed by a question from Participant B: "What do you mean by a specific example?" (subfigure 6). The participants were clearly stalling for time by conversing to fill the silence and repeating a part of Neut's comment. All three participants avoided eye contact, indicating that they were pondering their own opinions until another participant took action.

6 Discussion

When the robot designated a single speaker, the participants more easily discriminated the robot's behavior than when the robot adopted other speaker-designation behaviors. The three types of speaker-designation behaviors implemented on Neut repaired conversation lapses in different ways. Herein, we discuss the designation behaviors ap-propriate to different circumstances and why these behaviors are appropriate.

1. Designating an individual speaker can break the silence during a first-meet conversation. When Neut designated a specific person, the two non-designated participants simultaneously directed their gaze toward the designated speaker. As shown in the gaze distribution of the participants (Fig. 5, subfigure 2), obligating the designated person to speak reduced the speaking obligations of the remaining two participants. The silence was then broken by the designated speaker and the conversation continued (Subsect. 5.3). The results implied that participants acquired a sense of playfulness and maintained the conversation by treating the experiment as a game: "Who was selected by Neut as the next speaker?" This hypothesis was supported by remarks such as "yeah!" and "eh?" from the participants (Subsect. 5.3). Uninhibited conversation is important for shy young people who feel uncomfortable in group discussions. The individual designation behavior The of Neut possibly created an environment in which obligation to speak was combined with a sense of playfulness.
2. The all-of-you designation behavior is useful for breaking silences in a group-learning discussion. During this behavior, the participants were staring at each other (subfigure 4 in Fig. 6) and wondering whether their partner would speak next. When one of the speakers eventually spoke, the conversation continued (Subsect. 5.4). Consequently, a cooperative situation formed in which the participants listened to the opinions of others (Category 1"Statement of opinion" in Fig. 4). The atmosphere generated by the multi-designation behavior might facilitate cooperative participation by all participants, which is necessary in group-learning discussion.
3. The we-condition behavior can provide periods of silence for thinking or waiting in the classroom. In a representative case (Subsect. 5.5), all participants showed evasive eye gaze when engaged in their own thoughts (subfigure 6 in Fig. 7). During these periods of silent thought, the participants exhibited disorderly gazing in different directions, avoided the lines of sight of other participants, and did not speak. Apparently, the participants were attempting to extend the silence. Many utterances were apparently used for time-stalling (Category 4 "Stalling for time" in Fig. 4). Therefore, it was presumed that no particular person was obliged to speak, but a cooperative thinking situation had formed wherein the participants were pondering their contributions to the discussion. Thus, non-designation behaviors can provide students with several seconds of thinking time after asking a question and improve the learning experiences.

7   Conclusion

We analyzed whether three next-speaker-designation behaviors of a robot can promote cooperation in group discussions. The communication-enhancement robot (Neut) encourages participants to speak during periods of silence in multiparty human conversations. The effects of the speaker-designation behaviors were analyzed in multiparty conversation settings.

The results of quantitative and qualitative evaluations revealed the appropriate types of repair silence (three new behaviors expand on previous studies [17, 18]) under conversation settings and circumstances. These results will greatly contribute to promotion of building a communication-enhancement robot that can autonomously detect silence and behave in an appropriate manner to break the silence. Group discussions are divided into three stages: divergence, where various opinions are presented, evaluation, where the opinions that have emerged are examined, and finally, convergence, which leads to a conclusion. Our results can be used as a design guideline to determine which of Neut's behavioral patterns are suitable for such group discussions. For example, in the divergence stage, the we-condition behavior, which allows everyone to speak freely, and the you-condition behavior, which encourages each person to speak, are appropriate for the purpose. For the evaluation and convergence stages, using behaviors of the you-condition and the all-of-you condition are appropriate for the context. In the future, we will integrate these findings to develop such robot.

These findings are expected to contribute to the development of communication-enhancement robots, interaction designs for human–robot collaborative conversations, and the understanding of human social behaviors in multiparty conversations. However, several limitations remain to be overcome. First, our new perspective is only a hypothesis at this stage and the generality of the results must be verified in further experiments. Especially, we must evaluate whether the robots select the appropriate behaviors in a given conversation state. Second, further investigation whether the results were influenced by the robot's speech or by the difference in its gaze is necessary. Third, effects will be different when we test it in overseas people. In future work, we must analytically test whether the same utterances with conflicting eye gazes affect the participants' behaviors.

Acknowledgments. This research was partially supported by the Ministry of Education, Culture, Sports, Science and Technology under the Grant-in-Aid for Young Scientists [B] 16K16102.

Disclosure of Interests. The authors have no competing interests to declare that are relevant to the content of this article.

References

1. Adachi, H., Myojin, S., Shimada, N.: ScoringTalk: a tablet system scoring and visualizing conversation for balancing of participation. In: SIGGRAPH Asia 2015 Mobile Graphics and Interactive Applications (SA 2015), vol. 5. ACM (2015)
2. Adachi, H., Myojin, S., Shimada, N.: A co-located meeting support system by scoring group activity using mobile devices. In: Proceedings of the 7th Augmented Human International Conference 2016 (AH 2016), vol. 44. ACM (2016)
3. Bachour, K., Kaplan, F., Dillenbourg, P.: Reflect: an interactive table for regulating face-to-face collaborative learning. times of convergence. In: Technologies Across Learning Contexts. EC-TEL (2008)
4. Dagan, E., Segura, E.M., Flores, M., Isbister, K.: Not too much, not too little' wearables for group discussions. In: Extended Abstracts of the 2018 CHI Conference on Human Factors in Computing Systems (CHIEA 2018). ACM (2018). Paper LBW129, 6 pages
5. Faucett, H.A., Lee, M.L., Carter, S.: I should listen more: real-time sensing and feedback of non-verbal communication in video telehealth. In: Proceedings of the ACM Human Computer Interaction 1, CSCW, Article 44 (2017)
6. Fujita, K., et al.: Ambient Suite: enhancing communication among multiple participants. In: Proceedings of the 8th International Conference on Advances in Computer Entertainment Technology (ACE 2011), vol. 25. ACM (2011)

7. Ogawa, K., Hori, Y., Takeuchi, T., Narumi, T., Tanikawa, T., Hirose, M.: Table talk enhancer: a tabletop system for enhancing and balancing mealtime conversations using utterance rates. In: Proceedings of the ACM Multimedia 2012 Workshop on Multimedia for Cooking and Eating Activities CEA 2012 (2012)
8. Ohshima, N., Yamaguchi, Y., Ravindra, P., De Silva, S., Okada, M.: Sociable spotlights: the symbolic representation of interconnectivity for turn-taking. ICIC Express Lett. 6(12), 2981–2988 (2012)
9. Schiavo, G., Cappelletti, A., Mencarini, E., Stock, O., Zancanaro, M.: Overt or subtle? Supporting group conversations with automatically targeted directives. In: Proceedings of the 19th International Conference on Intelligent User Interfaces (IUI 2014), pp. 225–234. ACM (2014)
10. Schiavo, G., Mencarini, E., Cappelletti, A., Stock, O., Zancanaro, M.: Ambient influence for promoting balanced participation in group brainstorming (2014)
11. Shimizu, R., Takase, Y., Nakano, Y.I.: Audio based group conversation support system. In: Proceedings of the 2017 ACM International Joint Conference on Pervasive and Ubiquitous Computing and Proceedings of the 2017 ACM International Symposium on Wearable Computers (UbiComp 2017). ACM (2017)
12. Tausch, S., Hausen, D., Kosan, I., Raltchev, A., Hussmann, H.: Groupgarden: supporting brainstorming through a metaphorical group mirror on table or wall. In: Proceedings of the 8th Nordic Conference on Human-Computer Interaction: Fun, Fast, Foundational (NordiCHI 2014). ACM (2014)
13. Matsuyama, Y., Akiba, I., Fujie, S., Kobayashi, T.: Four-participant group conversation: a facilitation robot controlling engagement density as the fourth participant. Comput. Speech Lang. 33(1), 1–24 (2015)
14. Paulhus, D.L., Duncan, J.H., Yik, M.S.: Patterns of shyness in East-Asian and European-heritage students. J. Res. Pers. 36(5), 442–462 (2002)
15. Sakuragi, T.: Association of culture with shyness among Japanese and American university students. Percept. Mot. Skills 98(3), 803–813 (2004)
16. Kowner, R.: Japanese communication in intercultural encounters: the barrier of status-related behavior. Int. J. Intercult. Relat. 26(4), 339–361 (2002)
17. Ohshima, N., Fujimori, R., Tokunaga, H., Kaneko, H., Mukawa, N.: Neut: design and evaluation of speaker designation behaviors for communication support robot to encourage conversations. In: Proceedings of the 26th IEEE International Symposium on Robot and Human Interactive Communication, pp. 1387–1393 (2017)
18. Ohshima, N., Watanabe, T., Saito, N., Fujimori, R., Tokunaga, H., Mukawa, N.: Neut: "hey, let her speak." In: Stephanidis, C. (ed.) HCI 2015. CCIS, vol. 528, pp. 764–769. Springer, Cham (2015). https://doi.org/10.1007/978-3-319-21380-4_129
19. Riether, N., Hegel, F., Wrede, B., Horstmann, G.: Social facilitation with social robots. In: Proceedings of the Seventh Annual ACM/IEEE International Conference on Human- Robot Interaction (HRI 2012), pp. 41–48. ACM (2012)
20. Shimada, M., Kanda, T., Koizumi, S.: How can a social robot facilitate children's collaboration? Social robotics. In: ICSR 2012 (2012)
21. Woods, S., Dautenhahn, K., Kaouri, C.: Is someone watching me? - consideration of social facilitation effects in human-robot interaction experiments. In: International Symposium on Computational Intelligence in Robotics and Automation, pp. 53–60 (2005)
22. Hayamizu, T., Sano, M., Miyawaki, K., Mukai, K.: An interactive agent supporting first meetings based on adaptive entrainment control. In: Proceedings of the Sixth International Conference on Advances in Computer- Human Interactions (ACHI 2013), pp. 178–183 (2013)

23. Sano, M., Miyawaki, K., Sasama, R., Yamaguchi, T., Yamada, K.: A robotic introducer agent based on adaptive embodied entrainment control. In: Jacko, J.A. (ed.) HCI 2009. LNCS, vol. 5611, pp. 368–376. Springer, Heidelberg (2009). https://doi.org/10.1007/978-3-642-02577-8_40

24. Inoue, T., Guo, Z.: A conversational agent that uses turn-taking rules for supporting a non-native speaker. In: Collaborative Technologies and Data Science in Smart City Applications, Logos, pp. 1–9 (2018)

25. Xu, J., Liao, W., Inoue, T.: Speech speed awareness system for a non-native speaker. In: Proceedings of the 2016 International Conference on Collaboration Technologies and Systems, pp. 43–50 (2016)

26. Sacks, H., Schegloff, E.A., Jefferson, G.: A simplest systematics for the organization of Turntakin for conversation. Language **50**(4), 696–735 (1974)

27. Lerner, G.H.: Selecting next speaker: the context-sensitive operation of a context-free organization. Lang. Soc. **32**(2), 177–201 (2003)

28. Otsuka, K.: Conversation scene analysis. IEEE Signal Process. Mag. **28**, 127–131 (2011)

29. Petukhova, H., Bunt: Who's next? Speaker-selection mechanisms in multiparty dialogue. Neurosci. Lett. (2009)

30. Holm, S.: A simple sequentially rejective multiple test procedure. Scand. J. Stat. **6**(1), 65–70 (1979)

31. Sato, R., Takeuchi, Y.: Coordinating turn-taking and talking in multi-party conversations by controlling robot's eye-gaze. In: the 23rd IEEE International Symposium on Robot and Human Interactive Communication, pp. 280–285 (2014)

32. Stanton, C., Stevens, C.J.: Robot pressure: the impact of robot eye gaze and lifelike bodily movements upon decision-making and trust. In: Beetz, M., Johnston, B., Williams, M.-A. (eds.) ICSR 2014. LNCS (LNAI), vol. 8755, pp. 330–339. Springer, Cham (2014). https://doi.org/10.1007/978-3-319-11973-1_34

33. Komatsu, T., Kurosawa, R., Yamada, S.: How does the difference between users expectations and perceptions about a robotic agent affect their behavior? Int. J. Soc. Robot. **4**(2), 109–116 (2011)

34. Komatsu, T., Yamada, S.: Effects of adaptation gap on users variation of impression about artificial agents. Trans. Jpn. Soc. Artif. Intell. **24**(2), 232–240 (2009). (in Japanese)

35. Zaga, C., De Vries, R.A., Li, J., Truong, K.P., Evers, V.: A simple nod of the head: the effect of minimal robot movements on childrens perception of a low-anthropomorphic robot. In: Proceedings of the 2017 CHI Conference on Human Factors in Computing Systems (CHI 2017), pp. 336–341. ACM (2017)

36. Matsumoto, N., Fujii, H., Goan, M., Okada, M.: Minimal communication design of embodied interface. In: Proceedings of the 2005 International Conference on Active Media Technology (AMT 2005), pp. 225–230 (2005)

37. Matsumoto, N., Fujii, H., Okada, M.: Minimal design for human-agent communication. Artif. Life Robot. **10**(1), 49–54 (2006)

38. Jefferson, G.: Preliminary notes on a possible metric which provides for a standard maximum silence of approximately one second in conversation. Intercommunication series. In: 3. Conversation: An Interdisciplinary Perspective, pp. 166–196 (1989)

39. Hori, K.: Introduction to Facilitation (2004). (in Japanese)

40. Kugiyama, K.: A Book to Know the Fundamentals of Meeting Facilitation from the Beginning. Subarusya Corporation (2008). (in Japanese)

41. MorphVOX Junior (2019). Retrieved

42. Kikuchi, A.: Notes on the researchers using KiSS-18. Bull. Fac. Soc. Welfare Iwate Prefectural Univ. **6**(2), 41–51 (2004). (in Japanese)

43. Tagawa, N., Ogawa, K., Saito, K.: Identifying common topics in daily communication by saliency. Jpn. J. Interpers. Soc. Psychol. **6**, 71–79 (2006). (in Japanese)

44. Max Planck Institute for Psycholinguistics. The Language Archive - ELAN (2019). Retrieved
45. Cohen, J.: Weighted kappa: nominal scale agreement provision for scaled disagreement or partial credit. Psychol. Bull. **70**(4), 213–220 (1968)
46. Richard Landis, J., Koch, G.G.: The measurement of observer agreement for categorical data. Biometrics **33**(1), 159–174 (1977)
47. Callotti, M., Frith, C.D.: Social cognition in the we-mode. Trends Cogn. Sci. **17**(4), 160–165 (2013)
48. Zhao, X., Cusimano, C., Malle, B.F.: Do people spontaneously take a robot's visual perspective? In: 11th ACM/IEEE International Conference on Human-Robot Interaction (HRI) (2016)
49. Hutchby, I.: Conversation Analysis. SAGE Research Methods Foundations, pp. 1–21 (2019)
50. Tomasello, M.: Why We Cooperate. MIT Press, Cambridge (2009)
51. Trevathen, C.: Communication and Cooperation in Early Infancy: A Description of Primary Intersubjectivity, Before Speech. Cambridge University Press, Cambridge (1979)
52. Kujiraoka, T.: 'Live Together' with the development of Clinical, Minerva Shobo (2002). (in Japanese)
53. Enomoto, M., Den, Y.: An analysis of nonverbal behavior affecting participation-role taking in three party conversation. In: Proceeding of the Special Interest Group on Spoken Language Understanding and Dialogue Processing, vol. 38, pp. 25–30 (2003). (in Japanese)

Will You Work with Us to Design a Robot? Boys' and Girls' Choices of Anthropomorphic Robots According to Their Gender

Oronzo Parlangeli[1]([✉]) [iD], Margherita Bracci[1] [iD], Enrica Marchigiani[1] [iD],
Paola Palmitesta[1] [iD], Francesco Curro[1] [iD], Matteo Sirizzotti[2] [iD], and Stefano Guidi[1] [iD]

[1] Dipartimento di Scienze Sociali, Politiche e Cognitive, Università degli Studi di Siena, Siena,
Italy
oronzo.parlangeli@unisi.it
[2] LabVR – Santa Chiara Lab, Università degli Studi di Siena, Siena, Italy

Abstract. This study aimed to examine whether boys and girls demonstrate inclinations that drive them to select interactions with humanoid robots that share psychological and physical similarities with them and display gender characteristics aligning with their own. Forty-four students, aged 10 to 13, from two distinct primary school classes, engaged in a study where they interacted in a CAVE with a simulated humanoid robot with a gender of their choice, selected between male or female at the beginning of the procedure. They were instructed to assist the experimenter in the robot's design process. Subsequently, participants were assessed for any gender stereotypes.

The results indicate that children generally exhibit a preference for interacting with robots of their own gender rather than those of a different gender. Notably, the study suggests that the perceived level of agency assigned to gendered robots may be influenced by the extent of hostile sexism. Specifically, an increase in hostile sexism corresponds to an augmented perception of male robots as possessing agentic qualities. Conversely, a different pattern, only marginally significant, seems to emerge in relation to benevolent sexism, where an increase in benevolent sexism is associated with a heightened perception of female robots as agentic technology.

Keywords: Child-robot interaction · Gender stereotypes · Hostile and benevolent sexism · Anthropomorphism · Physical appearance

1 Introduction

It has been argued that in the elaboration of a conceptual category representing humans, gender attribution may be unavoidable (Søraa 2017); (Perugia and Lisy 2023). This categorization may influence both those who design robots with a higher or lower level of anthropomorphism, and those who use robots. Indeed, anthropomorphic robots manifesting a gender, whether male or female, are quite common within databases such as Robo-Gap (Perugia et al. 2022)) For the more than 250 robots in this database, moreover, it was shown that even when robots are seen as mainly gender neutral, they still manifest some references to the male or female gender (Perugia et al. 2022).

The increasing presence of gendered humanoid robots poses many challenges most of all for younger generations (Benitti 2012); (Toh et al. 2016). More and more often, children and adolescents witness to or actively participate in interactions with robots that exhibit physical characteristics shaping gender perception in relation to some roles or activity (Bernotat et al. 2017; (Reich-Stiebert and Eyssel 2017); (Parlangeli et al. 2023)). On one hand, this might facilitate interaction by triggering mental schemata and behavioral cues specific to the particular interactive context and task at hand. However, on the other hand, interactions based on projecting gender characteristics onto artificial systems can reinforce negative stereotypes and foster discriminatory behaviors (Rubegni et al. 2020).

This study was conducted to explore whether boys and girls manifest preferences leading them to choose to interact with humanoid robots which are similar to them and that exhibit gender characteristics corresponding to their own. Additionally, the study aimed to assess whether such potential choices imply a reference to gender stereotypes, both psychological and physical. To better specify the results, variables such as participants' tendency to anthropomorphize and their level of familiarity with robots were also considered.

2 Related Work

The attribution of human stereotypes and social categories to artificial systems is a bias that has long been documented and conceptualized as the Computer as Social Actors Theory - CASA - (Nass and Moon 2000); (Eyssel and Hegel 2012). This bias becomes more evident the more the artificial systems manifest anthropomorphic characteristics and, in those cases, reference to gender is particularly effective in directing the interaction (Siegel et al. 2009); (Kuchenbrandt et al. 2014); (Tay et al. 2014); (Nomura and Legato 2017); (Parlangeli et al. 2023). Among the most widely reported results, for example, is a positive effect related to the robot's judgment of appropriateness in performing a given task, the more congruence there is between the performance of that task and the related gender stereotypes (Eyssel and Hegel 2012); (Tay et al. 2014); Ladwig et al., 2018).

The tendency to attribute human characteristics to technologies also affects children. The relationships that children develop with robots have several characteristics in common with those they develop with humans. A study was conducted in which children between the ages of 9 and 15 had to play with a robot called Robovie (Kahn et al. 2012). When the experimenter interrupted the game and locked the robot into a closet, the children expressed their beliefs about the robot having mental states and being able to have social relationships. Furthermore, the children expressed complaints about the treatment inflicted on the robot and were convinced that it should not be subjected to physical or psychological abuse (Kahn et al. 2012).

Other studies have analyzed more directly the reference to gender stereotypes by children in interaction with robots. In some cases, children who had scant or no physical clues to refer to in order to determine the robot's gender, tended to see it as a boy (Cameron, et al. 2016); (Beran et al. 2011). (Song-Nichols and Young 2020) posed the question of whether children can be influenced in the processing of gender stereotypes by robots performing tasks that are or are not consistent with their gender stereotype.

In their study, children between the ages of 6 and 8 were first assessed with regard to their gender stereotypes. Subsequently, half of them watched videos in which gendered robots performed activities that conformed to their gender stereotype, while the other half watched them perform activities that did not conform. The children who viewed the counter-stereotypical videos subsequently demonstrated a decrease in gender stereotyping (Song-Nichols and Young 2020).

The tendency to elaborate gender stereotypes is quite precocious. Studies have shown that children as young as 3 years old can already see themselves as belonging to one gender (Fagot et al. 1986); (Martin et al. 1990). This identification later extends to other people. In terms of its temporal development, the path of gender identification in relation to artificial systems does not appear to be very far apart from that which occurs in relation to human beings. A study was conducted with Japanese participants, both children (5–7 years old) and adults (Okanda and Taniguchi 2021). In the course of the experiment, various non-human things were presented, such as more or less anthropomorphic robots, stuffed animals, as well as natural things (e.g. flowers). The results showed that children, not unlike adults, already at the age of 5–7 years show a tendency to perceive robots and machines as masculine. The bias also emerges for sunflowers, which are identified as feminine (Okanda and Taniguchi 2021).

Ozogul and colleagues (2013) tested the similarity attraction hypothesis - we tend to prefer what looks like us - with regard to artificial agents. In a first experiment, they showed that educational outcomes for middle school students are higher if the APA (Animated Pedagogical Agent) appears with female characteristics in the case of female students. The apparently female APA is also able to lead male students to better results than female students. In a second experiment, students were given the opportunity to choose the gender of the APA with whom they interacted. In this case, 76% of the female students preferred the female agent and 77% of the males the male one. The educational results achieved in the second experiment were better than in the first (Ozogul et al. 2013).

Further confirmation of the hypothesis that children may prefer robots of the same gender comes from studies by Sandygulova and O'Hare (2016; 2018). Specifically, in their 2018 study (Sandygulova & O'Hare, 2018) in which children of different ages interacted with the same robot that could, however, have both male and female voices, they found that children aged 5–7 years cannot discriminate the gender of the robot from the voice alone. These same children also prefer to deal with robots of their own gender, which is not the case for older children (9–12 years).

As highlighted by (Widder 2022), it is evident that the relationships between the gender of robots and the age of those interacting with them are still largely unexplored. Above all, the reasons why children of different ages might or might not prefer robots of a particular gender or with a particular physical appearance appear to be completely overlooked. It therefore seems necessary to fill this gap by exploring whether physical characteristics, such as the height of the robots, might play a role in determining the evaluation of the child-robot interaction. Furthermore, it seems relevant to analyze the relations between gender stereotypes and the choice/evaluation of a gendered robot.

3   The Study

The aim of the study was to investigate whether children tend to prefer robots that are more similar to them with regard to gender and physical appearance, and how much their choices are related to gender stereotypes. Thus the research questions were the following:

- **RQ1** - Do girls tend to choose a female robot and boys a male one?
- **RQ2** - Are children's preferences related to their tendency to anthropomorphize artificial systems and sexism?
- **RQ3** - Do children's preferences for robot gender vary with age?
- **RQ4** - Do children tend to interact with robots which are similar to them in their appearance (height)?
- **RQ5** - Do children refer to gender stereotypes when evaluating the traits of robots?
- **RQ6** - Does tendency to anthropomorphize artificial systems affect trait attributions?

4   Methods

Participants Forty-four pupils from two different classes participated in the study (sixth-grade: N = 19; average age: 10.8 years; eighth-grade: N = 25; average age: 12.9 years). There were 7 girls in the first class and 12 in the second.

Procedure and Materials. A form containing details about the study and requesting consent for participation was submitted to a school in Siena, Italy. The parent/carer of each pupil involved in the study was required to sign the form after discussing its contents with the child. The document explicitly outlined the confidentiality of the results and the anonymity of the responses. The study had previously obtained approval from the Ethics Committee for the Research in Humanities and Social Sciences of the University of Siena, Italy (CAREUS act 69/2022).

The experimental session took place at the Santa Chiara Lab of the University of Siena, which is equipped with an immersive virtual reality environment (CAVE: Cave Automatic Virtual Environment). This facility enables a three-dimensional digital representation of robots, facilitating the examination of preferences related to factors such as the physical appearance.

In a preparatory phase to the interaction, children were informed that the experimenters were implementing a robot. They were invited to help the experimenter in designing the robot. The height of participants was recorded before they entered the CAVE. They were also asked to choose the gender of the robot they would interact with (male or female).

The male virtual reality (VR) robot, referred to as Cosmo for the study, is a 3D model showing a humanoid male appearance. In parallel, the female robot was named Stella. Both robots were designed to be equivalent, aside from their gendered appearance (see Fig. 1).

Each child participated in the experiment individually. An experimenter was with each of them into the CAVE and acted as an assistant for the duration of the experiment.

Inside the CAVE, after wearing a 3D visor, participants were initially invited to explore the robot, moving closer and further away, left and right. Then they were invited

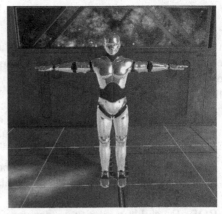

Fig. 1. The humanoid robots used in the study.

to adjust the robot's height by means of a simulated cursor, in a range between 100 and 180 cm by 10 cm steps. By default, both initially robots appeared 140 cm high.

The dialogue consisted of questions asked by the robot vocally and the selection of answers to these questions by the participant. The participant had to choose one of the possible answers simulated as buttons on a slider simulated in VR by means of a pointer. The slider was displayed between the robot and the child (see Fig. 2).

The first ten questions that the robot asked the participant were adapted from the Bem Sex Role Inventory questionnaire (Choi et al. 2009). This questionnaire measures the masculinity and femininity of individuals and, in this case, concerned the degree to which the participant believed the robot possessed a set of traits stereotypically associated with the masculine, agentic, assertive-dominant gender (five questions, e.g.: "Think about what the ability to make decisions is. Do you believe I can make decisions?"), and feminine, communicative, warmth and expressive (five questions, e.g.: "Think about what kindness is. Do you think I can be kind?"). The ten questions were presented in random order and answers were collected on a 7-point scale (1 = not at all; 7 = extremely) (see Fig. 2).

Four more questions were asked by the robot inviting participants to rate its appearance with regard to its gender: three questions on the degree of femininity, masculinity and gender neutrality respectively, and one question on perceived age. The answers on gender were collected on a 7-point scale. For the age judgment, participants were asked to rate at what point in life they would place the robot, on a scale of 1 to 100, where 1 = "a newborn child" and 100 = "a very old person". Also for these questions the answers were collected by means of the VR slider.

After the end of the interaction, the robot thanked the participant and the experience into CAVE ended. Overall, the interaction with the robot inside the CAVE lasted 4–5 min.

Once the interaction with the robot was completed, participants were administered a short questionnaire implemented in Google Forms. The questionnaire was administered online by means of a computer in a room next to the CAVE. The questionnaire was structured in 3 sections. In the first one, socio-demographic information about the participants were collected. This section also included questions aimed at detecting,

Fig. 2 Children inside the CAVE interacting with the robot

on a 7-point scale (1 = not at all; 7 = very much), the participants' familiarity with computers, robots, AI systems or cultural products of the Sci-fi genre.

The second section was made of some question of a standardized scale to measure the propensity to anthropomorphize technological systems by attributing mental states to them (e.g., intentions, conscious awareness, emotions such as shame or joy). This scale was the Individual Differences in Anthropomorphism Questionnaire (IDAQ) (Waytz et al. 2010). More specifically, five items were used (for example: "To what extent does technology - devices and machines for manufacturing, entertainment, and productive processes (e.g., cars, computers, television sets) - have intentions?"). The five items were rated on a 0 (not at all) to 10 (very much) scale.

The third session was the Ambivalent Sexism Inventory (ASI) for adolescents (Lemus. et al., 2008). This inventory measures sexist beliefs in adolescence. The scale consists of 20 statements for which participants were asked to express their agreement on a Likert scale from 0 to 5, where 0 = strongly disagree and 5 = strongly agree. The scale includes ten items for the evaluation of Hostile Sexism (for example: "Boys are physically stronger than girls" or "Girls should help their mothers at home more than boys") and ten items for Benevolent Sexism (for example: "In a disaster, girls ought not necessarily to be rescued before boys"; "Girls, compared to boys, tend to be more sensitive to other's feelings").

The scales IDAQ and ASI were translated into Italian and back-translated into English by a native speaker to check the correctness of their Italian version.

5   Results and Discussion

Sample Characteristics. Compared to eighth-grade students, sixth-grade students demonstrated a tendency to be more familiar with technology (5.29 vs. 4.57; p = 0.071), a greater tendency to anthropomorphize (23.4 vs. 15.1; p = 0.024), and higher levels of hostile (2.14 vs. 1.27; p = 0.002) and benevolent (2.91 vs. 1.66; p < 0.001) sexism (Table 1).

Table 1. Descriptive statistics about participants in the sample, divided by class

	Sixth-grade *(N = 19)*	Eighth-grade *(N = 25)*	
	M (SD)	*M (SD)*	*p-value*
Age (yrs)	10.8 (0.43)	12.9 (0.28)	<0.001
Height (cm)	146 (22.8)	163 (8.22)	0.007
FD	5.29 (1.12)	4.57 (1.45)	0.071
IDAQ	23.4 (11.9)	15.1 (11.3)	0.024
HS	2.14 (0.96)	1.27 (0.76)	0.002
BS	2.91 (1.17)	1.66 (0.86)	<0.001

FD = Familiarity with the Domain of robots; IDAQ = Individual Differences in Anthropomorphism Questionnaire; HS = Hostile Sexism; BS = Benevolent Sexism.

Preference for Robot Gender and Height. *(RQ 1–4.* 61.4% of participants (N = 27) chose the male robot, a probability not significantly different from chance in a binomial test (p = 0.174). We tested the association between participant gender and preference for the robot gender using Fisher's test for 2×2 contingency tables, combining the data collected from the sixth-grade and the eighth-grade students. The results showed a significant association between participant gender and chosen robot gender ($X^2(1) =$ 10.4, p = 0.001): girls preferred to interact with a female robot (N = 13, 68.4%) than with a male one (N = 6, 31.6%), and, vice-versa, boys preferred to interact with a male robot (N = 21, 84%) than with a female one (N = 4, 16%). We repeated the analyses separately for sixth-graders and eighth-graders, and in both cases the association between participant gender and preferred robot gender was significant: in each group participants tended to prefer to interact with a robot having their same gender (Table 2). With respect to RQ1, therefore, these results provide clear support for the hypothesis that children tend to prefer to interact with robots having their own gender over robots having a different gender.

To better understand the effect of the preference for same-gender robots, and test whether it was affected by participant gender or other factors, we coded in a new variable whether each participant had chosen to interact with a robot of their own gender (or not). This variable was then used as a dependent variable in a series of logistic regression models. As predictors, we used class grade, participants' gender, age, tendency to anthropomorphize (IDAQ), familiarity with the domain (computers, robots, AI systems

Table 2. Preferences for Robot Gender Among Male and Female Participants, divided by class.

A. Sixth-grade students				B. Eighth-grade students			
Participant Gender	Preferred Robot Gender		**Total**	Participant Gender	Preferred Robot Gender		**Total**
	Female	Male			Female	Male	
Female	5 (71.4%)	2 (28.6%)	7 (100%)	Female	8 (66.7%)	4 (33.3%)	12 (100%)
Male	1 (8.3%)	11 (91.7%)	12 (100%)	Male	3 (23.1%)	10 (76.9%)	13 (100%)
Total	6 (31.6%)	13 (68.4%)	19 (100%)	Total	11 (44%)	14 (56%)	25 (100%)
$\chi^2 = 5.487 \cdot df = 1 \cdot \varphi = 0.655 \cdot$ Fisher's p $= 0.010$				$\chi^2 = 3.205 \cdot df = 1 \cdot \varphi = 0.439 \cdot$ Fisher's p $= 0.047$			

Table 3. Results of the logistic regression analyses predicting preference for robots having the same (vs a different) gender as the participant. The estimated coefficients of the models are presented as Odd Ratios (OR).

Predictors	Mod. A		Mod. B		Mod. C		Mod. D		Mod. E		Mod. F	
	OR	p	OR	p	OR	p	OR	p	OR	p	OR	p
(Intercept)	3.40	**0.001**	3.37	**0.001**	3.70	**0.001**	3.64	**0.001**	4.20	**0.001**	3.85	**0.001**
gender [F-M]			0.64	0.229			0.66	0.265	0.69	0.359		
class [6-8th]					1.44	0.344	1.39	0.403	1.74	0.285		
FD									0.84	0.620	0.82	0.570
IDAQ									0.97	0.428	0.99	0.685
HS									1.65	0.487	2.15	0.267
BS									0.73	0.588	0.81	0.709
Observations	44		44		44		44		44		44	
R^2 Tjur	0.000		0.034		0.021		0.048		0.136		0.106	

FD = Familiarity with the Domain of robots; IDAQ = Individual Differences in Anthropomorphism Questionnaire; HS = Hostile Sexism; BS = Benevolent Sexism.

or cultural products of the Sci-fi genre – FD), hostile (HS) and benevolent (BS) sexism. Sum coding was used to encode the gender and class of participants, and all the continuous predictors were centered. Overall, we fitted 6 regression models (Table 3), with different combinations of predictors, starting from an intercept-only model (A), and adding single predictors (B. gender, C. class), or sets of predictors (D-F). The results are presented as OR in Table 3. In all the models only the intercept was significant, and in all cases the odds of participants choosing a same-gender robot were significantly higher than those of choosing a robot with a different gender (OR: 3.37–4.20, all p < 0.001). None of the predictors, individually or combined, were significant. Concerning RQ2 and RQ3, therefore, these results do not support the hypothesis that children's preferences for robot gender are related to their tendency to anthropomorphism, sexism or age. We must notice, however, that the sample size was rather limited for a logistic regression, so it is possible that the lack of significant effects of class and participant gender might have been due to lack of statistical power.

The average height set for the robots was 139.7 cm (SD = 13). Male robots were set higher (M = 143) than female robots (M = 135), but the difference was only marginally significant, t(28.69) = 1.80, p = 0.083. No significant differences were found across classes in the height set for the robot, t(30.386) = −0.88, p = 0.387. The height set for the robot was neither significantly correlated with participants' height (r = −0.11, p = 0.052), nor with any of the other variables collected about participants. Concerning RQ4, therefore, these results do not support the hypothesis that children tend to interact with robots which are similar to them in height.

Robot Perceptions: Age and Stereotypical Traits (RQ5-6). The mean age attributed to the robot was 24.2 years (SD = 12.6). The age of the robot did not vary significantly across robot genders, participant genders or classes. The mean of the agency scores (M = 3.86, SD = 0.98) of the robot was not significantly different from the mean of the communion scores (M = 3.74, SD = 1.28) in a related-samples t-test, t(43) = 0.86, p = 0.40.

We compared the levels of agency and communion attributed to the robots across participants' genders, classes, and robots' genders using independent sample t-tests. The degree of Agency did not vary significantly across any of the independent variables considered. The degree of Communion did not vary significantly across genders (of the robot or the participant), but did vary across classes: the sixth-grade students attributed a significantly higher level of communion to robots (M = 4.35) than the eighth-grade students (M = 3.27), t(40.79) = 3.06, p = 0.004.

However, when we conducted regression analyses of Agency and Communion scores, including as categorical predictors class, preferred robot gender or participant gender (all sum coded),[1] and as continuous predictors FD, IDAQ, HS and BS (all centered), in all the models only IDAQ and FD were significantly and positively associated with the levels of Agency and Communion attributed to the robot. None of the other categorical or continuous predictors were significant (Table 4).

In further regression analyses we tested whether HS and BS could be moderators of the stereotypical trait attributions, by allowing these variables to interact with robot gender. The analysis of the agency scores showed a significant interaction between HS and robot gender (F(1, 36) = 4.48, p = 0.041) and a marginally significant interaction between BS and robot gender (F(1, 36) = 3.33, p = 0.080). No significant interaction was instead found in the analysis of the communion scores. We followed up the significant interaction conducting an interaction contrast analysis comparing the slopes for the effect of HS and BS across robot genders. The results showed that the slope for HS varied significantly across robot genders (t(36) = 2.116, p = 0.041), and marginally also

---

[1] Since preferred robot gender was associated with participant gender, we never entered these predictors together in the analyses.

Table 4. Results of the multiple regression analyses predicting agency and communion levels attributed to the robots.

Predictors	Mod Agency 1		Mod Agency 2		Mod Communion 1		Mod Communion 2	
	B	p	B	p	B	p	B	p
(Intercept)	3.85	**<0.001**	3.85	**<0.001**	3.77	**<0.001**	3.77	**<0.001**
HS	0.26	0.289	0.24	0.317	0.20	0.482	0.21	0.465
BS	−0.13	0.532	−0.13	0.520	−0.01	0.969	−0.01	0.977
FD	0.24	**0.043**	0.25	**0.038**	0.15	0.286	0.14	0.310
IDAQ	0.03	**0.023**	0.03	**0.024**	0.05	**0.006**	0.05	**0.005**
class [6th-8th]	−0.05	0.775	−0.05	0.783	0.21	0.313	0.21	0.315
robot gender [F-M]	−0.02	0.872			0.02	0.921		
participant gender [F-M]			−0.07	0.628			0.05	0.772
Observations	44		44		44		44	
R^2/R^2 adjusted	0.314/0.203		0.318/0.208		0.409/0.313		0.410/0.314	

FD = Familiarity with the Domain of robots; IDAQ = Individual Differences in Anthropomorphism Questionnaire; HS = Hostile Sexism; BS = Benevolent Sexism.

the slope for BS ($t(36) = 1.799$, $p = 0.081$). Among all the estimated slopes (Fig. 3), however, only the one for the effect of HS on agency for a male robot was significantly higher than zero.

Lastly, we computed the bivariate linear correlations between Agency, Communion and all the individual scales (FD, IDAQ, HS, BS). Not surprisingly, in the light of the results of the regression analyses, anthropomorphism tendency was significantly and positively correlated with both agency ($r = 0.46$, $p < 0.05$) and communion ($r = 0.56$, $p < .01$), and technology familiarity with agency ($r = 0.44$, $p = 0.07$). Moreover, agency and communion were significantly correlated ($r = 0.63$, $p < 0.0001$).

Overall, these results provide partial support for the hypothesis related to RQ5 that children refer to gender stereotypes when evaluating gendered robots. While, in fact, the agency and communion levels attributed to the robot did not vary across robot genders in a stereotypical pattern, the significant interactions found in the analysis of the agency scores showed that the use of gender stereotypes might depend on the levels of sexism of the children. It is interesting to notice that the two types of sexism seem to have opposite effects on agency perception. The results also do support the hypothesis related to RQ6 that trait attributions are positively associated with children's tendency to anthropomorphism. The lower levels of IDAQ in 8th-grade students might thus explain the findings that these students also attributed lower levels of communion to the robots than 6th grade pupils.

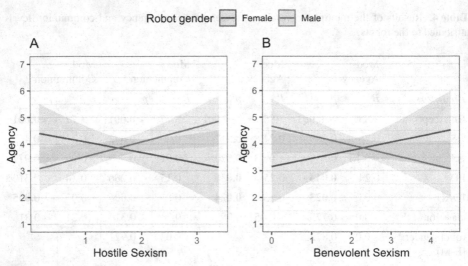

Fig. 3. Slopes for the estimated effects of (A) Hostile Sexism and (B) Benevolent Sexism on perceived Agency, as a function of robot gender.

6   Conclusion

Boys and girls show a tendency to prefer to interact with artificial systems that match their gender (Ozogul et al. 2013). With regard to the relationships between the psychological characteristics and the use of gender stereotypes, however, the results appear particularly complex. Given the almost always higher ratings of the sixth-grade pupils for all the scales used, the differences found between the two classes seem more referable to a more empathetic relationship that the younger pupils established with the robots and with the entire experimental setting.

Concerning the physical attributes of robots, there appears to be no discernible pattern supporting children's inclination towards choosing robots resembling themselves. Instead, the marginal difference in height between male and female robots, albeit not statistically significant, might be attributed to the influence of the male stereotype associated with a more robust physique.

The relationship found between the levels of agency attributed to male robots and hostile sexism (Lemus. et al., 2008) appears particularly relevant. From this relationship the possibility emerges that interaction with artificial systems that manifest gender may lead to discriminatory behavior in that male robots are seen as more positive (agentic) by those who report hostile sexist beliefs. The results obtained probably do not highlight the overall picture between sexism, hostile or benevolent, and robot gender, male and female, due to the small sample size. The possible pattern of relationships suggested here, therefore, deserves further investigation. A deepening of this knowledge could lead to interventions aimed more effectively at preventing negative behaviors in gender references by younger generations (Rubegni et al. 2020); (Zabel et al. 2021).

Acknowledgements. The authors would like to thank all pupils, as well as their teachers, who participated in this study. This study was partially realized with funds from the PNRR (project THE: spoke M_9.2.1) and PRIN (project FROB, 2022).

Disclosure of Interests. The Authors Have no Competing Interests to Declare that Are Relevant to the Content of This Article.

References

Benitti, F.B.V.: Exploring the educational potential of robotics in schools: a systematic review. Comput. Educ.. Educ. **58**(3), 978–988 (2012). https://doi.org/10.1016/j.compedu.2011.10.006

Beran, T.N., Ramirez-Serrano, A., Kuzyk, R., Fior, M., Nugent, S.: Understanding how children understand robots: perceived animism in child–robot interaction. Int. J. Hum. Comput. **69**, 539–550 (2011). https://doi.org/10.1016/j.ijhcs.2011.04.003

Bernotat, J., Eyssel, F., Sachse, J.: Shape it – The influence of robot body shape on gender perception in robots. In: Kheddar, A., et al. (eds.) Social Robotics, pp. 75–84. Springer International Publishing, Cham (2017). https://doi.org/10.1007/978-3-319-70022-9_8

Cameron, D., et al.: Congratulations, it's a boy! Bench-marking children's perceptions of the robokind Zeno-R25. In: Alboul, L., Damian, D., Aitken, J.M. (eds.) Towards Autonomous Robotic Systems, pp. 33–39. Springer International Publishing, Cham (2016). https://doi.org/10.1007/978-3-319-40379-3_4

Choi, N., Fuqua, D.R., Newman, J.L.: Exploratory and confirmatory studies of the structure of the bem sex role inventory short form with two divergent samples. Educ. Psychol. Meas. **69**, 696–705 (2009). https://doi.org/10.1177/0013164409332218

Eyssel, F., Hegel, F.: (S)He's got the look: gender stereotyping of robots. J. Appl. Soc. Psychol. **42**(9), 2213–2230 (2012). https://doi.org/10.1111/j.1559-1816.2012.00937.x

Fagot, B.I., Leinbach, M.D., Hagan, R.: Gender labeling and the adoption of sex-typed behaviors. Dev. Psychol. **22**(4), 440–443 (1986). https://doi.org/10.1037/0012-1649.22.4.440

Kahn, P.H., Kanda, T., Ishiguro, H., Freier, N., Severson, R.L., et al.: Robovie, you'll have to go into the closet now: children's social and moral relationships with a humanoid robot. Dev. Psychol. **48**(2), 303–314 (2012). https://doi.org/10.1037/a0027033

Kuchenbrandt, D., Häring, M., Eichberg, J., Eyssel, F., André, E.: Keep an eye on the task! How gender typicality of tasks influence human-robot interactions. Int. J. of Soc. Robot **6**, 417–427 (2014). https://doi.org/10.1007/s12369-014-0244-0

Ladwig, R.C., Ferstl, E.C.: What's in a name? An online survey on gender stereotyping of humanoid social robots. In: Proceedings of the 4th Conference on Gender & IT., pp. 67–69. Association for Computing Machine, New York (2018). https://doi.org/10.1145/3196839.3196851

Lemus, S., et al.: Elaboración y validación del inventario de sexismo ambivalente para adolescentes [Elaboration and validation of ambivalent sexism Inventory for adolescents]. Int. J. Clin. Health Psychol. Clin. Health Psychol. **8**(2), 537–562 (2008)

Martin, C.L., Wood, C.H., Little, J.K.: The development of gender stereotype components. Child Dev. **61**(6), 1891–1904 (1990). https://doi.org/10.2307/1130845

Nass, C., Moon, Y.: Machines and mindlessness: social responses to computers. J. Soc. Issues **56**, 81–103 (2000). https://doi.org/10.1111/0022-4537.00153

Nomura, T.: Robots and gender. In: Legato, M.J. (ed.) Principles of Gender Specific Medicine, 3rd edn., pp. 695–703. Academic Press, SanDiego (2017)

Okanda, M., Taniguchi, K.: Is a robot a boy? Japanese children's and adults' gender-attribute bias toward robots and its implications for education on gender stereotypes. Cogn. Dev.. Dev. **58**, 101044 (2021). https://doi.org/10.1016/j.cogdev.2021.101044

Ozogul, G., Johnson, A.M., Atkinson, R.K., Reisslein, M.: Investigating the impact of pedagogical agent gender matching and learner choice on learning outcomes and perceptions. Comput. Educ.. Educ. **67**, 36–50 (2013). https://doi.org/10.1016/j.compedu.2013.02.006

Parlangeli, O., Palmitesta, P., Bracci, M., Marchigiani, E., Guidi, S.: Gender role stereotypes at work in humanoid robots. Behav Inf Technol **42**(3), 316–327 (2023). https://doi.org/10.1080/0144929X.2022.2150565

Perugia, G., Lisy, D.: Robot's gendering trouble: a scoping review of gendering humanoid robots and its effects on HRI. Int J of Soc Robotics **15**, 1725–1753 (2023). https://doi.org/10.1007/s12369-023-01061-6

Perugia, G., Guidi, S., Bicchi, M., Parlangeli, O.: The shape of our bias: perceived age and gender in the humanoid robots of the ABOT database. In: 2022 17th ACM/IEEE International Conference on Human-Robot Interaction (HRI), IEEE Press, pp. 110–119 (2022). https://doi.org/10.5555/3523760.3523779

Reich-Stiebert, N., Eyssel, F. (Ir)relevance of gender? On the influence of gender stereotypes on learning with a robot. In: Proceedings of the 2017 ACM/IEEE International Conference on Human-Robot Interaction, pp. 166–176 (2017).

Rubegni, E., Landoni, M., Jaccheri, L.: Design for change with and for children: how to design digital storytelling tool to raise stereotypes awareness. In: Proceedings of the 2020 ACM Designing Interactive Systems Conference, pp. 505–518 (2020).

Sandygulova, A., O'Hare, G.M.P.: Investigating the impact of gender segregation within observational pretend play interaction. In: 2016 11th ACM/IEEE International Conference on Human–Robot Interaction (HRI), IEEE Press, pp. 399–406 (2016).

Sandygulova, A., O'Hare, G.M.P.: Age - and gender - based differences in children's interactions with a gender-matching robot. Int J of Soc Robotics **10**, 687–700 (2018). https://doi.org/10.1007/s12369-018-0472-9

Siegel, M., Breazeal, C., Norton, M.I.: Persuasive robotics: the influence of robot gender on human behaviour. In: 2009 IEEE/RSJ International conference on intelligent robots and systems, pp. 2563–2568 (2009). https://doi.org/10.1109/IROS.2009.5354116

Song-Nichols, K., Young, A.: Gendered robots can change children's gender stereotyping. In: Proceedings of CogSci2020, pp. 2480–2485 (2020).

Søraa, R.A.: Mechanical genders: how do humans gender robots? Gender Technol Dev **21**(1–2), 99–115 (2017). https://doi.org/10.1080/09718524.2017.1385320

Tay, B., Jung, Y., Park, T.: When stereotypes meet robots: the double-edge sword of robot gender and personality in human–robot interaction. Comput. Hum. Behav.. Hum. Behav. **38**, 75–84 (2014). https://doi.org/10.1016/j.chb.2014.05.014

Toh, L.P.E., Causo, A., Tzuo, P.W., Chen, I.M., Yeo, S.H.: A Review on the use of robots in education and young children. J. Educ. Techno. Soc. **19**(2), pp. 148–163 (2016). http://www.jstor.org/stable/jeductechsoci.19.2.148

Waytz, A., et al.: Who sees human? the stability and importance of individual differences in anthropomorphism. Perspect. Psychol. Sci. Psychol. Sci. **5**(3), 219–232 (2010). https://doi.org/10.1177/1745691610369336

Widder, D.G.: Gender and Robots: A Literature Review. (2022). arXiv preprint arXiv:2206.04716.

Zabel, S., Otto, S.: Bias in, bias out – the similarity-attraction effect between chatbot designers and users. In: Kurosu, M. (ed.) HCII 2021. LNCS, vol. 12764, pp. 184–197. Springer, Cham (2021). https://doi.org/10.1007/978-3-030-78468-3_13

Comparison of Robot Assessment by Using Physical and Virtual Prototypes: Assessment of Appearance Characteristics, Emotional Response and Social Perception

Juan-Carlos Rojas[1,3]([✉]) [ID], Jaime Alvarez[2], Arantza Garcia-Mora[1], and Paulina Méndez[4]

[1] School of Architecture, Art and Design, Tecnologico de Monterrey, 64700 Monterrey, Nuevo León, Mexico
jcrojasl@tec.mx

[2] Department of Design, Faculty of Engineering, Takushoku University, Tatemachi 815-1, Hachioji-shi, Tokyo 193-0985, Japan

[3] Institute for the Future of Education Tecnologico de Monterrey, 64700 Monterrey, Nuevo León, Mexico

[4] Graduate School of Engineering, Takushoku University, Tatemachi 815-1, Hachioji-shi, Tokyo 193-0985, Japan

Abstract. The integration of robots into society has prompted extensive exploration, extending over various fields such as education, healthcare, and industry. This paper delves into the classification of robot conception and emphasizes the increasing prevalence of robots in diverse applications. Particularly in healthcare, the implementation of robots has sparked debates regarding their positive and negative implications, necessitating a thorough understanding of their impact across different contexts. The authors proposed a healthcare robot aimed at providing emotional support for pediatric walking rehabilitation, emphasizing the importance of assessing both physical and emotional aspects through physical prototypes (PP) and virtual prototypes (VP). The study introduces a methodology for comparative analysis, focusing on appearance characteristics, emotional response, and social perception. Initial findings suggest that while observable aspects like color and shape are effectively compared, more intricate features require further exploration. The study also evaluates emotional responses using the SAM instrument, revealing comparable emotional aspects conveyed by both PP and VP. The RoSAS assessment further validates social and emotional aspects of the prototypes, highlighting differences in factors such as discomfort and warmth between PP and VP. These insights underscore the potential of VP for prototype assessment and suggest avenues for further research in this domain.

Keywords: Assessment design · Emotional response robot · Prototypes · Comparison perception

A. Marcus et al. (Eds.): HCII 2024, LNCS 14713, pp. 127–145, 2024.
https://doi.org/10.1007/978-3-031-61353-1_9

1 Introduction

The role of robots and their integration into society has awakened multiple perspectives of their study [1, 2] Currently, robots are present in fields as diverse as education [3, 4], health [5], and industry [6]. Robot conception can be classified in diverse ways [2, 7]; Nowadays, there are definitions and applications of robots that allow us to see them anywhere. Focusing on one type of application, the earliest robots' implementations in human care have shown favorable outcomes in their application and acceptance [5, 8, 9]. The high demand for the need to comprehend the robot's implementation, has detonated multiple assessment to ensure effectiveness. Because of this, attention has been focused on prototypes that help assess the impact on users [10] and play important roles within the design process [11, 12]. Prototyping has not only developed physically, but the physical prototypes (PP) also have transcended to virtual, augmented reality, and mixed formats [13–16]. Virtual prototypes (VP) represent a valid and advantageous option when evaluating products due to the multiple benefits [17]. Studies have already evaluated different types of electronic product prototypes and their respective [18, 19], as well as the emotional impressions of VP [20]. Focusing on our research, healthcare robots are a relevant topic due to multiple negative factors. The application of robots for medical uses has extended from technical aspects, opening debates on the positive and negative implications [5, 9, 21], thus making it necessary to understand their impact in different contexts. Alvarez and his colleagues [22] proposed a robot intended to provide emotional support to pediatric walking rehabilitation. Their design process started by clarifying the emotional functions of the robot and proposed the design of its shape and movements. This contribution focused on deepening the assessment of the PP of the robot and its VP from different perspectives such as appearance and emotional factors. The present study aims to continue evaluating the physical and appearance characteristics, emotional response, and social perception of the robot, by using PP and VP to compare the results and clarify the effectiveness of VP for robot design. Furthermore, we will explore information that will allow us to know the context of the exploration and evaluation of relevant aspects of robots such as physical and appearance characteristics, emotional response, and social perception. Our research will show a novel approach to assessment using PP and VP in order to compare and contribute to the use of prototypes in this field of research.

2 Related Work

2.1 Emerging Emotional Roles of Robots in Society

Research on human-robot interaction (HRI) consists of exploring how people and robots work together [23]. Robots are often designed with this interaction in consideration, which is why aspects of human social integration such as gestures, speech, or facial expressions are integrated [24]. Robots have intruded into every aspect of daily life. However, three niches are constantly trending in the advancement of robots. In education, interaction with students is associated with positive and negative values when robots are used as instruments or substitutes for educators [[4], p. 37]. In either case, socio-emotional involvement has a direct impact on pedagogical dynamics and its transformation [3]. In the industrial field, the interaction is perceived from a perspective of competitive advantages and productivity. Personal supplanting is the latent discussion; however, the current challenge of human-robot collaboration reveals the need to understand the current social and emotional aspects [6, 25]. Lastly, medicine is currently making the most progress in understanding HRI. There are different frameworks for categorizing human-robot interaction, from invasive to non-invasive or external devices [26]. These allow us to understand the potential impact. However, the promise and the most prominent role of robots is focused on assisting, rehabilitating, and accompanying people [27]. These roles have been extensively studied to determine the influence of physical-functional factors on emotional and social aspects. Factors related to direct contact with the person and their social environment, as well as technological constitution [5], are considered. Researchers aim to design, validate, and apply aspects of robot functions that affect the perception and experience of robots [9].

2.2 Increasing Dynamics of Robot Perception Evaluation

Since the 2000s, research in robot assessment has experienced a notable increase. The expansion of methods and methodologies for robot assessment has been concentrated on assessing the utilitarian, hedonic, and trust aspects of robots [28]. The pervasive integration of robots into various facets of life has accelerated to such an extent that designing and evaluating robots for their intended purpose has become imperative. The adaptation of a design must extend beyond purely physical aspects and encompass other functional dimensions [29]. The relevance of a design type, whether morphological or anthropomorphic, aims to have a targeted impact on the user. Quantifying positive or negative sensations should be a measurable aspect of robot design [30]. The seek for methodologies that generate and measure the effectiveness of new robot design proposals has evolved in recent years, particularly as robots are increasingly integrated into medical dynamics, as noted by Deegan et al. [31]. Accordingly, the repercussions of incorporating robots into socially emotional environments result in predictable and consistent social judgments within the environment. Understanding the impact of robot design and function is paramount in today's context [32, 33]. Spatola and Wadarczyk [34] mention that, despite the growing exploration of robot perception evaluation, new findings continue to emerge on how the morphism or anthropomorphism of machines is perceived. This is because multiple methods or tools are still being explored to ideally evaluate robots in their main aspects of interaction with humans. The most recent research on the impact of robots predicts a surge in their presence in society. However, it also warns of changes in perception, interest, and acceptance with each new robot proposal, underscoring the need for comprehensive assessment methods [35]. Furthermore, new research encourages investigations into design adaptations for robots to interact in a more friendly manner with people. This involves assessing the impact of their incorporation as part of the human social environment [36].

2.3 Robot Assessment Using Physical and Virtual Prototype

Prototyping excels as a highly valuable activity in the field of product development, opening up the possibilities of bringing design or inventions to tangible evaluations. The formulation and execution of strategies to create, build, or manufacture represent merely the initiation of a series of activities dedicated to prototype assessment [12]. Prototyping technologies, encompassing both physical and virtual fields, have demonstrated captivating potential across a spectrum of applications, ranging from ergonomic evaluation to training [13]. The evaluation of robots through the utilization of prototypes, whether they are physical or virtual, stands as an indispensable practice for the ongoing advancement of sophisticated robotic technologies. There is still a scarcity of studies that have analyzed whether VPs are comparable to the PPs in assessment of product attributes. However, recent research is contributing to the comparison between products that exist in both real and virtual versions. The results of these studies indicate that many aspects of perception are comparable, encompassing areas such as emotional engagement, sense of presence, and perceived quality [19]. The comparison between prototypes has been a significant area of exploration, and it has been enriched by gaining a better understanding of the formats in which prototypes are presented. While physical prototypes provide a practical insight into the robot's interaction with its environment, virtual models allow for the simulation of various scenarios and the optimization of design before implementation. Initially, comparisons between PP and VP were influenced by the technological capabilities of virtual representations. An example of this is the use of Computer-Aided Design (CAD) on PC monitors, where visual quality was not the primary focus of comparisons. Instead, aspects such as usability and cost savings were emphasized [14]. However, when the quality of visualization becomes comparable, the comparison between PP and VP enters the domain of formats and visualization scales, where the scale comparison aids in aligning the experience [15]. The study by Chu & Kao [37], it is demonstrated how the comparison between a real product and a screen visualization (iPad) yields similar effects in the assessment, particularly in highlighting negative aspects and passivity when using the screen. Another example of the utilization of multiple media is evident in an experiment where the use of videos and monitors is emphasized as an effective means for cost reduction and maintenance of PP [38].

3 Research Methodology and Application Processes

3.1 Objective

The primary objective of this paper is to introduce an explorative methodology designed to study the physical appearance characteristics, emotional response, and social perception associated with a prototype. The assessment framework encompasses three aspects: the impression of physical appearance, the measurement of emotional response, and social judgment perception. This methodological framework was implemented in the context of a pediatric walking rehabilitation robot, utilizing both its physical prototype (PP) and its virtual prototype (VP) iteration. The study aims to elucidate the discernible impact that different formats, represented by the PP and VP, may exert on users. A comprehensive exposition of all components comprising the methodology employed in this study is meticulously detailed below.

3.2 Methodology

Participants. The study sample comprised 60 students from the Faculty of Engineering and the Faculty of International Studies at the International Campus of Takushoku University in Hachioji, Japan. The sample was divided into two groups of 30 individuals each for the PP and VP cases, respectively. The age range of the students was between 18 and 27 years. Within the VP group, 18 participants reported normal vision, while 12 had corrected vision. In the PP group, 16 participants reported normal vision, and 14 had corrected vision. The majority of participants were Japanese, with few students from China, Taiwan, and Mexico.

Physical Prototype Stimuli. The robot utilized in this study is the one presented by Alvarez et al. [22] and subsequently analyzed by Navarro-Estrella et al. [39]. This PP exhibits the following physical characteristics: 1) The dimensions of the prototype are 230 mm wide × 230 mm deep × 435 mm high. 2) It is equipped with four omnidirectional wheels positioned at the base. 3) The remote operation is facilitated through a wireless controller. For visualization in this study, a light blue photoshoot background measuring 1.6 × 1.5 m was employed (see Fig. 1).

Fig. 1. The scene depicts the Physical Prototype on the left side and the Virtual Prototype on the right side.

Virtual Prototype Stimuli. The VP version was generated from a 3D model. The virtual modeling process was conducted using Fusion 360®. Renderings and animations were generated using KeyShot 10®, and final refinements were applied in Adobe Premiere® to ensure comparability with the scenes featuring the PP (see Fig. 1). The VP was showcased on a large-format SONY® LED TV screen (50 inches) to replicate the size and scale of the PP.

Assessed Robot Routines. Movement routines will be employed for the assessments applied to both the PP and VP versions. Table 1 presents the general movement routine in the order of application. Additionally, Table 2 outlines specific routines for evaluating the prototype in each of the two versions. The specific routines were applied randomly during the protocol.

Instruments. Three instruments were employed, each dedicated to assessing specific aspects described in this research. An online questionnaire was developed using the

Table 1. General Routine for prototype movements.

Routine Name	Time
Head Slide (fast)	During movement: 0.5 s each movement, 1 s back to its axis
Head & Body Rotation Clockwise (fast)	During movement: 0.5 s each movement, 1 s back to its axis
Sliding Displacement (fast)	During movement: 0.5 s each movement, 1 s back to its axis

Table 2. Specific Routines for prototype movements.

Routine	Time
Head Up-Down	During movement: 0.5 s up and down
	Four repetitions for a complete routine
Head Rotation Clockwise	During movement: 2 s
	Three repetitions for a complete routine
Head and Body Rotation Clockwise	During movement: 1 s
	Three repetitions for a complete routine
Head and Body Rotation Opposite Directions	During movement: 1 s
	Three repetitions for a complete routine

Qualtrics platform (https://www.qualtrics.com/), designed for visualization and completion on a mobile phone screen. The entire questionnaire was translated into Japanese for implementation. A comprehensive description of the three instruments is provided below.

Appearance Characteristics Questionnaire (ACQ): To gauge the impression of appearance in our methodology, we incorporated an instrument similar to those utilized in comparable studies [37, 40] emphasizing the evaluation of a product's appearance in real or virtual conditions. This instrument comprises five questions about dimensions, shape, weight, color, and material – essential physical attributes known to significantly influence the user's experience. Each question features five items describing elements of the appearance for assessment.

Regarding the measurements of the object: Look carefully at the robot for 10 seconds and choose the answer that is closest to reality.

(1) 30 mm × 330 mm × 435 mm (2) 230 mm × 230 mm × 435 mm (3) 430 mm × 430 mm × 635 mm (4) 130 mm × 130 mm × 135 mm (5) 270 mm × 270 mm × 475 mm

Regarding the weight of the object: Look carefully at the robot for 10 s and choose the answer that is closest to reality.

(1) 5kg (2) 7 kg (3) 10 kg (4) 15 kg (5) 25 kg

Regarding the color of the object: Look carefully at the robot for 10 s and choose the answer that is closest to reality.

☐ ☐ ☐ ☐ ■
(Tone 1, 2, 3, 4, 5)

Regarding the form of the object: Look carefully at the robot for 10 seconds and choose the answer that is closest to reality.

☐ ◻ ◯ ◯ ◯
(Shade 1, 2, 3, 4, 5)

Regarding the material of the object: Look carefully at the robot for 10 seconds and choose the answer that is closest to reality.

(1) Leather (2) Glass (3) Plastic (4) Wood (5) Metal

Emotional Response: Self-assessment Manikin Scale (SAM): This instrument was selected for its multifaceted features in measuring emotional responses. The Self-Assessment Manikin (SAM) was designed to gauge responses to objects and events with psychological impact on participants [41]. Notably, SAM serves as a tool free from cultural limitations in comprehension [42] and has seen recent applications in analogous studies [37]. The dimensions expressed by the pictorial elements—Valence, Arousal, and Dominance—enable participants to quantify the impact. Valence (or pleasure) delineates the degree of sadness or happiness experienced towards an object. Arousal (or activation) characterizes the calmness perceived, ranging from a relaxed and sleepy state to an excited state. Dominance (or control) gauges the extent to which a person feels in control of an object, ranging from out of control to completely in control. The measurement employed utilized a 5-point Likert Scale, with each value positioned beneath the corresponding pictorial element (see Fig. 2).

Robotic Social Attributes Scale (RoSAS): The selection of this instrument was predicated on its development as a standardized and psychometrically validated measure specifically designed to capture the social attributes attributed to machines. The Robot Social Attributes Scale (RoSAS) serves as an instrument for evaluating the fun + damental attributes associated with the perception of robots, while also examining how these perceived attributes might influence the quality of interaction with robots [33, 34, 43]. The RoSAS encompasses three distinct factors, comprising a total of 18 items. The Warmth factor incorporates adjectives such as happy, feeling organic, compassionate, social, and emotional. The Intelligence or Ability factor comprises additional adjectives including capable, responsive, interactive, reliable, competent, and compassionate.

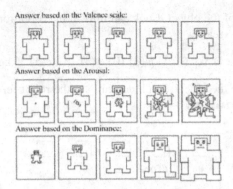

Fig. 2. Self-Assessment Manikin Scale [41, 42].

The Discomfort factor is linked to awkwardness and negative adjectives such as scary, strange, awkward, dangerous, awful, and aggressive. These three RoSAS factors have demonstrated their utility in analogous studies on robot perception [32, 40]. The measurement employed a 5-point Likert scale, ranging from "Not at all related" (1) to "Very related" (5) (see Fig. 3).

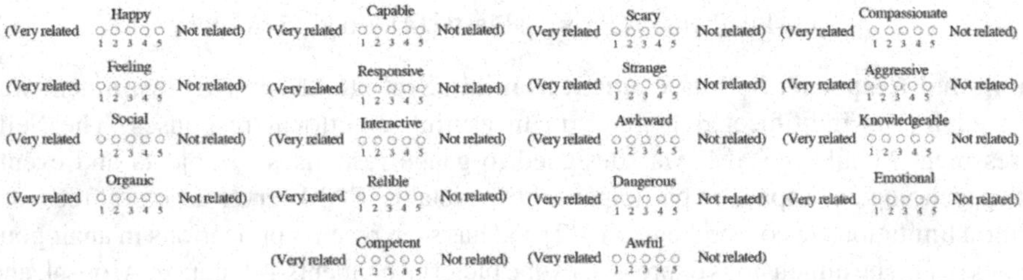

Fig. 3. Robotic Social Attributes Scale (RoSAS) items [33].

3.3 Procedure

The methodology was implemented at the Emotional Design Laboratory facilities located at the Hachioji International Campus of Takushoku University in Tokyo, Japan, from October to November 2023. As previously stated, this study aims to evaluate both the PP and VP using the three selected instruments. The procedural approach remained consistent across both cases (see Figs. 4 and 6). Subsequently, we will delineate related to each case.

PP procedure. A group of 4 people were invited to participate in the procedure, inviting them to scan a QR where they could read the information about the test, give their consent, fill in basic demographic data, and prepare for the start of the protocol. To assess without any type of sound distractor caused by the PP, participants used noise-canceling headphones.

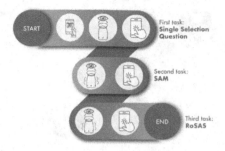

Fig. 4. Protocol scheme for PP assessment.

The protocol consisted of three tasks to be performed by the participants after watching the PP. The first task corresponded to the stationary PP assessment with the ACQ. The second task corresponded to the PP assessment with SAM after performing the general movement routine. The third task corresponded to the PP with RoSAS after performing the four specific routines in shuffle mode. Each specific routine was evaluated individually with RoSAS, this task was the longest to perform. In order to control the participants' watching, they performed a dynamic of frontal observation during PP movements, and when the routines finished, they turned around on the chair to answer the instruments without being able to watch the prototype (see Fig. 5). Except for the first task, for, it was given up to 60 s of prototype watching. The entire protocol took about 15–20 min, the first two tasks were the most time-consuming with 2–3 min in total, leaving the third task with more exposure time as each routine was evaluated with the RoSAS. The four specific routines were evaluated in 8–10 min.

Fig. 5. Images of the PP protocol procedure dynamics.

VP procedure. A group of 4–5 people was invited to participate in the procedure, inviting them to scan a QR where they could read the information about the test, give their consent, fill in basic demographic data, and prepare for the start of the protocol or this protocol, the prototype was displayed on the screen; there was no sonorization of the routine's movements.

The protocol for the VP entailed the same three tasks to be completed by participants following the observation of the VP displayed on the screen. The initial task involved assessing the stationary VP using the ACQ. The second task involved evaluating the VP's emotional response to SAM after engaging in the general movement routine. The

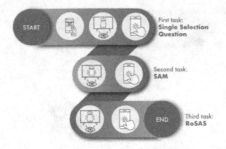

Fig. 6. Protocol scheme for VP assessment

final task entailed assessing the VP using RoSAS after performing the four specific routines in shuffle mode. In this protocol, display control was straightforward: once the movement routine concluded, the VP animation ceased, prompting participants to respond to the instruments (see Fig. 7). Similar to the PP protocol, except for the first task, which projected the VP image for 60 s, the entire VP protocol took approximately 15–20 min to complete.

Fig. 7. Images of the VP protocol procedure dynamics

4   Analysis and Results

All data collected from the Qualtrics platform were compiled for subsequent processing and analysis. Statistical analyses were conducted using SPSS 17.0 for Windows™ (IBM SPSS Inc., Chicago, IL, USA). The presentation of analyses and results will follow the sequence of the instruments used. The initial set of results pertains to the ACQ. Table 1 presents the evaluation of five characteristics for both the PP and VP perceptions. This outcome delineates the frequency with which each characteristic was selected. The table provides a comparative overview of the perceived dimensions, weight, color, and shape for both prototypes.

The subsequent result pertains to SAM. A comparison between the two samples was conducted using an independent T-student test. Table 4 presents the results for the three dimensions assessed in SAM. The analysis revealed that one of the three dimensions exhibited a p-value ($p < 0.05$) below the acceptable threshold. The results indicate that

Table 3. Appearance Characteristics Questionnaire Results.

Perceived Robot Appearance	Data	Physical	Virtual
Dimensions	135 × 130 × 130 mm	3	0
	135 × 130 × 130 mm	8	17
	435 × 330 × 330 mm	5	6
	475 × 270 × 270 mm	6	1
	635 × 430 × 430 mm	8	6
Weight	5 kg	7	4
	7 kg	6	1
	10 kg	8	9
	15 kg	6	14
	25 kg	3	2
Color	Tone 1	14	4
	Tone 2	**10**	**10**
	Tone 3	**4**	**14**
	Tone 4	2	2
	Tone 5	0	0
Shape	Shape 1	0	0
	Shape 2	5	10
	Shape 3	**22**	**18**
	Shape 4	3	2
	Shape 5	0	0
Material	Leather	0	0
	Glass	0	0
	Plastic	**29**	**30**
	Metal	1	0
	Wood	0	0

dominance for PP (M = 3.10, SD = 1.423) and VP (M = 2.83, SD = 1.020) showed a significant difference (t = 0.834, df = 58, p = 0.006).

The final set of results pertains to the application of the RoSAS to the four specific routines. Similar to the statistical analysis applied to SAM, an independent t-test was employed to compare the responses between the PP and VP. The test indicated that three out of the four routines exhibited significant differences (p < 0.05) in at least one of the RoSAS elements. Notably, the routine "Head Rotation Clockwise" did not show significant differences in the comparison of PP and VP. However, the routine "Head Up-Down" displayed significant differences in Emotional (t = −.129, df = 58, p =

Table 4. Self-Assessment Manikin Scale Results.

SAM	Physical Mean (Std.Dev)	Virtual Mean (Std.Dev)	F	Sig.
Valencia	3.87 (0.730)	3.83 (1.020)	1.506	0.225
Arousal	2.57 (0.858)	2.37 (1.066)	0.715	0.401
Dominance	3.10 (1.423)	2.83 (1.020)	8.134	**0.006**

0.002) and Dangerous (t = 1.816, df = 58, p = 0.023) elements. The detailed results are presented in Table 5.

Table 5. Robotic Social Attributes Scale (RoSAS) Result – Routine Head Up-Down.

RoSAS	Physical Mean (Std.Dev)	Virtual Mean (Std.Dev)	F	Sig.
Happy	2.13 (1.106)	2.47 (1.252)	1.997	0.163
Feeling	2.03 (1.098)	2.63 (1.159)	0.308	0.581
Social	2.03 (1.273)	2.53 (1.137)	0.202	0.655
Organic	2.33 (0.922)	2.83 (1.147)	1.197	0.278
Compasionate	2.40 (1.133)	2.70 (1.149)	0.137	0.712
Emotional	**2.00 (0.910)**	**2.63 (1.351)**	**10.825**	**0.002**
Capable	2.83 (1.206)	2.83 (1.053)	0.671	0.416
Responsive	2.43 (1.073)	3.10 (1.155)	0.020	0.887
Interactive	2.20 (1.157)	2.87 (1.042)	0.412	0.523
Reliable	2.33 (1.124)	2.73 (1.081)	0.047	0.830
Competent	2.80 (1.126)	2.83 (1.147)	0.043	0.836
Knowledgeable	2.83 (1.262)	2.97 (1.159)	0.145	0.705
Scary	4.43 (1.006)	4.27 (1.143)	0.501	0.482
Strange	3.87 (1.383)	3.53 (1.408)	0.281	0.598
Awkward	3.83 (1.262)	3.47 (1.252)	0.080	0.778
Dangerous	**4.67 (0.802)**	**4.20 (1.157)**	**5.452**	**0.023**
Awful	4.67 (0.802)	4.53 (0.900)	0.819	0.369
Aggressive	4.57 (0.971)	4.37 (1.033)	0.641	0.427

Subsequently, the "Head and Body Rotation Opposite Directions" routine exhibited significant differences in the analysis. This particular routine demonstrated notable distinctions in the Awkward (t = −2.593, df = 58, p = 0.000) and Dangerous (t = −1.852, df = 58, p = 0.039) elements. The detailed results are presented in Table 6. Concluding the analysis, the results for the "Head and Body Rotation Clockwise" routine are presented. This particular routine exhibited an elevated number of significant differences in RoSAS elements between PP and VP, mainly due to the discomfort factor. Happy (t = 2.6763, df = 58, p = 0.011) and Emotional (t = −0.218, df = 58, p = 0.022) are the first elements with significant differences. Subsequently, Scary (t = −1.120, df = 58, p = 0.024), Strange (t = −1.741, df = 58, p = 0.029), Awkward (t = −3.781, df = 58, p = 0.000), Dangerous (t = −2.196, df = 58, p = 0.000), and Aggressive (t = −1.406, df = 58, p = 0.010) showed significant differences. The detailed results are presented in Table 7.

Table 6. Robotic Social Attributes Scale (RoSAS) Result – Routine Head and Body Rotation Opposite Directions.

RoSAS	Physical Mean (Std.Dev)	Virtual Mean (Std.Dev)	F	Sig.
Happy	2.93 (1.337)	2.77 (1.305)	0.005	0.947
Feeling	1.87 (1.042)	2.37 (1.159)	0.524	0.472
Social	3.20 (1.031)	2.70 (1.317	2.489	0.120
Organic	2.53 (1.008)	2.70 (1.208)	1.374	0.246
Compasionate	3.10 (1.296)	3.20 (1.156)	.550	0.461
Emotional	2.73 (1.230)	1.83 (1.020)	3.338	0.073
Capable	2.87 (1.306)	2.93 (1.143)	0.595	0.444
Responsive	2.97 (1.217)	2.90 (1.208)	0.002	0.967
Interactive	2.83 (1.234)	2.70 (1.208)	0.310	0.580
Reliable	3.00 (1.234)	3.03 (1.159)	0.058	0.810
Competent	2.60 (1.163)	2.83 (0.986)	1.324	0.255
Knowledgeable	2.93 (1.230)	3.40 (1.192)	0.003	0.957
Scary	3.53 (1.432)	4.13 (1.167)	2.822	0.098
Strange	2.97 (1.377)	3.37 (1.450)	0.617	0.435
Awkward	**3.57 (1.373)**	**4.33 (0.844)**	**15.273**	**0.000**
Dangerous	**3.57 (1.501)**	**4.23 (1.278)**	**4.465**	**0.039**
Awful	4.37 (1.129)	4.50 (0.974)	1.158	0.286
Aggressive	3.67 (1.373)	4.20 (1.243)	1.751	0.191

5 Discussion and Conclusion

The primary aim of this paper was to introduce and illustrate a methodology designed for the comparative analysis of physical appearance characteristics and emotional perception within a prototype. This methodology seeks to make a valuable contribution to

Table 7. Robotic Social Attributes Scale (RoSAS) Result – Routine Head and Body Rotation Clockwise.

RoSAS	Physical Mean (Std.Dev)	Virtual Mean (Std.Dev)	F	Sig.
Happy	**3.10 (1.185)**	**2.60 (1.192)**	**6.846**	**0.011**
Feeling	2.60 (1.192)	2.60 (1.070)	1.024	0.316
Social	2.83 (1.711)	3.60 (1.003)	0.071	0.791
Organic	3.13 (1.456)	2.63 (1.245)	0.908	0.345
Compasionate	3.03 (1.326)	2.73 (1.143)	0.506	0.480
Emotional	**2.90 (1.125)**	**2.60 (1.037)**	**5.503**	**0.022**
Capable	3.07 (1.202)	3.23 (1.104)	0.063	0.803
Responsive	2.83 (1.341)	3.00 (1.174)	1.524	0.222
Interactive	2.83 (1.202)	2.60 (1.192)	0.444	0.508
Reliable	2.93 (1.322)	2.73 (1.143)	0.007	0.933
Competent	2.90 (1.408)	3.37 (0.999)	1.233	0.271
Knowledgeable	2.87 (1.230)	3.37 (1.159)	0.000	0.988
Scary	**4.07 (1.273)**	**4.50 (0.861)**	**5.337**	**0.024**
Strange	**3.43 (1.431)**	**3.63 (1.273)**	**5.030**	**0.029**
Awkward	**3.87 (1.167)**	**4.07 (1.258)**	**8.267**	**0.006**
Dangerous	**4.30 (1.119)**	**4.40 (1.037)**	**13.604**	**0.000**
Awful	4.43 (1.104)	4.53 (0.973)	2.967	0.090
Aggressive	**4.23 (1.073)**	**4.43 (0.935)**	**7.102**	**0.010**

the exploration of robot assessment and its validation for further development. Through the careful selection and integration of instruments, the methodology comprehensively addresses three pivotal dimensions: the visual impression of appearance, the elicited emotional responses, and the associated social perception. The study defines the application of this methodology in the context of a robot designed for walking rehabilitation, utilizing both a PP and VP. An underlying goal of this research is to gain insights into the impact of visualizing a VP through large-format displays and understand how such visualization devices can enhance the assessment process for products of this nature, particularly robots.

The initial finding of this research stems from the AQC application for the assessment and comparison of the two prototypes. The results presented in Table 3 offer an insightful overview of how participants perceived the prototypes during the assessment. This outcome reveals a discernible trend, with participants perceiving "the dimensions" of the prototype as the most distinguishable between them, while progressively aligning their perceptions of "the shape and material" across both prototypes. This information describes how the comparison is effective for observable aspects such as color, shape, or material, but penalizes the aspects of dimension and weight. The AQC instrument has demonstrated its value in prior studies [37, 40] with applications, in our study, it allows for the refinement of two crucial physical aspects, providing a foundation for delving into the perception of more intricate features. The second finding of this research was observed in the SAM application results. In the comparison between the two prototypes, it was obtained that control (dominance) perception was greater in PP than in VP. This finding cannot be said to be unfavorable, since the purpose of the SAM, as has been seen in other studies [15, 16, 37] is to show the emotional response evoked by the products. In our study, positively, valence, and arousal are comparable for the two prototypes, evidencing that the emotional aspects conveyed by the PP or by the VP through the screen are similar for a conscious comparison. Once again, the SAM is positioned as a tool capable of measuring emotional response and can be applied in this kind of research.

Based on the aforementioned information, the findings derived from the assessments using the RoSAS validated the social and emotional aspects of the prototypes. With a certain level of confidence in the SAM results, we can delve into the comparison between the PP and VP, discerning both differentiated and comparable aspects between the two prototypes. One aspect of to concert is a potential bias stemming from the participants' prior exposure to the general routine, as routines were randomly presented to participant groups, and all rotational movements of the prototypes were showcased during the specific routines. However, the RoSAS, like to the SAM, demonstrated its efficacy as an evaluation instrument, facilitating the comparison between the PP and VP. The obtained results provide pertinent insights into the three overarching factors assessed by RoSAS, consistent with observations from prior studies [15, 19, 33] where certain factors are observed to be predominant. In our study, as depicted in Tables 5, 6 and 7, the "discomfort" factor emerges as the most discernible distinction between PP and VP. Negative aspects are more pronounced in the VP, while the positive attributes of the "warmth" factor exhibit a slight prominence in the PP. Conversely, the "intelligence" factor does not demonstrate notable differentiation, suggesting similarity in this aspect between the two prototypes. We must emphasize that the emotional components revealed by the RoSAS and SAM findings demonstrate how the prototype visualization tools were capable of providing sufficient information for differentiated judgments on design aspects. These insights highlight areas that can be promptly adjusted in virtual product versions. Nonetheless, it is imperative to continue contrasting the results, as they may reveal a potential correlation between negative assessments of the VP and the PP. However, we have only scratched the surface of a methodology that holds further potential for prototype assessment. Although the independent assessment of each prototype enabled us to discern their impacts, the depth of the comparison revealed how engagement with a VP can provide both tangible and intangible aspects that can serve as substitutes. Furthermore, the visualization format introduces a new approach for validating prototypes at real scales.

The limitations of this research can be categorized into three aspects. The initial aspect pertains to the technical aspects associated with the VP. While the TV screen has proven effective in the methodology, greater attention should be devoted to controlling the scale quality and lighting conditions of the prototype scene development. The second aspect involves the limitations of the sample, which was confined to a university context. Nevertheless, this constraint serves to underscore the adaptability of the methodology within cultural contexts. Lastly, the third aspect concerns the conditioning of routines, an area that warrants exploration with alternative movements more closely aligned with the functions of the robot. In conclusion, the results of the assessments using physical and virtual prototypes showed some differences, but they were not highly significant. Hence, from an overall perspective, it can be said that using virtual prototypes of robots displayed on a high-definition screen at a 1:1 scale allows the assessment of appearance characteristics, emotional response, and social perception. It is particularly important to remark that the assessment methodology designed for this research considered two opposite dimensions of the robot: a tangible dimension (centered in the robot) assessed through appearance characteristics, and an intangible dimension (centered in users) assessed through emotional response and social perception. The perception of size was different, but users' responses for both PP and VP did not match the actual robot dimensions, a situation that may be fixed by placing a familiar object next to the robot. Weight also showed different results, but this characteristic is not relevant for interaction with robots like the one evaluated in this research. As a final consideration, this research focused on assessing the robot in a unidirectional way, in which the physical or virtual robot performed a set of movements, and the respondents evaluated it. For the case of assessing more complex human-robot interactions in which a robot performs a certain behavior as a response to the user behavior, it will be necessary to validate the efficacy of virtual prototypes displayed on a TV screen.

Acknowledgements. The authors would like to acknowledge the financial support to Tecnologico de Monterrey, in the production of this work and to the School of Architecture, Art and Design Research Group - Advanced Design Processes for Sustainable Transformation- of which we are part. We also extend our gratitude to the Faculty of Engineering of Takushoku University for providing the robot for the assessment, facilities, and equipment during this international collaborative research project. Special thanks to the student Betsy Leiva who actively participated in the development of the protocol during the international collaborative research project.

References

1. Weiss, A., Igelsböck, J., Wurhofer, D., Tscheligi, M.: Looking forward to a "robotic society"? Int. J. Soc. Robot. **3**(2), 111–123 (2011). https://doi.org/10.1007/s12369-010-0076-5
2. Ben-Ari, M., Mondada, F.: Robots and Their Applications. In: Ben-Ari, M., Mondada, F. (eds.) Elements of Robotics, pp. 1–20. Springer, Cham (2018). https://doi.org/10.1007/978-3-319-62533-1_1
3. Mubin, O., Stevens, C.J., Shahid, S., Mahmud, A.A., Dong, J.-J.: A review of the applicability of robots in education. Technol. Educ. Learn. **1**, 209–0015 (2013). https://doi.org/10.2316/Journal.209.2013.1.209-0015
4. Merdan, M., Lepuschitz, W., Koppensteiner, G., Balogh, R., Obdržálek, D.: Robotics in Education. Merdan, M.,Lepuschitz, W., Koppensteiner, G., Balogh, R., Obdržálek, D., eds. vol. 1023, Springer, Cham (2020). https://doi.org/10.1007/978-3-030-26945-6
5. Broadbent, E., Stafford, R., MacDonald, B.: Acceptance of healthcare robots for the older population: review and future directions. Int. J. Soc. Robot. **1**(4), 319–330 (2009). https://doi.org/10.1007/s12369-009-0030-6

6. Baratta, A., Cimino, A., Gnoni, M.G., Longo, F.: Human robot collaboration in industry 4.0: a literature review. Procedia Comput. Sci. **217**, 1887–1895 (2023). https://doi.org/10.1016/j.procs.2022.12.389

7. Sarrica, M., Brondi, S., Fortunati, L.: How many facets does a "social robot" have? A review of scientific and popular definitions online. Inf. Technol. People **33**(1), 1–21 (2019). https://doi.org/10.1108/ITP-04-2018-0203

8. van Straten, C.L., Peter, J., Kühne, R.: Child-robot relationship formation: a narrative review of empirical research. Int. J. Soc. Robot. **12**(2), 325–344 (2020). https://doi.org/10.1007/s12369-019-00569-0

9. Ricks, D. J., Colton, M. B.: Trends and considerations in robot-assisted autism therapy. In: 2010 IEEE International Conference on Robotics and Automation, IEEE, pp. 4354–4359 (2010). https://doi.org/10.1109/ROBOT.2010.5509327

10. Lauff, C.A., Kotys-Schwartz, D., Rentschler, M.E.: What is a prototype? What are the roles of prototypes in companies? J. Mech. Des. **140**(6), 061102 (2018). https://doi.org/10.1115/1.4039340

11. Nelson, J., Menold, J.: Opening the black box: developing metrics to assess the cognitive processes of prototyping. Des. Stud. **70**, 100964 (2020). https://doi.org/10.1016/j.destud.2020.100964

12. Elverum, C.W., Welo, T., Tronvoll, S.: Prototyping in new product development: strategy considerations. Procedia CIRP **50**, 117–122 (2016). https://doi.org/10.1016/j.procir.2016.05.010

13. Seth, A., Vance, J.M., Oliver, J.H.: Virtual reality for assembly methods prototyping: a review. Virtual Reality **15**(1), 5–20 (2011). https://doi.org/10.1007/s10055-009-0153-y

14. Gibson, I., Gao, Z., Campbell, I.: A comparative study of virtual prototyping and physical prototyping. Int. J. Manuf. Technol. Manage. **6**(6), 503 (2004). https://doi.org/10.1504/IJMTM.2004.005931

15. Kim, C., Lee, C., Lehto, M.R., Yun, M.H.: Affective evaluation of user impressions using virtual product prototyping. Hum. Factors Ergon. Manuf. Serv. Ind. **21**(1), 1–13 (2011). https://doi.org/10.1002/hfm.20210

16. Pontonnier, C., Dumont, G., Samani, A., Madeleine, P., Badawi, M.: Designing and evaluating a workstation in real and virtual environment: toward virtual reality based ergonomic design sessions. J. Multimodal User Interfaces **8**(2), 199–208 (2014). https://doi.org/10.1007/s12193-013-0138-8

17. Kerttula, M., Salmela, M., Heikkinen, M.: Virtual reality prototyping-a framework for the development of electronics and telecommunication products. In: Proceedings 8th IEEE International Workshop on Rapid System Prototyping Shortening the Path from Specification to Prototype, IEEE, pp. 2–11. Computer Society (1997). https://doi.org/10.1109/IWRSP.1997.618812

18. Chu, C. H., Kao, E. T.: A comparative study of design evaluation with virtual prototypes versus a physical product. Appl. Sci. (Switz.), **10**(14), 4723 (2020). https://doi.org/10.3390/app10144723

19. Pizzolante, M., Bartolotta, S., Sarcinella, E. D., Chirico, A., Gaggioli, A.: Virtual vs. real: exploring perceptual, cognitive and affective dimensions in design product experiences. BMC Psychol. **12**(1), 10 (2024). 10. https://doi.org/10.1186/s40359-023-01497-5

20. Kim, C., Lee, C., Lehto, M.R., Yun, M.H.: Affective evaluation of user impressions using virtual product prototyping. Hum. Factors Ergon. Manuf. **21**(1), 1–13 (2011). https://doi.org/10.1002/hfm.20210

21. Langer, A., Marshall, P.J., Levy-Tzedek, S.: Ethical considerations in child-robot interactions. Neurosci. Biobehav. Rev. **151**, 105230 (2023). https://doi.org/10.1016/j.neubiorev.2023.105230

22. Alvarez, J., Hara, E., Koyama, T., Adachi, K., Kagawa, Y.: Design of form and motion of a robot aimed to provide emotional support for pediatric walking rehabilitation. In: Lecture Notes in Computer Science (Including Subseries Lecture Notes In Artificial Intelligence and Lecture Notes in Bioinformatics), LNCS, Vol. 12780, pp. 403–419. Springer (2021). https://doi.org/10.1007/978-3-030-78224-5_28

23. Wada, K., Shibata, T.: Living with seal robots—its sociopsychological and physiological influences on the elderly at a care house. IEEE Trans. Rob. **23**(5), 972–980 (2007). https://doi.org/10.1109/TRO.2007.906261

24. Seo, S. H., Geiskkovitch, D., Nakane, M., King, C., Young, J. E.: Poor thing! would you feel sorry for a simulated robot? In: Proceedings of the Tenth Annual ACM/IEEE International Conference on Human-Robot Interaction, ACM, pp. 125–132. New York, NY, USA (2015). https://doi.org/10.1145/2696454.2696471

25. Sherwani, F., Asad, M. M., Ibrahim, B. S. K. K.: Collaborative robots and industrial revolution 4.0 (IR 4.0). In: 2020 International Conference on Emerging Trends in Smart Technologies (ICETST), pp. 1–5, IEEE (2020). https://doi.org/10.1109/ICETST49965.2020.9080724

26. Mohebbi, A.: Human-robot interaction in rehabilitation and assistance: a Review. Curr. Rob. Rep. **1**(3), 131–144 (2020). https://doi.org/10.1007/s43154-020-00015-4

27. Chita-Tegmark, M., Scheutz, M.: Assistive robots for the social management of health: a framework for robot design and human-robot interaction research. Int. J. Soc. Robot. **13**(2), 197–217 (2021). https://doi.org/10.1007/s12369-020-00634-z

28. Jung, M., Lazaro, M.J.S., Yun, M.H.: Evaluation of methodologies and measures on the usability of social robots: a systematic review. Appl. Sci. **11**(4), 1388 (2021). https://doi.org/10.3390/app11041388

29. Gonzalez, A., Garcia, L., Kilby, J., McNair, P.: Robotic devices for paediatric rehabilitation: a review of design features. BioMed. Eng. Online. Central Ltd. **20**, 1–33 (2021). https://doi.org/10.1186/s12938-021-00920-5

30. Bartneck, C., Bleeker, T., Bun, J., Fens, P., Riet, L.: The influence of robot anthropomorphism on the feelings of embarrassment when interacting with robots. Paladyn J. Behav. Rob. **1**(2), 109–115 (2010). https://doi.org/10.2478/s13230-010-0011-3

31. Deegan, P., et al.: Mobile manipulators for assisted living in residential settings. Auton. Robot. **24**(2), 179–192 (2008). https://doi.org/10.1007/s10514-007-9061-8

32. Stroessner, S.J., Benitez, J.: The social perception of humanoid and non-humanoid robots: effects of gendered and machinelike features. Int. J. Soc. Robot. **11**(2), 305–315 (2019). https://doi.org/10.1007/s12369-018-0502-7

33. Carpinella, C. M., Wyman, A. B., Perez, M. A., Stroessner, S. J.: The robotic social attributes scale (RoSAS). In: Proceedings of the 2017 ACM/IEEE International Conference on Human-Robot Interaction, Part F127194, pp. 254–262. New York, NY, USA: ACM (2017). https://doi.org/10.1145/2909824.3020208

34. Spatola, N., Wudarczyk, O.A.: Ascribing emotions to robots: explicit and implicit attribution of emotions and perceived robot anthropomorphism. Comput. Hum. Behav. **124**, 106934 (2021). https://doi.org/10.1016/j.chb.2021.106934

35. Cifuentes, C.A., Pinto, M.J., Céspedes, N., Múnera, M.: Social robots in therapy and care. Curr. Rob. Rep. **1**(3), 59–74 (2020). https://doi.org/10.1007/s43154-020-00009-2

36. Lei, X., Rau, P.-L.P.: Should i blame the human or the robot? Attribution within a human-robot group. Int. J. Soc. Robot. **13**(2), 363–377 (2021). https://doi.org/10.1007/s12369-020-00645-w

37. Chu, C.-H., Kao, E.-T.: A comparative study of design evaluation with virtual prototypes versus a physical product. Appl. Sci. **10**(14), 4723 (2020). https://doi.org/10.3390/app10144723

38. Bainbridge, W.A., Hart, J.W., Kim, E.S., Scassellati, B.: The benefits of interactions with physically present robots over video-displayed agents. Int. J. Soc. Robot. **3**(1), 41–52 (2011). https://doi.org/10.1007/s12369-010-0082-7

39. Navarro-Estrella, M., Rojas, J.-C., Hernandez, F. A., Alvarez, J.: Assessment of a robot design: a novel methodology using eye-tracking and semantic associations among undergraduate students´ contexts. In: 2023 World Engineering Education Forum - Global Engineering Deans Council (WEEF-GEDC), IEEE, pp. 1–6 (2023). https://doi.org/10.1109/WEEF-GEDC59520.2023.10343721

40. Dou, X., Yan, L., Wu, K., Niu, J. (2022). Effects of voice and lighting color on the social perception of home healthcare robots. Appl. Sci. (Switz.), 12(23). https://doi.org/10.3390/app122312191

41. Morris, J.D.: Observations: SAM: the self-assessment manikin an efficient cross-cultural measurement of emotional response 1. J. Advert. Res. **35**(6), 63–68 (1995)

42. Bradley, M.M., Lang, P.J.: Measuring emotion: the self-assessment manikin and the semantic differential. J. Behav. Ther. Exp. Psychiatry **25**(1), 49–59 (1994). https://doi.org/10.1016/0005-7916(94)90063-9

43. Angelopoulos, G., Rossi, A., Napoli, C. Di, Rossi, S. (2022). You are in my way: nonverbal social cues for legible robot navigation behaviors. In: 2022 IEEE/RSJ International Conference on Intelligent Robots and Systems (IROS), pp. 657–662 (2022). https://doi.org/10.1109/IROS47612.2022.9981754

Automotive Interactions and Smart Mobility Solutions

Research on Design Methods of Smart Service Systems Driven by Autonomous Vehicles

Ran Bei[✉]

South China University of Technology, Guangzhou 510006, China
ranbei@scut.edu.com

Abstract. The Smart Service Systems build perception and connection intelligence into the product itself. It focuses on intelligent products and combines big data, cloud computing, social computing, cognitive computing, the Internet of Things, mobile solutions, and other technologies to provide active, efficient, and user-centered services. Personalized, high-quality service process and service experience. The intelligent service system emphasizes the system structure, which has elements of system characteristics such as system resources, system subsystems, and their relationships, system operating rules, etc. The object of system process processing is service elements. As a typical smart product, autonomous vehicles drive the construction of smart systems, link service participants, and play an important role in the service process. For the design of Smart Service Systems driven by autonomous vehicles, service is the content of the design, and intelligence is the means to realize the service. This paper analyzes the types of intelligent service systems and the design innovation model driven by autonomous vehicles, constructs a design element and design content model, and proposes service system architecture design, information architecture design, and product functional specification design methods.

Keywords: Smart Service Systems · Autonomous vehicles · system architecture design · information architecture design · product functional design

1 Research Background

Technologies such as artificial intelligence, big data, and the Internet of Everything have greatly affected human mobility. The combination of the automobile economy, the digital economy, the network economy, the smart economy, and the algorithm economy has had a huge impact on smart cars represented by autonomous vehicles. In the field of design, industrial design methods cannot solve the design problem of Smart Service Systems using autonomous vehicles as media carriers. Artificial intelligence has become an important design resource, and the design object has changed from products to Smart Service Systems, triggering the innovation of design principles from functional modeling to smart service value experience. Design elements shift from focusing on the human-machine relationship to focusing on the relationship between smart service participants. Design tools have undergone changes that incorporate data thinking into qualitative analysis and deduction. This article studies the design methods of Smart Service Systems driven by autonomous vehicles.

A. Marcus et al. (Eds.): HCII 2024, LNCS 14713, pp. 149–158, 2024.
https://doi.org/10.1007/978-3-031-61353-1_10

2 Types of Smart Service System

The intelligent platform digitally connects intelligent products, service participants, and service processes to form the Smart Service System [1]. Social-ecological systems are divided into three basic types - Micro System, Mezzo System, and Macro System [2]. This article divides the Smart Service System into three types from three different perspectives: intelligent products, service participants, and intelligent platforms, with multi-service platform-oriented, multi-information channel-oriented, and multi-smart medium-oriented (Fig. 1).

2.1 Multi-service Platform Oriented

Macrosystems focus on the interactive relationship between systems composed of human intelligence and artificial intelligence and users. Through intelligent technologies such as cloud computing, cloud storage, and edge computing, we drive user activity behavior data collaboration on the system cloud, information collaboration on material flow, information flow, and capital flow, and service-based knowledge collaboration to realize human intelligence and artificial intelligence. Intelligent, systematic, and collaborative perception, identification, and management between entities drive the collaborative integration of human intelligence and artificial intelligence and the multi-platform integrated service innovation model created by crowd intelligence [3].

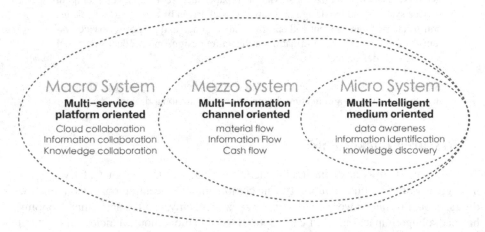

Fig. 1. Types of Smart Service System driven by autonomous vehicles

2.2 Multi-information Channel Oriented

Mesosystems focus on the interactive relationship between groups composed of human intelligence and artificial intelligence and users. Autonomous vehicles with active interaction capabilities participate in the construction of groups to complete material flow, capital flow, and information flow exchanges through the Internet, Internet of Things,

Internet of Intelligence, and social local mobile networks driving multi-information channel service innovation models [4].

2.3 Multi-intelligent Medium Oriented

Microsystems focus on the interactive relationship between human intelligence or artificial intelligence individuals and users. Autonomous vehicles with user activity behavior data acquisition, information recognition, and knowledge application capabilities, like biological humans, interact with users in an individual form, forming a service innovation model driven by intelligent service media.

3 Smart Service System Innovation Model

3.1 Service System Innovation Model

Autonomous vehicles are used in social service fields such as urban security, urban transportation, elderly care, municipal services, and health care, connecting transportation operators, data providers, and service providers to build an innovative platform service system model. Autonomous vehicles interact with users in the dimension of artistic conception, resulting in the transformation of user activities and behaviors from data, information, and knowledge, resulting in the systematic production of human mobility content, and the formation of autonomous vehicle services based on the social and cultural knowledge map of human mobility. The system innovation model embodies the characteristics of collaborative integration and group intelligence innovation. For the Service system innovation model driven by autonomous vehicles, autonomous vehicle service architecture, information interaction, and intelligent product design are required.

3.2 Service Information Innovation Model

Autonomous vehicles operated by transportation operators connect to other Autonomous vehicles, smartphones, smart terminals, and other smart facilities through the Internet, Internet of Things, Internet of Things, and local social mobile networks to obtain user activity behavior data and identify user activity behavior information. And discovering user activity behavioral knowledge. In the dimension of situational interaction, the intelligent service media connected by autonomous vehicles interact with users, producing professional human mobility content including material flow, information flow, and capital flow, and intelligent agents produce human mobility content, forming a human-based The service information innovation model of the mobility nature cognitive knowledge graph and the human mobility agent knowledge graph requires autonomous vehicle information interaction design and intelligent product design.

3.3 Service Product Innovation Model

The autonomous vehicle senses environmental data and user behavior data through the autonomous driving and service application sensing module and identifies the rules and patterns of user activity through calculation and analysis by the onboard central processor and transportation operators for autonomous driving and service implementation. Decision-making and forecasting in the process. In the dimension of physical environment interaction, autonomous vehicles interact with users to generate activity behaviors, complete the transformation from data and information to knowledge, generate user-produced human mobility content, and form an intelligent system based on the human mobility spatiotemporal service knowledge graph. The product service innovation model requires functional design and representation design.

4 Smart Service System Design Model

4.1 Design Elements Model of Smart Service System

Autonomous vehicles communicate and interact with users in three forms: individual, group, and system in the dimensions of the physical environment, situation, and artistic conception. They participate in the construction of three service innovation models intelligent service products, intelligent service information and intelligent service systems, and integrated services. Resources provide users with an effective, efficient, and satisfactory service experience.

As a systematic design thinking method, stakeholder-centered Smart Service System design has the following six main characteristics: (1) Use systematic design thinking and methods to design and develop services [5]. (2) From the design of individual system elements to the overall design of system relationships, from the design of internal factors of the system to the integrated design of external factors, and the design of creation to the design of things. (3) The five major elements of design are service participants, action, purpose, scene, and medium. (4) Emphasis on the collaborative co-creation of service participants, starting from the service journey, and paying attention to the service relationship between person-things-systems. (5) The implementation media of services are divided into tangible and intangible, and intangible services are realized through tangible hardware and software. (6) For experience, it aims to provide services that satisfy the service recipients and are more efficient and effective for the service providers [6].

This study proposes the design goals of the Smart Service System based on user activity behaviors, the accessibility of physical environment interaction at the instinctive level, the guidance of situational interaction, and the interactive experience of artistic conception. Combining the characteristics of the three smart service innovation models of autonomous vehicles, the Smart Service System design model (Fig. 2) expresses the design elements from five experience levels, covering the design elements of three model dimensions and five experience levels.

Three Service Model Dimensions. The service product innovation model is to be carried out with the task-oriented design in the dimension of physical interaction. The service information innovation model is to be carried out with the Matter-oriented design in the dimension of scenario interaction. The service system innovation model is to be carried out with the system-oriented design in the dimension of meaning interaction.

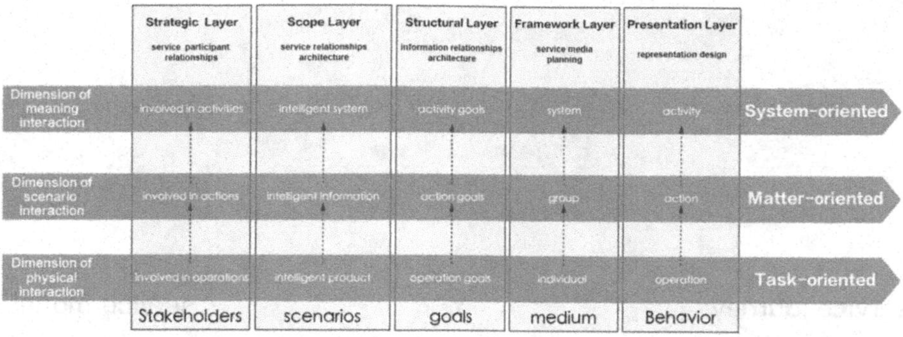

	Strategic Layer	Scope Layer	Structural Layer	Framework Layer	Presentation Layer	
	service participant relationships	service relationships architecture	information relationships architecture	service media planning	representation design	
Dimension of meaning interaction	involved in activities	intelligent system	activity goals	system	activity	System-oriented
Dimension of scenario interaction	involved in actions	intelligent information	action goals	group	action	Matter-oriented
Dimension of physical interaction	involved in operations	intelligent product	operation goals	individual	operation	Task-oriented
	Stakeholders	scenarios	goals	medium	Behavior	

Fig. 2. Design elements of Smart Service System Design Model

Five Layers of Experience. At the strategic layer, by identifying the person involved in operations, the person involved in actions, and the person involved in activities, service participants are identified. Through building service-participant relationships, service needs are mined. At the scope layer, build service relationships in intelligent product service scenarios, intelligent information service scenarios, and intelligent system service scenarios, and clarify service content. Scenarios refer to stories in which system and service participants perform tasks and activities under specific goals in a specific context. Designers plan how users use the system based on the design objects of the activities [7]. At the structural layer, service content is transformed into information relationships architecture and information requirements through operation goals (Motor goals), action goals (Do goals), and activity goals (Be-goals). At the framework layer, the hardware, software, personnel, and other service mediums, that implement the service are organized and planned, and the media functions are clarified. At the presentation layer, prototype the hardware and software service media that support the implementation of operations, actions, and activities.

4.2 Design Content Model of Smart Service System

Wei Wang et al. [8] proposed that service model, service journey, and service touchpoints are the three main parameters throughout the design of autonomous vehicle intelligent service systems based on user activity behavior. The service model focuses on grasping social, economic, cultural, and other values, identifying value propositions and service needs through organizational activities and forms that create and provide new value, and building a relationship between service elements to realize service value and meaning relationship; the service journey constructs the information relationship between service elements under the sequence chain of time and space; the service touchpoint indicates the area and moment of interaction between autonomous vehicle users, and the service organization or system uses autonomous vehicles to Touchpoints interact with users to generate service value [9]. Service design is the design of a person's experiences through many different touchpoints, which occur over time. On this basis, this study proposes the design content model for the Smart Service System (Fig. 3).

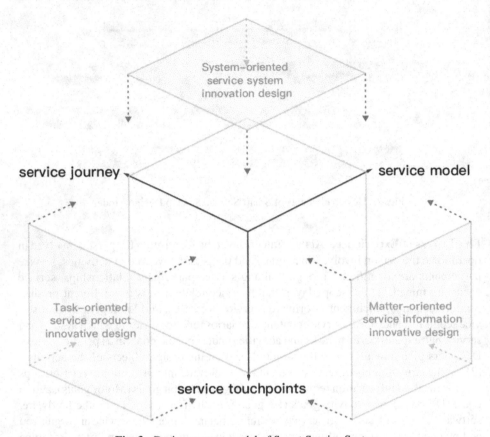

Fig. 3. Design content model of Smart Service System

System-Oriented Service System Innovation Design. Service providers, data providers, and transportation operators collaborate to build the Smart Service System innovation model. Focus on systematic service scenarios driven by autonomous vehicles, organize and plan autonomous vehicles and other service participants to meet the service value proposition, and build service relationships. The construction of a service relationship mainly depends on the needs of the service recipient and the business model and operating model of the service provider. Autonomous vehicles connect with other service providers to provide an efficient and user-friendly service process systematically, build a human mobility social-cultural knowledge graph based on the systematic production of human mobility content, and carry out service system innovation design based on service models and service journeys.

Matter-Oriented Service Information Innovative Design. Autonomous vehicles, data vendors, and transportation operators collaborate to build a multi-channel service information innovation model. Focus on autonomous vehicle-driven information service scenarios to satisfy service relationships, and identify the contact points of information interaction between autonomous vehicle-driven intelligent service media and users, as well as material flow, information flow, capital flow, etc. Based on the professional production of human mobility content and the production of human mobility content by agents, we build a cognitive map of human mobility properties and a knowledge map of human mobility agents and carry out innovative design of intelligent service information based on service models and service touchpoints.

Task-Oriented Service Product Innovative Design. All autonomous vehicles owned by transportation operators have built an innovative model of intelligent products and services with users. Focus on the service scenario to satisfy the information relationship and identify the media touchpoints for functional interaction between the autonomous vehicles and the user. Based on user-generated human mobility content, we build a human mobility spatiotemporal service knowledge graph, plan the functional specifications of autonomous vehicles, and carry out innovative design of intelligent service products based on service journeys and service touchpoints.

5 Smart Service System Design Methods

5.1 Service System Architecture Design

Service Participant Identification. Identifying service participants in the Smart Service System requires planning all stakeholders in the entire service life cycle and identifying their needs. To better realize the value proposition of stakeholders, designers need to plan the materialized and non-materialized service carriers that support service operation and implementation [10]. Compared with product design and interaction design, which build functional carriers and interactive media in physical and digital forms for users through functions and usage methods, Smart Service Systems provide stakeholders with service value in physical and digital forms through strategies and processes. Functional carriers and interactive medium Autonomous vehicles are the media for realizing services.

Service Needs Identification. The starting point of building a service blueprint is to stand in the customer's position, fully understand the customer's views and ideas, describe the type of service the customer wants, and express it in the form of a flow chart [11]. The service blueprint is related to the time dimension. It arranges the service elements experienced by customers in chronological order, showing the main functions of each service element and the connections between them. The service blueprint contains three main contents - user journey, touchpoints, and background processes, which help to intuitively display the service design process, the service participants involved, and the materialized and non-materialized carrier media that support service operation and implementation.

5.2 Information Relationship Architecture Design

Information Needs Identification. After the identification of service participants and mining of service requirements in the service system architecture phase, the information requirements within the service system need to be mined. Taking the CMR model (Fig. 4) as an example, C represents both non-materialized Content and materialized Container. The content and container are combined softly and hard, transforming into each other from the outside to the inside [12]. The M in CMR is based on the single-loop and dual-loop user Mental Model as the subject, and the Interaction Model is based on digital and non-digital information architecture levels as the object. The interaction model is divided into active interaction and passive interaction. In the process of interacting with the service carrier media, the feedback of the previous action can be converted into the feedforward of the next action, thereby establishing a relationship between Relationship and Requirement. Mapping relationships between persons, things, needs, and visions. The CMR model emphasizes that interaction content needs to match the mental model and interaction model, after defining the threshold. Use thresholds to guide users' vision and needs, derive demand-supply matching for interactive functions, content, and media, and build a dynamic transformation relationship between the functions and content of persons, things, and objects.

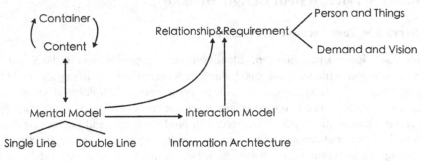

Fig. 4. CMR model

Information Relationship Building. The journey visualization tool mines social touchpoints, information touchpoints, and physical resource touchpoints based on user activities through touchpoints, conducts research on typical users through observation, in-depth interviews, etc., and conducts journeys around the real stories of the characters. The production of diagrams, and visualization tools that describe how users interact with services and the interactive relationships between systems, presents the relationships between persons, environments, and things in service design. The user journey map starts from the user's perspective and describes what happens at each stage of the user's experience, the touch points involved, the obstacles that may be encountered, etc., and displays the user's pain points. User journey maps usually integrate user experience maps to express the level of positive or negative emotions experienced by users during the entire interaction process and present user emotional flows. The user journey map is a visual expression of the entire story from the users' perspective. It presents the relationship between the user and the organization, services, and products over time. The user journey map helps designers and other service participants understand the users' needs and assists in design to bridge the gap between user expectations and system offerings.

5.3 Product Functional Specification Design

Functional Requirements Identification. Use the PSS-CMR model (Fig. 5) to transform from information relationship architecture design to product functional specification design [13]. The user mental model is the object of the service model and interaction model. The user's mental model and interaction model are the medium for the contact relationship with the outside world in the service model of the product service system. They are the Adaptation Functions (AF) that map the service and driving needs between the user and the product service system. Container design and content design of Interaction Functions (IF) [14]. Mental models and interaction models, through container and content design, map the relationships between functions and content between persons, things, and objects, as well as user needs and visions. PSS-CMR emphasizes that product service system design needs to match the corresponding user mental model, interaction model, and service model, and design corresponding product function specifications.

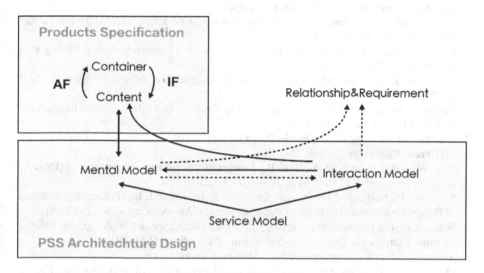

Fig. 5. PSS-CMR model

Product Prototype Building. Consider the main factors that affect the design results as design parameters and connect these factors with some logical relationship. The design of autonomous vehicle product prototypes must first parameterize the influencing factors, establish the relationship between parameters, and establish a parametric product prototype based on the relationship between parameter factors and design parameters.

6 Conclusion

This study combines the social-ecological system theory to summarize the service innovation driven by driverless vehicles into three modes: service system, service information, and service product. Service providers, data providers, and transportation operators collaborate to build the system-oriented system innovation model, which requires a service system architecture design based on service models and service journeys. Data vendors and transportation operators collaborate to build the matter-oriented service information innovation model, which requires a service information architecture design based on service models and service contacts. The autonomous vehicles owned by transportation operators have established the task-oriented service product innovation model, which requires the design of autonomous vehicle functional specifications and product characterization based on service journeys and service touch points.

References

1. Jiang, S., et al.: Service 4.0 and intelligent services—taking energy intelligent services as an example. Ind. Eng. J. (4), 1–9 (2021)
2. Charles, Z., Karen, K., Kirst, A.: Understanding Human Behavior and the Social Environment, 6th edn. Thomson Brooks Cole, Belmont (2004)
3. Luo, S.: Crowd intelligence innovation: a new innovation paradigm in the AI 2.0 era. Packag. Eng. 41(06), 50–56+66 (2020)
4. Qin, J., Cong, C.: Trust design in fund transaction system interaction design. Packag. Eng. 39(18), 78–82 (2018)
5. He, R., Hu, Y.: Study on design patterns and strategies in service ideation. Design (01), 40–49 (2015)
6. Moritz, S.: Service Design: Practical Access to An Evolving Field, 3rd edn. Köln International School of Design, Cologne (2005)
7. Carroll, J.M.: Making Use: Scenario-Based Design of Human-Computer Interactions. The MIT Press, Cambridge (2000)
8. Wei, W., Feng, Z., Wayne, L., Jim, B.: Designing the product-service system (PSS) for autonomous vehicles. IT Prof. Mag. 20(6), 62–79 (2018)
9. Sangiorgi, D.: Building up a framework for service design research. In: 8th European Academy of Design Conference, The Robert Gordon University, Aberdeen, pp. 415–420 (2009)
10. Forlizzi, J.: The product service ecology: using a system approach in design. In: Relating Systems Thinking and Design 2013 Symposium Proceedings, Oslo (2013)
11. Shostack, G.L.: How to design a service. Market. Serv. 16(1), 49–63 (2013)
12. Qin, J., et al.: Interaction design of the family agent based on the CMR+FBS ontology. Packag. Eng. 40(16), 108–114 (2019)
13. Maussang, N., et al.: Product-service system design methodology: from the PSS architecture design to the product specifications. J. Eng. Des. 4, 349–366 (2009)
14. Ran, B., Qin, J.: Product design of autonomous vehicles applied to intelligent logistics services. Packag. Eng. 42(06), 37–45 (2021)

From Passive to Active: Towards Conversational In-Vehicle Navigation Through Large Language Models

Huifang Du[1], Shiyu Tao[2], Xuejing Feng[1], Jun Ma[1($\boxtimes$)],
and Haofen Wang[1($\boxtimes$)]

[1] Tongji University, Shanghai, China
jun_ma@tongji.edu.cn, carter.whf carter@gmail.com
[2] Beijing Technology and Business University, Beijing, China

Abstract. In-vehicle navigation systems play a crucial role in the automotive intelligent cockpit and provide users with various functions. However, current systems make users suffer from passive experiences, which result in many inconveniences, such as low error prevention, limited user control, and insufficient user freedom. To address the existing limitations, we propose an interactive navigation paradigm based on conversations to enable users to actively engage in navigation, express their needs, and manage existing limitations. To explore the feasibility of this concept, we develop a simulated conversational navigation assistant based on prompting a large language model (LLM). The prompt designed for the LLM leveraged for conversational navigation is curated with tailored instructions and navigation functions. We conduct a subjective experiment to assess the impact on user perceptions of the conversational navigation system. Findings indicate that conversational navigation is deemed satisfactory, efficient, and more natural. Furthermore, users express that involvement with navigation during conversational navigation can reduce driver distraction, thus enhancing driving safety. This study highlights the potential to transform traditional navigation experiences into more engaging and efficient processes, paving the way for future research to further enhance user-centered navigation through additional external functions and optimized dialogue systems.

Keywords: Active interaction · Conversational in-vehicle navigation · Large language model

1 Introduction

In-vehicle navigation systems have become an integral part of the automotive intelligent cockpit, offering drivers a range of features and functionalities. Over the past few decades, in-vehicle navigation systems have undergone significant advancements, which can provide users with route planning [1], real-time traffic information [2], road condition forecasts [3], and personalized services to enhance

© The Author(s), under exclusive license to Springer Nature Switzerland AG 2024
A. Marcus et al. (Eds.): HCII 2024, LNCS 14713, pp. 159–172, 2024.
https://doi.org/10.1007/978-3-031-61353-1_11

their travel experience [4,5]. However, existing in-vehicle navigation systems are far from perfect from the perspective of human-computer interaction [6,7]. Users are passive recipients of information during the entire navigation process. The current navigation mode is characterized by limitations and a lack of flexibility, leaving users being passive recipients of information throughout the navigation process. This lack of active participation hampers the fulfillment of users' dynamic and diverse needs, leading to decreased driving efficiency and overall experience. The main inconveniences faced by users primarily include:

Low Error Prevention. Users often miss navigation instructions when they fail to understand the instructions promptly, resulting in the selection of incorrect routes. However, there is currently no interface available for users to convey their doubts to eliminate potential errors.

Limited User Control. When users deviate from the planned route based on their preferences or changing circumstances, the navigation system may persistently deliver alerts for several minutes. This not only confuses but also disrupts the overall navigation experience. Yet, it also lacks chances for users to express their intentions and control the situation.

Insufficient User Freedom. Users frequently encounter immediate needs when they reach a particular destination in navigation contexts, such as finding nearby amenities or exploring interesting locations. Unfortunately, the absence of an interface to freely communicate these needs often leads to users missing out on valuable information.

To overcome these limitations and enhance the user experience, it is crucial to provide a more flexible and interactive navigation interface that allows users to express their needs during the navigation process actively. Taking a human-centered approach, we explore a novel and interactive navigation paradigm based on conversations. This paradigm changes the way of traditional navigation by empowering users to actively engage in navigation with conversations and convey their needs at any time. In order to verify the feasibility of this concept, we develop a simulated conversational assistant designed for in-vehicle navigation. Recently, large language models (LLMs), such as GPT-4[1], Vicuna[2] and ChatGLM[3] have shown impressive adaptability to various tasks through in-context learning (ICL) using just a few examples [8–11]. The ability to generalize and learn from limited context is highly advantageous. We explore utilizing an LLM, GPT-4, to simulate an end-to-end assistant to address the aforementioned navigation limitations. The prompt tailored for navigation dialogues, including the *Context*, *Functions*, and *Example*, is designed for prompting LLMs. Our prompt can apply to all LLMs. External functions for navigation and searching places are also defined for LLMs to achieve the conversational navigation assistant. Figure 1 illustrates an example of the motivations and architecture of our assistant.

---

[1] https://arxiv.org/abs/2303.08774.

[2] https://lmsys.org/blog/2023-03-30-vicuna/.

[3] https://github.com/THUDM/ChatGLM-6B.

To evaluate the effectiveness of the interactive navigation and the impacts on user perceptions, we conduct a comprehensive experiment with 28 participants, who are asked to interact with our simulated navigation assistant in a static (non-mobile) driving vehicle. Participants are asked to complete questionnaires both before and after the test, assessing their perceptions regarding the assistant's naturalness, efficiency, satisfaction, and safety. The experimental results exceed expectations, with users reporting improved efficiency, naturalness of the interaction, and satisfactory experiences. Users also express positive reviews that actively participating in navigation can reduce driver distraction and enhance driving safety. This indicates that this interactive navigation paradigm can significantly enhance the overall driving experience. In summary, the main contributions of our work are as follows:

- We propose a flexible and interactive in-vehicle navigation paradigm that allows users to actively express their needs through conversation during the navigation process. The interactive navigation can help prevent driving errors, allow more user control, and enhance user freedom.
- We prompt an LLM using the in-context learning method to create a conversational navigation assistant. By organizing prompts with context, functions, and examples, the assistant can handle user queries, plan routes, and find points of interest effectively.
- We conduct a subjective experiment to evaluate the effects of the conversational navigation system. The results show that conversational navigation is satisfactory, effective, and more natural. Moreover, the involvement in navigation makes users more focused on driving, enhancing driving safety.

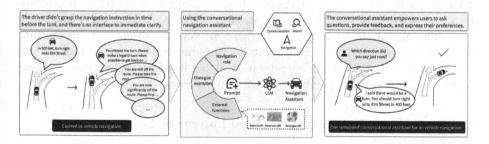

Fig. 1. An example of the motivations and the architecture of our conversational navigation assistant.

2 Related Work

With the development of Artificial Intelligence (AI), people are increasingly concerned about how to make in-vehicle navigation systems more user-friendly and smarter. This section explores related work in the area of in-vehicle navigation systems and the relevant technologies.

2.1   Advancements of In-Vehicle Navigation Systems

The debut of Iter Avto [12] marks the first application of navigation technology in the automotive field, laying the foundation for the subsequent development of navigation systems. Afterward, research on in-vehicle navigation systems early focused mainly on navigation accuracy while driving [13,14]. As functionalities improved over time, there was a shift towards studying innovations in human-computer interaction during the navigation process [15]. Visual touchscreen interfaces have become ubiquitous in contemporary vehicles, which are used to provide information related to navigation [16]. While touchscreens provide more versatility compared to traditional buttons and knobs, they have the drawback of potentially distracting the driver from the road. This distraction can increase the cognitive load on the user, posing a safety risk to the driving process [17]. In response to these challenges, Voice User Interface (VUI) has emerged as a viable solution, leading to significant advancements in in-vehicle navigation systems. These systems can offer voice prompts for distraction-free directions. In recent decades, in-vehicle navigation systems with VUI have evolved into essential parts of the modern automotive cockpit. These systems have undergone notable progress, offering users benefits such as route planning [1], real-time traffic updates [2], forecasts of road conditions [3], and personalized services aimed at enriching their journey experiences [4,5].

However, once users input their destination and the navigation begins in current in-vehicle navigation systems, it becomes challenging to intervene midway, leading to various issues. These encompass low error prevention, making it easy for users to select the wrong route when they do not promptly grasp navigation instructions. Furthermore, the user's control over the navigation system is constrained, particularly during deviations from the intended route, with continuous alerts disrupting the overall navigation experience. At last, users frequently encounter immediate needs during navigation, yet the absence of an interface for freely expressing these needs results in the omission of crucial information. Therefore, despite the system's strides in realizing key features, addressing these issues is imperative for an enhanced user experience.

2.2   In-Context Learning over Large Language Models

Recently, large language models (LLMs) [9,11,18] have shown emergent abilities [8] and have led to a new paradigm in creating natural language processing systems. Concretely, unlike traditional methods that rely on a well-selected, labeled training dataset [19,20], LLMs have introduced a new technique called in-context learning (ICL). By prompting LLMs with a few examples in the form of demonstration [21], they can generalize to various tasks like summarization, question answering, and code generation without updating parameters. The impressive effectiveness of ICL depends on two factors: the training of LLMs where the ICL ability stems from and task-specific demonstration examples in inference [21,22]. According to scale law [23] of the language model, larger models have better representation, and they also require more computational resources. In terms of selecting suitable examples for demonstrations, many methods extend the ICL capability by updating the model parameters using supervised [24] and self-supervised training [25]. Some studies improve ICL performance without optimizing parameters by using curated prompts. For example, few-shot settings are commonly adopted for ICL in the context of language model inference [26–28]. Showing intermediate reasoning steps of the examples, called chain of thought (CoT) [28], is an important strategy to boost ICL ability of LLMs. Self-consistency [29] generates multiple chains of thought and then takes the majority answer as the final answer. Using the technique of Tree of Thoughts (ToT), LLMs can make thoughtful decisions by considering many different reasoning paths and self-evaluating options [30]. The ReAct prompts LLMs to generate reasoning traces and task-specific actions while enabling the integration of external information and function [31].

In summary, the leverage of the ICL techniques to prompt LLMs is still a subject that is worth investigating. Our research expands upon previous studies and introduces prompts incorporating tailored instructions, external functions, and dialogue examples for interactive navigation.

3 Simulating a Conversational Navigation Assistant

We aim to enable users to actively participate in navigation through a simulated conversational navigation assistant. We describe how we achieve the navigation simulator by prompting LLMs. We also state the development setups and details.

3.1 Prompting Large Language Models

We investigate achieving this conversational navigation assistant using ICL prompting LLMs without updating the models' parameters. A prompt structure is designed to unify the prompts for the interactive navigation assistant. The prompt structure contains four modules, including *Context, Functions, Examples*, and *Conversation begin*. Figure 2 illustrates a prompt example.

Learning from general prompt engineering techniques [18,21,22], the prompt starts with the Context module that explains the role that the LLMs play, the tasks that the LLMs should perform and emphasizes. In our work, the LLMs will serve as in-vehicle navigation assistants through the use of conversational interactions. Note that the current location of the user is obtained in advance and fed to the LLM, which facilitates a better understanding of user dialogue for navigation. Following the Context, we state the Functions that LLMs can employ during the navigation. Specifically, we define three functions, including GetLocationInformation, Navigation, and GeoCoding. The GetLocationInformation function serves to provide details about a place, with search keywords or the geographic scope of the location as its input parameters. The Navigation function can provide routes to a destination using starting and ending points and can set user preferences, such as avoiding highways. GeoCoding can convert between addresses and geographic coordinates. This function takes as input either an address name or geographic coordinates. We use the Amap API to implement the three functions. The *search* API is used to implement the Get-LocationInformation function. The *direction* API is utilized for the Navigation function. The *georegeo* API is employed for the GeoCoding function. Afterward, a few examples are shown as demonstrations to boost LLMs' in-context learning abilities. In the examples, some tips are also provided in parentheses to assist LLMs in considering how to complete tasks. The "Conversation begin" represents the navigation conversation starts. Besides, the chat history will be continuously added to facilitate the in-vehicle navigation assistant in capturing context information accurately.

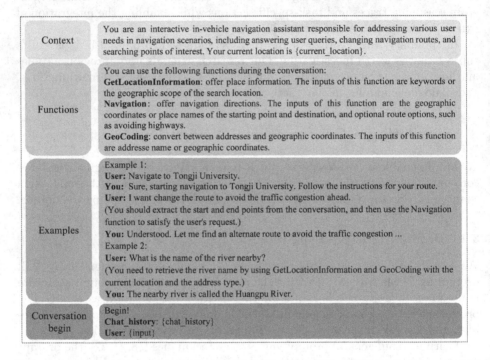

Fig. 2. A prompt example includes *Context*, *Functions*, *Examples* and *Conversation begin* instruction.

3.2   Developing the Navigation Assistant

We leverage the LLM GPT-4 with our designed prompt to develop the conversational navigation engine. We establish a RESTful API for conversational navigation. Utilizing this API, we develop an Android application to function as the graphical user interface (GUI). Furthermore, we add the functions of automatic speech recognition (ASR) and text-to-speech (TTS). We adopt Android SpeechRecognizer to facilitate speech-to-text conversion. Upon initialization of the navigation assistant, the ASR component is initialized and configured to listen to user input. This involves setting parameters such as language preferences, input mode (continuous), and audio source (microphone). The transferred users' text data is then passed to the conversational navigation engine for further processing. When the navigation assistant generates a response or provides information to the user, we employ the Android TextToSpeech class to provide spoken output. So participants can interact with the simulated navigation assistant using natural language like in real driving contexts. Note that we focus on exploring the feasibility of interactive conversational navigation, so the navigation instructions are not updated in real time based on addresses. Instead, we simulate outputting all navigation instructions to facilitate participants' experience of interactive navigation. During navigation, our conversational navigation system can assist users in responding to their inquiries, re-routing based on user needs, and expressing immediate needs. This interactive navigation effectively helps users prevent driving in the wrong directions, empowers users with control over navigation, and enables them to freely express their needs. Some conversation examples of the navigation simulator are shown in Fig. 3.

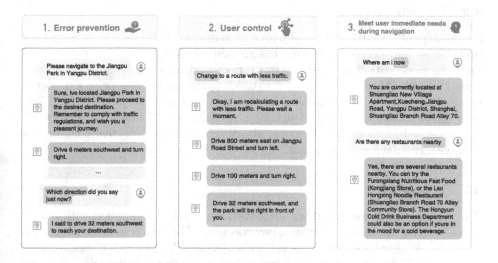

Fig. 3. Some conversation examples of our conversational navigation simulator.

4   Subjective Experiments

We evaluate the effectiveness of the interactive navigation and the impacts on user perceptions in this section.

4.1   Hypotheses

Previous research indicates that participants show more active engagement in expressing their needs during conversational interaction navigation tasks than in traditional passive forms of navigation. This active engagement enables them to more accurately plan routes after driving [32]. Additionally, some work suggests that conversations during navigation can reduce driver fatigue [33]. Therefore, we hypothesize that:

H1. The conversational navigation systems are perceived to be more effective and can increase user satisfaction with driving.

H2. Users perceive conversational navigation systems to offer enhanced safety benefits, contributing to a sense of security during navigation.

We ask participants to evaluate the conversational navigation system on various dimensions, including naturalness, efficiency, satisfaction, and safety, as adapted from previous studies [34–36]. Each aspect in these questionnaires is assessed using a 7-point Likert scale.

4.2   Participants

28 participants (P1-P28, 16 females and 12 males), including students from local universities and professionals from design and technology firms, were recruited for our experiments. These participants represent diverse academic backgrounds, ages 18 to 50 ($M = 32.78, SD = 5.45$). All participants have prior experience using either in-vehicle navigation systems or mobile navigation apps. Additionally, all participants have demonstrated proficiency in English, with TOEFL scores exceeding 88 or IELTS scores above 6.5, ensuring effective communication with the navigation assistant.

4.3   Procedure

The experiment is conducted within a stationary vehicle equipped with a 240° curved screen displaying a dynamic environment. The conversational navigation simulator is integrated into the vehicle's Human-Machine Interfaces, accessible via a tablet provided to participants before entering the vehicle (as shown in Fig. 4). Before starting the experiment, participants undergo a safety briefing, sign consent forms, etc. Each participant is provided with ten predefined navigation-related questions to ask during the experiment. The questions cover a range of topics such as clarification queries, requests for route replanning based on their preferences, and expressions of immediate needs during navigation (as illustrated in Table 1). The same questions for participants ensure consistency of experimental conditions and can help eliminate variables that could potentially affect the results. Participants are required to complete a questionnaire assessing their subjective perceptions of naturalness, efficiency, satisfaction, and safety both before and after interacting with the navigation system. Additionally, after each session, participants engage in a brief interview to elaborate on

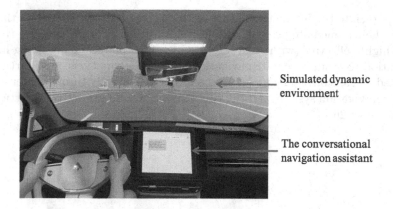

Fig. 4. The experimental environment. The environment aims to immerse participants in a driving scenario. The IVA simulator is set in front of the driver.

their experiences and feelings regarding the system. The entire testing process typically lasts approximately half an hour per participant.

Table 1. Ten predefined questions related to conversational navigation for participants during the experiment.

Topics	Questions
	Navigate to Fudan University
Clarifying queries	Where am I now?
	Which direction did you just mention?
	How many meters do I need to drive to the right?
Replanning routes	Change to the route with the shortest time
	I didn't follow the navigation route just now. Please reroute
	Replan a route with no traffic congestion.
Expressing immediate needs	What's the name of the river nearby?
	Are there any tourist attractions nearby?
	Are there any gas stations on the way to the destination?

4.4 Results

As illustrated in Fig. 5, the findings from the experiment reveal that users report significantly higher levels of satisfaction (with an average of 6.4 points) compared to their initial expectations (with an average of 4.9 points) before interacting with the conversational navigation system. They acknowledge that the system enhances the navigation experience by reducing repetitive instructions through its understanding of conversational context, leading to a smoother and more natural navigation process (with an average rating of 6.8 points). Furthermore, users appreciate the interactive nature of the navigation, which enables them to address their immediate personalized needs. Additionally, they perceive the system as highly effective (with an average rating of 6.9 points) in providing helpful information to ensure accurate navigation to their destinations. One participant expressed, "I can convey my preferences and queries directly through interactions with the navigation system, and the system can respond promptly." (Participant 12, male, age: 26).

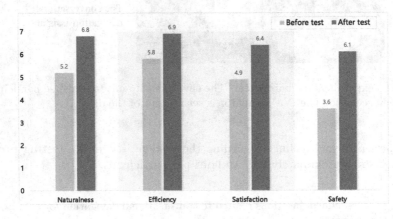

Fig. 5. User perceptions of naturalness, efficiency, satisfaction, and safety before and after the test.

In current navigation systems, once users input the starting and ending points, they receive navigation instructions passively throughout the whole journey. However, the passive interaction may lead to user fatigue or cause them to overlook these instructions, resulting in distracted driving. Interestingly, users initially had low expectations regarding the safety aspect of the interactive navigation system (with an average of 3.6 points), but after experiencing it, they gave higher ratings (with an average of 6.1 points). This can be explained by the fact that some users found that conversational navigation made them feel more engaged, which enhanced their perception of navigation instructions. This allows users to follow navigation prompts more consciously, ensuring driving safety. Additionally, it's worth mentioning that users feel reassured when they ask "Where am I now?" and receive specific information to confirm they are on the correct route during navigation. (P20, female, age: 35). Therefore, by incorporating more conversational interaction features, we can provide users with a greater sense of trust and safety, and improve user experience.

After analyzing the feedback from users, we have confirmed the validity of hypotheses H1 and H2. Our findings indicate that the conversational navigation system does have a significant impact on users' perceptions of naturalness, efficiency, satisfaction, and safety. This not only validates the significance of interactive conversational navigation but also demonstrates the advantages of LLMs in dialogue understanding for navigation.

5 Discussion

5.1 Insights of Our Work

We demonstrate the feasibility and value of the interactive conversational navigation system based on LLMs. The LLM GPT-4 has robust in-context learning capabilities, allowing it to understand user needs in navigation scenarios. Leveraging the prompts we designed and the associated functions, the LLM can effectively perform navigation tasks. By enabling users to actively participate in navigation through conversation, this approach overcomes the limitations of traditional systems and provides a more flexible and user-centered experience. Interactive conversational navigation helps prevent errors commonly seen in traditional systems where users may miss instructions or choose the wrong routes due to a lack of clarification. By allowing users to ask questions and express concerns during navigation, errors can be avoided and routes selected accurately. Additionally, the system gives users more control and freedom compared to traditional systems. Users can deviate from planned routes based on preferences or changing circumstances, leading to a more personalized and responsive navigation experience. Furthermore, this approach addresses the issue of limited user freedom by allowing users to freely communicate their immediate needs and preferences. Whether it's finding nearby amenities or exploring interesting locations, users can easily convey their requirements through conversation, enhancing their overall navigation experience. Users also show positive perceptions of the conversational navigation assistant.

In summary, our interactive conversational navigation system represents a step forward in the development of in-vehicle navigation. By addressing the limitations of traditional navigation systems, the user-centered approach has the potential to transform how users interact with navigation systems and improve their overall driving experience.

5.2 Limitation of Our Approach and Future

While the experimental results showcase significant enhancements in user satisfaction and efficiency through our interactive navigation paradigm, several shortcomings still exist. Our in-vehicle navigation system is in its early stages of development. Despite incorporating ICL to enhance the task performance of the LLM, the system may not be optimal in handling complex contexts. Future research will focus on expanding the capabilities of the assistant by incorporating additional external functions and optimizing the dialogue system to provide even more personalized and seamless navigation experiences. Moreover, it is also necessary to accumulate more dialogue data specific to navigation to train dedicated navigation models, thereby enhancing the accuracy of the dialogue.

Additionally, the relatively small participant pool of 28 individuals and the limited age range might introduce bias into the subjective evaluation outcomes. Additionally, our experiments were conducted within a simulated setting. Despite covering diverse navigation scenarios in the test questions, they may not fully capture the intricacies and variations present in real-world driving situations. Future investigations could delve into the efficacy of LLMs within authentic driving contexts to gain deeper insights into their potential for enhancing navigation system performance. Furthermore, extending the interactive navigation paradigm to encompass mobile devices could accommodate the requirements of various modes of transportation, such as pedestrians and cyclists. This expansion would contribute to a more comprehensive understanding of the paradigm's efficacy and adaptability across different user contexts and scenarios.

6   Conclusion

In conclusion, our work highlights the significance of enhancing in-vehicle navigation systems from a human-computer interaction perspective. By providing users with the chance to actively engage in navigation and express their needs through conversations, we significantly alleviate the limitations of existing navigation systems and create a more fulfilling driving experience. The simulated conversational assistant we develop serves as a proof-of-concept for this interactive navigation paradigm. The findings from our experiment support the feasibility and effectiveness of the interactive navigation paradigm and our method. By adopting an interactive conversational navigation paradigm, we have demonstrated the potential to transform the traditional navigation experience into a more engaging, user-centered, and efficient process.

Acknowledgments. The research was supported by the National Nature Science Foundation of China with Grant No. 62176185 and the Fundamental Research Funds for the Central Universities with grant Nos. 22120230032. We are grateful for the valuable and constructive feedback provided by all the anonymous reviewers.

Disclosure of Interests. The authors declare that they have no known competing financial interests or personal relationships that could have appeared to influence the work reported in this paper.

References

1. Aradi, S.: Survey of deep reinforcement learning for motion planning of autonomous vehicles. IEEE Trans. Intell. Transp. Syst. **23**(2), 740–759 (2020)
2. Seo, T., Bayen, A.M., Kusakabe, T., Asakura, Y.: Traffic state estimation on highway: a comprehensive survey. Ann. Rev. Control **43**, 128–151 (2017)
3. Subramaniyan, A.B., et al.: Hybrid recurrent neural network modeling for traffic delay prediction at signalized intersections along an urban arterial. IEEE Trans. Intell. Transp. Syst. **24**(1), 1384–1394 (2022)
4. Liu, H., Tong, Y., Han, J., Zhang, P., Xinjiang, L., Xiong, H.: Incorporating multi-source urban data for personalized and context-aware multi-modal transportation recommendation. IEEE Trans. Knowl. Data Eng. **34**(2), 723–735 (2020)
5. Huang, Z., Jingda, W., Lv, C.: Driving behavior modeling using naturalistic human driving data with inverse reinforcement learning. IEEE Trans. Intell. Transp. Syst. **23**(8), 10239–10251 (2021)

6. Tan, Z., et al.: Human-machine interaction in intelligent and connected vehicles: a review of status quo, issues, and opportunities. IEEE Trans. Intell. Transp. Syst. **23**(9), 13954–13975 (2021)
7. Muhammad, K., Ullah, A., Lloret, J., Del Ser, J., de Albuquerque, V.H.C.: Deep learning for safe autonomous driving: current challenges and future directions. IEEE Trans. Intell. Transp. Syst. **22**(7), 4316–4336 (2020)
8. Schaeffer, R., Miranda, B., Koyejo, S.: Are emergent abilities of large language models a mirage? arXiv preprint arXiv:2304.15004 (2023)
9. OpenAI. GPT-4 Technical Report. arXiv e-prints, page arXiv:2303.08774, March 2023
10. Du, Z., et al.: Glm: general language model pretraining with autoregressive blank infilling. In: Proceedings of the 60th Annual Meeting of the Association for Computational Linguistics (Volume 1: Long Papers), pp. 320–335 (2022)
11. Touvron, H., et al.: Llama 2: Open foundation and fine-tuned chat models. *arXiv preprint*arXiv:2307.09288 (2023)
12. D.Newcomb. From hand-cranked maps to the cloud: Charting the history of in-car navigation, January 2018. https://www.wired.com/2013/04/history-in-car-navigation/. Accessed 20 Jan 2020
13. Liu, R., Wang, J., Zhang, B.: High definition map for automated driving: overview and analysis. J. Navigation **73**(2), 324–341 (2020)
14. Arntz, A., Keßler, D., Borgert, N., Zengeler, N., Jansen, M., Handmann, U., Eimler, S.C.: Navigating a heavy industry environment using augmented reality - a comparison of two indoor navigation designs. In: Chen, J.Y.C., Fragomeni, G. (eds.) HCII 2020. LNCS, vol. 12191, pp. 3–18. Springer, Cham (2020). https://doi.org/10.1007/978-3-030-49698-2_1
15. Ma, J., Feng, X., Gong, Z., Zhang, Q.: From the parking lot to your gate: a need-centered approach for optimizing user experience in automated valet parking system. In: Stephanidis, C., Duffy, V.G., Streitz, N., Konomi, S., Krömker, H. (eds.) HCII 2020. LNCS, vol. 12429, pp. 150–165. Springer, Cham (2020). https://doi.org/10.1007/978-3-030-59987-4_11
16. Bruckner, S., Isenberg, T., Ropinski, T., Wiebel, A.: A model of spatial directness in interactive visualization. IEEE Trans. Visual Comput. Graphics **25**(8), 2514–2528 (2018)
17. Charissis, V., Papanastasiou, S.: Human-machine collaboration through vehicle head up display interface. Cognition, Technol. Work **12**, 41–50 (2010)
18. Brown, T., et al.: Language models are few-shot learners. Advances in neural information processing systems, 33, pp. 1877–1901 (2020)
19. Huifang, D., Zhang, X., Wang, M., Chen, Y., Ji, D., Ma, J., Wang, H.: A contrastive framework for enhancing knowledge graph question answering: alleviating exposure bias. Knowl.-Based Syst. **280**, 110996 (2023)
20. Huifang, D., Le, Z., Wang, H., Chen, Y., Jing, Yu.: Cokg-qa: multi-hop question answering over covid-19 knowledge graphs. Data Intell. **4**(3), 471–492 (2022)
21. Dong, Q., et al.: A survey for in-context learning. arXiv preprint arXiv:2301.00234 (2022)
22. Min, S., et al.: Rethinking the role of demonstrations: What makes in-context learning work? arXiv preprint arXiv:2202.12837 (2022)
23. Kaplan, J., et al.: Scaling laws for neural language models. arXiv preprint arXiv:2001.08361 (2020)
24. Wei, J., et al.: Symbol tuning improves in-context learning in language models. arXiv preprint arXiv:2305.08298 (2023)

25. Gu, Y., Dong, L., Wei, F., Huang, M.: Pre-training to learn in context. *arXiv preprint*arXiv:2305.09137 (2023)
26. Xu, R., Wang, Q., Mao, Z., Lyu, Y., She, Q., Zhang, Y.: k nn prompting: beyond-context learning with calibration-free nearest neighbor inference. arXiv preprint arXiv:2303.13824 (2023)
27. Honovich, O., Shaham, U., Bowman, S.R., Levy, O.: Instruction induction: from few examples to natural language task descriptions. arXiv preprint arXiv:2205.10782 (2022)
28. Wei, J., et al.: Chain-of-thought prompting elicits reasoning in large language models. Adv. Neural Inf. Process. Syst. **35**, 24824–24837 (2022)
29. Wang, X., et al.: Self-consistency improves chain of thought reasoning in language models. arXiv preprint arXiv:2203.11171 (2022)
30. Yao, S., et al.: Tree of thoughts: Deliberate problem solving with large language models. arXiv preprint arXiv:2305.10601 (2023)
31. Yao, S., et al.: React: synergizing reasoning and acting in language models. In: The Eleventh International Conference on Learning Representations (2022)
32. Antrobus, V., Large, D., Burnett, G., Hare, C.: Enhancing environmental engagement with natural language interfaces for in-vehicle navigation systems. J. Navigation **72**(3), 513–527 (2019)
33. Samson, B.P.V., Sumi, Y.: Are two heads better than one? exploring two-party conversations for car navigation voice guidance. In: Extended Abstracts of the 2020 CHI Conference on Human Factors in Computing Systems, pp. 1–9 (2020)
34. Zwakman, D.S., Pal, D., Triyason, T., Arpnikanondt, C.: Voice usability scale: measuring the user experience with voice assistants. In: 2020 IEEE International Symposium on Smart Electronic Systems (iSES)(Formerly iNiS), pp. 308–311. IEEE (2020)
35. Lee, M.K., Kiesler, S., Forlizzi, J., Srinivasa, S., Rybski, P.: Gracefully mitigating breakdowns in robotic services. In: 2010 5th ACM/IEEE International Conference on Human-Robot Interaction (HRI), pp. 203–210. IEEE (2010)
36. Cao, J., Zhang, J., Zhang, L., Wang, X.: The psychological structure and influence of interactive naturalness. Acta Psychologica Sinica **55**(1), 55 (2023)

Analysis of Influencing Factors on Advanced Driving Assistance System Purchase Intention in China

Hongwei Huang[✉] and Jun Ma

School of Automotive Studies, Tongji University, No. 4800, Cao-an Road, Shanghai 201804, China
2111304@tongji.edu.cn, majun.tongji@foxmail.com

Abstract. The number of vehicles with the introduction of Advanced Driving Assistance System (ADAS) is increasing. For this reason, it is becoming important to study the technology acceptance on how drivers can actively accept giving up some parts of the driving operation. Although there have been quite a lot of studies on consumers' purchase intention of new technologies and Technology Acceptance Models of ADAS, it is not common in the case of the purchase intention toward ADAS-equipped vehicles. This paper puts forward the concept of ADAS experience and discusses the relationship between related factors (ADAS experience, gender and age) and consumers' purchase intention of ADAS-equipped vehicles and establishes a theoretical model of consumers' purchase intention towards ADAS-equipped vehicles. The results indicate that the relationship between ADAS experience and consumers' purchase intention shows a V-shaped curve. There is a decline of purchase intention in the middle stage, and ADAS purchase intention is not completely positively correlated with consumers' ADAS experience. However, demographic characters are not highly relevant in purchase intention. These results can help automobile manufacturers seek new ways to increase sales of ADAS equipped vehicles.

Keywords: ADAS experience · Chinese consumers · purchase intention · NCA

1 Introduction

The number of road traffic accidents is one of the major societal problems and the 8th leading cause of death for people of all ages in the world today. According to estimated data from the WHO, 1.35 million people are killed each year [1]. Many accidents could be avoided if the automatic systems were used to provide the surrounding information and prompt the driver to slow down. ADAS cannot completely avoid accidents, but it could better protect us from some of the human factors and human error, which is the cause of most traffic accidents.

Surveys reveal that 81% of car crashes are direct effects of human mistakes [2]. To counteract traffic accidents, we could change human behavior, and adopt vehicle-related measures and physical road infrastructure-related measures. ADAS provides additional information from the car surrounding environment to support a driver and assist in implementing critical action [3].

As digitalization, multimedia, and networking have become core elements of automotive technology, the development of intelligent high-technology vehicles is accelerating [4]. Though ADAS technology and autonomous driving go hand in hand, they are not the same thing. ADAS are features that can be found in many modern cars, while autonomous driving is a system that allows a car to operate without human control. Essentially, ADAS is on a spectrum of autonomy that leads to full driving automation at Level Five. While autonomous driving is still around the corner for consumers, ADAS is here. The ADAS serves as a good bridge until advanced autonomous driving (L3-L5) vehicles are widely available. On the one hand, it provides consumers with the experience of cuttingedge technology, and on the other hand, it improves the safety of driving to some extent. For the last decades, ADAS has rapidly grown. Now, not only luxury cars but some entry-level cars are equipped with ADAS applications, such as Adaptive Cruise Control (ACC) [5].

In addition to the efforts of global governments and automobile manufacturers, consumers are also the key to the promotion of ADAS-equipped vehicles. 2021 is known as the "first year" of China's smart cars. Today, ADAS-equipped cars have become the "standard" of new products of major auto manufacturers, which is determined by the needs of consumers. Especially with the continuous improvement of Chinese people's income level, people's demand for cars is also increasing [6]. In terms of consumer performance, according to a survey conducted by McKinsey, 56% of Chinese consumers are willing to change car brands because of better intelligent connectivity; 76% of Chinese consumers prefer a combination of online and offline car buying models, and more than 33% of consumers Those who are willing to spend more than 4,000 yuan for the intelligent driving function. The Chinese market has become one of the "best markets" for smart cars to land [7]. On the other hand, consumers' purchase of ADAS-equipped vehicles will have a huge impact on the promotion of electric vehicles and the development of the entire industry. Therefore, it is very necessary to understand the factors of consumers' purchase of ADAS-equipped vehicles.

Tesla has successfully subverted the traditional automobile industry, launching popular products repeatedly. Tesla sold 471,462 vehicles in China. The reason that Tesla products are popular among Chinese consumer lie not only in the electric vehicle but in the ADAS functions provided. In addition, China is the world's largest automobile market. Domestic vehicle brands are also intensively focused on the development of ADAS technology. In the metropolis, especially in Shanghai, Chinese consumers there are highly exposed to the ADAS-equipped vehicles provided by Tesla and other domestic vehicle brands, including NIO, XPENG, etc., which are making great progress in ADAS technology.

Therefore, from the perspective of driving safety and the development of the national automobile industry, the positive development of ADAS-equipped vehicles is of paramount significance. Although some studies have shown that consumers are more likely to choose automobile brands with a long history that will bring the user a sense of security and trust [8], nowadays Chinese consumers showed great interest in ADAS. Because Chinese consumers can experience recent advances in ADAS from both online and offline channels. Especially when many car brands have experience stores in various cities, consumers have more opportunities to access ADAS technology than before, which enhances the ADAS experience in a way. The emergence of new forces in car manufacturing brings consumers a sense of technology that threatens traditional car manufacturers which still keep a great emphasis on the sense of luxury, so they will invest more in the research and development of ADAS. At the key point of the Chinese consumers' transition from traditional vehicles to ADAS-equipped vehicles, consumers' purchase of ADAS-equipped vehicles will have a huge impact on the promotion of ADAS-equipped vehicles and the development of the entire industry. Therefore, it is necessary to understand how the ADAS experience influences Chinese consumers to buy ADAS-equipped vehicles.

2   Materials and Methods

There are many theories used to investigate the adoption of technologies in different industries. Some of these are; the technology acceptance model (TAM) [9], diffusion of innovation (DOI) [10], technology, organization, environment (TOE), unified theory of acceptance and use of technology (UTAUT) [11,12]. Accordingly, existing researches that include reworks of the TAM and UTAUT were examined. For instance, Adell (2010) measured the extent of Driver Support System acceptance using a UTAUT model, proposing a modified UTAUT model based on the findings of the study on the effect of Performance Expectancy (PE), Effort Expectancy (EE), and Social Influence (SI) on Behavioral Intention (BI) with existing question items of the UTAUT model modified. But these theories generally apply when consumers have not experienced the new technology. Now a large part of Chinese consumers has already experienced ADAS to some extent, even some of them are deep experiencers, so the applicability of these theories in this study is not high. Online, the sharing of news, technology-related videos, and automobile bloggers on the Internet has promoted consumers' understanding of ADAS to a certain extent. With the development of China's auto industry, many auto companies have opened offline product experience stores, so that consumers can have more understanding and experience of ADAS. As autonomous vehicles are expected to revolutionize the automotive sector, as well as provision unprecedented value to consumers and society at large. Chinese consumers no longer only pay attention to the appearance, brand, luxury, etc. of vehicles, but have begun to demand a sense of technology and the experience of new technologies. This study explores how consumers' intention to purchase ADAS-equipped vehicles changes under different experience depths. As mentioned in a previous research, going against conventional wisdom, consumers' demographic characteristics, like age and gender, were not highly relevant in acceptance and intent to use ADAS functions [13]. Therefore, this study hypothesizes that:

Hypothesis 1: ADAS experience is necessary for purchase intention toward the purchase of ADAS-equipped vehicles or repurchase of ADAS-equipped vehicles.

Hypothesis 2: The deeper the ADAS experience of consumers is, the higher the intention to purchase ADAS-equipped vehicles or repurchase ADAS vehicles.

Hypothesis 3: Consumers' demographic characteristics (gender and age) are not highly relevant in purchase intention.

2.1 ADAS Experience

ADAS Experience. Prior knowledge plays various roles in affecting consumers' subsequent decision behaviors [14–16]. According to Kerstetter and Cho [15], prior knowledge includes three dimensions: familiarity, past experience and expertise. Our study focuses on past experience (i.e., ADAS experience) because it is one of the strongest variables influencing consumers' decision-making process, especially when consumers purchase ADAS-equipped vehicles [17]. An experiential view to customer behavior is first advocated by Holbrook and Hirschman (1982). Consumption is "a primarily subjective state of consciousness with a variety of symbolic meanings, hedonic responses, and aesthetic criteria" [18]. In this study, ADAS experience is constructed by Tenure, Frequency, and Depth. Tenure indicates how long people have been using the product. A good way to start measuring experience is by understanding how long-if at all-someone has been using a product. If someone's never used a product or seen an interface, then other experience questions do not matter. The longer people have been exposed to a product, the more likely they have used and encountered functionality in a product. Frequency indicates how frequently people use the product. Depth indicates how many features or functions of a product people use.

Purchase Intention. According to Laviage's research, a potential consumer usually goes through the stages of awareness, understanding, love, preference and conviction, before taking a purchase action [19]. Purchase intention refers to consumers' subjective inclination toward a certain product, which has been proven to be an important indicator to predict consumers' purchase behavior [20,21]. Consumers' experience will affect their purchase intention of the product or service. The higher the purchase intention is, the greater the probability of purchase is [22,23].

Theoretical Model. This study fully considers the characteristics of ADAS-equipped vehicles and uses research results for reference to construct the model of consumers' purchase intention: ADAS experience and purchase intention (see Fig. 1).

Fig. 1. The theoretical model

3 Research Design

ADAS-equipped vehicle demand is expected to grow significantly in China. Automobile manufacturers have been increasingly investing in the research and development of ADAS technology. The purpose of this research is to determine how ADAS experience influences the purchase intention of ADAS-equipped vehicles. Shanghai is the most appropriate location for data collection for this study because it has the highest number of ADAS-equipped vehicle consumers. The respondents are existing car owners in Shanghai. To deeply explore how the ADAS experience influences consumers to buy ADAS-equipped vehicles, a quantitative face-to-face interview was conducted. The questionnaire is comprised of two sections. The first section of the questionnaire focuses on the respondents' demographic characteristics, such as gender and age. The second section of the questionnaire includes questions about the study's constructs, including tenure, frequency, depth, and purchase intention. The questionnaire used in the study is presented in Appendix A. To ensure the reliability of the study, the scales used in this study are derived from mature scales that have been verified in the relevant literature. We paid 200 yuan to each respondent as a reward for attending the quantitative face-to-face interview. Finally, 127 respondents were chosen to participate in the study. As a result, the sample size is set at 127. The basic information about the subjects is shown in Table 1.

Table 1. Basic data of the respondents.

Sample	Category	Number	Percentage
Gender	Male	99	77.95%
	Female	28	22.05%
Age	18-25	18	14.17%
	26-34	56	44.09%
	35-54	53	41.74%

Table 2. The general rule of thumb [24]

d value	Implication
0 < d < 0.1	Small effect
0.1 <= d < 0.3	Medium effect
0.3 <= d < 0.5	Large effect
d >= 0.5	Very large effect

4   Results and Discussion

In this study, NCA (Necessary Condition Analysis) is used to determine the effect size of the ADAS experience to consumers' purchase intention. Originally developed by Dul (2016), the necessary condition analysis (NCA) is a relatively new approach and data analysis technique that enable the identification of necessary conditions in data sets (Dul, 2020) [24]. In the NCA, a small effect size indicates a small constraining effect; a large effect size indicates a large constraining effect, depending on theoretical support and the p-value. The effect size is calculated by dividing empty space by scope (d = C/S).

NCA Plot : ADAS Experience - Purchase Intention

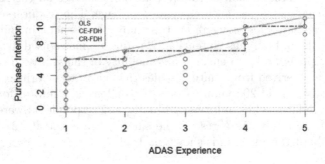

Fig. 2. The NCA Plot: ADAS experience - purchase Intention. OLS: ordinary least squares; CE-FDH: Ceiling Envelopment - Free Disposal Hull; CR-FDH: Ceiling Regression - Free Disposal Hull.

The effect size can have values between 0 and 1. Table 2 shows the general rule of thumb. Figure 2 shows a scatter plot with X = ADAS Experience and Y = Purchase Intention of 127 respondents' relationships for evaluating Hypothesis 1. According to the hypothesis of NCA, it is not possible to have cases with low level of Contractual detail (X) and high level of Innovation (Y). This means that the upper left corner of the scatter plot remains empty. The space without cases is called the empty space or ceiling zone. Two default ceiling lines are the Ceiling Envelopment - Free Disposal Hull (CE-FDH), which is a step function that can be used when X or Y are discrete with a limited number of levels or when the border is irregular, and the Ceiling Regression - Free Disposal Hull (CR-FDH), which is a straight trend line through the upper left corner points of the CE-FDH line. When a few cases are present in the otherwise empty space the ceiling line is not entirely accurate. The ceiling-accuracy (c-accuracy) is the percentage of cases on or below the ceiling line. By definition the CE-FDH line is 100% accurate and the CR-FDH line is usually not 100% ac-curate. A low c-accuracy indicates that the ceiling line may not properly represent the border between empty and full space, and another ceiling line may be selected.

Table 3 shows the results of NCA. According to the general rule of thumb above, the effect size of ADAS experience to purchase intention is 0.318(ce_fdh), greater than 0.3, which indicates that ADAS experience has a large effect size to purchase intention.

Table 3. The result of NCA

results	ce_fdh	cr_fdh
Ceiling zone	14.000	10.004
Contractual detail	0.318	0.227
Effect size	0.318	0.227
c-accuracy	100%	95.5%

Though the results of NCA show the necessity of ADAS experience to purchase intention, the discrete points still remain low level in the middle stage, as shown in the NCA plot. Therefore, there might exist a delicate relationship between ADAS experience and purchase intention in the middle stage. Figure 3 shows the plot of ADAS experience - purchase intention. In the plot, there is a decline in the middle stage, which means that ADAS purchase intention is not completely positively correlated with consumers' ADAS experience.

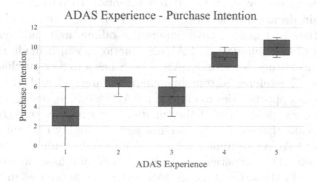

Fig. 3. The plot of ADAS experience - purchase intention.

As shown in Fig. 4(a), there is no evident difference between male and female in terms of purchase intention toward ADAS-equipped vehicles. Figure 4(b) indicates that there is no evident difference among age groups but a slight downward trend with age in terms of purchase intention toward ADAS-equipped vehicles.

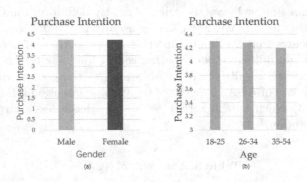

Fig. 4. The plot of Demographic Characters - Purchase Intention.

The results of the analysis provide some key findings. Specific discussions are as follows: H1 was valid, which means that ADAS experience is necessary for purchase intention. And according to the general rule of thumb, ADAS experience has a large effect size to purchase intention. Therefore, ADAS experience is a good predictor of consumers' purchasing decisions. However, the validity of H1 does not mean that there is a complete positive correlation between ADAS experience and purchase intention toward ADAS-equipped vehicles. H2 was not valid. There is a decline in the middle stage. Thanks to the quantitative face-to-face interview, some interesting discoveries are made. Although users in the third stage have ADAS experience offline, more information comes from the Internet. On the Internet, there are occasionally videos of ADAS-equipped vehicles having car accidents when Pilot or other functions are turned on. As a result, although this part of consumers has a deeper ADAS experience than the consumers in the previous two stages, they show no greater intention to purchase ADAS which causes a certain decline in the plot. Consumers in the fourth and fifth stages showed that they had more ADAS experience offline, and they had a clearer understanding of the boundaries of ADAS functions, which made them have a more optimistic attitude towards ADAS. ADAS has a higher purchase or repurchase intention. Therefore, Automobile manufacturers should give consumers more and various opportunities to experience ADAS offline, and focus on how to improve consumers' perception of the functional boundaries of ADAS. H3 was valid, which means that neither gender nor age was highly relevant in purchase intention toward ADAS-equipped vehicles. The results indicate that the relationship between ADAS experience and consumers' purchase intention shows a V-shaped curve. In the early stage, ADAS experience score was in the 1th and 2nd range, and purchase intention was showing an upward trend. In the middle stage, there is a decline of purchase intention. Therefore, ADAS purchase intention is not completely positively correlated with consumers' ADAS experience. However, demographic characters, like age and gender, are not highly relevant in purchase intention.

5   Conclusions

The main contribution of this study is the establishment of a theoretical model of the relationship between ADAS experience and consumers' purchase intention towards ADAS-equipped vehicles. According to the analysis in this study, ADAS purchase intention is not completely positively correlated with consumers' ADAS experience, but there is a decline in the middle stage, which shows a V-shaped curve, going against traditional wisdoms. At the same time, the conclusions of this study can be used as a reference for the Chinese government, consumers and relevant practitioners in the ADAS-equipped vehicle industry to increase the sales of ADAS-equipped vehicles, so as to reduce the traffic accident rate, promote the development of intelligent transportation and improve the market share of domestic automobile brands. The results show that: (1) neither gender nor age was highly relevant in purchase intention toward ADAS-equipped vehicles; (2) consumers' ADAS experience is necessary for their purchase intention toward ADAS-equipped vehicles; (3) ADAS purchase intention is not completely positively correlated with consumers' ADAS experience, but there is a decline in the middle stage. The results show that although the third part of consumers has a deeper ADAS experience than the consumers in the previous two stages, they show no greater intention to purchase ADAS, which causes a certain decline in the plot. That is also the cause of the deficiency of ADAS experience, which made the consumers vague about the functional boundaries of ADAS. Based on the above results, automobile manufacturers should give consumers more and various opportunities to experience ADAS offline, and focus on how to improve consumers' perception of the functional boundaries of ADAS, which will significantly increase sales of ADAS-equipped vehicles. Finally, this study also has some limitations, which can be continuously improved and deepened in follow-up research. In this study, respondents were mainly from Shanghai. The sample representation was slightly insufficient. In addition, there are many factors that affect consumers' purchase of ADAS-equipped vehicles, and the definition of ADAS experience could be broken down more finely, and some variables could be considered in future research to build a more comprehensive and reasonable research model.

A   Appendix

Questionnaire for the Study

Latent Variable	Coding	Item	Resources
Tenure	T1	I have used ACC and LKA for a long time	[25]
	T2	I have used ALC for a long time	
	T3	I have used Pilot for a long time	
	T4	I have used Display of the surrounding road environment for a long time	
Frequency	F1	I have used/experienced the ACC and LKA in daily life	[25]
	F2	I have used/experienced the ALC in daily life	
	F3	I have used/experienced the Pilot in daily life	
	F4	I have used/experienced the Display of the surrounding road environment in daily life	
Depth	D1	I know the functional boundaries of ACC and LKA	[25]
	D2	I know the functional boundaries of ALC	
	D3	I know the functional boundaries of Pilot	
	D4	I know the functional boundaries of the Display of the surrounding road environment	
Purchase Intention	PI1	An ADAS-equipped vehicle from an automobile manufacturer that focuses on the ADAS is the best choice for me	[26]
	PI2	The next time I change cars, I will give priority to ADAS-equipped cars	
	PI3	I'd like cars equipped with more ADAS functions	

References

1. Organization, W.H.: GLOBAL STATUSR EPORTON ROAD SAFETY 2018. Tech. rep. (2019)
2. Organization, W.H.: Global status report on road safety 2013: Supporting a decade of action. Tech. rep. (2013)
3. Ziebinski, A., Cupek, R., Grzechca, D., Chruszczyk, L.: Review of advanced driver assistance systems (ADAS). AIP Conf. Proc. **1906**(1), 120002 (2017). https://doi.org/10.1063/1.5012394
4. Yoon, B., Kim, J.: Trend of technology of Research and Development (R&D) about advanced car. Robot. Syst. **18**(2), 21–29 (2012)
5. Okuda, R., Kajiwara, Y., Terashima, K.: A survey of technical trend of ADAS and autonomous driving. In: Technical Papers of 2014 International Symposium on VLSI Design, Automation and Test, pp. 1–4, April 2014. https://doi.org/10.1109/VLSI-DAT.2014.6834940

6. With the Continuous Improvement of Living Standards, People's Demand for Cars Continues to Increase. https://cj.sina.com.cn/articles/view/6451924161/180908cc100100bawa

7. Fang, Y.: Experts' Perspectives China has become the "optimal market" for the implementation of smart cars. Bus. School **04**, 122 (2022)

8. Merchant, A., Rose, G.M.: Effects of advertising-evoked vicarious nostalgia on brand heritage. J. Bus. Res. **66**(12), 2619–2625 (2013). https://doi.org/10.1016/j.jbusres.2012.05.021

9. Venkatesh, V., Davis, F.D.: A theoretical extension of the technology acceptance model: four longitudinal field studies. Manage. Sci. **46**(2), 186–204 (2000). https://doi.org/10.1287/mnsc.46.2.186.11926

10. Ball, J., Ogletree, R., Asunda, P., Miller, K., Jurkowski, E.: Diffusion of innovation elements that influence the adoption and diffusion of distance education in health. Am. J. Health Stud. **29**(3) (2014). https://doi.org/10.47779/ajhs.2014.221

11. Rosenzweig, J., Bartl, M.: A Review and Analysis of Literature on Autonomous Driving, p. 57 (2015)

12. Yang, C.C., Li, C.L., Yeh, T.F., Chang, Y.C.: Assessing older adults' intentions to use a smartphone: using the meta-unified theory of the acceptance and use of technology. Int. J. Environ. Res. Public Health **19**(9), 5403 (2022). https://doi.org/10.3390/ijerph19095403

13. Zmud, J., Sener, I.N., Wagner, J.: Consumer Acceptance and Travel Behavior Impacts of Automated Vehicles. Tech. rep., Texas A&M Transportation Institute (Jan 2016)

14. Gursoy, D., McCleary, K.W.: Travelers' Prior Knowledge and its Impact on their Information Search Behavior. J. Hospitality Tourism Res. **28**(1), 66–94 (2004). https://doi.org/10.1177/1096348003261218

15. Kerstetter, D., Cho, M.H.: Prior knowledge, credibility and information search. Ann. Tour. Res. **31**(4), 961–985 (2004). https://doi.org/10.1016/j.annals.2004.04.002

16. Woloshyn, V.E., Paivio, A., Pressley, M.: Use of elaborative interrogation to help students acquire information consistent with prior knowledge and information inconsistent with prior knowledge. J. Educ. Psychol. **86**, 79–89 (1994). https://doi.org/10.1037/0022-0663.86.1.79

17. Consumer perceptions, understanding, and expectations of Advanced Driver Assistance Systems (ADAS) and vehicle automation - Christian Hoyos, Benjamin D. Lester, Caroline Crump, David M. Cades, Douglas Young (2018). https://journals.sagepub.com/doi/10.1177/1541931218621429

18. Holbrook, M.B., Hirschman, E.C.: The experiential aspects of consumption: consumer fantasies, feelings, and fun. J. Consumer Res. **9**(2), 132–140 (1982). https://doi.org/10.1086/208906

19. Lavidge, R.J., Steiner, G.A.: A model for predictive measurements of advertising effectiveness. J. Mark. **25**(6), 59–62 (1961). https://doi.org/10.1177/002224296102500611

20. Hill, R.J.: Review of belief, attitude, intention and behavior: an introduction to theory and research. Contemp. Sociol. **6**(2), 244–245 (1977). https://doi.org/10.2307/2065853

21. Yzer, M.: Reasoned action theory: persuasion as belief-based behavior change. In: The SAGE Handbook of Persuasion: Developments in Theory and Practice, 2 edn., pp. 120–136. SAGE Publications, Inc., Thousand Oaks(2012). https://doi.org/10.4135/9781452218410

22. Garbarino, E., Johnson, M.S.: The Different Roles of Satisfaction, Trust, and Commitment in Customer Relationships (1999)
23. Rosenbaum, M.S., Massiah, C., Jackson, D.W.: An investigation of trust, satisfaction, and commitment on repurchase intentions in professional services. Serv. Mark. Q. **27**(3), 115–135 (2006). https://doi.org/10.1300/J396v27n03_07
24. Dul, J.: Necessary Condition Analysis (NCA): Logic and Methodology of 'Necessary But Not Sufficient' Causality. SSRN Electronic Journal (2015). https://doi.org/10.2139/ssrn.2588480
25. Orlovska, J., et al.: Effects of the driving context on the usage of automated driver assistance systems (ADAS) -naturalistic driving study for ADAS evaluation. Transp. Res. Interdisciplinary Perspectives **4**, 100093 (2020). https://doi.org/10.1016/j.trip.2020.100093
26. Wang, S., Wang, J., Li, J., Wang, J., Liang, L.: Policy implications for promoting the adoption of electric vehicles: do consumer's knowledge, perceived risk and financial incentive policy matter? Transp. Res. Part A Policy Pract. **117**, 58–69 (2018). https://doi.org/10.1016/j.tra.2018.08.014

Advancing Adaptive Decision-Making for Intelligent Cockpit Layouts: Exploring Preferred and Sensitive Joint Angles Across Multi-Type Vehicles

Chengmou Li[1], Yang Yu[1], Baiyu Chen[2], Jiarui Chen[3], Yingzhang Wu[1], Jialin Liu[1], Wenbo Li[1(✉)], and Gang Guo[1]

[1] College of Mechanical and Vehicle Engineering, Chongqing University, Chongqing 400044, China
chengmou_li@stu.cqu.edu.cn, liwenbocqu@163.com
[2] China Automotive Engineering Research Institute Co., Ltd., Chongqing 400039, China
[3] Chongqing Changan Automobile Corporation Ltd., Chongqing 401133, China

Abstract. Understanding the driver's driving posture demand is a crucial prerequisite for achieving adaptive layout decision-making in intelligent cockpits, including preferred joint angles and sensitive joint angles (acceptable posture changes). However, differences in anthropometric characteristics across racial populations and the lack of field research limit the application of relevant conclusions to the Chinese driver. This study conducted a field test, inviting 90 participants (60 males) with typical body characteristics of Chinese drivers to perform real driving tasks in three occupant package layouts (Sedan, SUV, and MPV). The study utilized motion capture and post-image marking methods to obtain six major joint angles in the sagittal plane of the human body. A two-way mixed ANOVA was employed to assess the impact of gender and OPL factors on preferred and sensitive joint angles. The results indicated that, for the preferred driving posture, both gender and OPL factors had significant main effects on elbow, trunk, and thigh angle. Regarding sensitive joint angles, gender significantly affected elbow and shoulder angles, while OPL significantly affected elbow, shoulder, hip, thigh, and calf angles. This study extensively explored the driving posture preferences of Chinese drivers of different genders in various typical passenger vehicles, providing crucial guidance for future dynamic layout adaptive decisions in automotive intelligent cockpit.

Keywords: Automotive intelligent cockpit · Human-machine interaction · Chinese Driver posture · Driver joint angles · Field test

1 Introduction

The evolution of automotive intelligent cockpits [1] has significantly altered the requirements for the driver's posture, primarily driven by the challenges posed by the "3rd living space" [2]. The intelligent, personalized, and comfortable multi-scenario driving posture matching has become the new goal in today's automotive seats and cockpit layouts. To achieve this goal, advanced intelligent cockpits must possess adaptive layout decision-making capability. Based on travel scenarios and user characteristics, the cockpit automatically adjusts the human-machine interface to match the ideal driving posture, thereby enhancing the user's overall experience in safety, intelligence, efficiency, and pleasure.

To achieve adaptive layout decision-making in intelligent cockpits, it is essential to fully understand the driver's driving posture preferences in different cockpit layouts. In the field of ergonomics, extensive research has been conducted on the comfortable (preferred) joint angle ranges for driving postures. Rebiffé et al. [3] derived the comfortable joint angle range in the sagittal plane based on theoretical analysis. Porter et al. [4] experimentally found that the joint angles chosen by drivers were mainly smaller than the theoretical values using a simulator. Kyung et al. [5] suggested that driving posture studies should consider both comfort and discomfort evaluations, leading to recommended joint angles based on a filtering mechanism. These studies provide rich insights into the driver preferred postures. However, there are still many challenges in driving posture preferences for the Chinese driver population.

Firstly, although China is the most significant automotive consumer market, existing studies have primarily focused on European or North American populations, which may not accurately represent the preferred joint angles of Chinese drivers. According to Guan et al. [6], the average height of men and women in the United States are 176.9 cm and 162.9 cm, respectively. However, according to the latest data in China (GB/T 10000-2023), the average heights for Chinese men and women aged 18–70 are 168.7 cm and 157.2 cm, respectively. There are evident height and body proportion differences between these two populations, leading to incorrect conclusions regarding driving postures and seat positions [7]. Peng et al. [8] further confirmed this viewpoint, showing that compared to French participants, Chinese participants exhibited a more reclined trunk by 1.9° and a more open trunk-thigh angle by 3.8°. Nevertheless, this conclusion is drawn from a small sample size of 21 individuals in a simulator, limiting its practical applicability.

Moreover, the absence of field research brings more uncertainty to the ecological applicability of recommended driving posture angles. Simulated cockpits are often used as the preferred driving posture research environment [9]. According to Kyung et al.'s study [5], there is an inconsistency in driving posture between laboratory and real world. For instance, in the sedan layout, the neck, shoulders, elbows, and left hip joint angles are significantly larger under real-world conditions. In contrast, the angles of the wrists, knees, and ankles show the opposite result, larger under laboratory. Meanwhile, past research has always focused on the occupant package layout (OPL) of sedans, with little attention given to SUVs and MPVs. However, different OPL types have different cockpit layout dimensions and differentiated component adjustment ranges, potentially resulting in different preferences for driving postures [10].

In addition to considering the *preferred joint angles*, the driving postures should also delve into the dynamic change of joint angles under comfortable conditions. Postural changes during driving have been proven effective in alleviating fatigue, preventing musculoskeletal discomfort and pathology, serving as a theoretical foundation for developing active/passive motion seats, and representing the forefront of research in automotive ergonomics [11]. However, current research has only considered the variability of posture within individual drivers [8, 12], limiting the applicability of conclusions in scenarios where interior components dynamically change based on user needs. Exploring the dynamic change of comfortable joint angles under similar cockpit layout conditions (such as different brands of cars) can effectively complement acceptable posture changes theory for drivers. We define it as the *sensitive joint angles* under different OPL conditions to distinguish it from related research.

In summary, demographic and occupant layout factors on Chinese drivers' driving posture preferences must be explored in the real driving condition. This study aims to contribute valuable insights into the interior design of advanced intelligent cockpits and adaptive layout decision methods. Therefore, the primary objectives of this research are to explore the preferred and sensitive joint angles of drivers of different genders under various occupant package layout conditions (sedan, SUV, MPV) following real driving activities. The key questions addressed by this work are: a) How large are the preferred and sensitive joint angles after actual driving? b) How significantly do driver gender and occupant package layout factors impact preferred and sensitive joint angles?

2 Materials and Methods

2.1 Study Design

This study designed a field test based on a mixed method. Driver gender serves as the between-subjects factor, occupant package layout (OPL) as the within-subjects factor, and the preferred joint angles (average joint angles in the same type vehicle) and sensitive joint angles (maximum difference in joint angles in the same type vehicle) for three different vehicle types (Sedan, SUV, MPV) are considered as dependent variables. The joint angles are measured using motion capture equipment and image marking methods after real driving. This includes six key joint angles in the driver's sagittal plane, namely Elbow flexion (α), Shoulder flexion (β), Trunk inclination (γ), Trunk-thigh flexion (δ), Knee flexion (θ), and Foot-shank angle (η), as illustrated in Fig. 1.

Table 1. The main anthropometric data for Chinese male and female participants.

Gender	Stature [cm]	Fore arm length [mm]	Upper arm length [mm]	Calf length [mm]	Thigh length [mm]
Male (60)	171.0 ± 6.8	248.1 ± 15.3	302.1 ± 25.3	400.4 ± 31.7	473.8 ± 25.4
Female (30)	157.7 ± 5.7	226.8 ± 15.2	271.6 ± 21.6	357.7 ± 23.4	446.3 ± 30.8

2.2 Participants

Based on the driver demographic statistics released by the Chinese Ministry of Public Security in 2021, the male-to-female ratio among drivers is 1.97:1. Accordingly, this study recruited 90 participants from the Chinese driver population (60 males). Each participant underwent a preliminary screening process, holding a valid driver's license for at least one year and maintaining a driving frequency of three times per week or more. Participants were required to ensure sufficient rest the night before the experiment. Simultaneously, individuals experiencing discomfort or pain during the experiment were excluded. The male participants' ages ranged between 24 and 53 years, while the female participants' ages ranged between 23 and 50 years. Other relevant anthropometric measurements are presented in Table 1.

2.3 Study Procedure

The field test was conducted in an underground parking in Chongqing, China, to ensure safety and control environmental interference. Before the experiment commenced, all participants underwent measurements of anthropometric parameters. They were informed about the purpose and procedure of the experiment, as well as the safety aspects of the equipment, and were required to sign an informed consent form. Each participant was given sufficient time to familiarize themselves with the driving route and the adjustment methods for cockpit components, such as the steering wheel and seats. The experiment involved nine vehicles categorized as follows: Sedans (Ford Escort, Changan Eado, Mazda ATENZA); SUVs (Peugeot 4008, Changan CS75 PLUS, Honda CRV); MPVs (MAXUS G10, Buick GL8, Mercedes-Benz Vito).

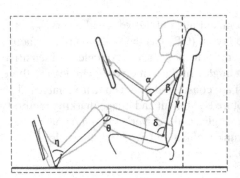

Fig. 1. Illustration of driving posture joint angles

Fig. 2. Standardized driving posture in field test

Once the experiment started, the cockpit components of all test vehicles were adjusted to their initial positions. The research workers assisted participants in donning motion capture devices (Xsens MVN Awinda) and completing calibration. After the data collection was stabilized, participants were instructed to re-enter the test vehicles and adjust components such as seats and steering wheels according to their individual driving preferences. Subsequently, participants were directed to drive along a predetermined route at a controlled speed of 15–20 km/h, with a driving duration of approximately two minutes. Participants were allowed to adjust cockpit components to achieve a comfortable driving posture throughout the driving process.

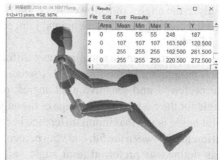

Fig. 3. The human biomechanical modeling in Xsens Analysis software

Fig. 4. Calculating driving posture joint angles using ImageJ

After determining the final components positions, participants were instructed to drive the vehicle to the route's endpoint and park while maintaining a standardized driving posture, as illustrated in Fig. 2. Specifically, participants were required to place their hands on the steering wheel at the 3 and 9 o'clock positions, with both arms naturally hanging down. The left foot was to rest on the footboard, while the right foot lightly touched the accelerator pedal, and the heel needed contact with the floor. Subsequently, the motion capture system recorded the joint angles of participants' driving postures, as depicted in Fig. 3. After completing the current vehicle's test, participants were asked to go to the next vehicle and undergo motion capture recalibration. The order of vehicles was randomized among different participants. In total, the experiment comprised 810 trials (90 participants * 9 vehicles). Free resting periods were allowed between different vehicles to ensure participants' mental well-being. Participants received 300 CNY upon completion of the experiment.

2.4 Data Acquisition and Processing

The full-body motion capture system (Xsens Technologies B.V., Netherlands) recorded driving postures. This system comprises the MVN Awinda, which includes 17 wireless motion trackers and body straps, along with recording software named MVN Analysis. The software defines a biomechanical model consisting of 23 segments to describe users' movement characteristics accurately. Advanced algorithms support precise estimation of the position, orientation, and joint angles of various body parts [13]. Janson et al. [14] experimented to assess the posture quantification capability of the Xsens system. The authors compared data collected with Xsens Awinda to a recognized method of measuring static postures [15], and the results indicated good agreement between the two methods, demonstrating the Xsens system's ability to capture the driver's posture accurately.

The definition of different joint centers and the sources of joint angles are outlined in Table 2. The MVN Analysis software can directly calculate the Elbow flexion, Knee flexion, and Foot-shank angle for the output biomechanical model. However, direct output is not available for Shoulder flexion, Trunk inclination, and Trunk-thigh flexion. Therefore, we exported sagittal plane images (right side) recorded by the software to analyze the angles of followed three joints. ImageJ [16] software was employed to digitize the coordinates of participants' joint centers and calculate joint angles, as illustrated in Fig. 4.

The average angle and maximum difference between the repeated measurements for each participant in the three OPL (Sedan, SUV, and MPV) were calculated to indicate the preferred and sensitive joint angles, respectively. For example, the preferred joint angle for the Sedan is the average of the angles for three Sedan vehicles, and the sensitive joint angle is the maximum difference between the angles for three Sedan vehicles. The difference between the 5th and 95th percentile of preferred joint angles for all participants was defined as preferred joint angle variability. Sensitive joint angle variability was defined as all participants' 90th percentile of sensitive joint angles.

Table 2. Definitions of the driving posture joint angles

Angle	Joint angle	Description	Source
α	Elbow flexion	Angle between upper arm and lower arm	MVN
β	Shoulder flexion	Angle between trunk and upper arm	ImageJ
γ	Trunk inclination	Angle between hip-shoulder vector and vertical	ImageJ
δ	Trunk-thigh flexion	Angle between thigh and trunk	ImageJ
θ	Knee flexion	Angle between thigh and shank	MVN
η	Foot-shank angle	Angle between foot plane and shank	MVN

2.5 Data Analysis

SPSS 26 (IBM Corp., Armonk, N.Y., USA) was used for statistical analysis. Two-way mixed analysis of variance (ANOVA) was employed to assess the impact of Gender and OPL on the preferred and sensitive angles of various joints. The Shapiro-Wilk Test was applied to check normality. In the case of violating the sphericity assumption, the Greenhouse-Geisser correction was utilized. The Box's test of equality of covariance matrices was performed to examine the homogeneity of covariance. Bonferroni post hoc tests were applied for pairwise comparisons. Simple main effects for different variables were examined when the interaction was significant. Boxplots were used to exclude any unreasonable outliers. A significance level of $p < .05$ was considered for statistical tests.

3 Results

3.1 Distribution of Preferred and Sensitive Joint Angle Difference

The mean, standard deviation, and variability of the preferred joint angles of all participants are presented in Table 3. The highest variability in preferred joint angles is elbow flexion at 57.9°, followed by trunk-thigh flexion at 31.0°. In descending order, shoulder flexion, knee flexion, trunk inclination, and foot-shank inclination exhibit the smallest and similar angle variabilities (26.7°, 25.5°, 24.6°, and 24.2°, respectively).

The distribution of sensitive joint angle ranges from all participants is shown in Table 4. The highest variability in sensitive joint angles is elbow flexion at 26.7°, followed by shoulder flexion, foot-shank inclination, knee flexion, and trunk-thigh flexion at 15.7°, 13.8°, 12.7°, and 12.6°, respectively. The trunk inclination exhibits the smallest variability at 10.0°.

Table 3. Variability statistics of driving posture preferred joint angles

Angle	Joint angle	Mean [°]	SD [°]	5th-95th % ile [°]
α	Elbow flexion	131.7	17.0	57.9
β	Shoulder flexion	33.0	8.0	26.7
γ	Trunk inclination	21.8	8.1	24.6
δ	Trunk-thigh flexion	107.7	9.3	31.0
θ	Knee flexion	122.6	7.6	25.5
η	Foot-shank angle	85.9	7.2	24.2

Table 4. Variability statistics of driving posture sensitive joint angles

Angle	Joint angle	Mean [°]	SD [°]	90th % ile [°]
α	Elbow flexion	14.9	8.7	26.7
β	Shoulder flexion	8.9	4.9	15.7
γ	Trunk inclination	5.8	3.8	10.0
δ	Trunk-thigh flexion	7.2	4.3	12.6
θ	Knee flexion	7.0	3.9	12.7
η	Foot-shank angle	7.4	4.8	13.8

3.2 Effects on Driving Posture Preferred Joint Angle Differences

Table 5 and Table 6 present the mean, standard deviation, and statistical test results of driving posture preferred joint angles, categorized by groups. Unless otherwise specified, all data are presented as mean ± standard deviation.

For α-preferred, there is no statistically significant interaction between gender and OPL, $F(2, 176) = 2.547$, $p = .081$, partial $\eta2 = .028$. The main effect analysis indicates: There is a statistically significant difference among different vehicle types, $F(2, 176) = 26.252$, $p < .001$, partial $\eta2 = .23$. SUV ($133.7 \pm 16.6°$, $p < .001$) and MPV ($132.4 \pm 17.4°$, $p < .001$) are significantly larger than Sedan ($128.9 \pm 16.9°$). SUV ($133.7 \pm 16.6°$) is also significantly larger than MPV ($132.4 \pm 17.4°$), $p = .02$. There is a statistically significant difference in gender groups, $F(1, 88) = 17.58$, $p < .001$, partial $\eta2 = .17$. Males ($136.4 \pm 15.1°$) are significantly larger than females ($122.2 \pm 16.9°$), $p < .001$.

For β-preferred, there is a statistically significant interaction between gender and OPL, F(1.757, 154.645) = 6.998, p = .002, partial η2 = .074. Simple main effect analysis reveals: Within the MPV type, there is a statistically significant difference in gender groups, F(1, 88) = 7.614, p = .007, partial η2 = .080. Males (35.7 ± 7.7°) are significantly larger than females (30.8 ± 8.2°), p = .007. In males, there is a statistically significant difference in the OPL groups, F(1.686, 99.492) = 27.920, p < .001, partial η2 = .321. Sedan (31.6 ± 7.9°) is significantly smaller than SUV (34.6 ± 7.6°, p < .001) and MPV (35.7 ± 7.7°, p < .001). In females, there is a statistically significant difference in the OPL groups, F(2, 58) = 11.795, p < .001, partial η2 = .289. Sedan (29.6 ± 8.1°, p < .001) and MPV (30.8 ± 8.2°, p = .016) are significantly smaller than SUV (33.0 ± 7.8°).

For γ-preferred, there is no statistically significant interaction between gender and OPL, F(1.752, 147.175) = 1.064, p = .341, partial η2 = .013. The main effect analysis indicates: there is a statistically significant difference among different vehicle types, F(1.752, 147.175) = 47.971, p < .001, partial η2 = .363. SUV (21.4 ± 7.7°, p < .001) and MPV (19.6 ± 8.2°, p < .001) are significantly smaller than Sedan (24.3 ± 7.8°). SUV (21.4 ± 7.7°) is also significantly larger than MPV (19.6 ± 8.2°), p = .001. There is a statistically significant difference in gender groups, F(1, 84) = 8.664, p = .004, partial η2 = .093. Males (23.7 ± 7.2°) are significantly larger than females (17.9 ± 8.6°), p = .004.

For δ-preferred, there is no statistically significant interaction between gender and OPL, F(2, 55.247) = 2.547, p = .081, partial η2 = .028. The main effect analysis indicates: There are no statistically significant differences among different vehicle types, F(1.783, 149.758) = 0.033, p = .968, partial η2 = .00039. There is also no statistically significant difference in gender groups, F(1, 84) = 0.259, p = .612, partial η2 = .003.

For θ-preferred, there is a statistically significant interaction between gender and OPL, F(1.574, 138.536) = 3.401, p = .047, partial η2 = .037. Simple main effect analysis reveals: Within Sedan, there is a statistically significant difference in gender groups, F(1, 88) = 5.123, p = .026, partial η2 = .055. Males (122.6 ± 8.1°) are significantly smaller than females (126.3 ± 5.4°), p = .026. Within SUV, there is a statistically significant difference in gender groups, F(1, 88) = 6.979, p = .010, partial η2 = .073. Males (121.7 ± 7.6°) are significantly smaller than females (126.0 ± 6.6°), p = .010. In males, there is a statistically significant difference in the OPL groups, F(1.618, 95.455) = 11.265, p < .001, partial η2 = .160. Sedan (122.6 ± 8.1°, p = .001) and SUV (121.7 ± 7.6°, p = .002) are significantly larger than MPV (120.1 ± 7.5°). In females, there is a statistically significant difference in the OPL groups, F(1.457, 42.246) = 22.681, p < .001, partial η2 = .439. Sedan (126.3 ± 5.4°, p < .001) and SUV (126.0 ± 6.6°, p < .001) are significantly larger than MPV (122.2 ± 7.4°).

For η-preferred, there is no statistically significant interaction between gender and OPL, F(1.827, 149.833) = 0.972, p = .374, partial η2 = .012. The main effect analysis indicates: There are no statistically significant differences among different vehicle types, F(1.827, 149.833) = 0.661, p = .505, partial η2 = .008. There is also no statistically significant difference in gender groups, F(1, 82) = 0.442, p = .508, partial η2 = .005.

Table 5. Means and standard deviations of the driving posture preferred joint angles in degrees by driver gender and OPL type groups

OPL	Gender	α [°]	β [°]	γ [°]	δ [°]	θ [°]	η [°]
Sedan	male	133.8 ± 14.8	31.6 ± 7.9	26.5 ± 6.4	108.0 ± 9.0	122.6 ± 8.1	86.1 ± 7.3
	female	119.1 ± 16.8	29.6 ± 8.1	19.9 ± 8.6	106.9 ± 9.9	126.3 ± 5.4	86.2 ± 7.1
SUV	male	137.9 ± 15.0	34.6 ± 7.6	23.3 ± 6.6	107.8 ± 8.7	121.7 ± 7.6	85.6 ± 7.3
	female	125.5 ± 16.8	33.0 ± 7.8	17.6 ± 8.6	107.5 ± 10.1	126.0 ± 6.6	86.4 ± 7.9
MPV	male	137.6 ± 15.3	35.7 ± 7.7	21.3 ± 7.7	108.1 ± 9.2	120.1 ± 7.5	85.8 ± 6.9
	female	122.0 ± 16.8	30.8 ± 8.2	16.2 ± 8.4	107.1 ± 10.2	122.2 ± 7.4	85.5 ± 7.1

Table 6. Two-way mixed ANOVA results for driving posture preferred joint angles

Group	α [°]	β [°]	γ [°]	δ [°]	θ [°]	η [°]
Male	136.4 ± 15.1	33.9 ± 7.9	23.7 ± 7.2	108.0 ± 8.9	121.5 ± 7.8	85.8 ± 7.1
Female	122.2 ± 16.9	31.1 ± 8.0	17.9 ± 8.6	107.1 ± 10.0	124.8 ± 6.7	86.0 ± 7.3
Sedan	128.9 ± 16.9	30.9 ± 8.0	24.3 ± 7.8	107.6 ± 9.3	123.8 ± 7.5	86.1 ± 7.2
SUV	133.7 ± 16.6	34.1 ± 7.7	21.4 ± 7.7	107.7 ± 9.1	123.1 ± 7.5	85.9 ± 7.5
MPV	132.4 ± 17.4	34.1 ± 8.2	19.6 ± 8.2	107.8 ± 9.5	120.8 ± 7.5	85.7 ± 6.9
		G&O **			G&O *	
	G ***		G **		G *	
	O ***	O ***	O ***		O ***	

Note: * 0.01 < p < 0.05, ** 0.001 < P < 0.01, *** p < 0.001. G: Main effect of genders group, O: Main effect of OPL group, G&O: Interaction effect between gender and OPL factor

3.3 Effects on Driving Posture Sensitive Joint Angle Differences

Table 7 and Table 8 present the mean, standard deviation, and statistical test results of driving posture sensitive joint angles, categorized by groups. Unless otherwise specified, all data are presented as mean ± standard deviation.

For α-sensitive, there is no statistically significant interaction between gender and OPL, $F(2, 162) = 2.483$, $p = .087$, partial $\eta2 = .03$. The main effect analysis reveals: There is a statistically significant difference among different vehicle types, $F(2, 162) = 22.112$, $p < .001$, partial $\eta2 = .214$. Sedan ($15.2 \pm 8.2°$, $p = .001$) and MPV ($18.3 \pm 9.0°$, $p < .001$) are significantly larger than SUV ($11.4 \pm 7.4°$). Additionally, Sedan ($15.2 \pm 8.2°$) is significantly smaller than MPV ($18.3 \pm 9.0°$), $p = .022$. There is a statistically significant difference in gender groups, $F(1, 81) = 8.851$, $p = .004$, partial $\eta2 = .099$. Males ($14.1 \pm 8.7°$) are significantly smaller than females ($16.6 \pm 8.3°$), $p = .004$.

For β-sensitive, there is no statistically significant interaction between gender and OPL, $F(2, 146) = 0.106$, $p = .900$, partial $\eta2 = .001$. The main effect analysis indicates:

There is a statistically significant difference among different vehicle types, $F(2, 146)$ = 10.468, p < .001, partial η2 = .125. Sedan (9.5 ± 5.4°, p = .005) and MPV (9.9 ± 4.5°, p < .001) are significantly larger than SUV (7.4 ± 4.4°). There is a statistically significant difference in gender groups, $F(1, 73)$ = 18.388, p < .001, partial η2 = .201. Males (8.7 ± 5.0°) are significantly smaller than females (9.4 ± 4.6°), p < .001.

For γ-sensitive, there is a statistically significant interaction between gender and OPL, $F(1.855, 146.559)$ = 4.203, p = .019, partial η2 = .051. Simple main effect analysis reveals: Within SUV, there is a statistically significant difference in gender groups, $F(1, 85)$ = 8.298, p = .005, partial η2 = 0.089. Males (4.7 ± 3.0°) are significantly smaller than females (6.2 ± 3.4°), p = .005. In males, there is a statistically significant difference in the OPL groups, $F(2, 108)$ = 7.028, p = .001, partial η2 = .115. Sedan (7.7 ± 4.4°, p = .035) and MPV (7.8 ± 3.7°, p = .002) are significantly larger than SUV (6.2 ± 4.3°).

For δ-sensitive, there is no statistically significant interaction between gender and OPL, $F(1.858, 152.387)$ = 1.038, p = .352, partial η2 = .012. The main effect analysis indicates: There is a statistically significant difference among different vehicle types, $F(1.858, 152.387)$ = 5.487, p = .006, partial η2 = .063. SUV (6.3 ± 3.9°) is significantly smaller than MPV (7.8 ± 3.8°), p = .005. There is no statistically significant difference in gender groups, $F(1, 82)$ = 0.722, p = .398, partial η2 = .009.

For θ-sensitive, there is no statistically significant interaction between gender and OPL, $F(2, 166)$ = 0.133, p = .875, partial η2 = .002. The main effect analysis indicates: There is a statistically significant difference among different vehicle types, $F(2, 166)$ = 3.336, p = .038, partial η2 = .039. However, no significant differences were observed in pairwise comparisons. There is no statistically significant difference in gender groups, $F(1, 83)$ = 1.463, p = .230, partial η2 = .017.

For η-sensitive, there is no statistically significant interaction between gender and OPL, $F(2, 158)$ = 0.288, p = .750, partial η2 = .004. The main effect analysis indicates: There is a statistically significant difference among different vehicle types, $F(2, 158)$ = 14.676, p < .001, partial η2 = .157. SUV (6.6 ± 4.8°, p < .001) and MPV (6.3 ± 3.9°, p < .001) are significantly smaller than Sedan (9.3 ± 5.2°). There is no statistically significant difference in gender groups, $F(1, 79)$ = 1.960, p = .165, partial η2 = .024.

Table 7. Means and standard deviations of the driving posture sensitive joint angles in degrees by driver gender and OPL type groups

OPL	Gender	α [°]	β [°]	γ [°]	δ [°]	θ [°]	η [°]
Sedan	male	15.0 ± 8.6	9.4 ± 5.8	6.4 ± 4.6	7.7 ± 4.4	6.2 ± 3.8	9.5 ± 5.4
	female	15.4 ± 7.4	9.6 ± 4.6	6.3 ± 4.6	6.9 ± 6.1	6.8 ± 4.1	8.9 ± 5.0
SUV	male	10.5 ± 7.2	6.9 ± 3.9	4.7 ± 3.0	6.2 ± 4.3	6.6 ± 3.7	6.7 ± 5.2
	female	13.2 ± 7.7	8.5 ± 5.2	6.2 ± 3.4	6.5 ± 3.3	7.1 ± 4.21	6.4 ± 4.0
MPV	male	16.8 ± 9.3	9.9 ± 4.7	6.2 ± 3.5	7.8 ± 3.7	7.8 ± 3.7	6.2 ± 4.0
	female	21.2 ± 7.8	10.0 ± 4.0	5.2 ± 2.7	7.9 ± 4.1	7.7 ± 4.4	6.4 ± 3.5

Table 8. Two-way mixed ANOVA results for driving posture sensitive joint angles

Group	α [°]	β [°]	γ [°]	δ [°]	θ [°]	η [°]
Male	14.1 ± 8.7	8.7 ± 5.0	5.8 ± 3.8	7.2 ± 4.2	6.9 ± 3.8	7.5 ± 5.1
Female	16.6 ± 8.3	9.4 ± 4.6	5.9 ± 3.7	7.1 ± 4.7	7.2 ± 4.2	7.2 ± 4.3
Sedan	15.2 ± 8.2	9.5 ± 5.4	6.4 ± 4.6	7.4 ± 5.0	6.4 ± 3.9	9.3 ± 5.2
SUV	11.4 ± 7.4	7.4 ± 4.4	5.2 ± 3.2	6.3 ± 3.9	6.8 ± 3.9	6.6 ± 4.8
MPV	18.3 ± 9.0	9.9 ± 4.5	5.9 ± 3.3	7.8 ± 3.8	7.8 ± 3.9	6.3 ± 3.9
			G&O *			
G **	G ***				
O ***	O ***		O **	O *	O ***

Note: * 0.01 < p < 0.05, ** 0.001 < P < 0.01, *** p < 0.001. G: Main effect of genders group, O: Main effect of OPL group, G&O: Interaction effect between gender and OPL factor

4 Discussion

This field research delves into the preferred and sensitive joint angles of Chinese drivers of different genders in three typical vehicles (sedan, SUV, and MPV). It also analyzes the impact of gender and OPL on both aspects. The following discussion presents the essential findings and compares them with relevant literature.

4.1 Factors Influencing the Driving Posture Preferred Joint Angles

The results of this study indicate that gender and OPL factors have differentiated effects on the preferred joint angles of driving posture, particularly those associated with the upper limbs and torso. Male drivers exhibit significantly greater Elbow flexion and Trunk inclination for all vehicle types than females. This suggests that Chinese males generally prefer a more reclined driving posture, while females prefer more bent elbow angles and a more upright backrest position. This difference may stem from two aspects: first it could be due to variations in upper limb lengths between genders. Kyung et al.'s [5] research suggests that the left limbs of the male population are noticeably longer, resulting in larger elbow joint angles. However, they also note that this difference may be influenced by height. Wolf et al.'s [12] study further supports this viewpoint, observing the phenomenon even when controlling for height. This study extends this conclusion to SUVs and MPVs. The other reason is these differences may arise from considerations of driving safety. Li et al.'s [17] research indicates that female drivers generally exhibit weaker driving skills. Female drivers might adjust their seat positions to be closer and the backrest angle smaller to achieve a broader driving view and maintain a more vigilant mental state. The findings of Haynes et al. [18] support this notion. In a laboratory experiment, participants demonstrated optimal work efficiency in an upright sitting position despite not being the most comfortable.

The comparison of vehicle types indicates that Sedans exhibit smaller elbow angles and greater trunk inclination. This suggests that drivers in Sedans tend to recline the seatback while moving the seat closer to the steering wheel. The comparison of shoulder angles further explains this phenomenon. Although no significant main effects were found, both male and female groups showed smaller shoulder angles in Sedans than in SUVs, reflecting a motion of bringing the upper limbs closer to the torso. Park et al.'s [10] research suggests that a more upright sitting posture is more prevalent in SUVs, aligning with this study's findings of lower trunk inclination. However, Kyung et al.'s [5] study indicates that Sedans have larger elbow angles, showing inconsistency with our study. This discrepancy could be attributed to differences in the gender distribution of the participant groups. In order to match the gender ratio of Chinese drivers, this study employed a 2:1 male-to-female strategy, while Kyung et al. [5] used a closer-to-1:1 ratio. Another interesting observation is that, in males, the shoulder angles in MPVs and SUVs are similar, but in females, the opposite is found.

The three joint angles related to the lower limbs present a relatively consistent trend. Trunk-thigh flexion and Foot-shank angle are unaffected by gender and vehicle type. The former ranges from 107° to 108°, and the latter falls within the interval of 85° to 86°. These findings provide crucial reference benchmarks for the design of passenger seating arrangements in vehicle cockpits. It means that drivers of different genders exhibit shared preferences in driving posture for these specific joint angles in different passenger vehicles. The development of vehicle models' passenger space layout should always consider the preferred angles for Trunk-thigh flexion and Foot-shank angle that can be satisfied by Digital Human Models (DHMs). Meanwhile, male Knee flexion is significantly smaller than that of females, which is consistent in both Sedans and SUVs. In contrast to the consistent conclusion for the upper limbs, the influence of gender on lower limb joint angles remains a topic for discussion. You et al. [19] found that gender affects knee angle and ankle angle in different cars, but Porter et al. [4] and Kyung et al. [5] did not observe a significant gender effect on these two angles, whether controlling for height differences or not. The seemingly contradictory conclusions could be attributed to differences in the participants' racial backgrounds. You et al.'s [19] study is based on a Chinese sample and yields results similar to this study. In a laboratory study, Park et al. [7] also found that Koreans had larger knee angles than the recommended angles in related research.

4.2 Factors Influencing the Driving Posture Sensitive Joint Angles

The range differences in sensitive joint angles across vehicle types remain a largely unexplored area. This study indicates that changes in upper limb posture range are influenced by both gender and OPL factors, while changes in lower limb range are primarily influenced by OPL. Males exhibit significantly smaller ranges of elbow and shoulder angles for all vehicle types than females. This suggests that males may more accurately find preferred upper limb postures during the user experience process for different vehicle types. This phenomenon could be explained from an evolutionary perspective. Males and females have different missions in reproduction and survival; males focus on hunting, while females focus on food gathering and child-rearing [20]. This requires males to possess the ability to adapt to new environments quickly. The upper limbs of the driver are crucial for lateral vehicle control [21] playing a decisive role in road adaptation and travel safety.

Besides, from the perspective of OPL differences, the range of joint angle variations in the driving posture for Sedans tends to be statistically greater than SUVs in most cases (except for knee flexion). In an experiment on the sensitivity of seat adjustments for preferred driving posture, Kyung et al. [22] found that drivers in SUV seats exhibited a stronger discomfort sensitivity than those in Sedan seats. For the minimum (5%) decrease in posture comfort rating, Sedan seats could be adjusted within a lateral range of 40 mm, while SUV seats could only be adjusted within a lateral range of 20mm. This finding aligns with the support from the current study. In the vehicle type comparison results, the sensitivity range for elbow flexion, shoulder flexion, and foot-shank angle in Sedans is significantly smaller than in SUVs. Trunk inclination and Trunk-thigh flexion also show smaller statistical trends. Additionally, this study reveals that MPVs exhibit the largest internal variations in elbow flexion, shoulder flexion, trunk-thigh flexion, and knee flexion among all vehicle types. This may be related to MPVs having optimal driving visibility and the largest range of cabin space for movement.

4.3   Comparison of Findings Related to Driving Posture

The results of this study were compared with those of Wolf et al. [12], as shown in Fig. 5. The critical difference between the two studies is that Wolf et al. [12] calculated inter- and intraindividual variability of drivers under Sedan seating conditions. In contrast, this study computed variability in preferred and sensitive joint angles under three different OPLs. The calculation methods for variability in both studies were similar. Compared with Wolf et al. [12], both preferred and sensitive joint angle variability in this study exhibited higher results. This can be attributed to differences in cockpit configurations. When a driver enters a new driving environment, an inevitable adaptation process is required, leading to greater angular variability. Additionally, it is noteworthy that the proportion of angular variability in both studies was similar, demonstrating a high level of consistency and indicating the validity of the measurement data.

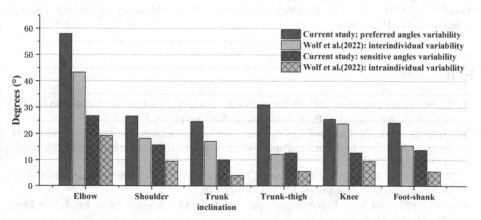

Fig. 5. The preferred and sensitive joint angles variability compared to Wolf et al. [12]

5   Conclusion

This study investigated the preferred and sensitive joint angles of Chinese drivers of different genders under real-world conditions in three vehicle types (Sedan, SUV, and MPV). The results indicate: (1) For preferred joint angles, Males exhibited significantly greater Elbow flexion and Trunk inclination in all vehicles. Sedan showed the smallest Elbow flexion but greatest Trunk inclination. Trunk-thigh flexion and Foot-shank angle were not influenced by gender or vehicle type. Males had significantly smaller Knee flexion than female drivers, a result observed in both Sedan and SUV. (2) For sensitive joint angles, Males showed significantly smaller ranges of motion in Elbow and Shoulder angles across all vehicles compared to females. In Sedan, the sensitive ranges of motion for Elbow flexion, Shoulder flexion, and Foot-shank angle were significantly smaller than those in SUV. MPV exhibited the largest internal variability in most joint angles (except Trunk inclination and Foot-shank angle).

In summary, this study delves into the driving posture preferences of Chinese drivers across different vehicle types, providing crucial insights for future adaptive layout decision-making in automotive intelligent cockpits. The research contributes to enhancing drivers' overall riding experience and offers profound insights into the development of automotive interior design, laying a solid foundation for meeting the ever-changing market demands. It is worth noting that this study addresses explicitly gender and vehicle factors in human factors research. However, other factors such as age, height, and BMI are equally deserving of further exploration.

6   Disclosure of Interests.

The authors have no competing interests to declare that are relevant to the content of this article.

Acknowledgments. This study is supported by National Natural Science Foundation of China (Grant 52302497), Horizontal Research Program—Predictive Modeling of Driving Posture Comfort 357344(H20211680).

References

1. Li, W., et al.: Intelligent cockpit for intelligent connected vehicles: definition, taxonomy, technology and evaluation. IEEE Trans. Intell. Vehicles (2023)
2. Dattatreya, P.H.: 22–1: *Invited Paper*: future automotive interiors - the 3rd living space. SID Symposium Digest of Technical Papers **47**, 263–266 (2016). https://doi.org/10.1002/sdtp.10659
3. Rebiffé, P.R.: Le siège du conducteur: son adaptation aux exigences fonctionnelles et anthropométriques. Ergonomics **12**, 246–261 (1969)
4. Porter, J.M., Gyi, D.E.: Exploring the optimum posture for driver comfort. Int. J. Veh. Des. **19**, 255–266 (1998)
5. Kyung, G., Nussbaum, M.A.: Specifying comfortable driving postures for ergonomic design and evaluation of the driver workspace using digital human models. Ergon. **52**, 939–953 (2009). https://doi.org/10.1080/00140130902763552

6. Guan, J., et al.: US truck driver anthropometric study and multivariate anthropometric models for cab designs. Hum. Factors **54**, 849–871 (2012)
7. Park, S.J., Kim, C.-B., Kim, C.J., Lee, J.W.: Comfortable driving postures for Koreans. Int. J. Ind. Ergon. **26**, 489–497 (2000). https://doi.org/10.1016/S0169-8141(00)00020-2
8. Peng, J., Wang, X., Denninger, L.: Effects of anthropometric variables and seat height on automobile drivers' preferred posture with the presence of the clutch. Hum. Factors **60**, 172–190 (2018). https://doi.org/10.1177/0018720817741040
9. Schmidt, S., Amereller, M., Franz, M., Kaiser, R., Schwirtz, A.: A literature review on optimum and preferred joint angles in automotive sitting posture. Appl. Ergon. **45**, 247–260 (2014). https://doi.org/10.1016/j.apergo.2013.04.009
10. Park, J., Choi, Y., Lee, B., Jung, K., Sah, S., You, H.: A classification of sitting strategies based on driving posture analysis. J. Ergon. Soc. Korea **33**, 87–96 (2014). https://doi.org/10.5143/JESK.2014.33.2.87
11. Schneider, L., Sogemeier, D., Weber, D., Jaitner, T.: Effects of a seat-integrated mobilization system on long-haul truck drivers motion activity, muscle stiffness and discomfort during a 4.5-h simulated driving task. Appl. Ergon. **106**, 103889 (2023). https://doi.org/10.1016/j.apergo.2022.103889
12. Wolf, P., Hennes, N., Rausch, J., Potthast, W.: The effects of stature, age, gender, and posture preferences on preferred joint angles after real driving. Appl. Ergon. **100**, 103671 (2022). https://doi.org/10.1016/j.apergo.2021.103671
13. Schepers, M., Giuberti, M., Bellusci, G.: Xsens MVN: Consistent Tracking of Human Motion Using Inertial Sensing (2018). https://doi.org/10.13140/RG.2.2.22099.07205
14. Janson, M., Wedmark, J.: Investigation of methods for quantifying sitting postures in cars
15. Park, J., Ebert, S.M., Reed, M.P., Hallman, J.J.: Development of an Optimization Method for Locating the Pelvis in an Automobile Seat. Procedia Manufacturing **3**, 3738–3744 (2015). https://doi.org/10.1016/j.promfg.2015.07.811
16. Abràmoff DMD Image Processing with ImageJ
17. Li, X., Yan, X., Wong, S.C.: Effects of fog, driver experience and gender on driving behavior on S-curved road segments. Accid. Anal. Prev. **77**, 91–104 (2015). https://doi.org/10.1016/j.aap.2015.01.022
18. Haynes, S., Williams, K.: Impact of seating posture on user comfort and typing performance for people with chronic low back pain. Int. J. Ind. Ergon. **38**, 35–46 (2008). https://doi.org/10.1016/j.ergon.2007.08.003
19. You, J., Qin, L., Zuo, P., Wang, X., Zhang, C.: Chinese drivers' preferred posture for sedans' seat ergonomic design. In: Long, S., Dhillon, B.S. (eds.) Man-Machine-Environment System Engineering, pp. 23–32. Springer, Singapore (2020)
20. Kheloui, S., et al.: Sex/gender differences in cognitive abilities. Neurosci. Biobehav. Rev. **152**, 105333 (2023). https://doi.org/10.1016/j.neubiorev.2023.105333
21. Xing, Y., Lv, C., Liu, Y., Zhao, Y., Cao, D., Kawahara, S.: Hybrid-learning-based driver steering intention prediction using neuromuscular dynamics. IEEE Trans. Industr. Electron. **69**, 1750–1761 (2021)
22. Kyung, G., Nussbaum, M.A., Lee, S., Kim, S., Baek, K.: Sensitivity of Preferred Driving Postures and Determination of Core Seat Track Adjustment Ranges, pp 2007-01–2471 (2007)

Research on Scenario-Based User Experience Evaluation Method for Intelligent Cars

Jin Lu[1][✉], Zaiyan Gong[2], and Jun Ma[1]

[1] College of Design and Innovation, Tongji University, Shanghai, China
lujin@ammi.cn
[2] HVR Lab, Tongji University, Shanghai, China

Abstract. With the rapid development of intelligent car technology, cars are no longer just means of transportation, but have become complex human-computer interaction systems. Therefore, user experience has become one of the key indicators for evaluating the performance of modern intelligent cars. This study explores three scenario-based intelligent car user experience evaluation methods, namely specification-centered evaluation method, journey-centered evaluation method, and demand-centered evaluation method, aiming to reflect the user experience level of intelligent cars comprehensively and accurately. This study compared and analyzed these three evaluation methods through user surveys and real vehicle tests, proving the superiority of the demand-centered evaluation method in terms of framework, content, results, and application. This method can effectively reflect the level of intelligent car user experience by evaluating the degree of satisfaction of user demands. This research provides an important reference for the design and definition of intelligent cars.

Keywords: Scenario · Intelligent car · User experience · User demand · Evaluation Method

1 Introduction

In recent years, the global automotive industry has developed rapidly in terms of intelligence. Cars have transformed from a simple means of transportation into an intelligent mobile space and become a complex human-computer interaction system. Today's intelligent cars are generally equipped with various advanced sensors and integrate multiple functions such as advanced driving assistance systems, Internet of Things connections, and infotainment systems [1]. The concerns of Original Equipment Manufacturers (OEMs) and consumers have changed from the performance of the engine to the experience of intelligent functions such as whether the infotainment system is rich in content and easy to use, and how complex the road the autonomous driving system can handle [2].

The intelligent car designs on the current market are mixed, and effective evaluation methods are needed to help improve the overall design level. Overly complicated technical means and functional configurations make the design of many intelligent cars flashy. Many seemingly cool functions may not bring actual value and may even bring negative effects. Correct evaluation can verify whether the design solves the problem or achieves the expected quality attributes, thereby providing effective guidance for design iterations or other related designs [3].

Changes in the attributes of automobile products have made user experience one of the key indicators for evaluating the performance of modern intelligent cars. The definition of user experience is a person's perception and reaction due to the use or expected use of a product, system, or service, so the scope of user experience includes the user's feelings about all aspects of use, brand image, product performance and use environment [4, 5]. User experience is one of the key evaluation indicators of human-computer interaction systems.

Currently, there are many models and methods used to evaluate the user experience of human-computer interaction systems [6]. Collins studied a method of using games to evaluate the user experience of human-computer interaction systems and applied it to the evaluation of computer speakers [7]. Olawole constructed an evaluation method based on cognitive psychology and user emotional factors, which can evaluate the user experience of institutional portals [8]. Kivijärvi's research found that comfort, pleasure, trust, and usefulness are all important factors in evaluating the user experience of the system interface [9]. In today's user-centered environment, system effectiveness, ease of use, learnability, efficiency, user satisfaction, error frequency, value, etc. are all important user experience evaluation contents. However, current research on user experience of human-computer interaction systems mainly focuses on the display interface, so there are limitations in the scope of interaction modalities. Moreover, since the evaluation subject is relatively fixed, it is difficult to adapt current evaluation indicators and methods to the evaluation of subjects other than the display interface.

Intelligent car is a special field in human-computer interaction systems. The interaction between the user and the intelligent car not only occurs on the display interface, but also includes more complex content such as voice interaction, hardware interaction, and interaction with external IoT devices. In addition, many tasks in automobile human-computer interaction require users to operate while driving the car. Users need to perform the main driving task and the secondary task at the same time [10]. As a result, it is difficult for current relevant evaluation methods to simultaneously satisfy comprehensiveness, accuracy, flexibility, and foresight when evaluating the overall user experience of intelligent cars.

This study proposes an evaluation system for intelligent car user experience based on car usage scenarios, which can accurately and quantitatively reflect the overall experience level of intelligent cars in different scenarios. The effectiveness of the evaluation system was verified through 30 user interviews and actual test results of 7 current mainstream production intelligent cars.

2 Theory and Methods

2.1 Exploring Intelligent Car User Experience Evaluation Methods

The user experience level of an intelligent car largely depends on the functions provided by the vehicle and the intelligent configuration behind the functions, because they are the main body in creating experience for users. The intelligent configuration of a car refers to a series of high-tech systems and hardware equipment integrated into the car, including automatic driving systems, infotainment systems, body hardware control systems, rich sensors, and actuators, etc., aiming to improve vehicle performance, safety, comfort, and convenience, etc. Take the autonomous driving system as an example, basic autonomous driving systems usually include basic functions such as adaptive cruise control, lane keeping assist, and automatic emergency braking. Higher-level autonomous driving systems also include more advanced autonomous driving decision-making algorithms and more advanced autonomous driving systems. Rich sensors enable high-end functions such as Navigate on Autopilot (NOA) and Full Self-Drive (FSD). The integration of these functions and configurations can improve driving safety and comfort and improve the driving experience by meeting users' needs to reduce driving burden. Compared with other intelligent products, intelligent cars have more ample space and richer usage scenarios, making it possible to integrate various intelligent configurations to create a high-quality user experience [11]. Research shows that consumers attach great importance to the intelligent configuration of cars, and for the same intelligent function, using different configurations and different designs will affect the actual use experience [12, 13].

To reflect the user experience level of intelligent cars accurately and quantitatively, we explored three scenario-based evaluation methods, using different ideas to convert the user experience level of intelligent cars with the intelligent functions and configuration of the vehicle.

Specification-centered evaluation method: directly disassemble the functions and configurations in the intelligent car, evaluate them one by one, and then summarize the results (see Fig. 1). The user experience of intelligent cars mainly comes from the intelligent functions and configurations of the equipment, which is also the most important difference between it and traditional cars [2]. Therefore, we tried to directly translate the evaluation of user experience into the evaluation of vehicle equipment functions and intelligent configuration.

This method is to disassemble the intelligent car into a series of functional sets, and then disassemble all the configurations that can provide each function to form a standard function list and configuration list to provide a basis for subsequent evaluation. Each function/configuration will be labeled with their commonly used scenarios. Then examine the configuration on the tested model based on the list, which includes testing which functions are implemented in each model and how these functions are implemented through specific configurations. Finally, the functions and configurations used by the vehicle are summarized, and the results are quantified by counting to achieve comparability between different models. For example, for the seat module of a intelligent car, the functions can be disassembled into seat heating, seat massage, seat ventilation, seat adjustment, seat vibration, etc. Among them, the configurations that can be separated from the adjustment functions of each part of the seat include a headrest moving module, a shoulder moving module, a waist moving module, a side moving module, a seat cushion moving module, a leg rest moving module, etc. If model A and model B have the same functions in the seat module, but model A lacks a seat cushion moving module and a leg rest moving module in the seat adjustment function, then it can be concluded that the user experience level of the seat module of model A is not as good as Conclusion for model B.

In summary, the core of this approach is to create a comprehensive list of features and configurations, and to reflect the differences between intelligent car functional designs through differences in the configurations used.

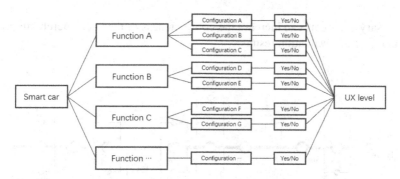

Fig. 1. Frame of specification-centered evaluation method

Journey-centered evaluation method: dismantle user behavior, analyze the functions and configurations involved in each step of behavior, conduct evaluations in sequence and summarize the results (see Fig. 2). Based on the above method, we also tried to use user behavior as clues to sort out functions and configurations. Because all functions and configurations equipped on intelligent cars generate value because they support user operations and behaviors, functions or equipment that are independent of user behavior should not be included in the scope of user experience evaluation even if they are equipped on the car [14]. Compared with specification-centered evaluation method, which lists all possible functions and intelligent configurations of intelligent cars without specific logic, using user behavior as a clue will make the final list more orderly and realistic.

The reliability of the evaluation results obtained using this method largely depends on the completeness of user behavior combing, so we first analyzed different users and their car usage behaviors, forming a series of car usage behavior slices. Taking the main driver leaving the car as an example (see Fig. 3), the actions that the user will inevitably take include: parking - parking - turning off the engine (fuel vehicle) - opening the door - getting off - closing the door - locking - confirming the locked status - staying away from the vehicle. When the user performs these inevitable behaviors, the user's behavior will change due to different conditions (time, location, environment, other users, etc.). For example, users need to observe their surroundings more carefully when opening the door in a small space compared to an open environment. Considering these complex and

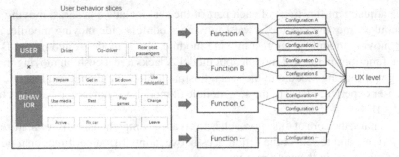

Fig. 2. Frame of journey-centered evaluation method

non-necessary situations can increase the completeness of the slice, thereby improving the accuracy of the evaluation results.

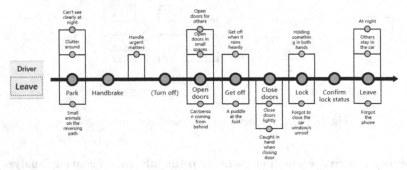

Fig. 3. Example of user behavior slice - driver leaves

After completing the construction of all user behavior slices, we analyzed the intelligent functions and configurations required by all user behaviors in each slice, and finally formed a slice-based function list and configuration list. When conducting evaluation, testers need to examine the extent to which the functions and configurations of the tested vehicle model can support the completion of user behavior slices. The more behaviors the tested vehicle model can support, the better the user experience. For example, when the user performs the door closing operation but fails to close the door at once because the force is too light, models equipped with electric door suction can automatically help the door close, which improves the closing experience compared with models that cannot help the user close the door automatically.

Demand-centered evaluation method: Split the car usage scenarios, analyze the user demands in each scenario and the functions and configurations of the vehicle used to meet the corresponding demands, evaluate each scenario in turn and summarize the results (see Fig. 4). The evaluation objects of the previous two methods are the functions and configurations of the vehicle, and the fundamental reason why users use the functions/configurations on the vehicle is because specific demands arise in specific scenarios and can be satisfied by the corresponding functions or configurations

[15, 16]. Therefore, we also tried to use the satisfaction of user demands in different scenarios as an evaluation object to reflect the user experience level of the vehicle.

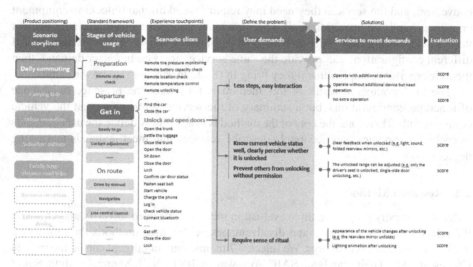

Fig. 4. Frame of demand-centered evaluation method

In this method, we first carefully split the car usage scenario. A scenario can be defined as a combination of the sequence of user actions and the extension under specific conditions. A scenario means a series of user actions under specific conditions. Compared with the user behavior slice in Method 2, the scope of the scenario is wider, and the content is richer. It can cover the interaction between the user's previous and subsequent behaviors and the role of different conditions on user behavior. For example, in the scenario where a user gets into a car, the user's action sequence includes sitting before adjusting the seat, updating the seat memory settings afterwards, adjusting the angle of the rearview mirror, etc. In addition to adjusting the seat under normal conditions, it may also include adjusting the seat while sport driving, adjust the seat when you have back pain, and other situations.

Only after scenario splitting is completed can we analyze all possible user demands, because user demands originate from scenarios and cannot exist without scenarios. User demands are determined by specific conditions and user behavior. For example, when a user first adjusts the seat and then updates the seat memory, since these are two independent interactive tasks, the user will need to make the transition between the two tasks more convenient. If the user feels back pain currently, then more waist support is needed. To conduct demand analysis without omissions, we decompose user demands into four dimensions, namely convenience, reassurance, comfort, and pleasure. The details are explained in Sect. 4.1.2.

We describe the way to meet demands as abstract "services" rather than specific functions and configurations to evaluate the degree of satisfaction of user demands. Because user demands themselves are not directly related to vehicle functions, if meeting user demands is a purpose, then functions/configurations are only means to achieve the purpose. Therefore, the evaluation content of this method is to examine whether the functions/configurations equipped with the vehicle can provide the services that users need in various scenarios. For example, users' demands when unlocking are fast and convenient, and the services they need may require no additional unlocking equipment or even no hands-on operation at all. There are many configurations that can implement these service descriptions, such as Bluetooth keys, touch-unlocked door handles, etc. If different configurations can provide the same services for a certain user demand, then the user experience improvement they bring in this scenario can also be the same.

The final evaluation result of this method is no longer the presence or absence of functions/configurations, but a summary of the service descriptions that the vehicle complies with. Therefore, the core of the method is to accurately define the user demands in each scenario slice and accurately describe services that meet demands to varying degrees.

2.2 Research Method

After theoretically proposing three evaluation methods, we need to verify and compare the effectiveness, advantages, and disadvantages of the three methods through actual vehicle testing and user surveys. We selected 7 mainstream intelligent cars in the current Chinese market. Their brands are SAIC Volkswagen, BYD, NIO, Xpeng, Leading, Smart and ZEEKR (see Fig. 5). We also invited 30 intelligent car users to conduct questionnaire interviews after participating in the vehicle experience. The participants were composed of 15 men and 15 women, aged between 20 and 45 years old.

Fig. 5. Some tested models

On the one hand, all participants were divided into 5 groups, and each group needed to simulate different car usage scenarios, such as daily commuting, long-distance family travel, etc. Participants were required to simulate their daily behaviors when using intelligent cars in corresponding scenarios on 7 models, such as unlocking and opening doors, getting in, and taking a seat, and resting in the car. During this process, users evaluate and record their experience with the vehicle model. After the experiment, each participant completed an experience satisfaction questionnaire and participated in a group interview to evaluate the user experience level of each vehicle model. On the other hand, professional testers tested 7 models according to three evaluation methods and recorded the test results accordingly.

By comparing and analyzing the results of user questionnaires and interviews of seven car models with the test results of testers, the accuracy of the results obtained by the three intelligent car user experience evaluation methods can be evaluated, thereby verifying the effectiveness of the evaluation methods.

3 Comparative Analysis of Three Evaluation Methods

We set the evaluation results obtained from user questionnaires and interviews as the user experience level benchmark of the vehicle under test, analyzed the consistency of the evaluation results obtained by the three methods with this benchmark, and investigated users' recognition of the three evaluation results. Degree, and finally a series of comparative analysis conclusions are drawn to illustrate the advantages, disadvantages, and effectiveness of each method. The specific content is shown in Table 1.

Table 1. Analysis results of three methods

	Specification-centered evaluation method	Journey-centered evaluation method	Demand-centered evaluation method
Stability of frame	**Poor** (Follow technological developments and changes)	**Medium** (User behavior is relatively stable, but functionality is constantly changing)	**Good** (Car usage scenarios, user demands and services are relatively stable)
Comprehensiveness of evaluation scope	**Poor** (Only function is involved)	**Medium** (Considering external conditions that affect user behavior)	**Good** (Considering multiple factors such as external conditions and the user themselves)
Flexibility in the evaluation process	**Poor** (Fully fixed)	**Relatively poor** (Basically fixed according to the set behavior)	**Good** (Adaptable according to scenarios and demands)
Targeting differentiated product positioning	**No** (No analytical perspective)	**No** (No analytical perspective)	**Yes** (Can analyze the experience of car models in different dimensions)
The generalizability of evaluation results	**Low** (Results will vary depending on competing products)	**Low** (Results will vary depending on competing products)	**Higher** (The results will not change due to competing products)
OEM department that can help	**Engineering**	**Engineering and Product**	**Engineering, Product and design**

3.1 Specification-Centered Evaluation Method

The evaluation results obtained by this method are ticks on a complete and non-duplicate list of the car's intelligent function configurations. This format is very straightforward and facilitates comparisons between different vehicle models. If a certain function/configuration of model A is not equipped on model B, then this is the difference in the user experience of the two cars. Although this method can reflect the experience differences between intelligent cars to a certain extent, it has the following two biggest flaws, which prevent it from truly reflecting the user experience level of intelligent cars:

1. Lack of consideration of conditions other than the function itself, and the evaluation results cannot reflect actual usage. Because when users drive a intelligent car, their experience will be affected by many aspects of the complex "human-vehicle-environment" system. Take a physical robot with an electronic display as an example. It can display anthropomorphic expressions when the system responds to user instructions. Although this function can enhance the emotional experience of voice interaction in intelligent cars, it does not work well when the vehicle is on complex roads or under light conditions. When driving at dark nights, dynamic expressions on the screen may attract the user's attention and increase cognitive load, causing driving distraction and reducing the user experience.
2. Because the evaluation results will vary depending on competing products, it is impossible to directly describe the user experience of the vehicle model through this method. The evaluation results obtained by this method are essentially a comparison of vehicle configuration and equipment, so the only conclusion that can be reached is that model A is equipped with 20 more functions than model B, and is equipped with 10 fewer functions than model C. In addition, only comparing configurations and equipment may lead to misguided guidance that the more intelligent functions/configurations the intelligent car has, the better the user experience will be.

3.2 Journey-Centered Evaluation Method

The evaluation results obtained by this method are also checked on the functional configuration list, but it has some advantages compared with the specification-centered evaluation method. This method maps functions/configurations to user actions. If a function/configuration corresponds to multiple user behaviors, it can be checked repeatedly and accumulated into the result, reflecting the different impact of functions/configurations on user experience. In addition, the method considers external conditions that may affect user behavior, making the results more relevant to actual usage.

However, this method also has many shortcomings. First, the stability of the method framework is insufficient. Although this method is based on user behavior, the evaluation object is still function/configuration. Functions/configurations will change rapidly with technological development, causing the evaluation content to change at any time. Secondly, it decomposes each user's actions into independent evaluation units and ignores the coherence of user actions, resulting in the lack of interrelated actions in the evaluation results. Take unlocking and opening the door as an example. In this method, these are two user actions that are used for evaluation respectively. However, in some models, the user will automatically unlock when opening the door, and the actual user experience is not divided into two parts. In this case, it would be unreasonable to evaluate the unlocking and door-opening parts separately and then add the results together. Then, this method focuses on the user's behavioral path, and the evaluation process needs to strictly follow the path sequence, which has poor flexibility. Finally, the evaluation results are not universal like the specification-centered evaluation method and will vary depending on competing products.

3.3 Demand-Centered Evaluation Method

The final evaluation result of this method is no longer a check on the function/configuration list, but a summary of the services that the vehicle can provide to meet user demands. Compared with the previous two methods, this method mainly has the following advantages:

1. The framework and content of this evaluation method are relatively stable. Functions and configurations will change rapidly with the development of technology and industry upgrading, but users' car usage scenarios, essential demands and corresponding service solutions are relatively fixed. Therefore, no matter how the functions and configuration of the vehicle change, if it can meet the demands of users, it can be considered a good user experience.
2. A demand-centered framework can incorporate various possible car usage conditions, user behaviors, and the impact between behaviors into experience evaluation, and use a more comprehensive evaluation scope to derive more accurate evaluation results. As mentioned in the example above, no matter what conditions and methods the user performs to unlock and open the door, they can all be classified into the "get in" scenario, and then the relevant user demands and services can be analyzed from the "get in" scenario.
3. This method provides different evaluation perspectives and can help different models or brands accurately analyze user experience in differentiated positioning. Since user demands are divided into four dimensions, the experience evaluation of the vehicle model in different dimensions can be obtained. For example, the experience level of model A in terms of convenience and pleasure. Car models or brands can choose the dimensions to be analyzed based on their own positioning or focus, so that they can analyze the differences between them and competing products in the segmented fields.
4. The user experience level of the tested model can be quantitatively obtained, and there is no need to compare with other models to present the results. The evaluation content of this method is the degree to which user demands are met, so there is a theoretical perfect score that can be used as a reference for the vehicle user experience level, that is, when all user demands are met. Testers can quantitatively describe the user experience level of the vehicle being tested by examining the gap between its user demand satisfaction and the full score. When the evaluation object is functions and configurations, there is no fixed reference standard, so the differences in user experience can only be reflected by comparing with other models.

In summary, the demand-centered evaluation method can effectively and accurately reflect the overall user experience level of intelligent cars by evaluating the degree to which user demands are met, and the framework and content of the method are relatively stable, solving the problems existing in other methods. It can be used to assist the OEM's engineering, product, and design departments.

4 Demand-Centered User Experience Evaluation Method for Intelligent Cars

4.1 Developing Demand-Centered Evaluation System

After verifying the effectiveness of the demand-centered evaluation method with actual tests and user surveys, we further developed the method and formed a relatively complete evaluation system. The detailed content includes: 1. Break down the user scenarios to a granularity that can be used for evaluation; 2. Describe users' demands in each scenario; 3. Describe services that meet user demands; 4. Establish a standard measurement method for deriving quantitative evaluation results; 5. Establish a labeling system for screening evaluation scope.

Breaking Down Scenarios. To comprehensively analyze car usage demands, complex car usage scenarios need to be broken down into granularity that can be used for evaluation. To this end, we have split the car usage scenario into three levels:

1. Scenario storylines. First, we referred to thousands of samples of vehicle usage surveys, clustered and integrated the survey results according to the dimensions of "user", "location" and "behavior", and summarized the five most important scenario storylines at present. They are daily commuting, carrying kids, urban recreation, suburban outings, and family long-distance road trips.
2. Stages of vehicle usage. Because the scenario storyline is too broad to deduce specific user demands, we expand the scenario storylines and obtain standard stages of vehicle usage by restoring the user's car use behavior. For example, when the user is in the arrival stage, he will go through the process of before arrival - parking - getting out - leaving (see Fig. 7). On the one hand, standardized stages of vehicle usage can provide a stable framework for the evaluation system, and on the other hand, they can cover all scenario storylines through permutations and combinations.
3. Scenario slices. The granularity of the stages of vehicle usage is not enough to explore user demands, so we further explored smaller car use behavior units and disassembled the stages of vehicle usage into scenario slices to form user experience touch points. To incorporate the interaction between users' own behaviors into the evaluation, the scenario slices need to include relevant user actions, such as "unlock and open the door" in "get in", "in-car environment adjustment" in "cockpit adjustment", navigation "Destination input and route planning" in "navigation", etc.

After splitting the car usage scenario into these three levels, we can more comprehensively and clearly sort out all the experience touch points of users using intelligent cars, which facilitates subsequent analysis of user demands (Fig. 6).

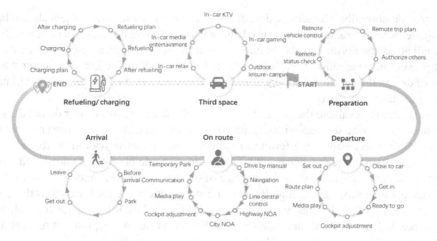

Fig. 6. Stages of vehicle usage framework

Analyzing User Demands. To avoid omissions, we divided the demands into four dimensions, and then analyzed and derived user demands in different scenarios along each dimension. After integrating ISO 9241, basic theories of design, automotive ergonomics, cultural research and other international standards and basic theories related to intelligent car user experience, we have divided the user demands of intelligent cars into: convenience, reassurance, comfort, and pleasure. Convenience means that it is easy for users to understand and learn various operations and page elements and interaction design are in line with public habits. Reassurance means that it is not easy to mis operate, the status is clear, injury is prevented, and people feel safe and trustful. Comfort means that the body feels relaxed, and fatigue is relieved, and entertainment You can have an excellent audio-visual immersion experience. Pleasure refers to feeling surprised, companionship and other emotional values, feeling warmth and being respected and understood. Taking "unlock and open the door" as an example, the user's demand for convenience is to unlock the vehicle and open the door with a few steps and simple interactions. The user's demand for reassurance is to be able to grasp the status of the vehicle and clearly perceive whether the vehicle is successfully unlocked or not, the demand for pleasure is the ritual feeling of being welcomed.

Each scenario slice contains a series of user actions and specific conditions, from which a variety of user demands can be derived. When unconventional conditions appear in the scenario slice, user demands will also change. For example, when the user's hands are occupied to unlock the door, the demand will change to open the car door from the outside conveniently and effortlessly. Therefore, the key to analyzing user demands is on the one hand to be based on the correct dimensions, and on the other hand to be able to comprehensively consider the impact of different conditions in different scenario slices.

Describing Services. Since user demands and functions/configurations are related to ends and means, we use various states rather than specific functions or configurations to describe different services that meet demands. For example, when the driver adjusts the cockpit environment while driving, he needs to be able to view navigation guidance information normally. The service description that can meet this requirement should be: No matter what interaction mode is used and what adjustment operation is performed, it will not affect the normal display of navigation information. Such a description method will prevent the evaluation from being affected by the specific design. No matter what kind of design the car model adopts, if it meets the description of the service, it will not reduce the user experience.

To accurately evaluate the degree to which a vehicle model meets user demands, we also need to describe services with different degrees of satisfaction under a user demand. For example, users want to use fewer steps and simple interactive operations to view car lock information in the car owner APP. The services should be divided into: 1. Directly display the car lock status on the home page of the car owner APP, and you can view it without any operation; 2. Through It takes one step to check the car lock status through the car owner APP; 3. It takes two steps or more to check the car lock status through the car owner APP. If different car models meet different service descriptions, it reflects the difference in their user experience levels.

Establishing Measurement Method. To quantify the user experience level, we first established a set of measurement standards for the service. Differences in user demand types lead to different services requiring corresponding quantitative scoring methods to accurately reflect the degree to which corresponding demands are met. There are mainly three scoring methods:

1. Score based on count, that is, points are given based on the number of service items that a car model meets in a user's demands. This method is suitable for situations where a requirement is met by multiple services and there is almost no difference in the contribution of each service to the user experience. For example, users want to have a clear and accurate location display in a complex parking lot. The corresponding services are: a. The car owner APP can record and accurately display the parking area information; b. The car owner APP can record and accurately display the parking floor information; c. The car owner The APP can record and accurately display parking space information. Under this requirement, models that meet different numbers of services will receive different scores.

2. Score accumulation, that is, each service has a corresponding score, and the demand score is equal to the sum of the scores of the services realized by the vehicle model. This method is suitable for situations where a demand is jointly satisfied by multiple services, and the contribution of each service to the user experience is different, and the demand can only be fully satisfied when all services are implemented. For example, users want to feel the comfortable environment in the car when they get in. The corresponding services are: a. The car owner APP supports making reservations in advance to set the air-conditioning temperature; b. The car owner APP supports making reservations in advance to turn on the seat heating; c. The car owner APP supports making reservations in advance. Turn on seat ventilation; d. The car owner APP supports making an appointment in advance to turn on the steering wheel heating. Under this requirement, the scores for each service are different, and a car model can get full scores only by implementing all services.

3. Take the maximum value of a single service, that is, each service has a corresponding score, and the demand score is equal to the maximum value of the service scores

achieved by the vehicle model. This method is suitable for situations where a demand can be satisfied by one service and multiple services can be substituted for each other. For example, users want to use fewer steps and simple interactive operations to check the car lock information in the car owner APP. The services should be divided into: a. Directly display the car lock status on the home page of the car owner APP, and you can view it without any operation; b. Through It takes one step to check the car lock status through the car owner APP; c. It takes two or more steps to check the car lock status through the car owner APP. Under this requirement, the points for each service are different. If a car model implements service a, it will directly receive full points.

We assigned weights to all scenarios and demands based on user questionnaires, and calculated scenario scores using a weighted average. First, the above-mentioned service metrics are used to obtain the demand score, and then the weighted average of the demand scores is used to obtain the scenario slice score. After multiple weighted averages, the stages of vehicle usage score, scenario storylines score and overall experience score can be obtained.

Establishing Labeling System. There are many types and quantities of scenarios and demands. To quickly filter out some scenarios and demands that we want to focus on, we have labeled the user demands in the evaluation system with the following two types of labels:

1. Module labels. The main content of such labels is the functional modules and hardware modules of intelligent cars, such as navigation, media, air conditioning, central control screen, passenger screen, etc. If the user demand or the service corresponding to the demand may involve a certain function or hardware module of the vehicle, then the demand will be labeled with the corresponding label, and one demand can be labeled with multiple labels. Module labels enable the targeted evaluation and optimization of existing functions and hardware configurations.
2. Experience labels. The main content of such labels is the attributes of people, objects, and environments, such as rear passengers, children, large items, hot weather, night, etc. Similarly, if the user's demands or the services corresponding to the demands may involve certain people, items, or environments, then the demands will be labeled accordingly. On the one hand, experience labels can help screen user demands; on the other hand, through permutation, combination and continuous refinement, they can sustainably deduce specific car usage scenarios and derive experience innovation points.

Finally, after completing the development of these aspects, a quantifiable demand-centered intelligent car user experience evaluation system was formed, which contains more than 100 scenario slices, more than 600 user demands and more than 1,000 services.

4.2 Applications of Demand-Centered Evaluation System

This demand-centered evaluation system has great application value for the intelligent car industry. It can not only help practitioners accurately evaluate the user experience level of vehicles, but also provide ideas and references for product definition.

In terms of evaluation, based on the evaluation of scenario slices, various experience evaluation results can be obtained by permutation and combination, which can be used for multi-angle product benchmarking analysis (see Fig. 8). In addition to the overall experience level of the car model, we can also get the score of the car model during a certain storyline, which can be used to benchmark against other car models on a specific storyline. We can also get the score of a car model on a certain evaluation indicator, which can be used to analyze the differences in positioning of different models or brands, or help different models or brands accurately analyze user experience based on differentiated positioning. In addition, by calculating the scores of certain types of user stages of vehicle usage, it can reflect the differences in experience performance of car models in specific links. Finally, we can get the user demand score with a certain type of label, which can be used to compare the differences in certain experience factors between models. Some test results are shown in Tables 2, 3, 4 and 5.

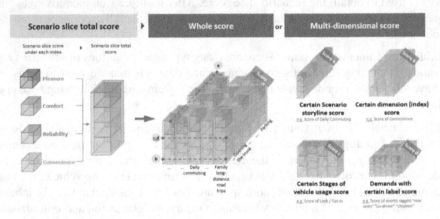

Fig. 7. Multi-angle interpretation of evaluation results

Table 2. Real cars test result sample from the angle of scenario storylines

	Daily commuting	Carrying kids	Urban recreation	Suburban outings	Family long-distance road trips
Model A	4.85	3.43	4.88	5.48	3.59
Model B	5.93	5.5	6.74	7.55	5.64

In terms of product definition, based on the scenario measurement scores and the weight of each scenario, the scope of scenarios to be optimized and the priority of product definition can be determined (see Fig. 9). If the scene weight of a scene slice is very high and its experience score is much lower than that of competing products, then the optimization priority of this event should be higher. After prioritizing all scenarios to be optimized for a vehicle model, product definers can examine which demands in

Table 3. Real cars test result sample from the angle of evaluation dimensions

	Convenience	Reassurance	Comfort	Pleasure
Model A	4.09	5.9	3.27	4.21
Model B	5.93	5.5	6.74	7.55

Table 4. Real cars test result sample from the angle of stages of vehicle usage

	Remote status check	Remote vehicle control	Remote trip plan	Authorize others	Close to car
Model A	5.46	1.2	8.26	3.3	5.12
Model B	7.86	5.69	5.86	2.48	2.89

Table 5. Real cars test result sample from the angle of labels

	Rear seats	Children	Snow	HUD	Light
Model A	1.93	7.06	4.67	6	3.96
Model B	3.69	2.48	6.73	8.76	4.13

the scenario are less satisfied according to priority, and then carry out optimization definitions.

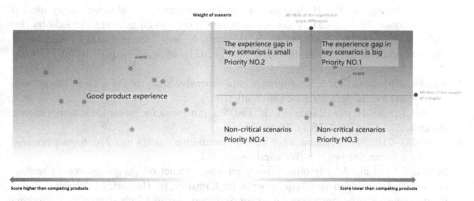

Fig. 8. Product definition priority screening method framework

5 Conclusion

This study explores three scenario-based intelligent car user experience evaluation methods and analyzes and compares the effectiveness of the three methods through user surveys and real vehicle tests. The results show that the demand-centered evaluation method can comprehensively, accurately, and quantitatively evaluate intelligent car users experience. This study also proposes a detailed process for building an evaluation system using demand-centered evaluation methods, including scenario layering, user demands analysis, service description, score calculation and labeling system. Through actual testing of 7 vehicles, this study verified the reliability and practical application value of the demand-centered intelligent car user experience evaluation system and provided a reference basis for relevant practitioners to evaluate intelligent car user experience and define intelligent car products.

Since the accuracy of the overall user experience evaluation results of a vehicle model is determined by the comprehensiveness of the scenarios and demands, this method also has certain limitations, that is, the scenario library and demands library need to be built comprehensive enough to obtain effective results. Although there are hundreds of scenarios and demands in the current library, which basically covers mainstream car use scenarios, there are still many long-tail scenarios that have not been included. We are still using experience labels to continue to improve the library. To solve this problem, our next research plan is to use AIGC to generate scenarios and demands. We hope that in the future, we can use the knowledge and capabilities of large language models to automatically fill the scenario library.

References

1. Tang, S., Ouyang, R., Tan, H.: Standardization of user experience evaluation: theory, method and promotion of high-quality development of Chinese intelligent vehicle industry. In: Duffy, V.G., Krömker, H.A., Streitz, N., Konomi, S. (eds.) International Conference on Human-Computer Interaction. Springer, Cham (2023). https://doi.org/10.1007/978-3-031-48047-8_27
2. Nakrani, P.K.: Smart car technologies: a comprehensive study of the state of the art with analysis and trends. Arizona State University (2015)
3. Venable, J., Pries-Heje, J., Baskerville, R.: FEDS: a framework for evaluation in design science research. Eur. J. Inf. Syst. 25(1), 77–89 (2016)
4. ISO: 9241–210: 2010 Ergonomics of human-system interaction - part 210: human-centered design for interactive systems. Technical report (2010)
5. Bergman, J., et al.: An exploratory study on how Internet of Things developing companies handle User Experience Requirements. In: Kamsties, E., Horkoff, J., Dalpiaz, F. (eds.) Requirements Engineering: Foundation for Software Quality: 24th International Working Conference, REFSQ 2018, Utrecht, The Netherlands, 19–22 March 2018, Proceedings 24. Springer, Cham (2018). https://doi.org/10.1007/978-3-319-77243-1_2
6. Hornbæk, K., Hertzum, M.: Technology acceptance and user experience: a review of the experiential component in HCI. ACM Trans. Comput.-Hum. Interact. (TOCHI) 24(5), 1–30 (2017)
7. Collins, K., Kanev, K., Kapralos, B.: Using games as a method of evaluation of usability and user experience in human-computer interaction design. In: Humans and Computers (2010)

8. Olawole, D.O.: User experience: tool for Human-Computer Interaction (HCI) design. AFRREV STECH: Int. J. Sci. Technol. **7**(2), 61–66 (2018)
9. Kivijärvi, H., Pärnänen, K.: Instrumental usability and effective user experience: interwoven drivers and outcomes of Human-Computer interaction. Int. J. Hum.-Comput. Interact. **39**(1), 34–51 (2023)
10. Blanco, M., et al.: The impact of secondary task cognitive processing demand on driving performance. Accid. Anal. Prev. **38**(5), 895–906 (2006)
11. Coppola, R., Morisio, M.: Connected car: technologies, issues, future trends. ACM Comput. Surv. (CSUR) **49**(3), 1–36 (2016)
12. Park, J., Nam, C., Kim, H.: Exploring the key services and players in the smart car market. Telecommun. Policy **43**(10), 101819 (2019)
13. Weyer, J., Fink, R.D., Adelt, F.: Human–machine cooperation in smart cars. An empirical investigation of the loss-of-control thesis. Saf. Sci. **72**, 199–208 (2015)
14. Kuniavsky, M.: Smart Things: Ubiquitous Computing User Experience Design. Elsevier (2010)
15. Vermeeren, A.P.O.S., et al.: User experience evaluation methods: current state and development needs. In: Proceedings of the 6th Nordic Conference on Human-Computer Interaction: Extending Boundaries (2010)
16. Harvey, C., et al.: In-vehicle information systems to meet the needs of drivers. Intl. J. Hum.-Comput. Interact. **27**(6), 505–522 (2011)

Exploring Electric Vehicle Charging Space Brand Market Factor and User Experience: A Case of the United States and China

Hao Lu$^{(\boxtimes)}$

Syracuse University, Syracuse, NY 13244, USA
hlu113@syr.edu

Abstract. With electric vehicles gradually replacing traditional petrol vehicles in the global market, charging stations usually provide a variety of different charging scenarios and modes to meet the needs of users in different usage scenarios. How to help brands establish standardized charging spaces in the US and China based on local user needs is a problem that needs to be solved. In this paper, we will take China and the United States, which have an advanced position in the global EV market, as an example, and use the exact same design research method to explore their charging space markets, investigate their user experiences, and ultimately compare and analysis them to draw conclusions that will help brands to establish standard charging spaces in China and the United States, as well as provide valuable references to the standardization of charging spaces on a global scale. Firstly, this paper will explore the charging space market in the two regions through literature review, cultural probes, and expert interviews; secondly, it will investigate the user experience in the two regions through observations, questionnaires, and interviews; and finally, it will compare and analysis the above data to draw conclusions. The final conclusions will be used to support the design of branded standardized charging spaces in China and the US and provide a reference for globalization and standardization.

Keywords: Charging Space · Brand Market Factor · User Experience

1 Introduction

According to the report of the US Department of Energy, the sales of electric vehicles from 2020 to 2021 almost doubled from 308,000 to 608,000. As of 2022, there are already 2,442,300 electric vehicles registered in the United States [1]. Similarly, in China according to the Ministry of Public Security statistics, as of the end of June 2023, the country's motor vehicle ownership reached 426 million, of which 328 million cars, 16.2 million new energy vehicles; in the first half of the new registration of new energy vehicles 3,128,000 vehicles, an increase of 41.6% year-on-year, hitting a record high. New energy vehicles accounted for 26.6% of the new registrations of automobiles [2]. China and the U.S. take the lead in EV sales across the board in 2022 [3].

A. Marcus et al. (Eds.): HCII 2024, LNCS 14713, pp. 218–237, 2024.
https://doi.org/10.1007/978-3-031-61353-1_15

2023 On June 19, the General Office of the State Council of China issued the "Guiding Opinions on Further Constructing a High-Quality Charging Infrastructure System", which makes specific deployment of the charging infrastructure construction [4]. The 14th Five-Year Plan mentions: focusing on the future trend of rapid growth of new energy vehicles, especially electric vehicles, the charging infrastructure still exists in the distribution is not perfect, the structure is not reasonable, the service is not balanced enough, the operation is not standardized enough and other issues [5]. On November 15, 2021, President Biden signed the Bipartisan Infrastructure Law, also referred to as the Infrastructure Investment and Jobs Act, which contains $7.5 billion in new funding for EV charging stations, makes EV charging infrastructure eligible for additional Federal funding programs, and provides funding for numerous other EV-related initiatives [6].

The situation in China and the United States is very different. There are several times more electric vehicle users in China than in the United States, China accounted for nearly 60% of all new electric car registrations globally [3]. Cities and road networks in China and the United States are also different, the density and distribution of population have a significant impact on the distribution of urban transport infrastructure [7]. At the same time, differences in cultural backgrounds and policies play a major role in the development of national infrastructure.

The paper has utilized a literature review to complete a preliminary understanding of the keywords of the problem. In the first part, the paper explored B-market (Brand market) factors of charging infrastructure and provide a comprehensive understanding of the charging space in China and the United States. It includes charging levels, charging costs, charging modes, number of users, number of charging infrastructures, charging infrastructure companies (competitive analysis), government programs and policies for charging infrastructure. In addition, the article has explored the literature's definition of UX, the process, and the methodology. The final part of the paper summarizes the factors from the first two parts and presents the current status of B-market (Brand market) factor and user experience.

Hence, emerging questions needs to be addressed, such as what kind of B-market factors need to be seen as determining the standardized development of charging stations? What kind of functionalities and operational journeys enhance the user experience of charging stations? What relationship exists between the charging station brand market and the user experience that can be used to optimize standardized charging stations across regions?

As shown in Fig. 1, this paper aims to explore the B-market factors, investigate user experience and analyze the relationship between them to optimizing cross-regional charging space, which is thought to assist to build brand image while meeting user needs and reduces costs by using standardized charging stations. First, the paper explores background and reviews the existing literature of user experience and B-market factors of EV charging space in The United States and China. Second, the paper explained the methods used for the above questions. Third, the paper presents the data collected by observation, survey and interview. Fourth, the results of the data analyses are presented. Finally, the conclusion, implication and contribution of this study are discussed.

In the literature review, the paper lists the six key factors of brand market about charging infrastructure in China and the United States. And two core component of user

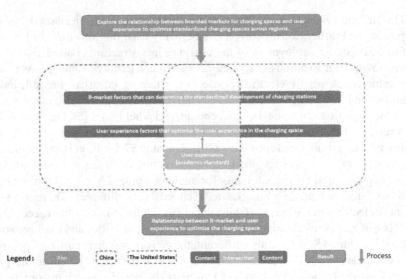

Fig. 1. Rationale of Design (Author-generated)

experience. However, as shown in Fig. 2, it is not clear what kind of relationship exists between brand market factors and user experience before, therefore, the paper utilizes a specific methodology to further explore the relationship between the two.

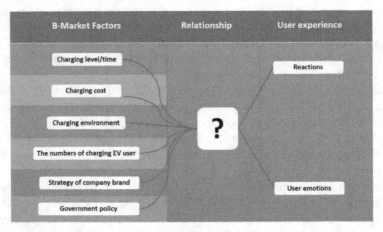

Fig. 2. Relationship between B-market and UX (Author-generated)

2   Methods

As shown in Fig. 3, this section introduced the proposed research objectives, the research methodology used, and the analytical methods used in this paper. This paper took China and The United States, which have an advanced position in the global EV market, as a case to study. In order to further explore the processes and experiences of EV users in the charging space in both the Chinese and American environments, the following section lists the research objectives that need to be accomplished. Finally, the analytical approach of the thesis will be presented.

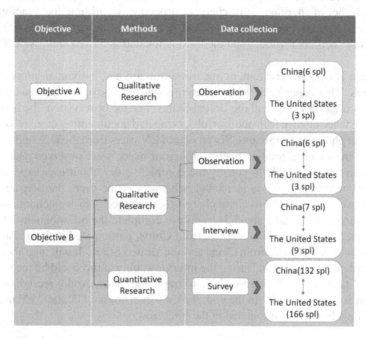

Fig. 3. The process of applying the methodology (Author-generated)

2.1 Research Objectives

A. Exploring the charging market factors in The United States and China.
B. Investigating the user experience factors in The United States and China.

2.2 Research Methods

As shown in Fig. 3, this paper utilized a mix of qualitative and quantitative research methods to collect data. The qualitative research included user interviews, behavioral tracking, and field observations, while the quantitative research included a user survey of EV charging spaces. This project employs observation in response to Objective A.

So, in China, the investigator selected charging spaces in Guangzhou, such as near hospitals, shopping malls, and residential areas. The first location is at Plaza Baiyun International Airport T2 Terminal P6 Parking Lot Station, the second is at No. 70, Zhongshan W. Road, Yuexiu District, Guangzhou City, Guangdong Province, China, the third is at No. 238, Peking Road No. 1 Street, Yuexiu District, Guangzhou City, China, the fourth is at No. 298, Yanjiang Middle Road, Zhuguang Street, Yuexiu District,

Guangzhou City, China, the fifth is at No. 33, Zhongshan S. Road, Yuexiu District, Guangzhou City, China, and the sixth is at No. 219, Zhongshan W. Road, Yuexiu District, Guangzhou City, China.

In the United States, the investigator selected charging stations in Syracuse and New York City. The investigator explored the sites and document the spatial layout, charging facilities, number of charging posts, charging procedures, and functional facilities. The first is located at 6031 Tarbell Rd, Syracuse, NY 13206, the second is located at 107 Essex St, New York, NY 10002, and the third is located at 59 Allen St, New York, NY 10002.

Objective B used observation, online questionnaire and individual interviews with the EV users. This paper selected the charging stations above which located in cities and highway areas in China and the United States. For the observation, the investigator stayed at a distance of 20 m from the user, observing and documenting the user's complete behavior with photos and drawings. Six groups of EV users from the U.S. and six groups of EV users from China, totaling twelve groups of users, were observed and recorded. This can help the paper able to portray the complete story about user experience and explore the common as well as incidental behaviors of the users. Participates will be asked to answer some questions about charging experience, views on charging stations and expectations. It will take about 5–10 min to complete the questionnaire. A total of 298 eV users, 166 from the U.S. and 132 from China, participated in the questionnaire. Participants will be EV users from China and the United States. It will take about 10–20 min to complete the interview. During the interview, only audio could be recorded after participants' permission. Neither will photographs be taken. Audio recording is not a requirement for participation. In the end, 9 eV users from the US and 7 eV users from China, totaling 16 users, participated in the interviews.

2.3 Methods of Analysis

As shown in the Fig. 4 [8], the above research methods presented and analyzed according to the iterative circle. Hence, the paper used content analysis and comparative analysis, respectively. The data collected in objective A and objective B on the Charging Spatial Environment in China and the United States will first be analyzed using content analysis and the results of this analysis will be further analyzed using comparative analysis and content analysis.

3 Result

3.1 Objective A

Observation of Components in the Charging Space

– Understand: The charging station as a whole space is characterized by its spatial layout as well as its composition.
– Observe: As shown in Fig. 5, Among them a. Safety signage was shown, b. EV parking signage was shown, c. Charging operation guide was shown, d. Ceiling in charging space was shown, e. Charge pile was shown, f. Garbage bin was shown, and g. Illumination in charging space was shown, g. shows illumination in charging space.

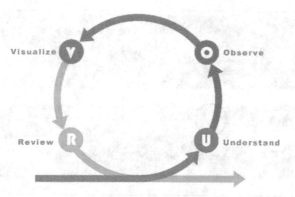

Fig. 4. Iterative circle (Research method)

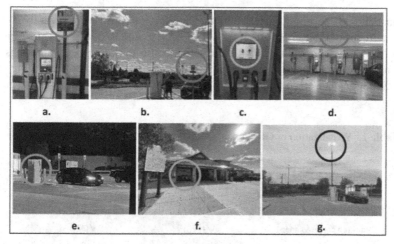

Fig. 5. Factors of The United States Locations from observation

As shown in Fig. 6, there are three outdoor charging stations and three charging stations located in underground parking lots. Among them a. shows the charging post, b. shows the carport inside the charging space, c. shows the fire extinguisher, d. shows the charging operation guide, e. shows the dedicated EV parking sign, f. shows the dedicated parking equipment, g. shows the illumination inside the charging space, h. shows the plus trash can, i. shows the Wi-Fi, j. shows the charging post, k. Shows the carport within the charging space. Specialized parking equipment is shown, g. Charging space illumination is shown, h. Trash cans are shown, i. Wi-Fi is shown, and j. Charging space security signage is shown.

– Visualize: As shown in Table 1, observations indicated that the design of charging spaces in China is more mature and complete than in the United States. The charging areas in China have a large number of safety signs, including fire signs and service phone numbers. Second, the observation of the Chinese charging spaces revealed that there were three outdoor charging stations, two of which had no shelters, compared to

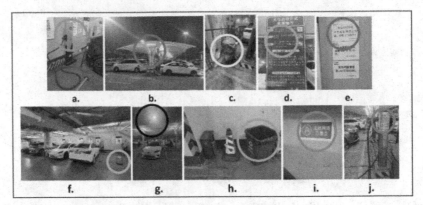

Fig. 6. Factors of China locations from observation

the unsheltered charging spaces where the charging facilities were severely corroded and a number of charging posts were out of service due to damage. Third, charging posts, operating instructions, and charging-specific parking space markings were present at a total of nine charging areas in both locations. Fourth, the charging spaces with garbage cans were significantly cleaner than the charging spaces without garbage cans.

Table 1. Visualization of Components of the charging space as well as the layout

Component	China(6)	The United States(3)
Charging pile	✓(6/6) ○	✓(3/3) ○
Operation Guide	✓(6/6) ○	✓(3/3) ○
Dedicated parking signage	✓(6/6) ○	✓(3/3) ○
Dedicated parking facilities	✓(2/6) ○ Parking space floor locks (auto branded charging stations)	✗
Illumination	✓(4/6) ○	✓(2/3) ○
Fire extinguisher	✓(6/6) ○	✗
Garbage bin	✓(3/6) ○	✓(1/3) ○
Sheds/ceilings	✓(5/6) ○ Two of the three outdoor charging stations have no shelters	✓(2/3) ○ There's an outdoor charging station with no shelter.
Safety sign	✓(6/6) ○	✓(1/3) ○
WIFI	✓(1/6) ○	✗

- Review: Based on the above observations, it suggested that:

• Compared to China, charging spaces in the U.S. lack safety and fire safety features.
• Charging stakes, charging instructions, and charging-space signage as the highest level are necessary components of a charging station.

- The lack of sheltered charging spaces can cause severe wear and tear on the facilities.
- Trash cans in the charging space can keep the charging space clean and tidy.
- Auto brands have different branding strategies for charging space than charging pile brands.

Observation of Charging Process

– Understand: The charging process, as the process that the user must go through in order to use the charging space, becomes an important factor.
– Observe: As shown in Fig. 7, the charging post EV connect at DeWitt Travel Plaza. If you are a veteran EV connect user, the whole process will take no more than three minutes. However, if you are a new EV connect user, you will need a download and registration process, which will take about 10 min.

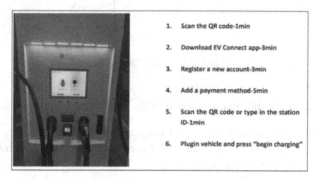

Fig. 7. Operating process in The United States charging space

As shown in Fig. 8, the operation steps within the charging space in China are categorized into two major groups, one is the car-branded charging piles and the other is the charging piles under the charging brand. Car-branded charging piles can be operated through a car-specific app for charging. The other type of charging brand charging pile has more steps, but they are similar. Take the steps within the charging station at Bai Yun Airport as an example, the steps are divided into: fetching the charging gun-1 min, connecting to the car-1 min, scanning or swiping the card-8 min and settling by cell phone or swiping the card-1 min.

Fig. 8. Operating process in China charging space

– Visualize: As shown in Fig. 9, charging spaces can be categorized into two types of users. First-time users and non-first-time users. Due to the long time of 5–10 min to download the software and register, it takes 10–15 min to complete the whole operation process. Second, depending on the charging brand, charging spaces branded by automobile companies can take a shorter time to complete the charging process as they are dealing with their own automobile users, but charging stations branded by charging companies are dealing with a more sophisticated user base.

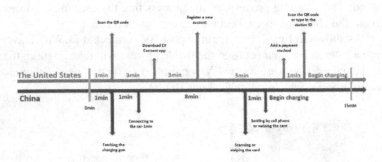

Fig. 9. Operation process for The United States and China

– Review: Based on the information shown in the above observations, it suggested that:

- New users need a longer and longer charging operation process
- Most car brands have charging stations for their own brand of charging users only, but with a shorter operation process.

3.2 Objective B

Observation of User Behavior

– Understand: The user experience is the most central factor to consider when it comes to how users interact with products and systems during their use. In order to effectively explore the relationship between user experience and brand factors, this section explores the complete behavior of users in the charging space.
– Observe: As shown in Fig. 10, the paper began with observations of users within the charging station. The observation location was in the charging space chosen for Objective A. The researcher maintained a distance of 20 m above the user to observe and record the user. The purpose was to explore the users' completed behaviors within the charging station and their interactions with the charging station.

As shown in Fig. 11, in observing charging stations in the China region, observers found user behaviors that were both the same and different from those in the U.S.: chatting, smoking, talking on the phone, eating, observing charging piles, sleeping inside the car, playing on the phone, waiting inside the car, waiting outside the car, and operating the charging.

Fig. 10. User behaviors in The United States charging space

Fig. 11. User behaviors in China charging space

- Visualize: As shown in the Fig. 12, the paper expresses the behaviors of Chinese and U.S. EV users in the charging space recorded by observation as a text map. Observing the charging pile, performing charging operations, sitting inside the car and waiting, and playing with the cell phone are the high-density behaviors in the behavioral interactions of users in both countries. Besides, eating, waiting outside the car, and sleeping inside the car are higher density behaviors in the intersection. Also, smoking behavior is very frequent in Chinese charging spaces. In additional, when users reacted with additional facilities such as eating, shopping and use the toilet near the charging space, the probability of these facilities being used by the charging users is very high.
- Review: Based on the information from the above observations, it suggested that:

- Most users will be more inclined to spend their charging waiting time in a recreational manner.
- Facilities attached to or in the vicinity of the charging space have a very high probability of being used by charging users.
- Geo-culture affects user behavior in the charging space to some extent.

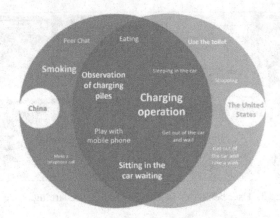

Fig. 12. Word Map-Behavior of EV user in charging space

Interview of the Numbers of EV Charging User. QUESTION: Have you ever had a really bad charging experience? Can you describe it?

When faced with this question, two out of seven Chinese respondents mentioned the term **number of users**. In the United States, four out of nine respondents mentioned the term number of users. In summary, six out of 16 users mentioned the term number of users. More than two-thirds of users provided additional explanations for their belief that too many charging users can lead to a lack of charging facilities and congestion, and some mentioned that the reason for failed charging experiences was due to the fact that the limited number of charging stations they found when they arrived at the charging space were all in use. However, at the same time, a user from the United States made the exact opposite point, arguing that the increased number of charging users would promote charging infrastructure and thus improve the user experience.

Interview of Government Policy. QUESTION: What kind of factors do you think affect the charging infrastructure and your experience with it?

When faced with this question, three out of seven Chinese respondents mentioned the term government policy. In the United States, six out of nine respondents mentioned the term government policy. In summary, nine out of 16 users mentioned the term. More than half the number of users mentioned government policies. And the message that emerges is that government policy will largely determine infrastructure development.

Interview of Strategy of Company Brand. QUESTION: How has the lack of standardization of charging space affected you?

Three out of seven Chinese users of car-branded charging stations mentioned the low cost of car-branded charging stations but the low number of charging stations in this question. Four-sevenths of Chinese customers use charging stations that are branded, and more than half of them cite poor quality environments and the unavailability of car-branded charging stations. Five out of nine U.S. respondents use car-branded charging stations, and more than half of them cite that there are well-located charging spaces that are not available to them or that cost more than the charging stations developed by their own car brand.

Questionnaire of Frequency Analysis of Demographic Variables. According to the following Table 2, the numerical characteristics of the demographic variables can be seen, reflecting the distribution of the respondents of this Chinese American questionnaire. The mean value represents the concentration trend and the standard deviation represents the fluctuation.

Table 2. Frequency Analysis of Demographic Variables in Chinese and U.S. Surveys

Variant	Options	Frequency (USA)	Frequency (China)	Percentage (USA)	Percentage (China)	Average (USA)	Average (China)	Standard deviation (USA)	Standard deviation (China)
Sex	male	125	110	75.30%	83.30%	1.25	1.17	0.433	0.37
	female	41	22	24.70%	16.70%				
Tram miles	300-400miles	36	15	21.70%	11.40%	2.04	2.43	0.773	0.91
	400-500miles	97	68	58.40%	51.50%				
	500-600miles	23	26	13.90%	19.70%				
	>600miles	10	23	6.00%	17.40%				
Home charging post	yes	117	84	70.50%	63.60%	1.3	2.43	0.458	0.48
	no	49	48	29.50%	36.40%				

According to the results of the questionnaire, it can be seen that the distribution basically meets the requirements of the survey. The results of the gender analysis of the United States are: 75.30% male and 24.70% female; the results of the gender analysis of China are: 83.3% male and 16.7% female. It can be concluded that the results of this survey are biased in favor of China as well as the United States of America's male willingness.

Questionnaire of Difference-in-Differences Test. According to the results of the independent samples T-test for China-US in the Table 3, it can be seen that there is a difference in the intention of each question in terms of gender, when the test of significance of the difference in terms of gender is less than 0.05, we believe that there is a difference in the intention of different genders in this question, when the test of significance of the difference in terms of gender is greater than 0.05, there is no difference in the intention of different genders in this question or there is less difference in intention.

Questionnaire of Impact of B-Market Factors on User Experience. As shown in the following Table 4, we can analyze and conclude which market branding factors in China US will have an impact on user experience. When the mean is closer to 1, the brand factor has a greater impact on user experience. When the average value is closer to 3, the brand factor has less influence on the user. So, we can conclude that the charging speed, the cost of use, the company's branding decisions and the layout of the new energy charging infrastructure will have a direct impact on the user experience. The number of users of new energy infrastructure and national policies have an indirect effect on user experience in China and the US.

Table 3. Analysis of Gender Differences on Various Issues in the United States of China

Analysis of gender differences on various issues	Sex	T(USA)	T(China)	Significant (USA)	Significant (China)
Are you now satisfied with the charging speed of the new energy charging infrastructure?	male	-1.228	1.237	0.221	0.218
	female				
Which of the following charging levels do you use the most??	male	2.472	0.232	0.015	0.817
	female				
What is your average time for a single charge?	male	-0.256	-0.209	0.798	0.835
	female				
Do you agree that reduced charging times would improve your experience with charging facilities?	male	-0.033	-1.994	0.974	0.056
	female				
Do you think the cost of using charging infrastructure can affect your charging experience?	male	0.205	1.78	0.838	0.083
	female				
Are you now satisfied with the cost of new energy charging infrastructure?	male	0.029	-0.89	0.977	0.375
	female				
Do you agree that a reduction in the cost of charging would increase your experience with charging facilities?	male	-0.571	2.634	0.569	0.012
	female				
Do you think the number of users of charging infrastructure can influence your charging experience?	male	-0.975	-0.64	0.331	0.523
	female				
Are you now satisfied with the number of users of the charging infrastructure?	male	-0.349	0	0.727	1
	female				
Do you agree that a decrease in the number of users of the charging infrastructure would increase your experience with the charging facility?	male	-1.434	2.657	0.153	0.011
	female				
Do you think company branding decisions for charging foundations can affect your charging experience?	male	0.694	-1.108	0.489	0.27
	female				
Are you currently satisfied with your company branding decisions for charging infrastructure?	male	0.707	-1.557	0.481	0.122
	female				
Do you agree that optimizing the branding decisions of charging infrastructure companies will increase your experience with charging facilities?	male	0.082	0.132	0.935	0.895
	female				
Do you think national policies on charging infrastructure can influence your charging experience?	male	0.233	-0.434	0.816	0.665
	female				
Are you now satisfied with the national policy on charging infrastructure?	male	0.181	-0.839	0.857	0.403
	female				
Do you agree that the optimization of national policies for charging infrastructure would increase your experience with charging facilities?	male	-1.282	0.151	0.202	0.88
	female				
Do you think the layout of charging infrastructure can affect your charging experience?	male	-0.434	0.677	0.665	0.5
	female				
Are you now satisfied with the layout of the charging infrastructure?	male	0.207	-0.356	0.837	0.722
	female				
Do you agree that standardized construction of charging spaces will go a long way towards enhancing the user's charging experience?	male	0.406	-0.463	0.685	0.644
	female				

Table 4. The Impact of B-market Factors on User Experience in the US Market in China.

The Impact of B-market Factors on User Experience				
Question	Average (USA)	Average (China)	Standard deviation (USA)	Standard deviation (China)
Do you think the charging speed of charging infrastructure can affect your charging experience?	1.13	1.08	0.34	0.266
Do you think the cost of using charging infrastructure can affect your charging experience?	1.41	1.42	0.697	0.711
Do you think the number of users of charging infrastructure can influence your charging experience?	2.27	1.8	0.533	0.486
Do you think company branding decisions for charging foundations can influence your charging experience?	1.56	1.46	0.51	0.598
Do you think national policies on charging infrastructure can affect your charging experience?	1.55	2.05	0.556	0.537
Do you think the layout of charging infrastructure can affect your charging experience?	1.29	1.14	0.7	0.344

4 Discussion

4.1 Network of Relationship

As shown in the Fig. 13, the fragmented views can be combined and summarized to analyze the relationship between B-market factors and user experience. By integrating these fragmented views, the relationship between B-market factors and user experience can be analyzed. In the following section, six B-market factors are discussed and analyzed.

Relationship Between Charging Level Factor and User Experience. Charging levels mean different charging times for users. The results of the observation in Objective A (Section 4.1.1.1) showed that new users require longer charging operation time. The observation in Objective B (Section 4.1.1.1) shows that most users will be more inclined to spend their charging waiting time in a recreational manner. The results of questionnaire in Objective B (Section 4.2.2.3) showed that the charging equipment of the charging infrastructure will have a direct impact on the user experience. Finally, based on the results of the observations in Objective A, Objective B and the questionnaire in Objective B, they can be connected to:

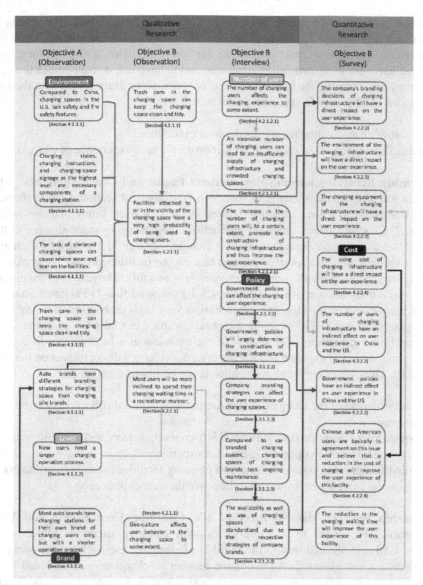

Fig. 13. B-market factors & User experience in the field of The United Stated and China (author generated)

- Charging time will have a direct impact on the charging user experience.
- Longer charging time will degrade the user experience.
- When faced with charging waiting time, users are more likely to choose other behaviors and amenities to try to improve their experience.
- Charging levels that are not standardized charging stations will lead to more frequent re-registration of the user's operation.

Relationship Between Charging Cost Factor and User Experience. The results of the objective B (Section 4.2.2.4) questionnaire viewed that 1) The using cost of charging infrastructure will have a direct impact on the user experience, and 2) Chinese and American users are in agreement on this issue and believe that a reduction in the cost of charging will improve the user experience of this facility. Hence, based on the two views drawn in Objective B, it can be linked together to:

- The cost of charging directly affects the user experience.
- A reduction in the cost of charging will improve the user experience of charging.

Relationship Between Charging Environment Factor and User Experience. The results of the observation of charging spaces in Objective A (Section 4.1.1.1) showed that 1) Compared to China, charging spaces in the U.S. lack safety and fire safety features, 2) Charging stakes, charging instructions, and charging-space signage as the highest level are necessary components of a charging station, 3) The lack of sheltered charging spaces can cause severe wear and tear on the facilities and 4) Trash cans in the charging space can keep the charging space clean and tidy. The results of the charge space observations in objective B (Section 4.1.1.1) showed that 1) Facilities attached to or in the vicinity of the charging space have a very high probability of being used by charging users and 2) Trash cans in the charging space can keep the charging space clean and tidy. Furthermore, The results of the questionnaire in Objective B showed that the environment of the charging infrastructure will have a direct impact on the user experience. Thus, based on the above results, it can be linked together to:

- The environment of the charging infrastructure will have a direct impact on the user experience.
- Adequate safety facilities, detailed spatial information, shelters, and cleaning facilities are important factors in optimizing the user experience.
- Detailed spatial information, shelters and cleaning facilities are important factors to optimize the charging environment to improve the user experience.

Relationship Between the Numbers of EV Charging User Factor and User Experience. The results of the Interviews with charging users for Objective B (Section 4.2.1.2.1) showed that 1) the number of charging users affects the charging experience to some extent, 2) An excessive number of charging users can lead to an insufficient supply of charging infrastructure and crowded charging spaces and 3) The increase in the number of charging users will, to a certain extent, promote the construction of charging infrastructure and thus improve the user experience. The results of the questionnaire for Objective B (Section 4.2.2.3) showed that the number of users of charging infrastructure have an indirect effect on user experience in China and the US. Therefore, based on the above points, it can be linked together to:

- The number of charging users will indirectly affect user experience.
- Excessive users can lead to congestion in the charging space and thus reduce the user experience.

- An increase in the number of users will also promote the development of charging infrastructure and improve the user experience.
- The number of charging users is a double-edged sword for user experience.

Relationship Between the Strategy of Company Brand Factor and User Experience. The results of the Observation of charging spaces in Objective A (Section 4.1.1.1) showed that 1) Most auto brands have charging stations for their own brand of charging users only, but with a shorter operation process and 2) Auto brands have different branding strategies for charging space than charging pile brands. The results of the questionnaire for Objective B (Section 4.2.2.4) showed that 1) Company branding strategies can directly affect the user experience of charging spaces, 2) Compared to auto branded charging spaces, charging spaces of charging brands lack ongoing maintenance and 3) The availability as well as use of charging spaces is not standardized due to the respective strategies of company brands. As such, based on the above points, it can be linked together to:

- Company branding decisions can directly affect user experience.
- Charging space of auto brands and charging brands are inconsistent due to differences in their respective branding strategies thus reducing the user experience.
- The charging brand's follow-up maintenance and cleaning of the charging space is an important factor that can improve the user experience.

Relationship Between the Government Policy Factor and User Experience. The results of the interview for Objective B (Section 4.2.1.2.1) showed that 1) Government policies can affect the charging user experience and 2) Government policies will largely determine the construction of charging infrastructure. The results of the questionnaire for Objective B (Section 4.2.2.4) showed that Government policies have an indirect effect on user experience in China and the US. Finally, based on the above points, it can be linked together to:

- Although government policy can indirectly affect user experience.
- Government policy can largely determine the construction of charging infrastructure.

4.2 Relationship Between B-Market Factors and User Experience

As shown in the Fig. 14, the paper presented six B-market factors and two user experience factors. The relationship between B-Market factors and user experience factors can be categorized into direct and indirect impact which direct impact have charging level, charging environment and charging cost, and indirect impact have the number of charging EV user, strategy of company brand and government policy. In additional, direct impact and indirect impact have both positively proportional and inversely proportional. User experience can be categorized into Reaction factor and Emotion factors.

Direct Impact. As shown in the Fig. 14, the brand market factors of charging level, charging cost, and charging environment have a direct impact on the user experience.

- Charge level

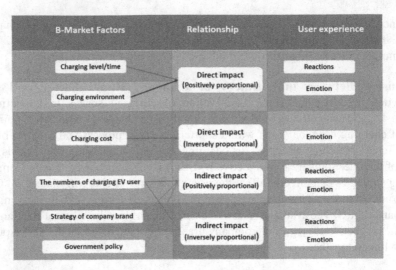

Fig. 14. Relationship between B-market factors and UX (Author-generated)

- Reaction: Charge level has a direct impact on user reaction, and this impact is positively proportional, meaning that when the charge level is improved, the user reaction will be improved.
- Emotion: Charge level has a direct impact on user reaction, and this impact is positively proportional, meaning that when the charge level is improved, the user's emotion will be improved.

– Charging cost

- **Reaction:** The cost of charging will have no impact on user reaction.
- **Emotion:** Charging cost will have a direct impact on user reaction, this impact is inversely proportional, meaning that when charging cost increases, user emotion reduces.

– Charging environment

- **Reaction:** The charging environment will have a direct impact on the user's reaction, and this impact is positively proportional, meaning that when the charging environment is optimized, the user's reaction will be enhanced.
- **Emotion:** The charging environment will have a direct impact on the user's reaction, and this impact is positively proportional, meaning that when the charging environment is optimized, the user's emotion will be enhanced.

Indirect Impact. As shown in the Fig. 14, the factors of the number of charging users, the strategy of the company brand, and the government policy have an indirect impact on the user experience.

– The number of charging users

The factor of the number of charging users is the only one in the B-market factor that has a double-edged character. Its impact on the user experience is not absolute and depends on the different needs of the user.

When users are more in need of their own charging environment as well as resources:

- Reaction: The number of charging users has an indirect impact on user reaction, which is inversely proportional, meaning that when the number of charging users increases, user reaction reduces.
- Emotion: The number of charging users has an indirect impact on user reaction, and this impact is inversely proportional, meaning that when the number of charging users increases, user emotion reduces.

When users are more in need of overall optimization of all charging environments:

- Reaction: The number of charging users has no impact on user reaction.
- Emotion: The number of charging users has an indirect impact on user reaction, and this impact is positively proportional, meaning that when the number of charging users is increased, user emotion will be enhanced.

– Strategy of the company brand

- Reaction: The strategy of the company brand has an indirect impact on user reaction, and this impact is positively proportional, meaning that when the strategy of the company's brand is improved, user reaction will be improved.
- Emotion: The company brand strategy has an indirect impact on user reaction, which is positively proportional, meaning that when the company's branding strategy is improved, the user's emotion will be enhanced.

– Government policy

- Reaction: Government policy has an indirect impact on user reaction, and this impact is positively proportional, meaning that when government policy is improved, user reaction will be improved.
- Emotion: Government policies have an indirect impact on user reactions, and this impact is positively proportional, meaning that when government policies are improved, user emotions will be enhanced.

5 Conclusion

This paper conducts a case study on the relationship between B-market factors of charging space and user experience in the United States and China, which has explored the relationship between B-market of charging space and user experience. The paper presents the iterative methodology used to accomplish the qualitative and quantitative research.

The result suggested that: The brand market factors of charging level, charging cost, and charging environment have a direct impact on the user experience. The factors of the number of charging users, the strategy of the company brand, and the government policy have an indirect impact on the user experience. Among them charging level, charging environment, strategy of the company brand and government policy have positive proportional impact on user experience.

In theoretical implications aspect, the conclusion of the research in this paper can help to fill the academic map on the relationship between brand marketing factors and user experience in charging space. In realistic meaning aspect, the conclusion of this paper can help establish standardized charging spaces or optimize charging spaces in more than just China and the United States. At the same time, the results of this paper can help auto brands and charging brand companies to optimize their strategies and help governments to optimize their policies about charging space. In the methodological value aspect, this research methodology allows for a targeted study of the market and user experience of charging space brands in different regions and backgrounds.

This paper may also have certain limitations in the research process: First, the literature review part, this paper may not be comprehensive enough to review the literature profoundly leading to the search for B-market factors is not comprehensive enough. The second is that this paper needs to adopt a research method that combines quantitative and qualitative research, so there may be some subjective content in the quantitative research, and there may be the limitation of insufficient samples in the qualitative research. In order to solve the deficiencies of the research in this paper, the following future development directions are suggested: First, to conduct more profound exploration and discovery of the literature review part to ensure that the B-market factor and the user experience factor are comprehensively explored and discovered. Second, expand the sample capacity, precise the research object of the sample, and increase the object variables, so as to conduct a more in-depth and comprehensive user research. At the same time, try to ensure the objectivity of the collected data, so that the conclusion is closer to the objective facts.

Acknowledgments. The authors have no competing interests to declare that are relevant to the content of this article. Appreciate for Professor Liu Zhen for the guidance. He provided the author with academic guidance, inspiration for ideas, research resources, and other assistance. Appreciate for the participants of the questionnaire and interviews. They provided the author with important data and literature resources needed for the research.

References

1. U.S. Department of Energy, "TransAtlas". https://afdc.energy.gov/transatlas/#/?fuel=ELEC. Retrieved 20 Oct 2023
2. Ministry of Public Security of the People's Republic of China. In the first half of 2023, the number of motor vehicles nationwide reached 426 million, and the number of drivers reached 513 million, and the number of new energy vehicles reached 16.2 million, 8 July 2023. https://app.mps.gov.cn/gdnps/pc/content.jsp?id=9106397. Retrieved 20 Oct 2023
3. IEA. Global EV Outlook 2023, IEA, Paris (2023). https://www.iea.org/reports/global-ev-outlook-2023. Retrieved 20 October 2023

4. Central People's Government of the People's Republic of China. Recent Series of New Energy Vehicle Policies Issued by the State Council, 25 June 2023. https://www.gov.cn/zhengce/202 306/content_6888250.htm. Retrieved 20 Oct 2023

5. General Office of the State Council. Guiding Opinions of the General Office of the State Council on Further Building a High-Quality Charging Infrastructure System, 19 June 2023. https://www.gov.cn/zhengce/zhengceku/202306/content_6887168.htm?eqid=ec2 704d7000051c5000000066492a01c. Retrieved 20 Oct 2023

6. The White House. Biden-Harris Administration Proposes New Standards for National Electric Vehicle Charging Network, 9 June 2022. https://www.whitehouse.gov/briefing-room/statem ents-releases/2022/06/09/fact-sheet-biden-harris-administration-proposes-new-standards-for-national-electric-vehicle-charging-network/. Retrieved 20 Oct 2023

7. Xing, X.: Comparison of Urban Development and Management Model of USA and China, July 2018. https://www.researchgate.net/publication/274567239_Reflections_on_the_simila rities_and_differences_between_Chinese_and_US_cities. Retrieved 20 Oct 2023

8. Milton, A., Rodgers, P.: Research methods for product design. Hachette UK (2023). https://www.laurenceking.com/products/research-methods-for-product-design

Visual or Auditory First? The Modality Shift Effect in Two-Stage Takeover Warning

Yang Wang[1], Chu Zhou[1(✉)], Xuesong Wang[2,3], and Shuo Yang[2,3]

[1] Department of Psychology, Fudan University, Shanghai 200433, China
zhouchu@fudan.edu.cn
[2] School of Transportation Engineering, Tongji University, Shanghai 201804, China
[3] Key Laboratory of Road and Traffic Engineering, Ministry of Education, Tongji University, Shanghai 201804, China

Abstract. Two-stage warning systems play a crucial role in ensuring safe and stable takeovers in conditional automated driving when drivers are engaged in non-driving-related tasks (NDRT). This study aims to investigate the effectiveness of visual and auditory warning modalities, particularly when NDRT have overlapping modality resources with the first-stage takeover warning. Two simulated driving experiments were conducted in a driving simulator, and we discovered that visual warnings were significantly more affected by the NDRT modality overlap than auditory warnings. The findings highlighted that modality overlap between takeover warnings and NDRT can negatively affect takeover stability. These results also indicate that it is imperative to take into account the modality shift effect and its first-stage modality while designing two-stage warning systems. Our results suggest that using auditory warnings in the first stage leads to a more stable takeover performance than visual warnings. We found that the modality of the initial takeover warning significantly influences drivers' attention allocation and alertness. These insights provide empirical support for the industrial design of two-stage takeover warning systems, paving the way for more diversified and effective automobile intelligent cockpit designs.

Keywords: Two-stage takeover warning · multisensory integration · modality shift effect

1 Introduction

In conditional automated driving (CAD, SAE Level 3), drivers are allowed to engage in non-driving related tasks (NDRT) that require a higher level of immersion and are unrelated to the driving task [6]. The distracting effect of NDRT not only diminishes the driver's perception of the surrounding environment, increasing the difficulty of making accurate responses during emergency takeovers, but also potentially elevates the risk of accidents [7]. The vehicle can perform all driving operations and monitor the surrounding environment, but the driver must be prepared to take over the vehicle when the request is issued.

Using two-stage takeover warning systems can promote a safer and more stable process, which is essential for a seamless driving user experience [8]. The first stage

A. Marcus et al. (Eds.): HCII 2024, LNCS 14713, pp. 238–248, 2024.
https://doi.org/10.1007/978-3-031-61353-1_16

of warning is an alert, which involves issuing a sound or an icon to regain drivers' attention to the road. The second stage is the takeover request (TOR), which requires an immediate takeover. The effectiveness of this alert is crucial, as it primes drivers for the impending need to take over control without necessitating immediate action. This nuanced warning strategy is vital for ensuring a smooth transition from NDRT back to driving focus, thereby enhancing overall takeover readiness.

The first-stage alert plays a pivotal role in re-engaging the driver's focus towards the driving task, particularly when they are immersed in NDRT. The modality of alerts might affect the speed of attention back into the loop [1]. Moreover, the NDRT modality affects drivers' ability to prepare for the takeover and degrades takeover performance [10], especially when NDRT has overlapping modalities with driving operations according to the multiple resource theory [14]. When modality demands overlap visual-manual tasks (such as texting), takeover performance decreases the most, while auditory tasks show similar performance to no-task conditions [13]. This suggests that the visual modality significantly impacts takeover performance in driving situations due to driving associated with high visual demands [2]. Furthermore, a shorter takeover reaction time (RT) is associated with auditory warning compared to visual warning [15]. However, how first-stage alert and NDRT modalities interact in takeover performance remains underexplored, especially when the NDRT has overlapping modality resources with the first-stage takeover alert.

Modality shift theory demonstrated that stimulus-response times are faster when the successive stimuli are consistent in modality compared to when they are not [9]. These discrepancies in reaction speed arise from differences in the allocation of attentional resources and levels of alertness due to the modality of the preceding stimulus. Therefore, it is essential to categorize the preceding stimulus modality before conducting behavioral analysis. Notably, reaction times are significantly longer when the pre-stimulus modality is visual than when it is auditory or audiovisual [11]. In the takeover process in automated driving, the warning-takeover actions parallel the stimulus-response pattern in simple reaction tasks. The theoretical and applied research trends may be aligned, but we still cannot confirm it. Based on the modality shift theory, this study aims to investigate the impact of different first-stage warning modalities on takeover performance, particularly when NDRT had overlapping modality resources with the alert in the two-stage takeover warning.

2   Experiment 1

2.1   Participants

A total of 24 participants (14 females, 10 males), divided into two groups, took part in this study. Their ages ranged from 19 to 27 years ($M=21.50$ years, $SD=2.27$ years). All participants had driving licenses in the People's Republic of China, and their average annual mileage was 2,375 km.

2.2   Experimental Design

Alert Type. Each participant experienced both abstract and speech alerts in the experiment. The alerts were issued four times per driving session, and participants had to drive two sessions. The issue sequence of two alerts was balanced across two driving sessions.

The time budget of the alert is 7 s, and the TOR is 5 s [3]. The abstract alert sound in the first stage was a "ding-dong" sound obtained from a domestic sound platform that allows open downloads. The content of the first-stage auditory alert was "Please pay attention", and the second-stage auditory TOR was "Please takeover the vehicle". The speech rate was 1.5 times faster than in the first stage to increase the sense of urgency and prompt the driver to take action to control the vehicle. Each alert has a duration of 1 s, and the total warning duration is 3 s. All auditory warnings were created using Baidu AI's text-to-speech synthesis feature, post-edited, and assembled using Adobe Audition CC 2021.

Dependent Variables and Measure. The dependent variables were divided into takeover performance and subjective assessment. Takeover performance included takeover speed and quality. The subjective assessment included task load measured by NASA-TLX and warning acceptance measured by usefulness and satisfaction questionnaire. NASA-TLX consisted of 6 items on a 10-point scale [5]. The usefulness and satisfaction questionnaire consisted of 9 items on a 5-point scale [12]. All the indicators are listed in Table 1.

Table 1. Dependent variables and indicators

Dependent variables	Dimensions	Indicator
Takeover Performance	Speed Quality	Takeover Time Speed Maximum deceleration Maximum lateral acceleration Lateral lane deviation Steering wheel angle
Subjective Assessment	Task Load Acceptance	NASA-TLX usefulness satisfaction

Procedures

2.3   Apparatus and Materials

The study was conducted in a Logitech G29 driving simulator consisting of a steering wheel, gas pedal, and brake pedal. A desktop computer provided the front view with an Intel Core i9-10900K processor and an NVIDIA Geforce RTX 2080Ti graphics card. The screen size is 23.8 in., and the resolution is 1920 × 1080. Engine and takeover warnings were played through computer headphones. The software SCANeR™ Studio from AV Simulation simulated the driving environment and recorded relevant driving variables. A conditionally automated driving system could take over longitudinal control (i.e., driving at a constant speed of 100 km/h) and lateral control (i.e., operating in the lane center) tasks.

The experimental setup includes the design of the road layout and the driving scenarios. The road layout for the experiment is designed as a circular highway with a total length of 20 km and a lane width of 3.5 m. The experimental driving scenario is a six-lane dual carriageway (three lanes in each direction). Random placements of houses and trees were made to enhance the realism of the scenario. The traffic flow was controlled at fewer than five vehicles per kilometer to prevent interference with the driver's vehicle takeover behavior and to ensure the quality of the takeover [4].

The vehicle maintains a speed of 100 km/h during autonomous driving. A real-time speedometer and tachometer are placed in the top right corner of the scene, and a digital speed head-up display is set at the bottom center of the screen to enhance the realism of the simulated driving experience (see Fig. 1). To reduce the learning effect from the driver's repeated takeovers, four different driving takeover scenarios are set up on the four straight segments of the road: a rear-end collision, lane closure, vehicle breakdown, and construction barriers. In all four driving takeover scenarios, the driver must take over the vehicle and change lanes to avoid obstacles.

Fig. 1. Experimental Scenario

2.4 Results

Takeover Performance. The results of the experiment were processed using the Python programming language. The data was cleaned, labeled, and sliced to facilitate analysis (see Table 2).

Table 2. Takeover Performance

	Abstract	Speech
Takeover Time (s)	2.75±1.04	2.78±1.05
Maximum deceleration (m/s2)	1.76±1.19	1.70±1.07
Break Padel (daN)	2.49±3.72	2.97±4.97
Maximum lateral acceleration (m/s2)	2.40±0.91	2.49±0.90
steering wheel angle (°)	18.35±7.76	18.53±6.65

Subjective Evaluation. A *t*-test was used for pairwise comparison of the elements of the auditory alerts (i.e., abstract, verbal). The *t*-test showed no significant difference between the two elements of the auditory alerts.

3   Experiment 2

3.1   Participants

A total of 21 participants (10 females, 11 males), divided into two groups, participated in this study. Their ages ranged from 19 to 30 years (M=22.86 years, SD = 3.20 years). All participants had driving licenses in the People's Republic of China, and their average annual mileage was 2,809 km.

3.2   Experimental Design

Takeover Warning. A 2 × 2 mixed design was conducted in this experiment. The first independent variable is the alert modality; each participant experienced visual and auditory alerts in the experiment. The second independent variable is NDRT modality overlap, and participants are assigned to only one condition where the alert's modality either overlapped with or separated from NDRT sensory demands. The alerts were issued four times per driving session, and participants had to drive two sessions. The visual alert was a red takeover icon performed in the center of the screen. The auditory alert used the speech alert in Experiment 1.

3.3   Results

Takeover Performance. The takeover performance indicators were tested for significance using mixed two-way variance analysis (ANOVA), with the NDRT modality overlap as a between-subjects factor and the first-stage warning modality as a within-subject factor.

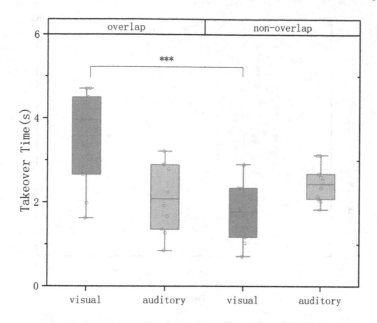

Fig. 2. Takeover Time

Takeover Reaction Time. The results showed no significant differences between the alert modalities, $F(1, 18) = 4.11$, $p = 0.058$, $\eta_p^2 = 0.19$. There was a significant difference between modality overlap and non-overlap, $F(1, 18) = 4.98$, $p < 0.05$, $\eta_p^2 = 0.21$. The NDRT modality overlapped the alert modality, making the takeover reaction times significantly higher than the NDRT modality non-overlapping. The interaction between alert modalities and NDRT modality overlap was significant, $F(1, 18) = 22.81$, $p < 0.001$, $\eta_p^2 = 0.56$ (See Fig. 2). The takeover reaction times were significantly higher when overlapping the visual alert modality with the NDRT modality ($p < 0.001$). However, there were no significant differences when using the auditory alert modality ($p = 0.263$).

Maximum Deceleration. The results showed no significant differences between the alert modalities, $F(1, 18) = 0.77$, $p = 0.39$, $\eta_p^2 = 0.05$. There was a significant difference between modality overlap and non-overlap, $F(1, 18) = 6.20$, $p < 0.05$, $\eta_p^2 = 0.28$ (see Fig. 3). The NDRT modality overlapped the alert modality, making the maximum deceleration significantly higher than the NDRT modality non-overlapping. The interaction between alert modalities and NDRT modality overlap was not significant, $F(1, 18) = 0.039$, $p = 0.85$, $\eta_p^2 = 0.002$.

Maximum Lateral Acceleration. The results showed no significant differences between the alert modalities, $F(1, 18) = 1.33$, $p = 0.26$, $\eta_p^2 = 0.069$. There was no significant difference between modality overlap and non-overlap, $F(1, 18) = 0.0002$, $p = 0.99$, $\eta_p^2 = 0.0001$. The interaction between alert modalities and NDRT modality overlap was significant, $F(1, 18) = 22.81$, $p < 0.05$, $\eta_p^2 = 0.56$ (Fig. 4). When the NDRT modality

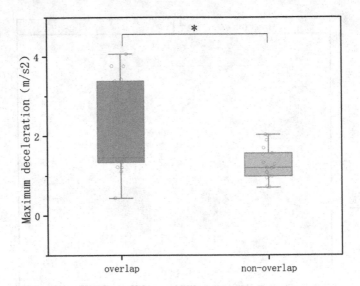

Fig. 3. Takeover Time

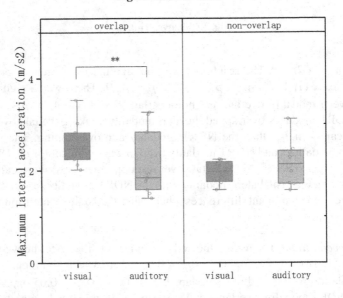

Fig. 4. Maximum lateral acceleration

overlapped the alert modality, the maximum lateral acceleration of visual alerts was significantly higher than that of auditory alerts ($p < 0.05$). However, no significant differences existed when the NDRT non-overlapped the alert modality ($p = 0.331$).

Driving Trajectory. Data on lane deviation and lane positions for 15 s post-takeover warning were selected and converted for analysis. A trajectory map illustrated the driver's post-warning vehicle control (Fig. 5). The lane deviation is set to start at 0 m, with higher values indicating greater distance from the center lane.

These results suggested that visual and auditory alerts had different impacts on the driver's trajectory when NDRT overlapped the alert modality. When the visual modality overlapped, it affected the takeover reaction time for lane change avoidance and the stability of the post-takeover trajectory. However, when the auditory modality overlapped, it only affected the takeover reaction time. Thus, using the auditory alert was more likely to maintain stability in the driver's post-takeover vehicle control in a two-stage warning system.

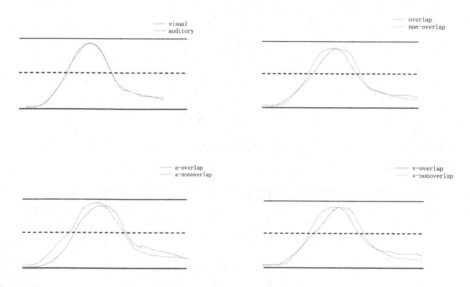

Fig. 5. Driving Trajectory

Subjective Evaluation

NASA-TLX. The results showed no significant differences between alert modality and modality overlap, $F(1, 18) = 0.06$, $p = 0.80$, $\eta_p^2 = 0.002$ (Fig. 6).

Acceptance. The results showed no significant differences between alert modality and modality overlap, $F(1, 18) = 3.43$, $p = 0.08$, $\eta_p^2 = 0.1$ (Fig. 7).

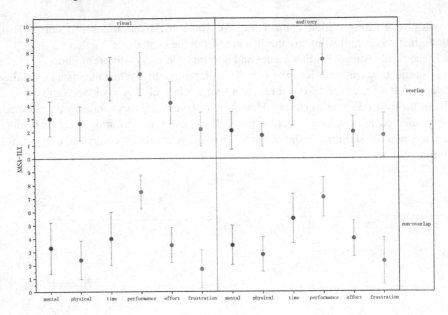

Fig. 6. NASA-TLX

satisfaction

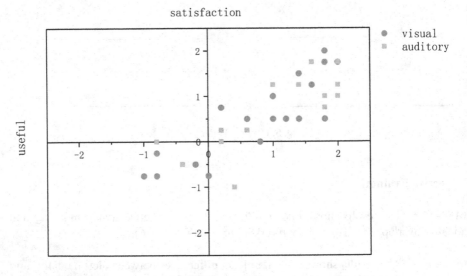

Fig. 7. Acceptance

4   Discussion

This study conducted two experiments to investigate the design of two-stage takeover warnings in autonomous driving scenarios. It explored the modality of the first-stage alerts and the interaction mechanisms with NDRT, examining the application of multi-sensory integration research in autonomous driving takeover.

The results showed that the two elements of auditory warning have advantages in different takeover performance indicators. The NDRT modality overlap significantly affected visual warnings more than auditory warnings. This conclusion aligned with the findings of Wandtner et al. that visual NDRT had a significant impact on drivers' takeover performance [13]. Moreover, the results indicated that when the alerts modality overlapped with the NDRT modality, it prolonged the time required for drivers to shift their attention from NDRT back to the road.

The overlap of drivers' modality by NDRT would inevitably lead to a decline in takeover stability. In terms of lateral control, the takeover stability of visual warning was significantly worse than that of auditory warning when NDRT overlapped the first-stage warning modality. In terms of longitudinal control, regardless of whether the visual or auditory warnings, the takeover stability was significantly worse when the NDRT modality overlapped the first-stage warning modality. This observation extended Wickens' Multiple Resource Theory from manual to automated driving. This conclusion further emphasized the significance of research on warning modality in autonomous driving scenarios. Moreover, it is imperative to take into account the modality shift effect and its first-stage modality while designing two-stage warning systems.

In conclusion, auditory modality as the first-stage alert modality could obtain a more stable takeover performance than visual warning in two-stage takeover warning systems. Different auditory alerts could be used according to the application scenario. Alert modalities would influence the drivers' attention allocation and alertness level. Therefore, designers could develop an integrated visual and auditory takeover warning system that intelligently selects the most appropriate alert modality based on the drivers' state, ensuring effective driver notification under various NDRT. The present findings have provided empirical support for the industrial design of two-stage takeover warnings facilitating diversified product design and enhancing product usability.

References

1. Bazilinskyy, P., Petermeijer, S.M., Petrovych, V., Dodou, D., de Winter, J.C.: Take-over requests in highly automated driving: a crowdsourcing survey on auditory, vibrotactile, and visual displays. Transport. Res. F: Traffic Psychol. Behav. **56**, 82–98 (2018)
2. Eriksson, A., Stanton, N.A.: Takeover time in highly automated vehicles: noncritical transitions to and from manual control. Hum. Factors **59**(4), 689–705 (2017)
3. Gold, C., Damböck, D., Lorenz, L., Bengler, K.: "take over!" how long does it take to get the driver back into the loop? In: Proceedings of the human factors and ergonomics society annual meeting. vol. 57, pp. 1938–1942. Sage Publications Sage CA, Los Angeles, CA (2013)
4. Gold, C., Körber, M., Lechner, D., Bengler, K.: Taking over control from highly automated vehicles in complex traffic situations: the role of traffic density. Hum. Factors **58**(4), 642–652 (2016)
5. Hart, S.G., Staveland, L.E.: Development of nasa-tlx (task load index): results of empirical and theoretical research. In: Advances in Psychology, vol. 52, pp. 139–183. Elsevier (1988)
6. International, S.: Taxonomy and definitions for terms related to driving automation systems for on-road motor vehicles. SAE International (2021)
7. Lee, S.C., Yoon, S.H., Ji, Y.G.: Effects of non-driving-related task attributes on takeover quality in automated vehicles. Int. J. Hum.-Comput. Interact. **37**(3), 211–219 (2021)

8. Ma, S., et al.: Take over gradually in conditional automated driving: the effect of two-stage warning systems on situation awareness, driving stress, takeover performance, and acceptance. Int. J. Hum.-Comput. Interact. **37**(4), 352–362 (2021)

9. Mannuzza, S., Kietzman, M., Berenhaus, I., Ramsey, P., Zubin, J., Sutton, S.: The modality shift effect in schizophrenia: Fact or artifact? Biological Psychiatry (1984)

10. Naujoks, F., Befelein, D., Wiedemann, K., Neukum, A.: A review of non-driving-related tasks used in studies on automated driving. In: Stanton, N.A. (ed.) AHFE 2017. AISC, vol. 597, pp. 525–537. Springer, Cham (2018). https://doi.org/10.1007/978-3-319-60441-1_52

11. Sun, Y.L., Hu, Z.H., Zhang, R.L., Xun, M.M., Liu, Q., Zhang, Q.L.: An investigation on the effect factors in the paradigm of multisensory integration. Acta Psychol. Sin. **43**(11), 1239 (2011)

12. Van Der Laan, J.D., Heino, A., De Waard, D.: A simple procedure for the assessment of acceptance of advanced transport telematics. Transp. Res. Part C: Emerg. Technol. **5**(1), 1–10 (1997)

13. Wandtner, B., Schömig, N., Schmidt, G.: Effects of non-driving related task modalities on takeover performance in highly automated driving. Hum. Factors **60**(6), 870–881 (2018)

14. Wickens, C.D.: Multiple resources and performance prediction. Theor. Issues Ergon. Sci. **3**(2), 159–177 (2002)

15. Zhang, B., De Winter, J., Varotto, S., Happee, R., Martens, M.: Determinants of take-over time from automated driving: a meta-analysis of 129 studies. Transport. Res. F: Traffic Psychol. Behav. **64**, 285–307 (2019)

Voice Revolution on Wheels: Porsche's Pioneering Journey into Next-Gen In-Car Interactions

Haoran Wen[1], Zixuan Qiao[1], Bin Zhang[1], Ruilu Yu[1], Xiaoxuan Ge[1], Yuan Zhang[1], Yu Zhao[1], Xianbo Wang[1], Yujie Ma[1], Mengmeng Xu[2(✉)], Yang Guo[2(✉)], and Jingpeng Jia[3(✉)]

[1] Beijing Key Laboratory of Applied Experimental Psychology, National Demonstration Center for Experimental Psychology Education (Beijing Normal University), Faculty of Psychology, Beijing Normal University, Beijing 100875, China
202328061044@mail.bnu.edu.cn
[2] Chapter of User Experience, Porsche Digital China, Shanghai 200120, China
[3] College of Special Education, Beijing Union University, Beijing 100075, China
tjtjingpeng@buu.edu.cn

Abstract. In the context of the smart era, in-car human-machine interaction (HMI) faces new opportunities and challenges. Voice interaction, as a crucial mode of HMI, presents fresh possibilities for a superior user experience (UX) in in-car interactions. Currently, Porsche, as a traditional automotive company, has certain shortcomings in the design of voice interaction and voice digital assistants (DA). This project addresses these gaps by approaching innovation and improvement in the DA domain from two dimensions: Visual Design (Avatar) and Dialogue Design. Following the principles of human-centered design (HCD), this initiative aims to provide feasible solutions for Porsche's transition towards intelligent in-car HMI.

Keywords: User eXperience · Human-Machine Interaction · Human-Centered Design · Digital Assistants · Generation Z

1 Introduction

In the era of smart technology, in-car HMI has become increasingly crucial in automotive design [1–3]. With the advancements in new technologies such as big data and AI, evolving user demands, and the rise of internet-based new players in the automotive industry, in-car HMI design is experiencing continuous innovation and rapid iteration. The central control system in cars, serving as the mediator for human-vehicle interaction, involves multi-dimensional perception, primarily utilizing visual, auditory, and tactile senses [4]. Faced with the growing complexity of information in in-car systems and continuous operational tasks, traditional single-modal interaction is insufficient to fully meet user needs. Multimodal interaction is considered the future trend.

H. Wen, Z. Qiao, B. Zhang, R. Yu and X. Ge—Contributed equally.

A. Marcus et al. (Eds.): HCII 2024, LNCS 14713, pp. 249–261, 2024.
https://doi.org/10.1007/978-3-031-61353-1_17

Voice interaction, as a vital component of multimodal interaction, is gaining increased attention in the field of in-car HMI. Its greatest advantage lies in its naturalness, allowing users to master the use of voice interfaces without the need for extensive learning. Consequently, in-car voice HMI helps reduce cognitive load resulting from touch-based interactions [5–7]. Voice DA, as carriers of voice interaction, often assume the role of an assistant, displaying intelligent and human-like characteristics, especially with the ongoing development of artificial intelligence.

Currently, various automotive manufacturers are exploring the possibilities of voice interaction in intelligent HMI. For instance, Mercedes-Benz's third-generation MBUX system is focused on developing more natural and context-aware intelligent voice interaction. It is set to support the integration of ChatGPT, aiming to create a "mind-reading voice assistant." BMW's eighth-generation iDrive system introduces a new voice assistant that is not only smarter but also capable of interpreting the driver's intentions and needs through recognizing their body language. However, compared to these continuously innovating traditional car manufacturers, Porsche's current intelligent voice assistant seems less intelligent and user-friendly. For example, the voice interaction feature in the latest Porsche Macan relies on touchscreen controls on the central screen and physical buttons on the left side of the steering wheel for activation. Once activated, the vehicle prompts the user to speak specific commands through voice and displays instructions on the central screen. While the vehicle demonstrates good recognition of specific voice commands, it struggles with vague instructions, leading to lower recognition accuracy. This lack of intelligence results in a lower frequency of user engagement with this feature.

The preliminary research indicates that Porsche's in-car voice HMI currently lags some high-end automotive brands in the dimension of intelligent transformation. The future trend of in-car HMI would be characterized by personalization, contextualization, experientialization, connectivity, and intelligence [8]. This poses a new challenge for Porsche's voice assistant. However, traditional evaluation methods focusing on utility, usability, and general satisfaction may not sufficiently address the DA topic. The evaluation of the new interaction/interface design and its emotional impact should center around three key metrics: excitement, high-tech feeling, and luxury feeling.

During the fall semester of 2023, 20 graduate students collaborated in four teams on two design briefs: Visual Design (Avatar) and Dialogue Design. Regular workshops, review sessions, and company visits were conducted to ensure that the outcomes provide Porsche Digital China with significant design and growth opportunities. To achieve this overarching goal, the following research questions were addressed:

- What are the characteristics of the target user groups?
- What are the typical user scenarios and journeys?
- What are the new design concepts to enable a rich and meaningful experience with the DA?

2 Methodology

2.1 User Research Process

All four project teams applied innovative methods in the user research process to advance their projects. It is adherence to this process that allowed us to handle tasks and complete the design efficiently and effectively [9, 10]. Through constructing user journey maps, we analyzed the UX and emotional changes during interactions with the car, identifying pain points in the current user journey map, such as the infrequent use of the DA due to unclear functionality. Affinity analysis, jobs-to-be-done (JTBD), mind mapping, MoSCoW, and C-Box were several novel thinking methods employed. We clustered the needs derived from 1v1 interview results into an affinity analysis chart, forming the basis for 20 identified JTBDs, elaborated in the results section. Each team brainstormed solutions and mind maps based on JTBD, subsequently forming MoSCoW and C-Box models. Prioritizing functions corresponding to requirements based on innovativeness and feasibility, we determined the preferred features for implementation, laying the foundation for subsequent innovative design. With the underlying logic of innovative design established, we proceeded with concept design, creating low-fidelity and high-fidelity user interface designs and illustrative storyboards in accordance with the user research process, visually presenting our innovative design concepts through hand-drawn sketches, images, and videos.

2.2 Interaction Quality

Interaction quality refers to the subjective feelings and experiences users have while interacting with digital products, such as the luxury, excitement, and high-tech feel associated with Porsche. Enhancing interaction quality can increase user satisfaction and loyalty, also contributing to brand image and reputation, akin to how Porsche is synonymous with luxury. Besides visual and operational experiences, interaction quality can encompass more senses, including sound, touch, and even taste [11, 12].

When it comes to luxury, most people might associate it with the exterior and interior of a car. Expressing luxury in DA posed a significant challenge in our design process. In later stages, we attempted to infuse luxury into the DA by making it more attuned to the driver's thoughts. For instance, Porsche's DA recognizes the driver's emotions and physiological state through an in-car camera, adjusting ambient lighting and playing suitable music to enhance the driver's mood and driving state [13]. When the owner approaches the car, external lights illuminate to help quickly locate the vehicle. We believe that, in subsequent iterations, we deepen our understanding of luxury and better incorporate it into the DA to continually meet user expectations.

Excitement focuses on the application of technology and hardware in the car to bring a sense of excitement, stimulation, and vitality during both riding and driving experiences [14]. We aspire to evoke this feeling not only through Porsche's car performance but also in the DA. For example, our project includes a simulated "push-back" sensation. When the driver selects the exhilarating driving mode, the driver's seat provides a lifelike push-back sensation corresponding to the vehicle's speed to assist in intensifying the feeling of excitement. The DA, integrated with various connected electronics, aims to deliver an exhilarating and engaging experience to users.

High-Tech Feeling involves incorporating advanced technology into the car's functionality and design to provide a more intelligent, comfortable, and convenient experience [15]. Existing technologies include intelligent DA systems, multimedia entertainment systems, wireless charging, and automatic parking. We aim to innovate on this foundation, driving technological progress based on user needs. For instance, one team designed intelligent ambient lighting that adapts to outdoor temperature and in-car music. The DA recognizes the interaction partner's vocal range, distinguishing between high and low frequencies to reduce children's impact and interference with the driver, resulting in a safer and more comfortable driving experience.

2.3 HCD

The goal of HCD is to ensure high usability, encompassing the ease of use and management of products, as well as the alignment of product features with user needs. The general process includes determining scenarios and users, identifying requirements, building design solutions and development, evaluating the product, and repeating these steps to further refine and optimize the product [16]. Preliminarily defining the target users and scenarios is the first and crucial step. Each project team, starting from the information provided by Porsche Digital China, continuously explored and refined their Personas and Context through interactions with experts, ultimately solidifying these aspects. During the rapid usability testing phase, each project team invited 12 peers to participate in testing the outcomes, forming peers' usability results. Non-team peers who experienced the interaction process with low-fidelity design prototypes filled out the user experience questionnaire (UEQ) [17, 18]. We utilized data analysis to assess whether our designs met user expectations. We consider this data crucial for future iterations, providing valuable insights into which aspects of interaction quality might be lacking or missing in our designs. By observing the data from all four teams, the dimension of joy appeared to be the most challenging to design. Through inquiries about user experiences, the teams iteratively improved their designs, addressing points that, while novel to us, might be burdensome for users. This process fully embodies the HCD principles of the project.

3 Results

3.1 Friendly Assistant

Many commuters wish to have a unique, luxurious, and better-serviced DA during their journeys, with enhanced capabilities in health management, parking assistance, and more. Users often feel limited by the insufficient capabilities of existing DA. We aim to design a DA that improves the driving experience for users during their commute and proactively provides services. Users can initiate the DA through voice or gesture commands, generating effective instructions. Based on the information provided by the DA, users can receive personalized services and health-related information. We have created a storyboard to illustrate this concept, as shown in Fig. 1.

Meet Linlin, a 35-year-old born into a warm middle-class family in a relatively small city. Coming from intelligent parents, she graduated from a prestigious university and is passionate about planning and creativity. Linlin joined a renowned advertising company, starting from the grassroots level and gradually rising to become a leader in the industry, eventually serving as the planning director in a large enterprise. In the following JTBDs, the focus is on proactive interaction:

- Enhance the usability and intelligence of the DA comprehensively.
- Provide users with proactive interaction experiences in different scenarios.
- Deliver more personalized services and experiences to users.
- Assist users in effectively and efficiently learning the available DA functions.
- Enable users to experience the luxurious interior ambiance.

We created a high-fidelity prototype, as shown in Fig. 2. This design effectively helps users access a friendly DA model with a luxurious feel, catering to the navigation, traffic, and health needs of the target users during their daily commute. It also records users' interactions with the DA, enhancing their sense of luxury and showcasing their personal and value attributes.

Fig. 1. The user scenario.

3.2 Mountain Conqueror

Young trail running enthusiasts often struggle to find satisfying driving routes during their trail running adventures, and ensuring safety while driving becomes a challenge. Currently, they attempt to address this issue by browsing trail running videos shared on social media. However, these videos tend to be overly subjective and contain a lot of irrelevant information. To solve this problem, we designed an AR-based DA called "Alpineer," which interacts with users through DA and the windshield. A successful design would enable users to understand every detail without physically being on the

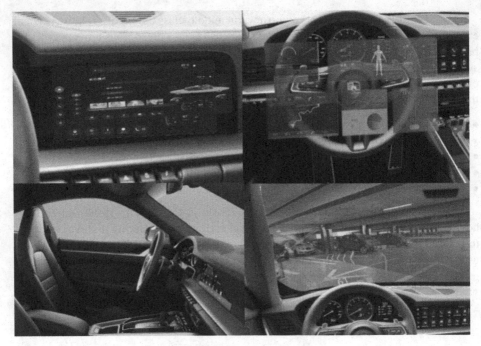

Fig. 2. The high-fidelity prototype.

trail, empowering them to quickly identify potential dangers during the driving process and promptly mark them for attention. We have created a storyboard to illustrate this concept, as shown in Fig. 3.

Meet Bohan, a 24-year-old founder of an art studio. He graduated from college in Beijing, currently unmarried, and pursues a life that is free, individualistic, and tasteful. Balancing work and life, he enriches and perfects his successful life, gaining a circle of friends with similar tastes and mutual recognition, sharing his achievements. In the following JTBDs, the focus is on the trail running process:

- Plan trail running trips quickly and conveniently.
- Complete trail running safely.
- Have a good driving experience during trail running.
- Obtain advanced data after trail running, recording achievements.
- Achieve self-fulfillment during trail running.

We created a high-fidelity prototype, as shown in Fig. 4. The simulated trail running system helps users plan their trips and choose suitable trail running routes, start gatherings with friends, and confirm weather conditions through the interface to ensure driving safety and select appropriate clothing. During trail running, when oncoming vehicles are detected on winding mountain roads, the system automatically makes mountain obstacles transparent and marks the oncoming vehicles, greatly ensuring user safety. After trail running, users can share trail running data with teammates and record their experiences.

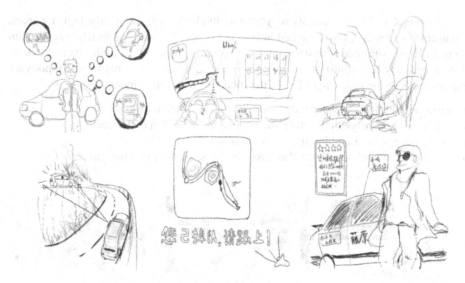

Fig. 3. The user scenario.

Fig. 4. The high-fidelity prototype.

3.3 Business Partner

Some Porsche owners need to conduct business cooperation and negotiations in their cars. During the journeys to pick up business partners, they choose to use this time for some ice-breaking and brief discussions. Unforeseen situations often arise. To facilitate cooperation and provide a better experience, designing a small DA for car owners would be very helpful. This DA can accompany the owner intimately at any time, reminding of safety issues in a warm and intelligent manner during the journey and providing accurate and timely prompts. At the same time, it can also provide Porsche customers with a sense of luxury and technology, as well as a comfortable cabin experience. Such a design would help ease the atmosphere of negotiations, promote deeper conversations, and deliver an extraordinary luxury experience to customers through the DA. We have created a storyboard to illustrate this concept, as shown in Fig. 5.

The target audience consists of young individuals with relatively high incomes, regardless of gender, mostly located in first-tier cities. They are primarily employed in finance, internet-related industries, and entrepreneurship, with a high level of education. Some may be enthusiasts of performance or modified cars, but most are not very experienced. In the following JTBDs, the focus is on business meetings:

- Enjoy an intelligent connected in-car system anytime, anywhere.
- Create a constantly comfortable and understanding cabin experience.
- Design convenient and intelligent multimodal in-car HMI.
- Provide users with an all-weather assistant for safe and punctual travel.

Fig. 5. The user scenario.

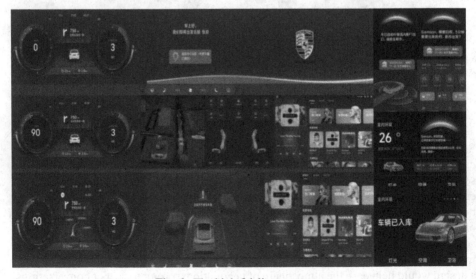

Fig. 6. The high-fidelity prototype.

We created a high-fidelity prototype, as shown in Fig. 6. The product's basic functions are well-equipped and practical. It can help users record schedules and accurately locate, adjust in-car hardware devices through voice and controls, including adjusting seat angles, steering wheel temperature, etc., greatly enhancing the user's driving experience. At the same time, it can recognize the outdoor and indoor environment, provide reminders for unsafe distances, ensuring driving safety.

3.4 Elegant Assistant

Users expect the in-car voice DA to provide real-time weather conditions at the destination, enabling the driver to decide whether to continue the journey. It should also offer information on nearby facilities such as restaurants and charging stations, eliminating the need for users to be distracted by operating their phones during driving. The DA should navigate based on traffic conditions, choosing the optimal route. When children are present, the DA should be able to communicate with them and provide assistance. In situations where the driver or passengers experience negative emotions, the DA should use gentle music and lighting to soothe their mood. We have created a storyboard based on these requirements, as shown in Fig. 7.

The user profile is Dawei, with a doctoral degree, working in Beijing, married with two children. His motto is "Find the joy of life in the turns." Driven by the desire to provide a comfortable and convenient travel experience for his family, he seeks both a performance-driven and luxurious driving experience. He also wishes to experience the convenience brought by the latest technology anytime, anywhere, achieve success in his career, and create better family conditions. In the following JTBDs, the focus is on family travel:

- DA always understands my words and helps me like my capable assistant.

Fig. 7. The user scenario.

- Every day, DA can be considerate and caring like a friend.
- The central control interface is always easy to understand and use.
- Whenever friends see my car, they think I am a person with taste.

We created a high-fidelity prototype, as shown in Fig. 8. Through elegant lighting design, it exudes luxury and technology, not only alleviating negative emotions in certain situations but also providing users with abundant information during family travel, making the journey more enriching and enjoyable.

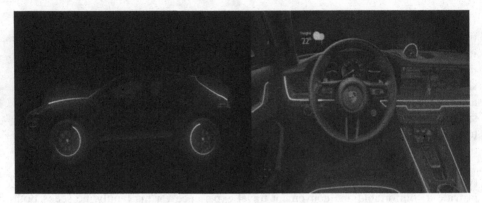

Fig. 8. The high-fidelity prototype.

4 Discussion

Through In this innovation project, we focused on addressing three research questions and used this foundation to unfold the design, attempting to explore the future vision of Porsche HMI. The target user groups addressed by the four project teams differ, but the characteristics of these users are quite similar. Porsche owners, across the teams, seek driving sensations while emphasizing personalized expressions. This individuality manifests in different forms as the target user groups evolve. For example, in the Mountain Conqueror, the personalized needs of the target users are reflected in the dimensions of speed and driving sensation. They derive a sense of self-fulfillment from the enjoyment of speed, victory, and conquest.

Throughout the project, we identified the most typical user scenarios, such as commuting, including daily commuting and family travel. Three out of the four teams focused their exploration on the commuting scenario. The current user journey is not perfect, and the suboptimal level of HMI experience is attributed to the lack of intelligence in the DA. Addressing this phenomenon, the innovative design process of the project provides an answer to the final question. Although each team derived different innovative solutions, overall, we aimed to design an intelligent DA with multi-modal interactions that respects and satisfies users' personalized needs, fully supporting the HMI process. The goal is to deliver a smart and user-friendly DA that provides a rich and meaningful interactive experience for users.

4.1 Feedback from Porsche

Representative members from the four teams visited Porsche Digital China for project presentations and received valuable feedback from the company. In the process of considering interaction quality, there is a need to pay closer attention to persona characteristics, assessing whether the quality aligns with the characteristics of the target users. For example, it should be considered whether women need to experience a sense of technology in the interaction process. While the current design is comprehensive, there is a desire for future designs to focus on a unique and exciting point during the design phase. When considering intelligent connectivity design, decisions should be made based on real usage scenarios and user needs. For instance, determining whether users need to interact with and control all furniture in the car.

They believe that the project has achieved excellent results, starting from its initial form and evolving through discussions and reviews. Porsche, as a traditional automotive company, emphasizes the importance of innovative design and values. The company expressed satisfaction with the project's ideas and designs in the theme of digital innovation for DA. They appreciate the divergent and innovative thinking, unburdened by commercial constraints. They look forward to future collaborations and hopes to produce valuable products for users, the company, and society through these theoretical approaches.

4.2 Reflections

In this project, transdisciplinary collaboration and the exchange of professional knowledge played a pivotal role, bringing forth more possibilities through the integration of diverse academic backgrounds. Each team could leverage the expertise of its members, approaching the same issues from different professional perspectives, thus avoiding cognitive biases during the project. For instance, during conceptual design, a team member dedicated to the visual design had experience in smart home IoT, contributing innovative concepts connecting cars with home appliances. This novel idea was reflected in the project outcomes of that team. In creating high-fidelity prototypes, team members with a foundation in visual communication ensured the visualization of innovative design ideas across all teams, showcasing their technical proficiency.

Every step of the project emphasized a HCD philosophy, a guiding principle we followed throughout the design process. Results produced under the premise of a thorough understanding of target users, their needs, and contexts are more likely to gain market acceptance and genuinely satisfy user requirements. Challenges arose in defining target users and scenarios, such as incongruities between income levels, actual car usage needs, and brand positioning. This experience underscores the importance of exploring and understanding user needs more profoundly in practice, relying on in-depth exploration rather than mere initial assumptions. The rapid usability testing phase provided valuable feedback, serving as a crucial basis for improving the prototypes. Yet, as the test participants were not actual Porsche users, there might be limitations in ecological validity. This highlights the necessity for involving real users at every stage of product design to mitigate potential issues stemming from "pseudo-needs" and "pseudo-experiences."

Through regular learning and practical experiences, we established a foundation of professional knowledge. Leveraging the characteristics of project-based learning, we immersed ourselves in the role of corporate employees, providing feasible and innovative strategies for the company. The exchange of knowledge among classmates and the advantage of interdisciplinary collaboration enabled us to analyze existing problems critically and propose innovative solutions from different perspectives.

4.3 Prospects

Based on the valuable insights provided by Porsche Digital China, we believe that there is still room for progress and improvement in the future of this project. The exploration and implementation of interaction quality in DA design faced challenges, requiring a deeper understanding and innovation in achieving a sense of luxury, excitement, and technology. In designing the DA, we attempted to incorporate a sense of luxury into the interaction between the user and the car—a novel but complex concept. In future work, we need to dive into the real expectations of users regarding these sensations to better integrate them into DA design. Continuous iteration and testing are essential to enhance the achievement of interaction quality.

While the data collected from rapid usability testing provides important references for design iteration and optimization, we need to be aware of its limitations. Usability test scores may be influenced by subjective factors or may not fully reflect users' true experiences. Therefore, in subsequent iterations, we should rely more on in-depth feedback and observations from real users, as well as comprehensive analysis and optimization based on multiple sources of data.

Whether it is future improvements in this project or other design projects, we must continue to uphold the basic principles of design and draw on the valuable experiences gained in this research, such as interdisciplinary collaboration, challenges in interaction quality, and HCD principle. In the backdrop of the intelligent era, where technology continually undergoes iterative innovation, as graduate students in user experience, we need to explore and utilize innovative methods to discover genuine user needs. Only then can we leverage cutting-edge technological advancements to meet user needs and deliver more perfect design products.

References

1. Maedche, A., et al.: AI-based digital assistants: opportunities, threats, and research perspectives. Bus. Inf. Syst. Eng. **61**, 535–544 (2019)
2. Sachdev, S., Macwan, J., Patel, C., Doshi, N.: Voice-controlled autonomous vehicle using IoT. Procedia Comput. Sci. **160**, 712–717 (2019)
3. Mahajan, K., Large, D.R., Burnett, G., Velaga, N.R.: Exploring the benefits of conversing with a digital voice assistant during automated driving: a parametric duration model of takeover time. Transport. Res. F: Traffic Psychol. Behav. **80**, 104–126 (2021)
4. Chattaraman, V., Kwon, W.S., Gilbert, J.E., Ross, K.: Should AI-Based, conversational digital assistants employ social-or task-oriented interaction style? A task-competency and reciprocity perspective for older adults. Comput. Hum. Behav. **90**, 315–330 (2019)

5. Cui, S., et al.: Beyond car human-machine interface (HMI): mapping six intelligent modes into future cockpit scenarios. In: International Conference on Human-Computer Interaction, pp. 75–83 (2023)
6. Zhu, Y., Tang, G., Liu, W., Qi, R.: How post 90's gesture interact with automobile skylight. Int. J. Hum.-Comput. Interact. 38(5), 395–405 (2022)
7. Pullin, G., Treviranus, J., Patel, R., Higginbotham, J.: Designing interaction, voice, and inclusion in AAC research. Augment. Altern. Commun. 33(3), 139–148 (2017)
8. Yardım, S., Pedgley, O.: Targeting a luxury driver experience: design considerations for automotive HMI and interiors. Int. J. Des. 17(2), 45–66 (2023)
9. Visser, F.S., Stappers, P.J., Van der Lugt, R., Sanders, E.B.: Contextmapping: experiences from practice. CoDesign 1(2), 119–149 (2005)
10. Gray, C.M.: Languaging design methods. Des. Stud. 78, 101076 (2022)
11. Liu, W., Lee, K.P., Gray, C.M., Toombs, A.L., Chen, K.H., Leifer, L.: Transdisciplinary teaching and learning in UX design: a program review and AR case studies. Appl. Sci. 11(22), 10648 (2021)
12. Kokotsaki, D., Menzies, V., Wiggins, A.: Project-based learning: a review of the literature. Improv. Sch. 19(3), 267–277 (2016)
13. Desmet, P.M., Xue, H., Xin, X., Liu, W.: Demystifying emotion for designers: a five-day course based on seven fundamental principles. Adv. Des. Res. 1(1), 50–62 (2023)
14. Desmet, P., Hekkert, P.: Framework of product experience. Int. J. Des. 1(1), 57–66 (2007)
15. Liu, W., et al.: Designing interactive glazing through an engineering psychology approach: Six augmented reality scenarios that envision future car human-machine interface. Virtual Reality Intell. Hardware 5(2), 157–170 (2023)
16. Norman, D.A.: Design for a Better World: Meaningful, Sustainable, Humanity Centered. MIT Press, Cambridge (2023)
17. Schrepp, M., Hinderks, A., Thomaschewski, J.: Design and evaluation of a short version of the user experience questionnaire (UEQ-S). Int. J. Interact. Multimedia Artif. Intell. 4(6), 103–108 (2017)
18. Zhu, D., Wang, D., Huang, R., Jing, Y., Qiao, L., Liu, W.: User interface (UI) design and user experience questionnaire (UEQ) evaluation of a to-do list mobile application to support day-to-day life of older adults. Healthcare 10(10), 2068 (2022)

User Interaction Mode Selection and Preferences in Different Driving States of Automotive Intelligent Cockpit

Yuanyang Zuo[1]([✉]) [iD], Jun Ma[1,2] [iD], Zaiyan Gong[2], Jingyi Zhao[2], and Lizhuo Zang[2]

[1] College of Design and Innovation, Tongji University, Shanghai, China
zuoyy@tongji.edu.cn
[2] School of Automotive Studies, Tongji University, Shanghai, China

Abstract. The purpose of this study is to investigate the user's interaction modality choices and preferences in vehicle intelligent cockpits under different driving states. The driving state is divided into three driving scenarios: before departure, during driving, and halfway parking through a user-centered user journey approach, combining Don Norman's theory of emotional systems. Data collection is conducted using questionnaire and interview methods to produce outputs on preference frequencies and correlations. In the questionnaire, it is found that users show significant interaction preferences in different driving states. Users have the most task preferences while driving, with the interaction behavior of navigating to a destination being the most frequent. A qualitative study in the interview indicates users' modal preferences in different tasks as well as users' focus on topics. After conducting user research, a multimodal combination method has been proposed to partition the input and output modes of interaction. The findings provide targeted guidance for automakers and designers to better meet user interaction needs in different driving scenarios and enhance the user experience and safety of automotive smart cockpits.

Keywords: Interaction Tasks · Interaction Modes · User Preferences · Automotive Intelligent Cockpit

1 Introduction

With the rapid development of intelligent cockpit-related technologies, the design of automotive intelligent cockpits has become more and more critical, as it directly affects the driver's interactive experience and safety in the vehicle. In the field of automotive human-computer interaction (HCI), the design experience of intelligent cockpits should start from the user's demand and integrate contextual knowledge from the design field into the provision of functional services. Human interaction with the world is essentially multimodal [1, 2]. We use multiple senses, sequential and parallel, passively and actively, to explore our environment, confirm expectations about the world and perceive new information. User's cognition is based on multi-modal sensory experiences such as visual, tactile, auditory, olfactory, and gustatory stimuli recognition and interpretation

© The Author(s), under exclusive license to Springer Nature Switzerland AG 2024
A. Marcus et al. (Eds.): HCII 2024, LNCS 14713, pp. 262–274, 2024.
https://doi.org/10.1007/978-3-031-61353-1_18

feedback [3, 4]. While the cockpit visual experience dominates, the research and application of voice technology, tactile technology, eye movement technology and olfactory technology are also widely carried out [5, 6]. There are also studies on establishing comfort models based on user experience [7, 8]. Jaimes and Sebe surveyed multimodal HCI research with a particular emphasis on computer vision [9]. Dumas et al. investigated multimodal principles, models, and frameworks and proposed that multimodal interfaces can improve task efficiency [10]. Lalanne et al. investigated fusion engines for multimodal inputs [11]. Humans can process information faster and better when it is presented in multiple forms [12]. Reeves identified the following guideline for multimodal user interface design: multimodal systems should be designed for the widest range of users and usage environments. Designers should support the best mode or combination of modes expected in a changing environment (e.g., private office versus driving a car) [13].

In this paper, we focus on exploring users' interaction modality choices and preferences in automotive intelligent cockpits under different driving states in order to deepen our understanding of drivers' demands. Comprehending these preferences not only helps to improve the driver's interaction experience, but also enhances the practicality and safety of the cockpit system in various driving scenarios. By conducting in-depth research on user interaction needs under different driving states and modes, the interaction input and output are subdivided, and a multimodal combination method is developed. We expect to provide powerful guidance to automakers and designers to ensure that intelligent cockpit systems meet user expectations while enhancing the overall experience of driving a vehicle. This study fills the research gap on the selection and preference of user interaction modes under different driving states, and provides a practical reference for future automotive cockpit design.

2   Method

2.1   Study Design

The theoretical basis is combined with user journey method [14] and Don Norman's three levels of emotional system [15]. The main research object of this study is user interaction mode selection and preferences, so the methods of questionnaire and interview are employed to conduct targeted research on users, as shown in Fig. 1.

2.2   Questionnaire Method

Participants. To obtain effective quantitative results, we surveyed 210 owners of intelligent cockpit cars in China's first-tier cities with a quota of 1:1:1:1 for Beijing, Shanghai, Guangzhou, and Shenzhen respectively.

Tools. To ensure a sufficient sample size and objectivity of data collection, "Questionnaire star", an online placement questionnaire platform, was used for questionnaire data collection. Given the presence of ranking questions and a substantial volume of data, "SPSS" software was used for data frequency analysis, multiple response analysis and factor analysis. "Origin" software was utilized for data visualization.

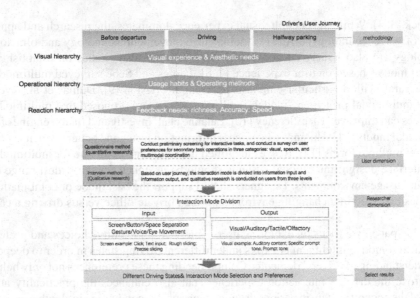

Fig. 1. The schematic of research methodology.

Questionnaire Design. The questionnaire was designed with 11 questions centered around the research object, mainly including "Frequency of Function Use Survey" and "Modal Preference Study" for different functional tasks, as shown in Fig. 2.

Quest ion No.	Structures	Content	Outputs
1	Technical expectations	What new technology are you most excited about regarding the interaction modality of smart cockpits? (Multiple choice question)	User technology expectations
2	Frequency of Function Use Survey	Of the common car-machine interaction tasks used in driving, which do you use most frequently? (Sorting questions Top5)	Frequency of interaction functions for different driving states
3		Of the common car interaction tasks used before departure, which do you use most frequently? (Sorting questions Top5)	
4		Of the common vehicle-machine interaction tasks used during a stopover, which do you use most frequently? (Sorting questions Top5)	
5	A Survey of Needs for Traditional Physical Interaction	Which functions do you think need to retain physical buttons (multiple choice)	Physical Button Function Sorting
6	Investigate for visual interaction and voice interaction (matching functions & different states)	For which driving tasks in which driving states do you prefer visual interaction? (Sorting question, top5)	Interaction form choices and preferences in different driving states
7		For which driving tasks in which driving states do you prefer auditory interaction? (Sorting question, top5)	
8		For which driving tasks in which driving states do you prefer multimodal (e.g., visual, auditory, and haptic interactions) collaboration? (Sorting question, top5)	
9	Central Control, Voice Interaction and Natural Interaction Views and Opinions	What is your opinion on the existence of the following features of the center screen (rating question)	Perspectives on the center screen
10		What are your views on the following features of voice interaction (rating question)	Perspectives on Voice Interaction
11		If there were other means of natural interaction (e.g., eye movement interaction, spaced gestures, or EEG interaction), what would you prefer it to do? (Sorting questions Top3)	Perspectives on Other Interactions

Fig. 2. Questionnaire design structure.

2.3 Semi-structured Interviews

Participants. To obtain accurate and professional survey feedback results from the perspective of users, 12 practitioners (25–36 years old, M = 29) working on interaction design or automotive industry were selected in the qualitative survey design of the interview.

Interview Design. The outline for the semi-structured interviews [16, 17] centered around four components: information input, information output, experience evaluation, final communication. To ensure comprehensiveness, professionalism, and structure in the interview content, these components were further categorized into three types: closed questions, open questions, and topic probes, as shown in Fig. 3. The interviews lasted approximately 50 min per person.

Event selection and design were derived from questionnaire findings (task frequency ranking):			Driving
Event 1, before departure. (A) Check vehicle's range, tire pressure, and other status. (B) Open and close the doors, windows, and trunk. (C) Log into car phone account and connect to phone Bluetooth			simulation platform
Event 2, during driving. (D) Navigation destination. (E) Play music recommended by software. (F) connect/make phone calls.			experiment
Event 3, halfway parking. (G) Search songs. (H) Modify music software to play playlist/change current radio station. (I) Open the video entertainment software to watch recommended videos/karaoke			
Classify	Serial No.	Interview information	3 events in
Information input	1	What tasks are typically accomplished using a touch screen (tap, type, swipe, rough slide) during information input?	total; interviews were conducted at
	2	What tasks are typically accomplished using the keys (click, swipe/scroll, square position, center position) during information input?	the end of each event;
	3	What tasks are typically accomplished using air gestures during information input	(closed questions)
	4	What tasks are typically accomplished using voice during information input?	
	5	What task is typically accomplished using eye movements during information input?	
Information output	6	What tasks are typically accomplished using visuals (content/glances/ambience-afterglow confirmation, etc.) during information output?	
	7	What tasks are typically accomplished using hearing (content/alarm tones/prompts, etc.) during information output?	
	8	What is generally accomplished using the sense of touch (vibration/bodily sensation) in the information output?	
	9	What do you think of the interaction role of olfactory interaction in information output? In what scenario tasks would you prefer it to occur?	
Experience evaluation	10	What are some of the best interaction experiences during use?	(open questions)
	11	What were some of the interactions that felt bad during use?	
	12	Have you ever used eye movements (gaze control)? What scenarios and tasks do you think are appropriate?	
	13	In what form would you like the information to be presented? How would you like to interact with the information?	
Final communication	14	What do you see as the shape of the broad interface in the next 3-5 years?	(topic probes)
	15	What do you think will be the typical driving scenarios for L4+ autonomous driving states?	
	16	What are your expectations for the future visual experience of intelligent cockpits?	
	17	What are your expectations for the interaction design of intelligent cockpits under autonomous driving?	

Fig. 3. Semi-structured interview design structure.

Through the desktop research, the LYNK&CO 08 automobile is selected as the task operation entity, as shown in Fig. 4. Users start the interview survey after completing the following three groups of event tasks within the simulated cockpit platform (the events are selected from the results of the task frequency in the questionnaire study, and the driving sub-tasks with the top three frequencies are selected in each driving stages):

Event 1, before departure. (A) Check vehicle range and tire pressure status. (B) Open and close doors, windows, and trunk. (C) Adjust seat and steering wheel position.

Event 2, during driving. (D) Set the navigation destination. (E) View the navigation overview, road conditions in the surrounding area, and points of interest. (F) Make and receive a phone call.

Fig. 4. Simulated cockpit platform.

Event 3, halfway parking. (G) Input search songs. (H) Modify music software playlist/changing current radio station. (I) Adjust interior air conditioning temperature, airflow and direction.

The interviews are structured in a funnel shape, with the user being asked broader questions first, and relatively focused questions later.

2.4 Data Analysis

Two Key Components. 1. Analyze users' interaction choice preferences for information input and information output and other concerns after completing the three driving task events. 2. Analyze users' evaluation of their experience and future outlook on the interaction forms of interaction output and input.

Data Coding. All data were coded using the coding strategies: structural coding, descriptive coding, process coding, and in-vivo coding [18]. Structural coding was used to organize interview responses according to the questions answered [19]. The remaining strategies were able to uncover driver expectations and their corresponding effects on information preferences. Descriptive coding summarized responses into words or phrases. Process coding analyzed responses through observable and conceptual actions, such as gestures or areas that participants pointed to [20]. These behaviors were recorded by the researcher as field notes during the interviews and supplemented using audio recordings after the experiment. And finally, in-vivo coding recorded the exact phrases used by the participants. This process was completed independently by two qualitative searchers, who then compared the results to create a list of collaboratively exported codes. By categorizing the types of codes used, it allowed for a consistent approach to the coding of the interview data. For each type of code, multiple loops were run until a theoretical saturation point was reached (to reduce the risk of subjectivity in the analysis) [21]. The number of times participants mentioned codes was also tracked. It can be noted that the frequency tends to be greater than the number of participants. This is because each participant may mention the code more than once in their responses.

3 Results and Discussion

3.1 Questionnaire Results

Frequency of Function Use Survey (Question 2nd, 3rd, 4th). SPSS software was used to develop a multiple response analysis of the data from the ranking questions to derive the frequency of each option and the order of precedence, as shown in Fig. 5. And the frequency of the ranking order was calculated using the Reverse Allocation Method (RAM) to derive the total ranking, as shown in Fig. 6.

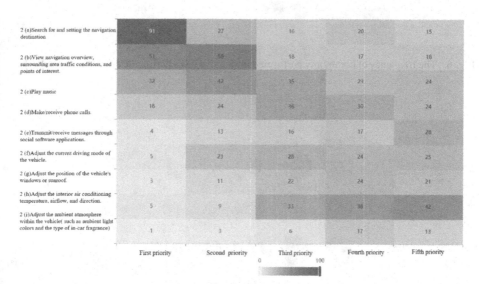

Fig. 5. A heatmap depicting the prioritized frequency of commonly used in-vehicle HCI tasks during driving.

Among the common vehicle-machine interaction tasks used while driving, the following are used more frequently: searching for and setting the navigation destinations (118), viewing navigation overview, surrounding area traffic conditions and points of interest (94), and playing music (75), as shown in Fig. 6. Among the common vehicle-machine interaction tasks used before departure, the following are used more frequently: checking vehicle's range, tire pressure, and other status indicators (116), opening the car windows and sunroof (70), and adjusting and storing the rearview mirror settings (63). Among the common vehicle-machine interaction tasks used for halfway parking, the following are used more frequently: searching for music (82), making/receiving phone calls during a halfway parking (68), and opening the audio-visual entertainment software to watch recommended videos or engage in karaoke singing (62).

Investigation for Visual Interaction and Voice Interaction (Question 6th, 7th, 8th). As shown in Fig. 7, there are generally many tasks selected for driving, with navigating destination being the highest during driving (196). Among the three driving stages, the overall frequency of "during driving" is the highest.

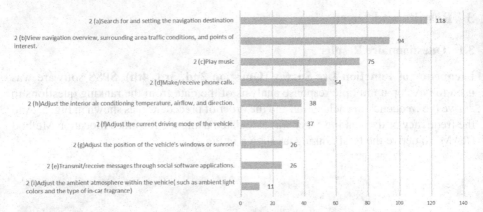

Fig. 6. The frequency of commonly performed interactive tasks during the driving process-RAM.

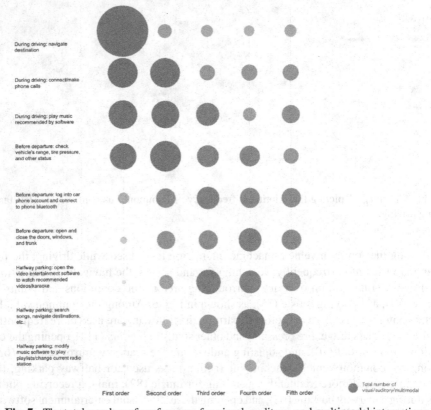

Fig. 7. The total number of preferences for visual, auditory, and multimodal interactions.

As shown in Fig. 8, the navigating destination in "during driving" stage is the top ranked. Fu's research has analyzed that full-touch mode consumes less visual and manual resources compared to traditional mode, but has higher requirements for navigation tasks [22]. To complete operational task of navigating destinations in "during driving" stage, users prefer visual interaction (36.2%) and multi-modal collaboration (36.2%). When making phone calls and playing songs in "during driving" stage, users prefer voice interaction (26.2%; 24.8%) or multimodal interaction (14.3%; 16.7%). When inputting songs etc. in "halfway parking" stage, users prefer to use voice interaction (20.5%) or multimodal interaction (21%) for collaborative operations.

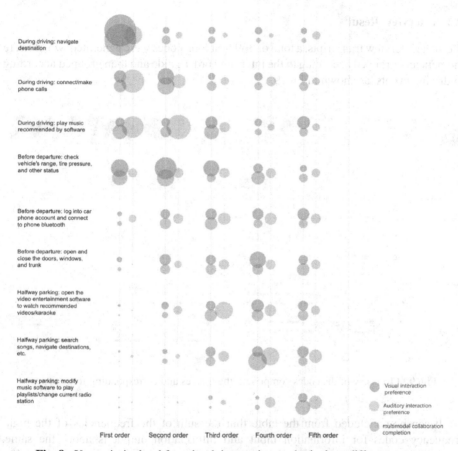

Fig. 8. User priority level for subtask interaction modes in three different stages.

Technical Expectations & A Survey of Needs for Traditional Physical Interaction (Question 1st, 5th). The new technologies that users consider most desirable for the interaction modality of the intelligent cockpit are: generative artificial intelligence (39), air gesture (36) and electroencephalographic interaction (33).

The functions that users believe need to be retained in the physical buttons in the vehicle's intelligent cockpit are: answering phone calls (116), quick-open map navigation (112) and air conditioning on/off and temperature adjustment (102).

Central Control, Voice Interaction and Natural Interaction Views and Opinions (Question 9th, 10th, 11th). The user scores of the screen and voice interactions in the questionnaire are mainly used to verify the outliers (if any). The results indicate that among the contents related to vehicle control adjustments, users most prefer to use: adjusting the seat and steering wheel position (66), opening the car windows and sunroof (61), adjusting the volume, cabin temperature, and air conditioning airflow (61), and adjusting and storing the review mirror setting (56).

3.2 Interview Results

From the interview transcripts, a total of 369 first loop codes were generated, which were thematically grouped according to the interview order guide and then grouped according to driving events, as shown in Fig. 9.

Classification	Serial No.	Event 1, before departure: (A) Check vehicle's range, tire pressure, and other status. (B) Open and close the doors, windows, and trunk. (C) Log into car phone account and connect to phone Bluetooth. (f=117)	Event 2, during driving: (D) Navigation destination. (E) Play music recommended by software. (F) Connect/make phone calls. (f=110)	Event 3, halfway parking: (G) Search songs. (H) Modify music software to play playlist/change current radio station. (I) Open the video entertainment software to watch recommended videos/karaoke. (f=142)
Information input (f=189)	1 (f=31)	(A) (4)	(D) (7); (E) (4)	(G) (7); (H) (6); (I) (3)
	2 (f=51)	(B) (11); (C) (8)	(F) (8)	(G) (7); (I) (3); accuracy (6); convenience (8)
	3 (f=66)	(B) (12); (C) (2); safety (8)	(E) (7); (F) (6); zoom size (3); up and down selection (5); familiarity (2); user habits (3)	(H) (2); directionality (5); maneuvering for different passengers (3); convenience (6)
	4 (f=20)	/	(E) (7); (F) (8); complexity of realization (3); points of interest (2)	/
	5 (f=21)	Confirmation of the accuracy of the information (1); safety (4)	Points of interest (3)	Driving task relevance was weak (3); modifying music to play the song list (2); browsing for attention (2); convenience (4)
Information output (f=180)	6 (f=89)	(A) (10); confirmation of the accuracy of the information(3); with or without alarm (4); screen (6)	(D) (9); (E) (10); (F) (11)	(G) (10); (H) (12); (I) (11); safety (3)
	7 (f=59)	(A) (9); vehicle malfunctions (7); erratic tire pressure (5); seat belt tips (3)	(F) (11)	(G) (8); (H) (7); sound cues (3); speech input (2); modal input-output consistency (2); conformity to cognitive rules (2)
	8 (f=30)	(C) (4); somatic contact (4); direct (3); convenience (4)	/	(H) (8); (I) (7)
	9 (f=2)	/	Sense of atmosphere (2)	/
Experience evaluation (f=113)	10 (f=32)	Safety (10); voice function (7); convenience (6); gesture recognition (4); pet mode (3); voice & button wake-up function (2)		
	11 (f=20)	Accuracy of voice commands (8); vertigo (6); visual fatigue (3); HUD picture quality (3)		
	12 (f=26)	While driving (3); turning/reversing (3); afterimage feedback (1); rearview mirrors (6); assisting other interaction modality use (6); safety (7)		
	13 (f=35)	There being primary and secondary (6); multimodal (5); cause information interference (4); multiple screen displays (4); simplified forms of interaction (4); safety (4); personalization (3); voice (3); and optimal modal presentation (2);		
Final communication (f=83)	14 (f=26)	Multiple (9); large (8); rich in screen carriers (6); progressively simplified (3)		
	15 (f=17)	Short distances (3); playing with mobile phones (7); playing games (4); driving main task changes (3)		
	16 (f=22)	Convenience (6); enhanced interaction outside the vehicle (4); visual interaction inside the vehicle (4); view outside the vehicle (3); complexity (3); visual driving load balance (2)		
	17 (f=18)	Safety (7); inclusiveness (3); technology (6); scenario-oriented (2)		
High frequency words: safety (f=43); convenience (f=34); accuracy (f=20)				

Fig. 9. Overview of the codes comprising the themes and corresponding frequencies.

It can be concluded from the table that the sum of the frequencies of the high-frequency codes for information input and information output is about the same. The high-frequency words throughout the interview experiment are safety (f = 43), convenience (f = 34), and accuracy (f = 20).

In "Information input", the total number of high-frequency word (3, air gesture) is highest (f = 66). All participants agree that the task of (B) Open and close the doors, windows, and trunk can be done by air gesture. Seven participants agree that the task of (E) Play music recommended by software, can be done by air gesture. Six participants agree that the task of (F) Connect/make phone calls, can be done by air gesture. Participants' high-frequency keywords for this interaction are safety (f = 8), directionality (f = 5), user habits (f = 5), and up-down selection (f = 5).

In "Information output", the total number of high-frequency words (6, visual) is highest (f = 89). Most participants think that the task of (A) Check vehicle's range, tire pressure, and other status requires visual output (f = 10), where the high-frequency words are screen (f = 6), with or without alarm (f = 4), and confirmation of the accuracy of the information (f = 3). Most participants agree that the driving tasks in Event 2 and Event 3 requires visual information output, with users more concerned about safety (f = 3).

In interview 13 (Forms of Information Presentation) in "Experience evaluation", the most frequent contents proposed by the participants are that "they want the presentation of information being primary and secondary (6), being multimodal (5), and to avoid causing information interference (4)".

In interview 14 (Future Interface Forms) in "Final communication", the majority of participants believe that the interface forms in the future should be multiple (f = 9), the interface screens would become larger (f = 8), and the form of screen carrier would be richer (f = 6).

An interesting finding is that in the grouping of high-frequency words in the interviews, the total frequency of "during driving" is lower compared to "before departure" and "halfway parking", which is different from the results of the frequency of driving task in the questionnaire.

3.3 Slicing of HCI Tasks

Based on the research conducted through questionnaires and interviews, qualitative and quantitative results of user interaction mode selection and preferences in different driving states have been obtained. To apply these results in practical design, we further carry out interaction mode division from the researcher dimension, which is presented through a case study.

In order to obtain a more refined user operation process, the driver's active input and vehicle system output content are sliced through multiple modalities to complete HCI tasks, as shown in Fig. 10. Based on the questionnaires, modal analysis was conducted on high-frequency tasks to search for new multimodal interaction combinations beyond traditional interaction modes, achieving task segmentation and interaction slicing for different interaction dimensions. The interaction mode can be divided into input and output. The input of interaction mode refers to the system receiving and processing a variety of different modes of input data, including text, image, voice, gesture, etc. It can enable the system to understand the user's intention more comprehensively and provide a richer and more intelligent interaction experience. In this paper, it is divided into five categories: screen, buttons, air gestures, voice, eye tracking/head turn direction. Taking the "Screen" category as an example, its interactive input behaviors are divided into click, text input, rough slide and precise slide. The output of interaction mode include text, image, voice, graphical interface, tactile feedback, etc. By effectively integrating these modes, the system can offer a richer and more personalized interaction experience to meet users' demand. In this paper, the output of interaction mode is divided into four categories: visual, auditory, olfactory, tactile. Taking the "Auditory" as an example, its interactive output behaviors are divided into text content, specific alert sound and alert sound. Detailed descriptions and specifications of interaction actions for interaction behaviors are provided, as in this study where the interactive behavior of "Click" in "Screen" input is defined as "Single screen click".

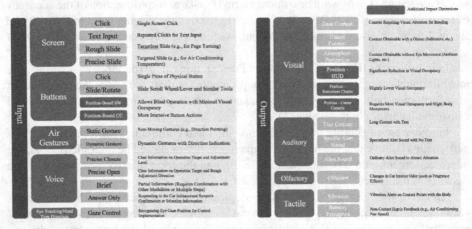

Fig. 10. Slicing of HCI tasks through multiple modalities.

As shown in Fig. 11, the case study on task "Open car windows and sunroof" is finally selected due to its high frequency among the tasks before departure and diversity in interaction modes. It is segmented into five subtasks: "Select window target", "Confirm opening", "Specify range", "Open half of the sunroof", "Specify range". By comparing commonly used modes (buttons/voice) and feasible multimodal forms according to steps to accomplish this task, the differences in operational steps and interaction behaviors are analyzed and multimodal analysis methods are developed. In this case study task, each color box represented a different category of input and output, and the vertical arrangement of the box represented the simultaneous execution of tasks and the implementation of multiple interactive forms. Traditionally, button or voice interaction mode is commonly used during the process of opening car windows and sunroofs. However, it is concluded that multimodal interactions that include both air gestures and voice can achieve more convenient interaction operations.

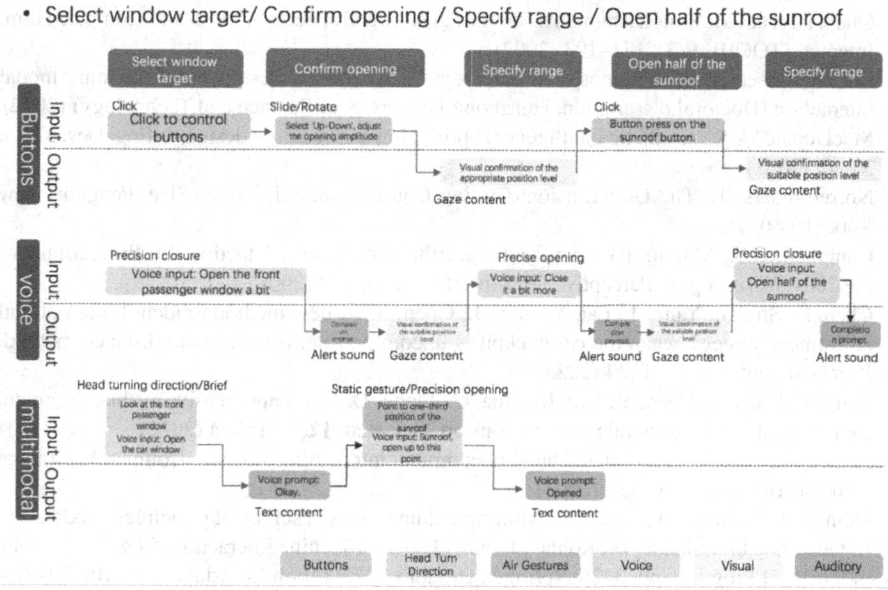

- Select window target/ Confirm opening / Specify range / Open half of the sunroof

Fig. 11. Case study of multimodal analysis methods.

4 Conclusion

In this paper, we use user-centered approach to explore user choices and preferences for interaction modes in vehicle intelligent cockpits in different driving stages. The integration of questionnaire and interview methods enriches the understanding of Don Norman's three levels of emotional system, providing comprehensive data support through quantitative and qualitative analyses for different driving stages. In the questionnaire survey, users have different interaction preferences under different driving stages, which indicates that the design of different interaction preferences under different driving states is meaningful. Interview results unveil trends in users' modal preferences for specific tasks and highlight their focus on relevant topics. Finally, the interaction input and output are subdivided through user research, and a multimodal combination method is proposed by taking the interaction task of opening car windows and sunroofs as an example. These findings provide substantial guidance for automotive manufacturers and designers, enabling them to meet users' interaction needs in various driving scenarios and enhance the overall user experience and safety of intelligent vehicle cockpits.

Disclosure of Interests. The authors have no competing interests to declare that are relevant to the content of this article.

References

1. Bunt, H., Beun, R.J., Borghuis, T. (eds.): Multimodal Human-Computer Communication: Systems, Techniques, and Experiments, vol. 1374. Springer, Cham (1998). https://doi.org/10.1007/BFb0052309

2. Quek, F., et al.: Multimodal human discourse: gesture and speech. ACM Trans. Comput.-Hum. Interact. (TOCHI) **9**(3), 171–193 (2002)
3. Liu, J.: Research on automotive interior space experience design based on multimodal interaction (Doctoral dissertation, Huazhong University of Science and Technology) (2022)
4. MacDonald, A.S.: Aesthetic intelligence: optimizing user-centred design. J. Eng. Des. **12**(1), 37–45 (2001)
5. Norretranders, T.: The User Illusion: Cutting Consciousness Down to Size. Penguin, New York (1999)
6. Campbell, C.S., Maglio, P.P.: A robust algorithm for reading detection. In: Proceedings of the 2001 Workshop on Perceptive User Interfaces, pp. 1–7 (2001)
7. Chen, F., Shi, H., Yang, J., Lai, Y., Han, J., Chen, Y.: A new method to identifying optimal adjustment strategy when the car cockpit is uncomfortable: optimal state distance method. PeerJ Comput. Sci. **9**, e1324 (2023)
8. Yang, J., Xing, S., Chen, Y., Qiu, R., Hua, C., Dong, D.: A comprehensive evaluation model for the intelligent automobile cockpit comfort. Sci. Rep. **12**(1), 15014 (2022)
9. Jaimes, A., Sebe, N.: Multimodal human–computer interaction: a survey. Comput. Vis. Image Underst. **108**(1–2), 116–134 (2007)
10. Dumas, B., Lalanne, D., Oviatt, S.: Multimodal interfaces: a survey of principles, models and frameworks. In: Lalanne, D., Kohlas, J. (eds.) Human Machine Interaction: Research Results of the MMI Program, pp. 3–26. Springer, Heidelberg (2009). https://doi.org/10.1007/978-3-642-00437-7_1
11. Lalanne, D., Nigay, L., Palanque, P., Robinson, P., Vanderdonckt, J., Ladry, J.F.: Fusion engines for multimodal input: a survey. In: Proceedings of the 2009 International Conference on Multimodal Interfaces, pp. 153–160 (2009)
12. Van Wassenhove, V., Grant, K.W., Poeppel, D.: Visual speech speeds up the neural processing of auditory speech. Proc. Natl. Acad. Sci. **102**(4), 1181–1186 (2005)
13. Reeves, L.M., et al.: Guidelines for multimodal user interface design. Commun. ACM **47**(1), 57–59 (2004)
14. Stickdorn, M., Schneider, J.: This is Service Design Thinking: Basics, Tools, Cases. Wiley, BIS Publishers, New York (2012)
15. Norman, D.: The Design of Everyday Things: Revised and Expanded Edition. Basic Books, New York (2013)
16. Fowler, F.J., Jr.: Survey Research Methods. Sage Publications, New York (2013)
17. Kvale, S., Brinkmann, S.: Interviews: Learning the Craft of Qualitative Research Interviewing. Sage, New York (2009)
18. Wicks, D.: The coding manual for qualitative researchers. Qual. Res. Organ. Manage. Int. J. **12**(2), 169–170 (2017)
19. Namey, E., Guest, G., Thairu, L., Johnson, L.: Data reduction techniques for large qualitative data sets. Handb. Team-Based Qual. Res. **2**(1), 137–161 (2008)
20. Corbin, J., Strauss, A.: Techniques and procedures for developing grounded theory. In: Basics of Qualitative Research, 3rd edn. Sage, Thousand Oaks, CA, USA, pp. 860–886 (2008)
21. Bowen, G.A.: Naturalistic inquiry and the saturation concept: a research note. Qual. Res. **8**(1), 137–152 (2008)
22. Fu, R., Zhao, X., Li, Z., Zhao, C., Wang, C.: Evaluation of the visual-manual resources required to perform calling and navigation tasks in conventional mode with a portable phone and in full-touch mode with an embedded system. Ergonomics **66**(10), 1633–1651 (2023)

Speculative Design and Creativity

Guided Fantasy: A Research Method
for Innovative Products

Adriano Bernardo Renzi[✉]

MobileLive Inc. , Toronto, ON M5J 1A7, Canada
adrianorenzi@gmail.com

Abstract. Larry Tesler developed the first experimentation with Guided Fantasy in 1973, together with Tim Mott, at the Parc labs at Xerox. The method was one of many user-centered methods used to test usability at the lab (Moggride 2007, p.48.). While research methods and usability testing such as heuristic evaluation, think-aloud protocol, cooperative evaluation, etc., help investigate pain points and usability issues, and map users' expectations and mental models, the Guided Fantasy allows researchers to map how a new system should be structured based on users' cultural conventions and references. It allows designers and developers to build a new product together with users. This paper presents the remapping of the method 50 years later, through three experiments conducted in both in-person and remote contexts, detailing the process and results for discussion and new learnings. The three projects used for the experiments described here are related to project management, banking systems and telecom service.

Keywords: UX research · UX methods · Innovation

1 Introduction: Innovation A Subsection Sample

Innovation has been commonly used in the industry to represent new products, new services, new processes, new apparatuses, and new ways of thinking, not necessarily following the scientific definitions for the characterization of its typology.

One of the major problems in innovation management is that there is not a single definition between researchers, policymakers, and authorities. Innovation is deprived of innovative thinking, which means creating new things.

Kogabayev and Maziliauskus (2017) from their finance context base their studies about innovation on many different authors – Rowe and Boise (1974), Dewar & Dutton (1986), Rogers (1995), Utterback (1994), Afuah (1998), Fischer (2001), Garcia & Calantone (2002), McDermott & O'Connor (2002), Pedersen & Dalum (2004), and the Frascati Manual (2004) –, but narrow down the definitions of innovation from 4 researchers:

Urabe (1988): "generation of a new idea and its implementation into a new product, process or service, leading to the dynamic growth of the national economy and the increase of employment as well as to a creation of pure profit for the innovative business enterprise. Innovation is never a one-time phenomenon, but a long and cumulative process of a great number of organizational decision-making processes, ranging from the phase of generation of a new idea to its implementation phase. New idea refers

A. Marcus et al. (Eds.): HCII 2024, LNCS 14713, pp. 277–289, 2024.
https://doi.org/10.1007/978-3-031-61353-1_19

to the perception of a new customer need or a new way to produce. It is generated in the cumulative process of information-gathering, coupled with an ever-challenging entrepreneurial vision. Through the implementation process, the new idea is developed and commercialized into a new marketable product or a new process with attendant cost reduction and increased productivity".

- Schumpeter (1982): "regards innovation as the economic impact of technological change, as the use of new combinations of existing productive forces to solve the problems of business".
- Twiss (1989): "a process that combines science, technology, economics and management, as it is to achieve novelty and extends from the emergence of the idea to its commercialization in the form of production, exchange, consumption".
- Afuah (1998): "new knowledge incorporated in products, processes, and services – classified according to technological, market, and administrative/organizational characteristics".

Although innovation can bring definitions from different points of view, there are many common characteristics, independent of the diverse areas of knowledge. They all refer at some point to change, to impact, and novelty for society, technology, processes, and market.

Different authors also categorize innovation based on different perspectives:

- Schumpeter, from his economics lens, presents five types of innovation: (1) New, still unknown in the sphere of consumption, benefit, or new quality known good, (2) Opening new market opportunities for well-known products, (3) Reorganization of production, leading to the erosion of some established therein monopoly, (4) The discovery of new sources of raw materials or semi-finished products, (5) A new, more efficient method of production that is not associated with scientific discovery.
- Davydenko (2011) classifies innovation into 7 categories based on: (1) application (2) STP stages, (3) intensity, (4) pace, (5) scope, (6) effectiveness, and (7) efficiency.
- Siauliai (2013) classifies into 3 main types: (1) basic – basis of major inventions, marks the beginning of new, previously unknown products or processes based on new scientific principles, (2) improving – small but important improvement of products, processes, services, and (3) Fake – External modify products or processes that do not lead to a change in their consumer characteristics.
- (Zizlavsky 2014) points to the Oslo Manual as a commonly used substantive typology of innovation terms and cites the four main types of innovation recognized: (1) product innovations, (2) process innovations, (3) marketing innovations, and (4) organizational innovations (OECD, 2005).

Adding to the presented types of innovation from the cited authors, innovation can also be measured by degrees. Based on Schumpeter's theory, which repeatedly emphasized that radical innovations play a key role in economic development, Zizlavsky (2014) summarizes the degrees of innovation into:

- Radical – represents the introduction of revolutionary new technologies (e.g. Kock, 2007).
- Incremental – gradual improvement of existing technology, with quantifiable impacts on business (e.g. Garcia and Calantone, 2002).

- Rationalization – involves the prevention and elimination of production losses while using existing business elements optimally.
- Disruptive – disrupts the existing market or create entirely new markets (Christensen, 1997)

The author differentiates innovation from invention and places them as part of the same process, as invention is only the first step in a long process, during which a good idea is transformed into a widely applicable, effective product. Invention and innovation often take place separately and it may take many years (15–20 years according to Bill Buxton - Interaction America 2013) before an invention can be applied in practice to become innovation – and many inventions never reach this stage.

2 Research for Innovation

The Parc labs at Xerox is often mentioned as a historical mark when talking about the first steps of research in human-computer interaction. It was a key part in the transition from the 1st wave to the 2nd wave of interaction (Renzi et al. 2018). Within this scenario, Larry Tesler developed the method Guided Fantasy in 1973. Together with Tim Mott (both from Parc labs at Xerox), they created many user-centered methods that often would test usability at the lab between 1974 and 1975 (Moggridge 2007, p. 48.)

The Guided Fantasy was used to help create what would be the future first word editor, together with future users of the software. They interviewed secretaries, editors, and copywriters to have a better sense of users' daily experiences and to help build a new system from scratch based on users' needs and expectations. Together with users, they started designing the structure, features, visuals, and interactions for the text editor. Recorded interviews from Moggridge's book "Designing interactions" show that this research proposal was mainly related to radical innovation products.

The process presented by Tesler and Mott while creating the editor system calls attention to the Guided Fantasy method, as there was no pre-built, or even defined, editing system that participants could interact with. Editors were put in front of a computer with nothing on display and moved a disconnected mouse around to make imaginative interactions. Participants were asked to explain and show their working process, while imagining using a text editing system, At the time people used pencils, erasers, and typewriters. Participants would imagine technological possibilities non-existent at the time and show how it should be built.

From Moggride's (2007) series of interviews, Tim Mott describes: "when we got to the part of deleting the text, they (editors) said they wanted to select the whole thing, just like they did when underlining or scratching whole phrases. Until that moment, the way to select pieces of text was by marking the beginning and the end of the section and activating 'SELECT'. Nobody had thought of using the mouse to draw throughout the text [...] characteristics we see in text editing systems come directly from this research project with people who worked with text editing all their lives, and we would ask: how would you like to do this?".

Throughout my research about Guided Fantasy origins and process, not a lot of references aside from Tesler and Mott could be found in scientific publications. The ones related to the terminology are focused on psychological recovery, learning, or creative stimulus, a very different topic from technology innovation. These references are not considered relevant to this paper.

While research techniques and usability testing such as heuristic evaluation, think-aloud protocol, cooperative evaluation, etc., help investigate pain points and usability issues, and map users' expectations and mental models, the Guided Fantasy allows researchers to map how a new system should be structured based on users' cultural conventions and references (Renzi 2016). The method invites users to build together how a system should work and look based on their own experiences and expectations.

The 3 experiments described in this paper show that the method can bring users as co-designers in creating interaction structures, informational spaces, and new displays based on how they think a system should work, and bring understanding of their whole experience journey with a system, an ecology of systems or service. The experiments presented in this paper were about 3 very different projects and conducted in 3 different contexts: (A) management system, (B) banking app, and (C) telecom website.

For a better comparison of factors, objectives, and results, each phase of the Guided Fantasy will describe the 3 experiments in detail in this paper.

3   Guided Fantasy in 3 Experiments

The goals of each project, depicted as experiments, were distinct and connected with innovation categories in different ways. In experiment A (management), the use of Guided Fantasy helped understand how design studio owners in Brazil were thinking/planning project management and how a management system should look to better help them plan and strategically manage many projects at the same time.

The participants invited for these sessions were all (12) designers and owners of design agencies with 2–12 employees range – categorized as micro and small businesses by IBGE (Instituto Brasileiro de Geografia e Estatística). The participants were from all 3 types of managers (educated, adaptive, and intuitive[1]), according to the categorization presented in the thesis (Renzi 2016) "User Experience: the journey of Designers in their studio's management processes using a fantasized system based on an ecosystem of cross-channel interaction".

For experiment B, Guided Fantasy helped build a new Bank app from scratch, based on customers' journeys and needs while interacting with the bank. The previous app was considered outdated and customers mainly used the website (and physical branches) to connect with the bank. The goal was to structure, organize, and create shortcuts based on customers' daily financial interactions and needs, and cross-reference with technology possibilities and bank strategies. The participants for this experiment were customers of the bank from the Emiliano Regina region in Italy and categorized by generation type: millennials, Gen X, and baby boomers[2].

---

[1] *Educated manager - the manager who has formal education in management; Adaptative manager - the manager that transfers knowledge from other areas to his/her management challenges; Intuitive manager - the manager with no previous knowledge and has built management experience throughout the years as the agency owner - Renzi 2016, p.210.*

[2] *Baby Boomers, born between 1954 and 1964, are commonly considered to have the most difficulties with digital media and the Internet; Generation X, born between 1964 and 1982, are considered, globally speaking, the active workforce with entrepreneur characteristics; Millennials (Gen Y), born between 1981 and 1998 (Fig. 3), is a generation marked by the turn of the millennium and important technological evolutions. – Renzi et al. 2020, p.83.*

In experiment C, Guided Fantasy was used to help structure and reorganize the display of information in a telecom website - encompassing the homepage and 2nd information pages within a 1-click action. Opposed to experiments A and B, the participants for this experiment C had all the existing features and actions to start from, when building their new system. The invited participants were customers and non-customers of the telecom company, responsible financially for their wireless account living in Canada – millennials, X, and baby boomer generations. This was a continued study from the results collected previously using Prioritization Matrix (Renzi and Agner 2023) that helped understand what customers consider to be the most important information and features on a telecom website, the focus of this experiment is connected to customers of a telecom company (not to be mentioned here because of non-disclosure contracts).

3.1 Setting up the Research Sessions

Experiment A (management system) was conducted individually in 2014, and in person, with invited designer-managers. Pens, pencils, colored pencils, blank A4 papers, and 2 cardboard matrixes simulating different sizes of displays (phone, iPad) were used in every session. The participants were part of a series of research sessions and recruited after being categorized as one of the 3 manager types (educated, adaptive, or intuitive), through a chain of contacts in Rio de Janeiro – following recruiting guidance described as chain of contact from "Delphi method to explore future scenario possibilities on technology and HCI" - Renzi and Freitas 2015.

The sessions were held in their own design agencies, at the most appropriate time slot selected by each participant. The session duration varied between 35 and 65 min (Renzi 2016, p.148–158).

For experiment B (bank app), in 2020, a total of 30 people participated, organized by generation type on different days (Millennial on day one, get x on day two, baby boomers on day 3). On each day, a 10-person group from the same generation was divided into two smaller groups of 5 and the guided fantasy was the longest part of a series of workshop activities, leading to a total duration of 4 h each day. The recruiting was done through an Italian recruiting agency, following characteristics that would represent variations of each generation. The participants were from the region of Emiliano Regina, Italy, representing the highest number of customers for the bank – also the bank headquarters location.

For the Guided Fantasy part, each group received a stack of papers with printed phone templates, pencils, pens, colored pencils, and markers, where each group would create and discuss ideas, mimicking interaction with a bank app to fulfill tasks.

The experiment C (telecom website), in 2022, had a total of 20 participants. The sessions were conducted individually and remotely through video conference, where the researcher would share access to a mural board with each participant. The duration of each session varied between 30 and 60 min, where participants would be presented with information areas to be organized into basic templates of the homepage, profile page, and secondary page (1-click). The recruiting and video interviews were done through usertesting.com and a set of parameters were set to help filter participants. Although the sessions were not organized by generation, as in experiment B, the filtering process was planned to have representation from generations millennial, X, and baby boomer. The participants were financially independent, responsible for their own wireless account, a minimum income of 50k, at least a high school degree, and to be a resident of Canada.

Due to remote interview possibilities, it was possible to recruit participants from a range of cities throughout Canada (from Vancouver to Hallifax).

3.2 Conducting the Research Sessions

Following the same topic (management) from previous interviews with the designer-managers, each session in experiment A started with warm-up questions about their company, types of projects, and management in general. To have participants start creating the system, a series of situational contexts were shared with them and specific project management tasks were proposed. The participants verbalized what types of features they would need to fulfill the tasks and plan strategically, to soon after draw how the system should be organized visually. While drawing the system, the designer-managers would explain how the system would work and what would be their process of managing multiple projects at the same time.

Experiment B gathered 2 groups of 4–5 people each day and the 4-h session would start with 3 warm-up insights collected from previous interviews to start group discussions about interactions with the bank. The insights presented would have points of view from different generations to see what would be the opinions from each group. The session moved forward to specific situational tasks for discussion and a priority matrix (Renzi and Agner 2023) session with features proposed by bank stakeholders, before starting the Guided Fantasy procedure (Fig. 1).

Fig. 1. Participants discuss and organize features and actions in prioritization matrix templates as a base to start drawing ideas of how an app should look like.

The Guided Fantasy phase would present situations and tasks for the groups and they would discuss among themselves while drawing on the phone templates how the system should look like and how the interactions should happen to fulfill the tasks. After each group confirmed which ones would be the official drawings, they would present the ideas and explain the actions and processes to fulfill tasks in the imagined system.

As experiment C was performed remotely, the pencil drawing and coloring process was adapted to creating and reshaping preset basic polygonal shapes available in the Mural app. Similar to the previous experiences, this one also started with warm-up questions to know more about participants' interests and journeys when entering their telecom website. Based on the insights collected in the warm-up section, tasks would be suggested for participants and they would draw polygonal shapes and organize the information as they saw fit when interacting with the website, putting together how the system should look and organized – Fig. 2. The features used in experiment C are substituted by letters and numbers in Figs. 2 and 5, due to non-disclosure contracts.

Fig. 2. Mural board in which users would help organize and create shapes to show how the website should be organized

4 Results

Experiment A (management system) presented very clear patterns of organization of the information for multiple project management and how to best display them. Similar ideas were brought up by participants from the 3 types of management experience categories (educated, adaptive, and intuitive). It was interesting to notice that higher knowledge on the subject led to more detailed and more complex structures, therefore the managers from the category educated created systems more complex and detailed than the ones from the category adaptive and even more than the ones from the category intuitive. The differences in complexity were more obvious in parts related to finance management, where the intuitive managers would express thinking based on in and out cashier flows and the other two would include prospecting, marketing, investments, etc. – Fig. 3a and 3b.

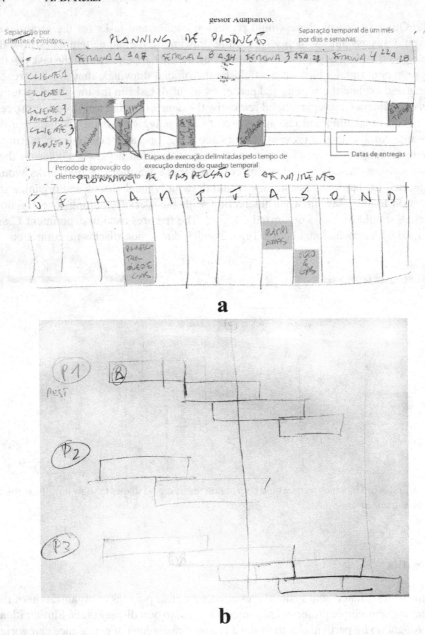

Fig. 3. a. Example of drawing creation from Guided Fantasy, where one participant organizes different phases of a project in separate rows, creates precedents and duration by columns of weeks and general overview of projects by columns of months. b. Example of drawing creation from Guided Fantasy, where one participant organizes different phases of 3 projects in separate rows, creates precedents and duration by columns of weeks.

In experiment B (bank app), participants would discuss ideas and get to a final agreement before presenting the drawings. Patterns of ideas were easily noticeable, but also unique ideas that led to interesting discussions. The created displays would bring more information/feature organization planning than drawings of shapes and forms. The features discussed previously in the prioritization matrix provided a structured and objective thinking of what should go where and how the interaction should go – Fig. 4.

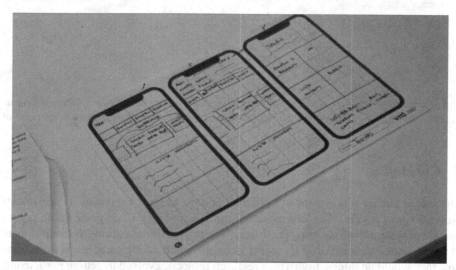

Fig. 4. Example of drawing creation from Guided Fantasy, using smartphone template, where one of the groups organizes the features and displays of the bank app.

Since experiment C was conducted remotely, the forms and shapes rearranged by participants were more simple, as they used preset shapes from the Mural app board. The shapes were re-dimensioned to represent areas of information and similar patterns of thinking were easy to spot – Fig. 5. Participants reorganized proposed features according to their interests and experience from regular usage of telecom websites. For experiment C, indicating areas of information sufficed to guide the project, since the telecom company has design guidelines to use in any change of the website structure.

Besides information areas, participants presented how the connections and interaction should work and how some information content could be interchangeable and highlighted (A, B, C, D - E on the left figure).

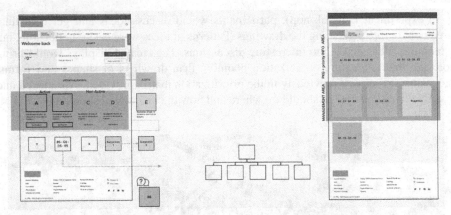

Fig. 5. Example of display creation from Guided Fantasy, using Mural board, where each participant organizes the features and the information of the website according to his/her point of view.

5 Conclusion

The guided fantasy was adapted to 3 different context scenarios and in all 3 experiments presented great results to: understand users' thinking processes, and guide the designing process of systems with the help of real users. The original idea of setting the environment to the closest expectation of an inexistent technology and asking participants to describe how they would do things, from Tim's research projects, evolved to getting participants to express their thoughts not only verbally, but also visually – through drawing ideas, organizing spaces, creating shapes, and categorizing information.

The 3 experiments showed that the starting of visual expression should be sparkled by a precedent action to help set context, set references, set boundaries, and to warm up the thinking process. All presented experiments had something precedent and sometimes integrated into the Guided Fantasy session:

- experiment 1 (management) started with an exploratory semi-structured interview, followed by controlled topics discussion based on interview results that merged into the Guided Fantasy proceedings;
- experiment 2 (bank app) had a previous interview to map general characteristics and select participants for the Guided Fantasy session. For the session itself, statements collected from the interviews were presented for a discussion panel to start the session, followed by a prioritization matrix to present features and items and organize them by importance (from users' perspective). The set of boundaries by features led to the starting discussion for the Guided Fantasy proceedings;
- Experiment 3 (telecom website) was one full session with each participant, starting with an interview to set up the context, followed by a prioritization matrix to help users express the importance order of items and help participants in the thinking process of what is important to them before starting the Guided Fantasy.

The 3 experiments showed that it is ok for the participants to look for references (of how something works, of how something looks like, how is a specific brand, etc.)

themselves to help them create. There will always be people with more and people with less creativity abilities, and the best way to encourage drawing and creation seems to be helping participants drag creation from their own experiences. The use of templates (physical and digital) helped to set boundaries, create references, and connect to familiarity and understanding, even if the participants decided not to create from the template during the session. This was learned in the 1st experiment and re-used in the 2 other experiments, leading to a gradual learning/improving journey for the method.

Experiment 2 relied on phone templates to help participants connect with their own experience and draw on it, while using shapes and forms in the remote experiment (3) was fundamental for the participants and supported the lack of physical presence, drawing materials, and unfamiliarity with the app. In order for experiment 3 to be successful, it was important to bring learnings from previous experiments with a prioritization matrix in a remote environment (Renzi and Agner 2023).

Although the experiment (1) with less usage of templates can lead to a more free imagination creation, it is harder to get the sparkling point of the drawing. It required a much longer introductory conversation with the participants than the other 2 experiments. As the template becomes more prominent in the other 2 experiment sessions, the faster is the sparkle point. But it can limit possibilities of expansion of creativity – leaving it to the researcher to adapt as he/she feels the engagement of participants and how comfortable they are to express ideas.

Each variation of the guided fantasy was important to understand and improve the experience of the research method and not affect the results and goals of each project:

As experiment 1 was more related to radical innovation (Zizlavsky 2014) and understanding the designer-manager thinking process, it was better to have a more free session for creation. The sessions helped map the whole project management process of the 3 types of managers (Renzi 2016) – "a new, still unknown in the sphere of consumption, benefit, or new quality" (Schumpeter 1982).

Experiment 2 had free creation sessions with pencil and paper, but also had boundaries from preset features by stakeholders and technology possibilities of the banking industry. Nevertheless, brought up incremental and disruptive innovations (Zizlavsky 2014), leading to changes in intellectual property contract between the companies involved in the project, and to become a reference to future bank apps in Europe – "reorganization of production, leading to the erosion of some established therein monopoly" (Schumpeter 1982).

Experiment 3 was the one with less space for drawing actions, due to the characteristics of the project, and had the most boundaries from the limited number of features offered by telecom providers. The project brought incremental and rationalization innovation ideas (Zizlavsky 2014) related to the organization of information and personalization of service based on customers' interest – "a new, more efficient method of production that is not associated with scientific discovery." (Schumpeter 1982).

References

Moggridge, B.: Designing interactions. In: MIT Press, 766f. Massachusetts (2007)

Kolubayev, T., Maziliauskus, A.: The role of innovation for efficiency of investments. In: Science and Studies of Accounting and Finance Problems and Perspectives, November 2016

Dewar, J.L., Dutton, J.: The adoption of radical and incremental innovations: an empirical analysis. Manage. Sci. 32(11), 1422–1433 (1986). https://doi.org/10.1287/mnsc.32.11.1422

Rowe, A., Boise, B.: Organizational innovation: current research and evolving concepts. Public Adm. Rev. 34(3), 284–293 (1974)

Utterback, J.: Mastering the Dynamics of Innovation: How companies can seize opportunities in the face of Technological Change. Harvard Business School Press. Boston, MA (1994)

Mcdermott, C., O'Connor, G.: Managing radical innovation: an overview of emergent strategy issues. J. Prod. Innov. Manag. 19(6), 424–438 (2002)

Pedersen, C.R., Dalum, B.: Incremental versus radical change - the case of the digital north denmark program. In: 10th International Schumpeter Society Conference, 2004. Bocconi University, Milano, Italy (2004)

Fischer, M.: Innovation, knowledge creation and systems of innovation. Ann. Regional Sci. 35, 199–216 (2001)

Rogers, M.: Diffusion of Innovation, 4th edn. The Free Press, New York (1995)

Manual, F.: Main Definitions and Conventions for the Measurement of Research and Experimental Development (R&D). A Summary of the Frascati Manual. OCDE/GD (94)84 (2004)

Urabe, K.: Innovation and Management: International Comparison. Walter de Gruyter, Berlin, New York (1988)

Schumpeter, J.: Theory of economic development. J. Econ. Literature 20(3), 1049–1059 (1982)

Twiss, B., Goodridge, M.: Managing Technology for Competitive Advantage: integrating technological And Organizational Development: From Strategy To Action. Trans-Atlantic Publications, Philadelphia, PA, USA (1998)

Afuah, A.: Responding to structural industry changes: a technological evolution perspective. Ind. Corp. Chang. 6(1), 183–202 (1998)

Davydenko, L.: Fundamentals of economic theory: principles, problems, politics of transformation. international experience and Belarusian Vector Of Development. Manual, Minsk (2011)

Siauliai, A.: The essence of the concept of "Innovation" as an economic category and economic systems management. Electron. Sci. J. http://www.uecs.ru, Date: 31.10.2013 (1979)

Zizlavsky, O.: An analysis of innovation classification and typology: a literature review. In: Crafting Global Competitive Economies: 2020 Vision Strategic Planning & Smart Implementation Conference proceedings, Milan (2014)

Kock, A.: Innovativeness and innovation success: a meta-analysis. ZFBF Spec. Issue 2, 1–21 (2007)

Garcia, R., Calantone, R.: A critical look at technological innovation typology and innovativeness terminology: a literature review. J. Product Innov. Manage. 19(2), 110–132 (2002)

Christensen, C.M.: The Innovator's Dilemma: When new Technologies Cause Great Firms to Fail, p. 1997. Harvard Business School Press, Boston (1997)

Renzi, A.B., Fiuza, J., Muniz, J.V.A.: Experiência do usuário pervasiva no planejamento de viagens: mapeando modelo mental e criando personas. In SPGD 2018 proceedings, v.1. Rio de Janeiro (2018)

Renzi, A.B., et al.: User experience journey with multiple devices and telepresence during quarantine. Ergodesign & HCI Journal. Rio de Janeiro. N.1, v.8 jan-jun (2020)

Buxton, B.: Why eBay is a better prototyping tool than a 3D printer, the long nose, and other tales of history. In: Interaction South America Conference. Recife, Brazil (2013)

Renzi, A.B.: Experiência do usuário: a jornada de designers nos processos de gestão de suas empresas de pequeno porte com utilização de sistema fantasiado em ecossistema de interação cross-channel [thesis]. Escola Superior de Desenho Industrial - UERJ. Rio de Janeiro, Brazil (2016)

Renzi, A.B., Agner, L.: Prioritization matrix to highlight business opportunities. In: Design, User Experience, and Usability. 12th International Conference, DUXU 2023. Proceeding, part I, pp. 38–50. Copenhagen, Denmark (2023)

Renzi, A.B., Freitas, S.: The Delphi method for future scenarios construction. In: APPLIED Human Factors and Ergonomics Conference. Procedia Manufacturing, vol. 3, pp. 5785–5791, Las Vegas, USA (2015)

Reform and Practice of "Foundation of Innovation and Entrepreneurship" Course Based on "Three Phases and Six Segments" Experiential Teaching

Xiaoshi Chen[1,2] and Jixu Zhu[1,2(✉)]

[1] Guangzhou City University of Technology, Guangzhou, China
zhujixu@gcu.edu.cn
[2] SEGi University, Kota Damansara, Malaysia

Abstract. With the arrival of the era of "Mass entrepreneurship and innovation" in China, a large number of innovation and entrepreneurship courses have been opened in colleges and universities. However, the current courses mostly focus on theoretical teaching and ignore the problem of ability cultivation. In order to stimulate students' innovative thinking and entrepreneurial potential, this study explores the effect of applying the "three phases and six segments" experiential teaching mode in the course of "Foundation of Innovation and Entrepreneurship". The teaching mode includes three stages of pre-course preparation, in-course implementation and post-course consolidation, as well as six segments of designing, creating, experiencing, sharing, constructing, and transferring, emphasizing that students can acquire knowledge and ability in practice through "hands-on, experience and feeling". In this study, two classes were selected for comparative experiments, one adopting the experiential teaching mode and the other adopting the traditional lecture method. The results show that the experiential teaching mode can significantly stimulate students' interest in learning, cultivate their innovative thinking, and improve their entrepreneurial awareness and ability compared with the traditional teaching mode. This study verifies the application effect of experiential teaching mode in innovation and entrepreneurship courses, and provides a reference for the reform of related courses.

Keyword: Three phases and six segments · Experiential teaching · Foundation of Innovation and Entrepreneurship · Curriculum reform

1 Introduction

China's economic and social progress towards a new phase, coupled with the adoption of an innovation-driven development strategy and the onset of the "mass entrepreneurship and innovation" era, has led to an unprecedented emphasis on innovation and entrepreneurship education in higher education institutions [1]. In the context of a national emphasis on fostering innovation and entrepreneurship, the Ministry of Education has mandated that all universities offer a course titled "Foundation of Innovation and Entrepreneurship." The objective of this course is to equip students with essential knowledge and skills necessary for entrepreneurship, including a comprehensive understanding of the fundamental principles and methodologies of entrepreneurship. Additionally, students will gain familiarity with the legal and regulatory frameworks, as well as relevant policies, governing entrepreneurial activities. The course aims to cultivate students' entrepreneurial mindset, enhance their sense of social responsibility, foster their innovative thinking, and develop their entrepreneurial capabilities. Ultimately, the course seeks to facilitate students' engagement in entrepreneurial endeavors, promote employment opportunities, and foster holistic personal growth [2]. However, the current "Foundation of Innovation and Entrepreneurship" course in China's colleges and universities generally focuses on theoretical teaching and ignores the problem of ability cultivation, resulting in poor course results and limited enhancement of students' innovation and entrepreneurship awareness and ability [3]. Therefore, how to reform the traditional knowledge-transferring teaching of "Foundation of Innovation and Entrepreneurship" and build a teaching mode that can stimulate students' innovative thinking and entrepreneurial potential is an urgent problem to be solved.

Xing et al. (2016) proposed that experiential teaching should be student-centred, experience-based, and team-based, and the implementation process includes five links: clarifying the goal, transforming the role, implementing the experience, providing guidance, and summarizing and reflecting [4]. At present, researchers both domestically and internationally have looked at the reform of entrepreneurship courses from a variety of perspectives. The key findings of their studies are as follows: According to Gao et al. (2022), successful experiential learning involves teachers and students as well as students and themselves in a state of interaction and dialogue, continuously satisfying the students' three psychological needs of "autonomy," "competence," and "relationship," and gradually enhancing and strengthening entrepreneurial motivation [5]. According to Yang et al. (2020), the main objective of innovation and entrepreneurship education is to cultivate students' innovative spirit, entrepreneurial awareness, and entrepreneurial ability. Teachers should also modify students' perspectives, allow students to work hands-on in the classroom, actively engage in experiential activities, and fully stimulate students' enthusiasm and interest in learning [6].

In summary, experiential teaching emphasizes students' subjective participation and intuitive experience, which can promote the internalization and application of knowledge. However, the existing entrepreneurship course reforms such as the case teaching method still have the problem of theorization, and there are fewer studies on the combination of experiential teaching with innovation and entrepreneurship courses, so the related research and practice need to be expanded. This study introduces the "three phases and six segments" experiential teaching mode, takes the course of "Foundation of Innovation and Entrepreneurship" as the object of study, and actively explores the teaching concept, process and method to stimulate the students' entrepreneurial interests and potentials, and improve the teaching effect of the innovation and entrepreneurship course. The research findings hold theoretical and practical significance as they can serve as a guide for the reform of China's innovation and entrepreneurship course.

2 The "Three Phases and Six Segments" Experiential Teaching Model

Experiential teaching originated in the early 20th century from the American philosopher Dewey's "learning is experience" idea [7]. The so-called "experiential teaching method", that is, according to the cognitive process, cognitive characteristics of students, in the learning preparation stage, classroom teaching stage, the continuation of the post-course stage and evaluation and analysis of the stage highlights the "experience", with the active participation of students, active exploration, active thinking, active The students' active participation, active exploration, active thinking, active operation and independent activities are characterized [8]. The practical part of entrepreneurship education adopts experiential teaching activities, which can not only encourage students to learn entrepreneurial knowledge actively and consciously, but also, more importantly, it is easier to arouse the participation of various psychological factors of students and have a direct impact on the entrepreneurial literacy of entrepreneurial ability, entrepreneurial personality and entrepreneurial emotions and other non-intellectual factors, so as to make the students' psychological and behavioral intermingle, promote each other, and develop together in the experience. The students' psychology and behavior will be intertwined, mutually promoted and jointly developed in the experience.

The specific process of teaching implementation needs to be centered on the teaching objectives, with the teaching principles as the guideline, based on the teaching content, supplemented by the necessary forms of teaching, and the design of the teaching implementation process is crucial to the development of the course in the later stage [9]. Since this study is the implementation of experiential teaching in the course of "Foundation of Innovation and Entrepreneurship", the following will be in accordance with the teaching process of the implementation of experiential teaching mode, and the teaching process mainly includes three stages of pre-course preparation, in-course implementation and post-course consolidation, as well as six segments of designing, creating, experiencing, sharing, constructing, and transferring, constituting a "three phases and six segments" teaching mode, to give full play to the effect of experiential teaching [9]. As shown in Fig. 1.

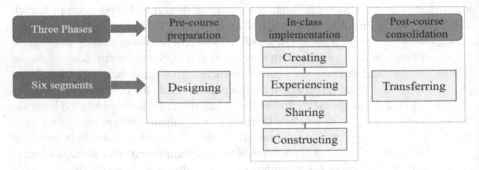

Fig. 1. Foundation of Innovation and Entrepreneurship "three phases and six segments "Teaching Mode

1. Pre-course preparation

Teachers clarify the teaching objectives and determine the knowledge, skills and emotional attitudes that students can obtain. According to the teaching content to choose the appropriate form of experience, such as role-playing, group practical training tasks, etc., and design the teaching situation related to the content of the course, to enhance students' interest in learning. Group students and assign roles, prepare teaching materials to help students have a deeper understanding of knowledge. At the same time, prepare course evaluation forms for students' self-reflection after the activities.

2. In-course implementation

First of all, the teacher guides the students to enter the situation, independent exploration to obtain preliminary experience. Then, through the project-driven, task-oriented approach, the organization of experiential activities, set the corresponding interactive training tasks, student teams to complete the results of the display and sharing. In this process, students experience the whole process in specific situations, and the teacher observes and guides them at the right time. Then, students are organized to share their experiences, and the teacher summarizes the key points of knowledge. Finally, help students to build a complete knowledge system.

3. Post-course consolidation

To encourage learning through competitions, arrange for students to take part in hands-on activities like refining business plans, polishing entrepreneurial projects, and competing in various innovation and entrepreneurship competitions like China International College Students' "Internet+" Innovation and Entrepreneurship Competition, "Challenge Cup" China University Student Entrepreneurship Planning Competition, etc. This will enable students to apply what they have learned to solve practical problems, link theory to practice, and enhance their practical ability. At the same time, course evaluation is carried out to promote students' reflection on the learning process.

3 The Application of "Three Phases and Six Segments" Experiential Teaching to the Teaching Design of "Foundation of Innovation and Entrepreneurship"

3.1 Course Overview

Foundation of Innovation and Entrepreneurship is a mandatory innovation and entrepreneurship class (32 credit hours/2 credits) for students from all majors across the university, and each teaching class is composed of students from different colleges and majors in the university, with cross-fertilization of majors. Through the teaching of knowledge, students can understand the basic knowledge and business process of starting and running a business, and develop their entrepreneurial awareness and entrepreneurial literacy [10]. In the teaching process, "experiential" teaching methods are adopted, through the inter-disciplinary formation of entrepreneurial teams, entrepreneurial project simulation exercises, interactive practical training tasks around the core knowledge of entrepreneurship, students through the use and practice of entrepreneurial core skills necessary to complete the business plan and roadshow report, so as to enhance the entrepreneurial ability of the students and the ability to find employment. The program is designed to enhance students' entrepreneurial ability and employability.

The course is centered on the knowledge and ability required for entrepreneurship, and the course content is divided into Module 1 Entrepreneurial Cognition and Team Formation, Module 2 Innovative Thinking Training and Project Screening, Module 3 Entrepreneurial Project Determination and Market Evaluation, Module 4 Marketing 4P Plan, Module 5 Entrepreneurial Resources and Startup Funding Prediction, Module 6 Business Model Analysis, Module 7 Sales Revenue Prediction, Module 8 Entrepreneurial Financial Analysis, Module 9 Entrepreneurship Financing and Risk Analysis, Module 10 Entrepreneurial Project Roadshow and other ten modules [11].

3.2 Teaching Objectives of the Course

Through the teaching of "Foundation of Innovation and Entrepreneurship" course, students can master the basic knowledge needed to carry out entrepreneurial activities, recognize and analyze entrepreneurs, entrepreneurial opportunities and entrepreneurial resources dialectically, cultivate the innovation and entrepreneurship ability, resource integration ability, teamwork and communication ability needed to carry out innovation and entrepreneurial activities, and encourage the new generation of entrepreneurs to have the mission of the times and responsibility. Entrepreneurs should have the mission and responsibility of the times, and have a sense of social responsibility and national sentiment. The objectives of knowledge, ability and literacy are achieved through course teaching [12]. As shown in Fig. 2.

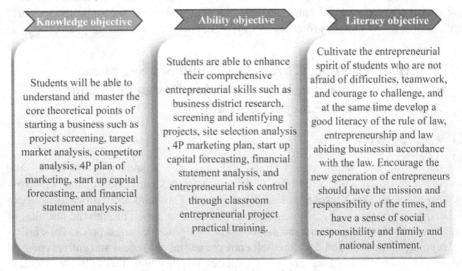

Fig. 2. Teaching objectives of the course

3.3 Teaching Session Design

Business model analysis is very important in the Foundation of Innovation and Entrepreneurship course. Drucker, a master of modern management, once said, "The competition between companies today is not between products, but between business models" [13]. Business model is the operation mode of an enterprise, which is one of the basis and core elements of enterprise profitability [14]. Business model not only determines the operation mode of the enterprise, but also determines the competitive advantage and market position of the enterprise, and its importance to the enterprise cannot be ignored [15]. Therefore, business model analysis is a key content for students to learn. In this paper, we take "Module 6 Business Model Analysis" as an example, and describe the teaching process based on the "three phases and six segments" experiential teaching method. The specific design is shown in Table 1 below.

Table 1. Instructional design for business model analysis

Three phases	Six segments	Content	lesson time
Pre-course preparation	Designing	(1) Define the teaching objectives: to understand the meaning of business model and business model components, through the learning focus on cultivating students to be able to apply the business model canvas reasoning tools, to master the business model design and development of ideas and so on (2) Design situation: create an Internet start-up company situation, students group role-playing (3) Grouping and role allocation: Divide students into 5–6 people for a startup team, assign different positions (4) Preparation of teaching materials: Prepare the course evaluation form, business model canvas, cases and related materials	Extra-curricular hours: 105 min

(*continued*)

Table 1. (*continued*)

Three phases	Six segments	Content	lesson time
In-class Implementation	Creating	(1) To provide students with an understanding of the concept of business models by teaching the concepts and giving examples; (2) To understand the importance of business model analysis for entrepreneurial ventures; (3) Introduce the business model analysis tool - business model canvas; (4) Entering into the situation, students play their respective roles to explore the business model	In-class time: 50 min
	Experiencing	Teachers organize hands-on tasks: (1) Business model design for a pancake stand (15 min); (2) Business model canvas design in conjunction with their group's project (15 min)	In-class time: 30 min
	Sharing	(1) Sharing the results of the group discussion on the business model design of the pancake stand (20 min); (2) Sharing the business model canvas of the group's entrepreneurial project (20 min)	In-class time: 40 min
	Constructing	(1) Intergroup mutual evaluation form assessment feedback (5 min); (2) Teacher's comments, summarize the key knowledge points: business model components logical relationship (10 min)	In-class time: 15 min
Post-course consolidation	Transferring	After-class assignments: (1) Case study - free book rental earns millions of dollars a year, analyze its business model using canvas; (2) Participate in an on-campus and off-campus entrepreneurship competition and be responsible for analyzing the business model of that entry	Extra-curricular hours: 75 min

Table 2. Course Assessment Methods and Contents

Course Assessment Methods and Contents			proportions
Process assessment (50%)	Attendance, theoretical studies (multidimensional assessment)	Learning attendance 20%	20%
		Learning progress 40%	
		Learning discussions 40%	
	Participation in practical training tasks for entrepreneurial projects (multiple assessment subjects)	Intergroup assessment 40% (attitude, reporting of learning outcomes, cooperation)	30%
		Team leader (CEO) assessment 20% (observation of process, overall evaluation)	
		Teacher critique 20% (observing process, summarizing and evaluating)	
Outcome-based assessment (50%)	Participation in China International College Students' "Internet+" Innovation and Entrepreneurship Competition (individual assessment)	Each student participates in China International College Students' "Internet+" Innovation and Entrepreneurship Competition as a project leader, 1 person, 1 project, everyone participates, 3–10 team members	10%
	Business plan (personal assessment)		20%
	Project Roadshow Reporting (Team Assessment)	Student mass judging 50%	20%
		Teacher assessment 50%	
Total			100%

3.4 Course Assessment Methods and Content

In this paper, we design experiential teaching evaluation in experiential teaching mode, and adopt the course performance evaluation method combining process assessment and outcome assessment, in which process assessment accounts for 50%, including attendance and theoretical learning accounts for 20%, and participation in entrepreneurship project practical training tasks accounts for 30%. The outcome assessment

(50%) includes 10% participation in the China International College Students' "Internet+" Innovation and Entrepreneurship Competition, 20% submission of individual entrepreneurial plan and 20% group entrepreneurial project roadshow reporting assessment [11]. As shown in Table 2.

4   Analysis of Teaching Effectiveness

In order to verify the effect of the "three phases and six segments" experiential teaching mode, the authors carried out a comparative experiment in the teaching of two classes of the "Foundation of Innovation and Entrepreneurship" course, in which: class 1 as the control class, the "Foundation of Innovation and Entrepreneurship" of the class adopts the traditional theoretical teaching method; class 2 as the experimental class, the "Foundation of Innovation and Entrepreneurship" course used the "three phases and six segments" experiential teaching mode. Class 2 is the experimental class, in which the course of "Foundation of Innovation and Entrepreneurship" adopts the experiential teaching mode of "three phases and six segments"; students in the experimental class and the control class adopt the same method for the final assessment after the semester, except for the different modes. The SPSS statistical software was used to analyze the teaching effect of the two modes of teaching by conducting independent sample t-tests on the final grades of the two classes. The specific analysis results are shown in Table 3 below.

Table 3. Comparative Analysis of Teaching Effectiveness of Two Teaching Models

Group	Mean value	T	Sig (Two-tailed)
Class 1 (control class)	77.55	2.906	.004**
Class 2 (experimental class)	82.52		

Note: * indicates differences at the significance level of 0.05, ** indicates differences at the significance level of 0.01

The results of the experiment are shown in Table 3, and the independent samples t-test of the two classes showed that $T = 2.906$ and $P = 0.004 < 0.01$, which indicated that there was a highly significant difference between the two modes of teaching and learning at the 0.01 level of significance. Further comparison of the mean value shows that the average grade of students in class 2 (experimental class) is significantly higher than that of class 1 (control class), which indicates that compared with the traditional teaching method, the application of the "three phases and six segments" experiential teaching mode in the teaching of "Foundation of Innovation and Entrepreneurship" is more effective than the traditional teaching method and can significantly improve the students' learning outcomes. The learning outcomes of the students can be significantly improved.

5 Conclusions and Recommendations

Through the research on the application effect of the "three phases and six segments" experiential teaching mode in the course of "Foundation of Innovation and Entrepreneurship", it is found that the experiential teaching mode can better stimulate the students' interest in learning than the traditional theoretical lecture teaching method, especially suitable for the innovation and entrepreneurship courses with strong applicability. The experiential teaching mode allows students to conduct role-playing, scenario simulation, project exploration and other practical experiences by constructing situations, so as to turn abstract knowledge into concrete experiences, thus promoting the internalization and application of knowledge. In the whole process of experiential learning, students can improve their innovative thinking and entrepreneurial awareness, and complete the comprehensive development from knowledge acquisition to ability cultivation to quality improvement. The research results show that the experiential teaching mode emphasizes the organic unity of knowledge transmission, ability cultivation and quality improvement, and is an effective teaching mode for cultivating students' innovation and entrepreneurship literacy. Therefore, promoting the application of experiential teaching mode in the teaching of innovation and entrepreneurship courses is an effective way to improve the teaching effect of entrepreneurship courses. The specific measures are as follows.

1. Improve teachers' understanding of the concept of experiential teaching and provide more diversified experiential opportunities in the design of teaching in order to realize the effects of experiential teaching. Organize seminars on experiential teaching theory to enhance teachers' understanding of the experiential teaching concept; encourage teachers to design courses with diversified activities such as situational experience, role-playing, and project-based practical training to provide rich experiential opportunities.
2. Encourage school-enterprise cooperation and build entrepreneurial situations that are close to reality. Establish a platform for school-enterprise cooperation to promote the docking between teachers and enterprises; teachers organize field visits and project internships for students in cooperative enterprises to set up real business situations and enhance the applicability of teaching.
3. Strengthening process evaluation and timely tracking of students' learning experiences and effects in the process of experiential teaching. Increase formative assessment, such as learning logs, presentation evaluation, etc., to provide timely feedback on students' learning effects; interview and investigate students' learning experiences to adjust and improve teaching methods; continue to expand the application research of experiential teaching in innovation and entrepreneurship courses to enrich the teaching mode and methods.
4. Strengthening the cultivation of teachers' experiential teaching design and implementation skills; organizing workshops on experiential teaching methodology to train teachers' teaching design skills; encouraging teachers to evaluate each other's experiential teaching programs to improve their ability to apply them. Conduct more empirical research to explore the application effect of experiential teaching. Collect and publicize successful experiential teaching cases.

Acknowledgement. The research is funded by Key Research Base of Humanities and Social Sciences in Universities of Guangdong Province: Research Base for Digital Transformation of Manufacturing Enterprises (2023WZJD012).

References

1. Li, L.: A pair-split teaching method based on subject regression in the course of Fundamentals of Innovation and Entrepreneurship. Logistics Eng. Manage. **45**(01), 176–178+173 (2023)
2. Xu, P., Wang, X., Yang, J., et al.: Innovative design and practice of teaching innovation and entrepreneurship fundamentals. Innov. Entrepreneurship Theory Res. Pract. **5**(12), 24–27+86 (2022)
3. Yu, T., Lin, B.: Research on the application strategy of CDIO concept in the teaching of innovation and entrepreneurship basic course. Innov. Entrepreneurship Theory Res. Pract. **5**(17), 13–15 (2022)
4. Xing, Y., Lu, B., Shi, J., et al.: Exploration of student-oriented experiential teaching mode-from knowledge to wisdom. Res. High. Eng. Educ. **2016**(05), 122–128 (2016)
5. Gao, X., Ma, L.: New exploration of experiential teaching mode in university entrepreneurship education: using self-determination theory as a tool. J. Hebei Univ. (Philos. Soc. Sci. Ed.) **47**(06), 99–109 (2022)
6. Yang, M., Ma, Y.: Exploration and application of experiential teaching in innovation and entrepreneurship basic course. J. Sichuan Cadre Correspondence Coll. **03**, 101–104 (2020)
7. Schratz, M., Westfall-Greiter, T.: Learning as experience: a continental European perspective on the nature of learning. Phenomenological pedagogy and vignette research: University of Innsbruck (2015)
8. Zhang, H.: E-course of college badminton curriculum based on multimedia platform: an experiential teaching method. RISTI (Revista Iberica de Sistemas e Tecnologias de Informacao) **E5**, 106–115 (2016)
9. Zhai, Y.: Research on the application of experiential teaching in the teaching of international trade practice in secondary vocational education. Guangdong Technical Normal University (2023). https://doi.org/10.27729/d.cnki.ggdjs.2023.000382
10. Liu, Z., Chen, X.: Blended teaching design based on online courses–a case study of "Fundamentals of Innovation and Entrepreneurship" course. Technol. Wind **28**, 55–57 (2021)
11. Liu, Z., Chen, X.: Research on the path of enhancing teaching effect of basic course of innovation and entrepreneurship-taking Guangzhou City Polytechnic as an example. Mod. Commun. **15**, 1–3 (2021)
12. Chen, X.: Innovative design and practice of teaching fundamentals of innovation and entrepreneurship-taking Guangzhou City Polytechnic as an example. Qual. Mark. **22**, 58–60 (2021). https://doi.org/10.19392/j.cnki.1671-7341.202128019
13. Jaworski, B., Cheung, V.: Creating the Organization of the Future: Building on Drucker and Confucius Foundations. Emerald Publishing Limited (2023)
14. Chen, J., Guo, Z., Tang, Y.: Research on B2C E-commerce business model based on system dynamics. Am. J. Ind. Bus. Manag. **9**(04), 854 (2019)
15. Zhou, Y., Zhang, L., Lu, R.: The impact of network ties on SMEs' business model innovation and enterprise growth: evidence from China. IEEE Access **10**, 29846–29858 (2022)

Framework for a Project Methodology in Design - Interactions in Speculation and Fictional Futures

Susana Leonor[1](✉) ⓘ and David Palma[1,2](✉) ⓘ

[1] ISMAT, Rua Dr. Estêvão de Vasconcelos, n°. 33, 8500-656 Portimão, Portugal
{susana.leonor,david.palma}@ismat.pt

[2] FAUL, Pólo Universitário, Rua Sá Nogueira, Alto da Ajuda, 1349-063 Lisboa, Portugal

Abstract. Exploring concepts such as speculation, fiction, and critical design in disciplines where creativity overcomes is an approach to identifying potential development, innovation, and future possibilities in contemporary societies according to a set of rational, evolutionary, and sequential data. We presented a framework that guides the students through steps throughout the creative process, allowing them to substantiate concepts, proposals, and utopian and dystopian visions of possible futures. The different dimensions used in this framework can potentially overcome students' creative limitations regarding what they consider factual truth toward more holistic, altruistic, and transformational visions. The exploration and creation of future scenarios are driven by the possibility of conceiving new potential forms of interaction and behaviors between humans and machines, which also requires critical reflection on their purpose and possible consequences. This approach enables a renewed vision regarding Human-Computer Interaction (HCI) - how we engage with it and integrate technology positively within an artifact, system, experience, or service. Above all, underlying the pedagogical practice, the project methodology identified here through this proposed framework is the learning of the global contexts with which the designer has to work, aware of the impact of his projects in the short and long term, and that he also has the transformational role with society, the environment, and ethics. With this paper, we aim to contribute to a framework that enables the introduction of speculative and factional approaches to design students in higher education.

Keywords: Human-computer Interaction · Speculative design framework · Design Education

1 Introduction

Design is commonly introduced and approached in higher education as a professionalizing field that allows for solving problems and emerging issues, especially of a commercial nature—adapting and shaping itself in the face of social and technological development throughout history, with increasing concern and connection to HCI issues. However, in parallel, new approaches in the design field also emerge, promoting reflection on discursive and critical thinking regarding what we project, as well as the exploration of alternative future scenarios, such as speculative design [5] and design fiction [2], which challenge literal thinking and have the potential not only to address emerging questions but also to anticipate challenges and future scenarios.

This article presents the analysis briefing framework and final results of a selection of projects obtained by a group of students through a speculative project methodology in the discipline of Advanced Design Project for the conclusion of undergraduate studies in design. Throughout their course, these students have already had the opportunity to learn, explore, and participate in various design projects, applying different conceptual and methodological processes and technical competencies that constitute the founding basis of this final project.

The final project's pedagogical objective is to amplify future professionals' skills that emerge from current and future challenges the students will face, with a critical look at new alternative speculative possibilities in which the habits of the future are no more than a set of actions and practices designed in the past and the present.The results obtained in the last three years by implementing this project's methodological framework allow us to identify a significant convergence between Human and Technology, even with the emergence of complex themes such as climate change, the extinction of specimens, or the transformation of social behaviors, among others. Especially as technology becomes increasingly immersive to enhance individual and collective experiences, improving the quality of life and emotions through the design interaction.

The framework is composed of 6 phases:

1- presentation of the briefing, understanding the challenge and context;
2- divided into two timelines:
   2a)- research and diagnosis on the topic of the briefing through research and application of participatory methods;
   2b)- research and analysis of future trends (micro, macro, and meso), and analysis and exploration of fictional and speculative works (art, literary, cinematographic, others);
3- data crossing to build the future scenario and personas;
4- ideation for a proposal;
5- modeling the result;
6- inversion for the near future, with an innovation proposal that will introduce and evolve to the speculated future.

It is possible to identify a pattern in the results of the different students. Regardless of the theme of the proposed project, they present proposals that challenge and explore future scenarios integrating systems, products, and services centered on the technological domain, with a focus on HCI.

2 Framing Speculative Design and Design Fiction in Higher Education in Design

In higher education, it is possible to identify several pedagogical practices that have introduced speculative design or design fiction concepts, exploring the past, present, and future. Some of these practices and theories continue to be an exploratory object, intersecting with other methodologies such as design thinking, which, through a set of tools, leads students to reflections that introduce them to significant questions about their human condition. It is a clear opportunity that brings creative development and critical thinking to the next level for the future professional designer.

The role of speculative or fictional design is to structure a set of questions, identify a set of problems, and allow the generation of alternative scenarios by evaluating the problems and subduing with What if? [5]. Therefore, responding by exploring the human and machine relationship becomes increasingly inevitable as the ultimate possible alternative for human functioning.

When exploring this field, it is essential to highlight the different temporal dimensions and, as well as the past, analyze and understand the prospective evolution of technology and HCI. [12] describe the concept of the speculative past as a possibility for students to explore the past intersection between social, economic, and technological historical contexts. Interconnecting the past with the present and reflecting on the future has even justified the choice of the year to speculate on a specific problem. Despite the hypothetical date, it gives the student a frame to build the project narrative.

According to [13], regular project methodologies focus on identifying future perspectives for desirable scenarios and simulation of evolutionary models of the present instead of privileging the identification of extreme events that may impose a dystopian creative process, which allows responding to problems of extreme crisis and rupture. [8] presents several techniques that have introduced these skills into the learning context, for example, science fiction prototyping [8], where the most complex problems can produce new technological proposals, allowing them to diverge into new problems.

Foresight methodologies [3], which have been playing a role in the debate between peers, have been fundamental in triggering a set of ideas with potential future scenarios and variables that influence the field of development and research. Catastrophes, extreme scenarios, or vulnerability are increasingly part of everyday life. Hence, developing skills that allow students to act creatively and quickly to drastic transformations is necessary for greater resilience. Nevertheless, in the case of speculative design, according to [5], its main objective is to develop a vision according to a critical context to reflect on a less positive vision about the application of technology and to create awareness about the dangerous aspects of technology. Often in the form of satire so that the disruptive form can have a more significant impact on the rationale and the associated risk [11].

The dimension that [13] characterize as speculative design materializes in dystopia the danger of technology through the inability to see beyond, the limitations that can affect contexts and decisions, and the risks that can affect humanity. [14] Give us an example of this by reviewing frameworks that already identify flaws in the construction of scenarios, which incorporate improving the integration of the interaction between technology and humans, the possibility of error, and a more inclusive approach to different publics.

According to [16], the connection that allows better results is the development of speculative thinking as a bridge between design and HCI. For that, the authors reviewed and adopted speculative thinking processes, methods, logic, or practice by mapping methods for constructing scenarios in HCI (Fig. 1) and integrating multidisciplinary areas, mainly debuting the link with design processes. Therefore, the convergence of these visions is necessary, and we will briefly frame the relationship between how these visions converge.

FUTURES STUDIES METHODS		SYNERGIES WITH HCI
1.Behavioral techniques (Intuitive)	Delphi method	Interview
		Fictional reviews
	Workshop	Futures workshop
	Scenario-based method	Story Complete method
		Speculative video
2.Monitoring (interpretive)	Environmental scanning	Fieldwork
3. Simulation and Modeling (Computational)	Human computation	Rapid prototyping
		Probes
4.Reflection (Critical)	Action learning	Observation

Fig. 1. Futures Studies Methods, by the authors, according to [16].

3 Framing HCI in Speculation and Fictional Futures

Much like design fiction, speculative design represents approaches within the design field that enable the envisioning of alternative future scenarios, providing space for reflection and the conception of new challenges concerning the world we desire for the future [5]; [2]. These approaches also deter predictable solutions based on the current reality and encourage questioning and critical reflection on relevant social, political, and ethical issues [17].

In this context, it is usual to identify examples of speculative and fictional projections where technology plays a central role, involving human interaction with technological artifacts designed to simplify life in society and the environment [5]. This statement reinforces the discussion of being surrounded by digital stimuli characterized by constant connection and interactivity with electronic devices, progressively altering daily life, communication methods, and consumption patterns [4].

Likewise, a predetermined view of the future and advancements in human interaction with technological artifacts has become familiar and expected through various entertainment mediums, such as science fiction films and series. For instance, 'Minority Report' [15] depicts a future scenario where, in addition to new social habits and behaviors, it showcases and utilizes prototypes of interactive screens similar to those we have today. However, in this case, interaction occurs through gestures and hand movements, akin to a conductor's motions in an orchestra [2]. This portrayal exemplifies how to introduce new narratives and envision future scenarios with the relationship between technology and interaction design. Nonetheless, speculative and fictional design allows the exploration of less predictable scenarios and facilitates questioning and critical reflection on future possibilities.

Given the exploratory nature of speculative and fictional design in constructing future scenarios and their relationship with technology, it is natural for HCI fields to have a growing interest in and involvement in these approaches. HCI is central to interaction design, involving integrating digital technologies into product design. This intersection of knowledge areas begins in the 1990s with the increased incorporation of digital technology into household objects, aiming to problematize and develop digital communication technologies while considering human interaction [11].

Combining a speculative design approach with the field of interaction enhances, on one hand, reflection, and critique on aspects of technology, society, and sustainability; on the other hand, it enables the projection of future scenarios and introduces new resources and methods to guide researchers in interaction areas to anticipate new forms and concerns associated with human-technology usability and interaction, applicable in both professional and research contexts [10].

An example is the work of researcher [10], proposing a set of resources called 'reflective modes' designed to assist researchers and professionals in HCI areas in strengthening the quality and responsibility of design future work, articulating research construct, guiding the generation of new directions for their research, and analyzing their work and that of others. This approach goes beyond mere speculation without direction or focus [10].

Similarly, [9] explore a multi-stage methodology based on fictional speculation with engineering design students and graduates to facilitate the ideation process for automotive user interface design. They emphasize that methods focused on speculative and fictional design generate future scenarios projects and conceptualize new perspectives on interaction and the relationship between humans and technology.

Furthermore, it is possible to identify the use of the speculative approach in participatory contexts, involving different types of communities and addressing issues such as racial and social exclusion, providing participants with a reflection on the future of culture and possible pathways [18]; [19]. [20] illustrate how speculative design and ethnographic processes allow for collective exploration and construction of hypothetical futures. In this case, researchers focused on individuals' personal and emotional relationships with the urban environment, enabling the joint discovery of new technological devices and services and the exploration of the social, political, and ethical implications of emerging technologies and urban transformations.

In this sense, approaches such as speculative design and design fiction are reflected in research methods and processes that can empower different design areas to consider future scenarios and the extrapolation of technological artifacts and their interaction with humans.

4 Framework for a Pedagogical Methodology for Learning Scenarios

The methodological framework encourages students to overcome their creative limitations towards speculative dimensions (utopian or distortive) anchored in holistic principles at the process design's genesis. However, the framework focuses on the positiveness of the future scenarios, followed by a step back towards a more conscious present in constructing that envisioned future.

From a formal point of view, the framework is composed of 6 phases and implemented in a timeframe of 15 weeks (see Fig. 2):

Phase 1 - presentation of the brief, understanding of the challenge and context;

Phase 2 - divided into two timelines:

2a) research and diagnosis on the topic of the briefing through research and application of participatory methods and,

2b) research and analysis of future trends (micro, macro, and meso), and analysis and exploration of fictional and speculative works (art, literary, cinematographic, others);

Phase 3 - data crossing to build the future scenario and personas;

Phase 4 - ideation for a proposal;

Phase 5 - modeling the result;

Phase 6 - inversion for the near future, with an innovation proposal that will introduce and evolve to the speculated future.

Describe the aspects that we took into consideration throughout the development and, above all understand the objectives, taking into account that:

- Phase 1 - Presentation of the briefing, understanding the challenge and context:

    The briefing does not usually characterize a specific problem relating to humanity vs technology; it has secondary questions with a complementary topic that leads students to reflection and a starting point for their research (phase 2). The literature review has categorically identified contexts that describe perverse emerging technologies, highlighting the undesirable effects of new technologies [13]. Or problems related to replacing humans with artificial intelligence [6]. However, opening the briefing allows students to look for other questions about their interests, leading to pragmatic issues such as the climate effect, gender, capitalism, ethics, and ecosystems [11]. This gives freedom for critical thinking about a vision of the future, built through the research developed in phase 2, to arrive at speculative thinking.

- Phase 2 - Is divided into two timelines:

    - 2a)- Research and diagnosis on the topic of the briefing through research and application of participatory methods;

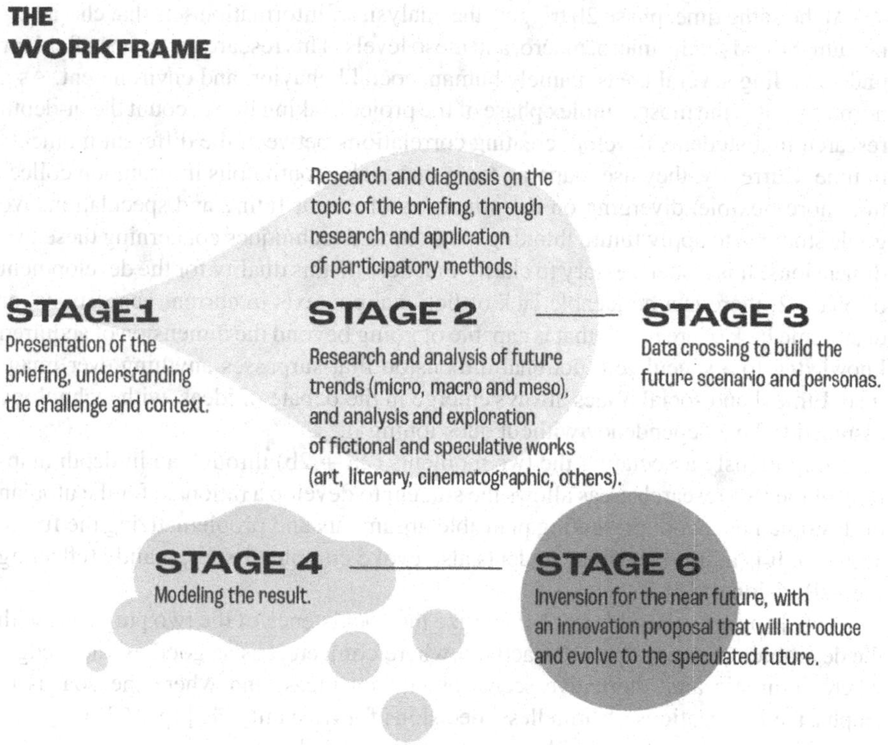

THE WORKFRAME

Research and diagnosis on the topic of the briefing, through research and application of participatory methods.

STAGE 1

Presentation of the briefing, understanding the challenge and context.

STAGE 2

Research and analysis of future trends (micro, macro and meso), and analysis and exploration of fictional and speculative works (art, literary, cinematographic, others).

STAGE 3

Data crossing to build the future scenario and personas.

STAGE 4

Modeling the result.

STAGE 6

Inversion for the near future, with an innovation proposal that will introduce and evolve to the speculated future.

Fig. 2. The Workframe for Advanced Design Project, by the authors.

As [12], the relationship between the past and the future is an opportunity to frame an auto-ethnographic account, which in this framework (phase 2a) allows us to encourage the student to not only understand the context of the challenge and its evolution over time, as well as the socio-economic context of the purpose of the briefing. It also allows the student to exercise awareness about the necessary evolution of contexts, especially technological context, for incremental innovation and how this is achieved through history. In the same way that researchers like [17] take a journey into the past to subsequently project future scenarios through *'speculative ethnography,'* in which they follow the sequence of analyzing the present, past, trends, and future [17].

– 2b)- Research and analysis of future trends (micro, macro, and meso), and analysis and exploration of fictional and speculative works (art, literary, cinematographic, others);

At the same time, phase 2b triggers the analysis of information sets that characterize future trends at the micro, macro, and meso levels. This research is an open field for understanding several areas, namely human, social behavior, and environment. As a normative, it is the most complex phase of the project, taking into account the in-depth research that students develop, creating correlations between the different moments in time. Currently, they use mapping tools that make continuous information collection more flexible, diverging on the principles of a near future and speculation. We guide students to apply future thinking methods and techniques concerning these two dimensions. It is also necessary to clarify that despite this duality for the development of phase 2, there is a noticeable lack of fictional contexts in current generations, or even some lack of creativity that is capable of going beyond the dimension of acquired knowledge to a speculated, fictional dimension that surpasses anything ever imagined. Ethical and social issues always emerge in the debate of ideas, with technology assumed to be a dependency without questioning it.

Continuously associating the two moments (2a + 2b) through an in-depth mapping of the two research areas allows the student to develop a rationale for the utopian or dystopian decision, presenting plausible arguments and problematizing the future scenario. It is at this stage that students also evoke complex issues, mainly reflecting the A/B vision of [5].

As [7] analyze, the authors characterize the coexistence of the two purposes, with the desirable one being: "(...) an activity where conjecture is as good as knowledge, where futuristic and alternative scenarios convey ideas, and where the goal is to emphasize implications of 'mindless' decisions for humanity" [7] (p. 1624).

- Phase 3 - Data crossing to build the future scenario and personas:

Students must develop through the crossing of data and converging to develop a dystopian or utopian vision to be constructed by the student. In this way, we intend not to inhibit the student from their positivist view of human-machine interaction. On the other hand, the future risks associated with post-human existence have never been questioned by students as an approach to the total extinction of humanity. Regarding the construction of scenarios and personas, [14] in the field of future studies, developing a future scenario is understanding the dynamics to lead to transformations in the future and, in this way, aligning the vision and strategy so that they converge toward the same purpose (strategic foresight). In this stage, students create a probable future rather than a preferable one [5], within equally linear personas. At this stage, support is needed to complement the critical thinking gap.

- Phase 4 - Ideation for a proposal:

This stage is the most critical moment for the students in this framework because they tend to extrapolate ideas that are similar to the present; it needs tools and support to help them achieve the speculative dimension. Nevertheless, throughout this process, we were also able to characterize the profile of the students most capable of crossing different levels, especially students who usually have a gaming hobby or interest in sci-fi or have a solid creative and intellectual capacity. As [9] confirm:

"prior knowledge may also generate fixative biases in the designer's thinking. Primarily for novice designers, and to some extent for experienced ones, too, creative idea generation can be enhanced through provision of a repository of ideas or ideation tools that are driven by technical knowledge or based on analogical reasoning. We posit that having a knowledge resource consisting of the speculative advancements in technology and science found in fiction novels, magazines, blogs, short stories, or essays could complement the existing design idea generation tools." (p. 080801–2).

Fundamentally, it is at this stage that the influence of technologies on students' imagination is identified since most proposals are leveraged on artifacts, services, and experiences, which challenge new technological possibilities, especially interaction. The interaction is designed with a positive perspective, oriented to human needs, and systematized for the individual or the community.

- Phase 5 - Modeling the result:

After the ideation phase, students must develop and model their ideas and concepts. This stage becomes more comfortable for students, where they apply the creative and technical skills as a designer and a creative, and they apply the knowledge they acquire during the course in the production and finalization of design projects. However, it is essential to note that many of the scenarios and ideas that students design, due to time management considerations and the need to meet presentation deadlines, end up as digital mock-ups and images that help explain their narratives. According to [1], there is a potential to explore diverse techniques, particularly with low-tech techniques and material, which can enrich the narrative and have the potential to lead to different interpretations. Producing an iterative effect between the audience and the designer through the aesthetic potential that prototyping can introduce into the speculative proposal.

- Phase 6- Inversion for the near future:

This stage is the last phase of the framework we present. At this point, we propose to the student a journey back to the near present, in which we ask them to reflect and map out how their speculative future proposals can have a starting point in the present. This phase is the most important, as it is when the student can have a holistic, reflective, and comparative vision regarding the projects they have undertaken throughout the course. It is a phase in which students realize that projecting future scenarios through a speculative design approach allows them to anticipate what no one has yet considered could arise and how this anticipation can activate and sensitize them to regress to the present. This regression can translate into possible alternative ideas and concepts for their projects.

It is equally important to emphasize that projects and the work framework only sometimes progress smoothly. Unexpected events, delays, and different ideation blocks from students may arise in different years. This reality is also part of the process and should be identified similarly to the presented framework.

5 Results

In this section, we present some projects developed by various students, emerging from the framework presented in this article. The distinct proposals for speculative future scenarios that we have selected reinforce how projecting alternative futures enhances the ideation and design of new services and technological artifacts aimed at interacting with humans.

Flow Powered by Delta Project. Delta Flow Results from a Student's Work, Focusing on Repositioning the Delta Brand for 2060, a Leading Portuguese Coffee Brand in Portugal.

In this project, based on her research and development through different stages of the presented methodology, the student envisions a scenario for 2060 where urban spaces are highly technological, and human evolution is conditioned at the auditory level. Cities will become silent spaces, leading citizens to greater efficiency in work and education with fewer chronic effects.

In this future Delta Flow scenario, spherical capsules (Fig. 3) are introduced, allowing moments of decompression and isolation in urban centers reminiscent of the current cultural tradition of coffee consumption in Portugal.

This project introduces a new lifestyle and illustrates new interfaces for digital interaction. For example, reserving a moment in a Flow capsule is done through screens that perform retina recognition. This proposal encourages reflection on digital security, interaction, and usability of new products and services in an environmental scenario. The academic year 2020–21.

Fig. 3. Flow Powered by Delta Project, by Ana Silva student.

Delta Pod. Delta Pod is Another Example of a Delta Project. In This Proposal, the Student, Through Her Research, Envisions a Revolution in Transportation and Mobility by 2060. It Presents a Society Where We Are All Digitally Interconnected and Supported by Artificial Intelligence Devices. In This Scenario, for Example, Transportation Systems Have no Human Drivers, Roads Are Made of Solar Panels, and There is Monitoring of

CO2 Footprint for Transportation, Enabling Society to Have a Greater Awareness of How to Commute.

In this future vision, the student envisions the Delta Pod (Fig. 4) - a robotic transportation system that can be requested through interfaces installed on personal electronic devices. It represents a new perspective on the future experience of mobility and interaction with intelligent robotic vehicles through electronic devices. Because Delta is a coffee brand, the student emphasizes the end of coffee production, and the project raises questions about the evolution of the senses through technological artifacts that are environmentally sustainable. The academic year 2020–21.

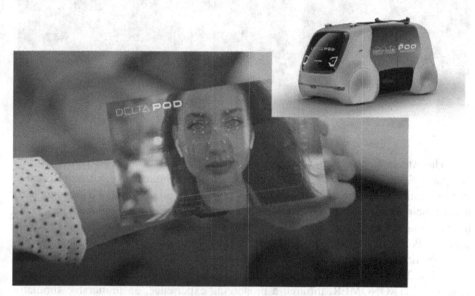

Fig. 4. Delta Pod, by Carlota Carvalho.

Yuskin. From a Project Based on Nomadism Culture and Forward-Thinking, Created by a Traveling Society, YUSKIN Emerges (Fig. 5). It Proposes an Intelligent Suit for 2050 with Nanotechnology and Photogenic Crystals, Enabling Greater Sustainability, Durability, and Heat Retention. It Focuses on the Future of Clothing Concerning Cost, Durability, and Usability, Intersecting with Textile Waste and Fast Fashion Issues.

Additionally, this speculative textile product is designed to allow users to customize colors and shapes by connecting to Personal Electronic Devices, enabling a unique piece to take on distinct configurations. The academic year 2021/22.

Astronomer - from Earth to Mars. Astronomer is the Result of a Project that Aimed to Reflect on the Experience of Visiting a Museum in 2050.

In this project, the student proposes to explore the human fascination with the exploration of Mars, envisioning a museum for 2050 that allows for an immersive experience of visiting Mars without the need to leave Earth.

In this context, the student provides context for the emergence of this interactive museum:

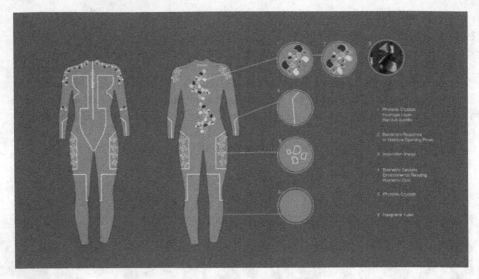

Fig. 5. Yuskin, by Yolanda Freitas.

"The American space agency - NASA, and the aerospace systems manufacturing company - SPACEX, led by Elon Musk, launched a joint venture to expand their Research and Innovation Center in the European continent and found in Portugal a strategic partner for their scientific research. In collaboration with the European Space Agency and the Portuguese Space Agency - ESA, the partnership advanced in the city of Lagos, in southern Portugal, considered the ideal location for this endeavor due to its geographical conditions and historical background of enormous symbolism in global maritime expansion. Thus, the Science Center in Lagos transformed into the Astronautics Science Center - ASTRONOMER, through a pioneering experience, an immersive simulator of space exploration and colonization of Mars. The great patron is Elon Musk, who has become the ambassador for this grand undertaking." (storytelling developed by the student).

This museum proposal for the future is based on an immersive and interactive experience using a suit with a helmet that allows the user to see, hear, taste, touch, and breathe as if they were on Mars. Astronomer (Fig. 6) results in an idea that challenges technological advancements in the field of interaction, intersecting different areas of knowledge such as interaction design, equipment design, engineering, information design, and textile design. Similarly, this proposal also validates the different stages of the presented framework. For instance, in this project, the student envisions the possibility of future development of these suits with technological advancements in motion/biometric capture systems and smart fabrics, based on the mapping and initial identification of megatrends, intersecting with references associated with science fiction stories. Through this project, the student also sought to make a statement about the possible colonization of Mars, so that it does not happen like the colonization on Earth. As a manifesto so that the experience can remind us of respect for the usufruct and efficient management of resources.

As an analogy to the severe consequences of what is happening, in a rhetoric of cause and effect by the usurpation of nature. The academic year 2022/23.

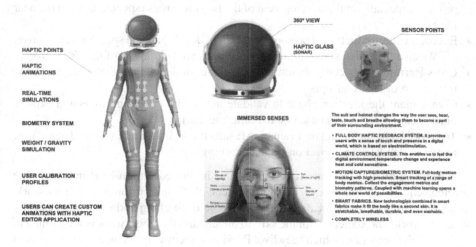

Fig. 6. Astronomer - From Earth to Mars, by Inês Crisóstomo student.

We chose to compile and present a set of projects from students of different years, exemplifying the diversity of possible outcomes in response to various proposed design assignments, demonstrating how new concepts of interfaces and technological artifacts can naturally emerge from the projection of alternative future scenarios carried out by our working framework. Empowering students throughout the process to reflect critically on the future of technology and its relationship with humans, addressing aspects such as interaction, usability, and sustainability. We also encourage them to consider how we can positively engage with and integrate technology into products, systems, or services.

6 Conclusion

The framework presented here and the respective results are some of the projects developed over the last three years, and they also represent several dimensions that influenced national and international contexts.

The positive aspects identified are mainly in the development of the student, namely:

- The openness of students to understanding project methodologies and mixed methods, where they also develop an understanding of their creative methods;
- Understanding of their role as designers and ability to develop projects with deep critical thinking through research and research;
- Training to develop complex projects based on open briefings;
- Develop skills in HCI by integrating technology according to purpose and need.

The systemic and critical analysis of the results also allowed researchers to draw some conclusions, namely:

- Empower students with peer-to-peer debate to confront difficulties and differences, but above all, to fill in any gaps;
- Implement a task management methodology to support the student throughout the process, especially in the development of the two proposals (speculation and the near future);
- Encourage the production of prototypes as part of developing the speculative narrative. We also identified some future avenues for the development of this framework:
- Cross-learning with computational engineering students for greater depth in the integration of HCI concepts;
- Complement the ideation phase to validate ideas with co-design tools and explore other speculative visions based on the future scenario;
- To propose a future model for evaluating results through a quantitative and qualitative matrix to validate the impact on student learning.

The integration of this curriculum unit at the higher education level influences the development of the mindset of future designers. With this, through our framework, we aim to stimulate and educate designers capable of thinking and reflecting critically about the world and society, with the skill to understand that their work is not limited to perceiving the present in which they live. Providing them with the necessary resources to visualize, alter, and positively influence the future.

References

1. Auger, J.: Speculative Design: Crafting the Speculation. Digital Creativity, pp. 11–35, Routledge, London (2013). https://doi.org/10.1080/14626268.2013.767276
2. Bleecker, J.: Design Fiction: A Short Essay on Design, Science, Fact and Fiction, Near Future Laboratory. Near Future Laboratory, Los Angeles (2009). Recuperado em julho 2, 2023, em http://www.nearfuturelaboratory.com/2009/03/17/design-fiction-a-short-essay-on-design-science-fact-and-fiction/
3. Daheim, C.: Emerging Practices in Foresight- Chapter 8. The Knowledge Base of Futures Studies 2020. Association of professional futurists, Washington D. C. (2020)
4. Dunne, A.: Hertzian Tales: Electronic Products, Aesthetic Experience, and Critical Design. MIT Press, Cambridge (2008)
5. Dunne, A., Raby, F.: Speculative Everything: Design, Fiction, and Social Dreaming. The MIT Press, Cambridge (2013). https://doi.org/10.1093/jdh/epv00
6. Harari, Y.: Homo Deus. Bogot´a: Penguin Random House (2016)
7. Johannessen, L.K., Keitsch, M.M., Pettersen, I.N.: Speculative and critical design—features methods and practices. In: Proceedings of the Design Society: International Conference on Engineering Design, pp. 1623–1632 (2019). https://doi.org/10.1017/dsi.2019.168
8. Johnson, B.: An updated practitioners guide to science fiction prototyping- Chapter 12. In: The Knowledge Base of Futures Studies 2020. Association of professional futurists, Washington D. C. (2020)
9. Kotecha, M.C., Chen, T., McAdams, D.A., Krishnamurthy, V.R.: Design ideation through speculative fiction: foundational principles and exploratory study. J. Mech. Des. **143**(8) (2021). https://doi.org/10.1115/1.4049656
10. Kozubaev, S., Elsden, C., Howell, N., et al.: Expanding modes of reflection in design futuring. In: Proceedings of the 2020 CHI Conference on Human Factors in Computing Systems, pp. 1–15. Association for Computing Machinery, New York (2020)

11. Malpass, M.: Critical Design in Context History, Theory and Practice. Bloomsbury Academic, London (2017)
12. Nooney, L., Brain, T.: A 'speculative pasts' pedagogy: where speculative design meets historical thinking. Digit. Creat. 218–234 (2019). https://doi.org/10.1080/14626268.2019.168 3042
13. Pinto, J.P., Ramírez-Angulo, P.J., Crissien, T.J., Bonett-Balza, K.: The creation of dystopias as an alternative for imagining and materializing a university of the future. Futures (2021). https://doi.org/10.1016/j.futures.2021.102832
14. Scupelli, P., Wasserman, A., Brooks, J.: Dexign Futures: A Pedagogy for Long-Horizon Design Scenarios, DRS 2016-Future-Focused Thinking. DRS, Brighton (2016)
15. Spielberg, S.: Minority Report. Twentieth Century Fox (2002)
16. Zhu, L., Chao, C., Fu, Z.: How HCI integrates speculative thinking to envision futures. J. Futures Stud. Beijing, China (2023). ISSN 1027-6084
17. Dong, F., Sterling, S., Schaefer, D., Forbes, H.: Building the history of the future: a tool for culture-centred design for the speculative future. In: Proceedings of the Design Society: Design Conference, vol. 1, pp. 1883–1890 (2020). https://doi.org/10.1017/dsd.2020.63
18. Baumann, K., Stokes, B., Bar, F., Caldwell, B.: Infrastructures of the imagination. In: Proceedings of the 8th International Conference on Communities and Technologies (2017). https://doi.org/10.1145/3083671.3083700
19. Bray, K., Harrington, C.A.: Speculative blackness: considering Afrofuturism in the creation of inclusive speculative design probes (2021). https://doi.org/10.1145/3461778.3462002
20. Stals, S., Smyth, M., Mival, O.: UrbanIxD: From Ethnography to Speculative Design Fictions for the Hybrid City (2019). https://doi.org/10.1145/3363384.3363486

Teaching Method Innovation and Practice for Information and Interaction Design in the Context of New Liberal Arts

Zhen Liu(✉) (iD)

School of Design, South China University of Technology, Guangzhou 510006,
People's Republic of China
liuzjames@scut.edu.cn

Abstract. Strong measures to deepen the reform of undergraduate education and teaching include stimulating interest through mutual integration and interaction, reforming teaching and learning by complementing each other, and encouraging questioning through action and understanding. The university will take the implementation of the new liberal arts research and reform practice project as an opportunity to promote the realization of liberal arts education, real change, new change, deep change, accelerate the construction of the new liberal arts, and vigorously cultivate first-class liberal arts talents of the 'Three Creative' (innovation, creativity, and entrepreneurship). However, in the new historical period, the difficulty of how to break through and improve the quality of industrial design talents training still exists, especially how to improve the quality of information and interaction design talents training under the implementation of the new liberal arts construction idea of combining engineering and literature, so as to achieve the goal of vigorously cultivating the 'Three Creative' first-class liberal arts talents. Therefore, this paper is aimed to improve the quality of experimental and innovative information and interaction design talents training in the construction of national first-class undergraduate industrial design program under the new liberal arts construction idea, and to contribute to the goal of cultivating 'Three Creative' first-class liberal arts talents through the innovation and practice of information and interaction design teaching method. This paper proposes the framework of 'the implementation plan and implementation method of information and interaction design teaching method innovation and practice in the context of new liberal arts' through a mixed research method of theory construction and case practice, which assists to achieve the goal of cultivating the 'Three Creative' first-class liberal arts talents with the themes, perspectives, and countermeasures and application of innovation.

Keywords: Teaching · Method · Innovation · Creativity · Entrepreneurship · Practice · Information · Interaction Design · New Liberal Arts

1 Introduction

At present, in order to implement the goal of high-quality development of China [1], implement the spirit of the National Education Conference [2], implement the requirements of the new Liberal arts construction work conference [3], comprehensively promote the construction of new liberal arts, and build a world-class and Chinese characteristics of liberal arts talent training system, the General Office of the Ministry of Education launched the first batch of new liberal arts research and reform practice projects [4] in March 2021. The new liberal arts, based on the existing basis of traditional liberal arts, reorganizes the courses of various majors in the discipline to form the intersection of liberal arts and science, that is, integrates modern information technology into philosophy, literature, language and other courses, so as to provide students with comprehensive interdisciplinary learning to expand knowledge and cultivate innovative thinking [5].

In recent years, South China University of Technology (SCUT) [6] earnestly implements the spirit of the National Education Conference, focuses on the innovative development needs of liberal arts education, strengthens the top-level design of liberal arts education reform, gives full play to the advantages of coordinated development of multidisciplinary schooling and the geographical advantage of being located in the Guangdong-Hong Kong-Macao Bay Area [7], vigorously pushes forward the connotation construction of the liberal arts majors, firmly grasps the core point of comprehensively improving the ability of talent cultivation, accelerates the formation of a high level of talent cultivation system, and strives to the university has been exploring and practicing the cultivation of talents with all-round development in ethics, intellect, physicality, aesthetics and labor. Strong measures to deepen the reform of undergraduate education and teaching include stimulating interest through mutual integration and interaction, reforming teaching and learning by complementing each other, and encouraging questioning through action and understanding [8]. As such, the university will take the implementation of the new liberal arts research and reform practice project as an opportunity to promote the realization of liberal arts education, real change, new change, deep change, accelerate the construction of the new liberal arts, and vigorously cultivate first-class liberal arts talents of the "three innovation" (innovation, creativity and entrepreneurship) [9].

In addition, the subsequent talent training goal of the School of Design, South China University of Technology, is based on the idea that design drives social innovation and development and creates a better life, and aims to cultivate innovative design talents with international vision and high-level talents with disciplinary innovation and research ability [10]. The industrial design major has successfully become a national first-class undergraduate major development curriculum in year 2020 [11]. The direction of information and interaction design [12] is the school's experiment in the innovation of the industrial design profession. Its idea is consistent with the 'cross-integration' of the construction of new liberal arts, that is, the cross-integration of liberal arts and engineering has become an important means to promote the construction of disciplines. However, in the new historical period, the challenges of how to break through and improve the quality of industrial design talents training still exists, especially how to improve the quality of information and interaction design talents training under the implementation of the new liberal arts construction idea of combining engineering and literature, need to be addressed so as to achieve the goal of vigorously cultivating the 'Three Creative' first-class liberal arts talents. These are the significance and status quo of the implementation of this study.

Therefore, this paper is aimed to improve the quality of experimental and innovative information and interaction design talents training in the construction of national first-class undergraduate industrial design program under the new liberal arts construction idea, and to contribute to the goal of cultivating 'Three Creative' first-class liberal arts talents through the innovation and practice of information and interaction design teaching method, which assists to make innovative contributions to the education and training of the front and reserve personnel of China's independent innovation in the field of high-tech and independent intellectual property.

2 Method and Research Framework

In order to improve the quality of experimental and innovative information and inter-action design talents cultivation in the construction of national first-class undergraduate industrial design program in the light of idea of establishing new liberal arts, this paper proposes a framework of 'the implementation plan and implementation method of information and interaction design teaching method innovation and practice in the context of new liberal arts' through a mixed research method of theory construction and case practice, which is integrated pedagogy theory, art theory, and design theory, to carry out research on related issues.

2.1 Theory and Framework

In the light of teaching philosophy of South China University of Technology, in the construction of the national first-class undergraduate industrial design experimental class, teaching, scientific research and social service are integrated into the talent training process of information and interaction design, adhering to the people-oriented, moral education first, ability first and all-round development, and focusing on enhancing students' social responsibility to serve the country and the people, which is to improve students' innovative spirit of courage to explore and practical ability to solve problems, and strive to train nation builders and successors with all-round development of moral, intellectual, physical and beauty. Therefore, as shown in Fig. 1, the research framework of teaching method innovation and practice of information and interaction design in the context of new liberal arts includes target orientation, concept cultivation, collaborative innovation, teaching and research, curriculum class, and project practice.

Target Orientation. Target orientation is interacted with three aspects i.e., concept cultivation, collaborative innovation, and teaching and research. Based on its own educational foundation and conditions, South China University of Technology has clearly put forward the goal positioning of high-quality, 'Three Creative' (innovation, creativity, and entrepreneurship) and international talent training, and is committed to training modern composite application-oriented first-class new liberal arts talents in new ways, new models, and new methods.

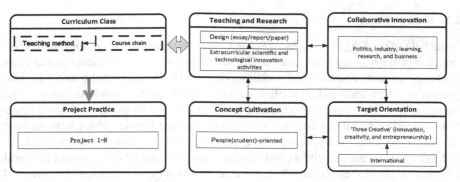

Fig. 1. Research framework of teaching method innovation and practice of information and interaction design in the context of new liberal arts.

Concept Cultivation. In the information and interaction design talent training concept, 'people(student)-oriented' is also the design principle of information and interaction design, to establish diversified and personalized talent training concepts, and pay attention to the comprehensive training of students' comprehensive quality.

Collaborative Innovation. The resultant force that drives the overall improvement of talent training quality through collaborative innovation has evolved into politics, industry, learning, research, and business. Innovation is the result of the cooperation of the whole society and various departments, which is in line with the trend of the times, the law of innovation, and the first-class new liberal arts talent training approach.

Teaching and Research. Teaching and research is integrated with target orientation concept cultivation, and collaborative innovation, in which the teaching thought of 'unity of teaching and scientific research' is updated via the teaching content with scientific research results of extracurricular scientific and technological innovation activities, so that the latest scientific research results can be embedded into the classroom, the textbook, and the minds of students. In teaching, the teaching mode is updated by integrating research experience and research thinking, and the innovative thinking mode of finding problems, limiting problems, solving problems, and implementing plans are imparting to students. Integrated with scientific research topics, students will be guided to design (essay/report/paper) and extracurricular scientific and technological innovation activities. Through participating in scientific research practice, students feel and understand what they have learned, through which the student personal experience assists to stimulate the spirit of innovation and cultivate innovation ability.

Curriculum Class. The whole model of information and interaction design course chain is designed with method of improving the quality of classroom teaching for curriculum class that is related to teaching and research.

Project Practice. Three innovation oriented project chain overall model is through implementing curriculum class associated project one to N.

2.2   Case Practice

In the light of teaching philosophy of South China University of Technology, in the construction of the national first-class undergraduate industrial design experimental class, teaching, scientific research and social service are integrated into the talent training process of information and interaction design, adhering to the people-oriented, moral education first, ability first and all-round development, and focusing on enhancing students' social responsibility to serve the country and the people, which is to improve students' innovative spirit of courage to explore and practical ability to solve problems, and strive to train nation builders and successors with all-round development of moral, intellectual, physical and beauty. Therefore, as shown in Fig. 1, the research framework of teaching method innovation and practice of information and interaction design in the context of new liberal arts includes target orientation, concept cultivation, collaborative innovation, teaching and research, curriculum class, and project practice.

Curriculum Class Design. The whole model of information and interaction design course chain is designed with method of improving the quality of classroom teaching for curriculum class that is related to teaching and research.

3   Results

3.1   Characteristics for 'Three Creative' Talents

Previous studies on the 'Three Creative' Talent Characteristics Model [13] show that gender of the background trait has a significant impact on the formation of the university students' personality. As shown in Fig. 2, there are four personality traits that have a significant positive impact on innovation, creativity, and entrepreneurship potential, which are Extraverted, Observant, Judging, and Assertive, and the indicators of entrepreneurial potential are entrepreneurial Motivation, entrepreneurial Aptitude and entrepreneurial Attitude.

In addition, the method of inviting overseas famous scholars to give joint lectures makes the orientation of students' international talent training goals clearer and more specific.

3.2   Strategy for 'Three Creative'

The design strategy to curriculum class design for 'Three Creative' is based on the following research question: how to construct a student-oriented multi-course ecological path to achieve the goal of cultivating 'Three Creative' first-class liberal arts talents and provide design strategies for teaching methods and project practice.

Subsequently, as shown in Table 1, a total of 256 teaching-hour course chain has been designed for the design strategy to curriculum class design for 'Three Creative', which contains a chain of six courses that are Fundamentals of Forming (Composition, Design Basic), Overview of Industrial Design, Product Design Methodology, Information and Interaction Design (II) Service Design, Design Management, and Design

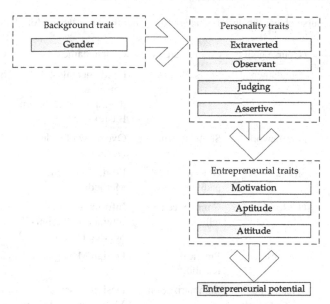

Fig. 2. Traits to entrepreneurship potential of the 'Three Creative' Talent Characteristics Model.

Research Method and Academic Writing. The course chain is aiming for fundamentals, framework, method, case, tactics, and academic, to achieve respectively outcomes such as skills, strategy structure, objective pathway, confidence storytelling, practical feasibility, and summarization.

3.3 Teaching Method for 'Three Creative'

Teaching methods such as practical teaching, class-work design, preliminary scientific research, inquiry teaching, field teaching, and case teaching, in the Curriculum Class acts as interaction approaches between Course Chain of the Curriculum Class and Project Practice that includes Project 1: characteristics for 'Three Creative' talents, Project 2: design strategy for 'Three Creative', Project 3: design method for 'Three Creative', Project 4: special subject for Information and Interaction Design: service experience design for social innovation, Project 5: competition for 'Three Creative (innovation, creativity and entrepreneurship)', and Project 6: design academic conference paper writing. Hence, the framework of teaching method innovation and practice of information and interaction design in the context of new liberal arts is updated in detail as shown in Fig. 3.

Project 1: Characteristics for 'Three Creative' Talents. In line with the traits to entrepreneurship potential of the 'Three Creative' Talent Characteristics Model (Fig. 2), is the outcome of the Fundamentals of Forming (Composition, Design Basic) class in the course chain through practical teaching method as shown in Fig. 3. Students have been systematically taught with fundamental principles and knowledge of basic forming (composition and design) through the form of point, line, surface, space and light as a whole process chain, as shown in Fig. 4, so that students can independently carry out fundamental forming (composition and design) and be familiar with the whole process

Table 1. The course chain: the design strategy to curriculum class design for 'Three Creative'.

Course sequence	Course goal	Course outcome	Course name	Course hour
1	Fundamentals	Skills	Fundamentals of Forming (Composition, Design Basic)	64
2	Framework	Strategy structure	Overview of Industrial Design	32
3	Method	Objective pathway	Product Design Methodology	48
4	Case	Confidence story telling	Information and Interaction Design (II) Service Design	64
5	Tactics	Practical feasibility	Design Management	32
6	Academic	Summarization	Design Research Method and Academic Writing	16

of forming design that assists to cultivate students' fundamental ability to find and solve problems, master the fundamental knowledge of the design process and composition process of forming, and have the preliminary ability of design procedures, which indicates characteristics for 'Three Creative' talents of the students in terms of traits to entrepreneurial potential on background, personality, and entrepreneurship.

Project 2: Design Strategy for 'Three Creative'. It is the outcome of the Overview of Industrial Design class in the course chain via class-work design method as shown in Fig. 3, from which students can master principles and knowledge of industrial design, and cultivate ability to identify problems and propose solutions, master approach of the industrial design process and development process, and have the initial ability to implement industrial design theory as shown in Fig. 5. The project and the class can be associated with international target orientation, as shown in Fig. 3, and to foster 'Three Creative' (innovation, creativity, and entrepreneurship) in terms of funding, competition (the Project 5), and subsequent academic conference paper writing and publication (the Project 6). For example, the students' outcome (Project 2), a circular design strategy for industrial design (Fig. 4), has been co-taught and collaborated with Prof. Dr. Mohamed Osmani, Loughborough University, United Kingdom (UK), and further developed and won a national level innovation and entrepreneurship training project [14] that has been successfully accomplished in the end with a published paper called 'Experience Economy and Green Economy Research in China: A 30-Year Bibliometric Analysis' [15].

Project 3: Design Method for 'Three Creative'. It is the outcome of the Product Design Methodology class in the course chain using preliminary scientific research

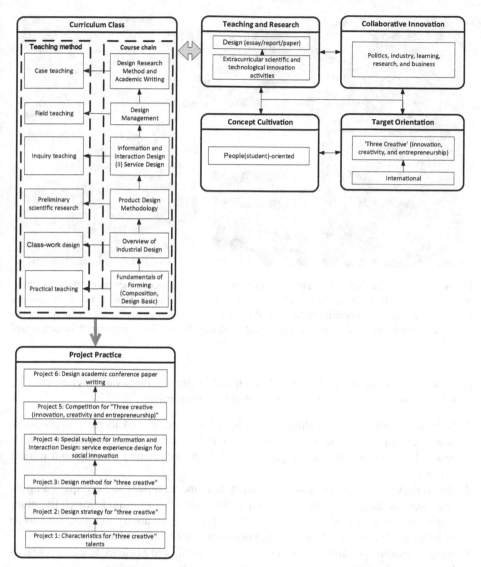

Fig. 3. Updated research framework of teaching method innovation and practice of information and interaction design in the context of new liberal arts in detail.

method as shown in Fig. 3, from which the students have been systematically taught with principles and knowledge of product design methodology through the methods of looking, learning, asking, making, testing, evaluation and selection, communication and expression, so that they have the ability to independently and deeply explore the needs of users via a user research oriented product design project, as shown in Fig. 6, and are familiar with the total process of design in line with the Double Diamond model from Design Council UK [15] including discover, define, develop, and deliver (4D)

Fig. 4. Students' outcome (through the form of point, line, surface, space and light as a whole process chain) of the Fundamentals of Forming (Composition, Design Basic) class in the course chain through practical teaching method for Project 1: characteristics for 'Three Creative' talents in line with the traits to entrepreneurship potential of the 'Three Creative' Talent Characteristics Model.

process, with idea of design iteration through understanding, observation, visualization, and review. As such, the students will be able to demonstrate:

1. Knowledge and Understanding: an ability to understand and identify appropriate strategies and research methods for a given activity; and an ability to understand how research techniques, methodologies, and methods are applied to assist and inform given activity.
2. Subject-specific cognitive skills: an ability to manage, reflect and critique complex and inter-related ideas and concepts; an ability to identify relevant research literature and other sources of primary and secondary data; and an ability to reflect on choice of research strategy, methodology, methods and statistical validation.
3. Subject-specific practical and professional skills: ability to evidence relevant research literature and other sources of primary and secondary information.
4. Key/transferable skills: an ability to be self-motivating when tackling problems and to plan their work tasks in an effective manner; and an ability to communicate ideas in an appropriate form.

Further, the students can master the principles and knowledge of product design methodology, and cultivate students' ability to find and solve problems, in which they have the preliminary ability of design procedures and design practice referring to user-centered design, and cultivate their design practice ability; and master common product design techniques (look, learn, ask, make, test, evaluate and select, communication and expression).

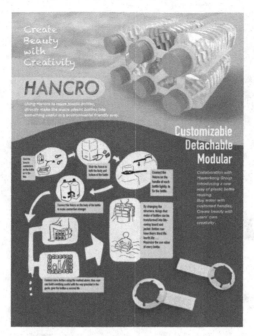

Fig. 5. Students' outcome (a circular design strategy) of the Overview of Industrial Design class in the course chain via class-work design method for Project 2: design strategy for 'Three Creative'.

3.4 Special Subject for Information and Interaction Design: Service Experience Design for Social Innovation

Project 4: Special Subject for Information and Interaction Design. Service experience design for social innovation is the outcome of the Information and Interaction Design (II) Service Design class in the course chain featuring inquiry teaching method as shown in Fig. 3, from which the principles and knowledge of service design have been systematically taught to students in the form of service design methods and cases, so that they can have the ability to independently and deeply explore the needs of users, and are familiar with the whole process of product-service-system design via a service experience design for social innovation design project, as shown in Fig. 7 and Fig. 8. Hence, the project focuses on enabling students to master the following aspects of service design research:

1. Knowledge and understanding: be able to understand and master appropriate service design strategies and methods to serve specific service design research activities; and to understand how to use service design techniques, methodologies, and methodological steps to assist and guide specific social service design activities.
2. Subject-specific cognition: ability to manage, reflect and criticize, synthesize and cross boundary ideas and concepts; ability to find relevant service design research literature and other primary and secondary data; and ability to reflect on service design research strategies, methodologies, methodological steps and statistical arguments.

Fig. 6. Students' outcome (a user research oriented product design project via Double Diamond model with idea of design iteration through understanding, observation, visualization, and review) of the Product Design Methodology class in the course chain via preliminary scientific research method for Project 3: design method for 'Three Creative'.

3. Subject specific practice and technical expertise: ability to provide evidence for relevant service design research literature and other primary and secondary information resources to forming a service experience design for social innovation knowledge.
4. Key/transferable techniques: when confronted with problems and service design plan research work tasks, the students will be self-motivated to carry out the work in an

effective way; ability to work effectively as part of a team; ability to critically evaluate the work of oneself and others; and able to communicate ideas in an appropriate way to share a service experience design for social innovation wisdom.

Moreover, students can master principles and knowledge of service design topics, and cultivate their ability to find and solve problems; master the knowledge of service design process with an initial ability of service design procedures; master the thematic techniques of service design (knowledge of service design, service design methods, and service design cases), and have an ability of product-service-system design (mainly referring to user-centered collaborative design), cultivating their' practical ability of collaborative service experience design for social innovation from its data, information, knowledge to wisdom.

For instance, since modern Chinese Neo-Confucianism (CNC) is considered one of the three main social ideological trends in China, which is also the primary ideological representative of modern Chinese cultural conservatism [16]. Unfortunately, CNC has been trapped in a dilemma of lacking recognition and appreciation in today's China. Hence, Journey to the Neo-confucianism project, as shown in Fig. 7, aims to publicize the philosophy of CNC through the combination of digital technology and CNC, to guide young people to explore, realize and understand the core views of CNC, and enhance their cultural confidence and cultural identity. Additionally, at present, the excellent traditional marriage custom culture is faced with the distress of the inheritance of the times. On the one hand, it is from the traditional alienation such as "sky-high bride price" and "vulgar marriage trouble". On the other hand, it is from the emergence of some excellent cultural forms of inheritance, and has not kept up with the development of the times. At the same time, few studies have directly paid attention to the inheritance and dissemination of traditional wedding customs culture in Guangzhou, which is directed by service design. In the context of the current times, young people have new requirements and expectations for the forms of traditional culture. Thus, under the current social background of the inheritance and reform of the wedding custom culture, Excellent traditional wedding culture project, as shown in Fig. 8, has been set to explore the inheritance status and background of Guangfu's excellent traditional wedding custom, and investigates the feasibility of design innovation. Guided by the service design thought, this project uses the double drill process method to design, and obtains the service design of the traditional wedding custom culture based on the excellent traditional wedding custom culture of Kuazilu. The new digital entertainment technology is used to empower the excellent traditional culture, create a living historical and cultural district experience museum, and put forward new suggestions and possible reform directions for the inheritance of the traditional marriage culture in Guangfu.

Furthermore, the project and the class can be associated with international target orientation, as shown in Fig. 3, and to foster 'Three Creative' (innovation, creativity, and entrepreneurship). For example, the above-mentioned students' outcomes, the Journey to the Neo-confucianism project (Fig. 7) that has won the 3rd price of the the user experience design award (UXDA) 2022 international competition across the China after four rounds of competition [17], and Excellent traditional wedding culture project (Fig. 8), have been co-taught and collaborated with Prof. Dr. Mohamed Osmani from Loughborough

University, United Kingdom (UK), and Prof. Dr. MARCELO MARCIO SOARES from Brazil.

3.5 Competition for 'Three Creative'

Project 5: Competition for 'Three Creative (Innovation, Creativity and Entrepreneurship)'. It is the outcome of the Design Management class in the course chain implementing field teaching method as shown in Fig. 3, from which the principles and knowledge of design management have been systematically taught to students through subjects such as design environment, design overview, management overview, accounting and finance, marketing and brand communication, design and innovation, so that the students can have the ability of independent innovation and entrepreneurship, and be familiar with the total process of design management through a further developed project from above-mentioned the service experience design for social innovation design (Project 4), aiming for competition of 'Three Creative (innovation, creativity and entrepreneurship)' via establishing a feasible business plan/model/canvas, as shown in Fig. 9. Thus, on completion of the project, the students will be able to demonstrate:

1. Knowledge and understanding: be able to understand and master appropriate design strategies and methods to serve specific design management activities; be able to understand how to use management techniques, methodologies, and methodological steps to assist and guide specific design activities.
2. Subject-specific cognition: ability to manage, reflect and criticize, synthesize and cross boundary ideas and concepts; ability to find relevant design research literature and other primary and secondary data; and ability to reflect on design research strategies, methodologies, methodological steps, and statistical arguments.
3. Subject specific practice and technical expertise: the ability to provide evidence for relevant design management research literature and other primary and secondary information resources.
4. Key/transferable skills: when confronted with problems and planned research work tasks, the students can be self-motivated to carry out the work in an effective way with ability to work effectively as part of a team, and ability to critically evaluate the work of oneself and team mates; and able to communicate ideas in an appropriate way to share design management wisdom in terms of 'Three Creative'.

In addition, the students can master the principles and knowledge of design management, and cultivate their abilities to find and solve problems; master knowledge of design management process with ability to manage design procedures; master the commonly used design management techniques (from the design tradition and source, academically, realistically at the company/entrepreneurship level and the designer's ideal level), and have the design management ability, and cultivate their theoretical and practical abilities of design management for 'Three Creative (innovation, creativity and entrepreneurship)' competition practice to show their entrepreneurial potential.

For example, as above-mentioned the students' outcome (Project 2), a circular design strategy for industrial design (Fig. 4), has been further developed and won a national level innovation and entrepreneurship training project. In addition, all the students of

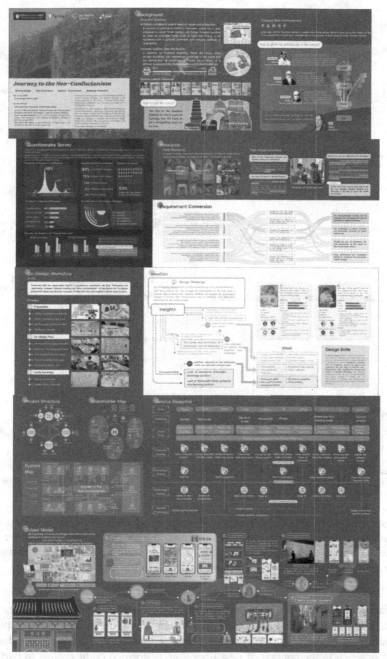

Fig. 7. Students' outcome, Journey to the Neo-confucianism (a service experience design for social innovation design project), of the Information and Interaction Design (II) Service Design class in the course chain via inquiry teaching method for Project 4: special subject for Information and Interaction Design: service experience design for social innovation.

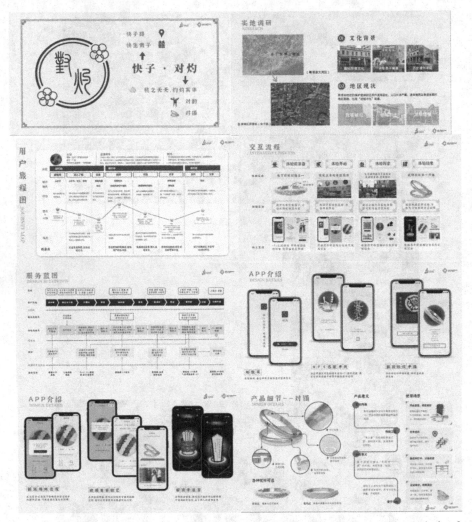

Fig. 8. Students' outcome, Excellent traditional wedding culture (a service experience design for social innovation design project), of the Information and Interaction Design (II) Service Design class in the course chain via inquiry teaching method for Project 4: special subject for Information and Interaction Design: service experience design for social innovation.

undergraduate industrial design experimental class (2020) who have been gone through all the course chain and total process of the framework of 'the implementation plan and implementation method of information and interaction design teaching method innovation and practice in the context of new liberal arts', formed eight groups to participate the user experience design award (UXDA) 2023 international competition, and the eight groups past first around [18], of which the Excellent traditional wedding culture project (Fig. 8) (Project 4) has won the Best Business Plan Award and 2nd price of the UXDA 2023 international competition across the China after four rounds of competition [19].

Fig. 9. Students' outcome, business plan/canvas to 'Journey to the Neo-confucianism' (a service experience design for social innovation design project), of the Information and Interaction Design (II) Service Design class in the course chain via inquiry teaching method for Project 4: special subject for Information and Interaction Design: service experience design for social innovation.

3.6 Design Academic Conference Paper for 'Three Creative'

Project 6: Design Academic Conference Paper Writing. It is the outcome of the Design Research Method and Academic Writing class in the course chain adopting case teaching method as shown in Fig. 3, from which the principles and knowledge of design research methods and academic writing have been systematically taught to students in the form of introduction of design research, research objectives and research directions, research methods, results, discussion and conclusion of design cases, so that they can have the ability of independent thinking and be familiar with the total process of design research methods and academic writing for their projects, thesis, and academic papers via a further developed paper from above-mentioned prophase projects of the course chain such as design strategy for 'Three Creative' (Project 2), design method for 'Three Creative' (Project 3), special subject for Information and Interaction Design: service experience design for social innovation (Project 4), competition for 'Three Creative (innovation, creativity and entrepreneurship)' (Project 5), and design academic conference paper writing (Project 6), aiming for concluding a total outcome for the the course chain to 'Three Creative (innovation, creativity and entrepreneurship)' in terms of academic, as shown in Fig. 9. Therefore, this project focuses on enabling students to master the following design research methods and academic writing aspects:

1. Knowledge and understanding: be able to understand and master appropriate design strategies and methods to serve specific design research activities; can understand how to use research techniques, methodologies, and methodological procedures to assist and guide specific design research activities.

2. Subject-specific cognition: the ability to manage, reflect and criticize, synthesize and cross boundary ideas and concepts; ability to find relevant design research literature and other primary and secondary data; ability to reflect on design research strategies, methodologies, methodological steps, and statistical arguments.
3. Subject specific practice and technical expertise: the ability to provide evidence for relevant design research literature and other primary and secondary information resources.
4. Critical/transferable skills: ability to critically evaluate your own and others' work when confronted with problems and planning research tasks; and able to communicate ideas in an appropriate way for their projects, thesis, and academic papers.

Furthermore, the students can master principles and knowledge of design research methods and academic writing, and cultivate their abilities to find and solve problems; master the knowledge of design research method and academic writing process, with an ability of academic writing procedures; master design research methods and academic writing techniques (research introduction, research objectives and research directions, research methods, results, discussion and conclusion), and have the ability to engage in academic writing (to cultivate students' collaborative practice ability of design research methods and academic writing) for their projects, thesis, and academic papers.

For instance, as above-mentioned the students' outcomes such as (Project 2) a circular design strategy for industrial design (Fig. 4) and (Project 4) Journey to the Neo-confucianism project (Fig. 7), have been further developed to published papers respectively, namely, 'Experience Economy and Green Economy Research in China: A 30-Year Bibliometric Analysis' [15] and 'A New Transmission Mode of Chinese Neo-Confucianism with Digital Technology via User Experience Design: A Case for Guan-hai Lou' [20] for presented and published in 12th International Conference on Design, User Experience, and Usability (DUXU 2023), affiliated to International Conference on Human-Computer Interaction (HCI International) 2023, Copenhagen, Denmark. Additionally, a paper called 'Designing a Robot for Enhancing Attention of Office Workers with the Heavily Use of Screen' [21] from a student undergraduate graduation thesis topic has been presented and published in the HCI International 2023 by a student who has been gone through all the course chain and total process of the framework of 'the implementation plan and implementation method of information and interaction design teaching method innovation and practice in the context of new liberal arts'.

4 Discussion and Conclusion

The feature of this paper are to improve the quality of experimental and innovative information and interaction design talents cultivation in the construction of national first-class undergraduate industrial design program in the light of idea of new liberal arts establishing, for which a framework of 'the implementation plan and implementation method of information and interaction design teaching method innovation and practice in the context of new liberal arts' has been proposed and updated (Fig. 3) via a mixed research method of theory construction and case practice, to integrate pedagogy theory, art theory and design theory, in the development of related issues. The results reveal that with the new liberal arts construction idea to improve the quality of experimental innovation information and interaction design talent cultivation in the construction of national first-class undergraduate industrial design program, it can be done through the innovation and practice of information and interaction design teaching methods to achieve the goal of cultivating the "three creativity" first-class liberal arts talents with the following themes, perspectives, and countermeasures and the application of innovation:

1. Theme innovation: this paper builds a bridge between the teaching method innovation and practice reform of information and interaction design under the background of new liberal arts, including target orientation, cultivation concept, teaching and research, collaborative innovation, curriculum, classroom and project practice.
2. Perspective innovation: from the content perspective of "three-creativity oriented project chain overall model" and "information and interaction design course chain overall model", the professional application field of "three-creativity" and information and interaction design courses in education, art and design has been expanded in a certain sense.
3. Countermeasures and application innovation: in order to implement the spirit of the National Education Conference, implement the requirements of the Working Conference on the construction of the new Liberal arts, comprehensively promote the construction of the new liberal arts, and build a world-class and Chinese characteristics of the liberal arts talent training system, the General Office of the Ministry of Education launched the first batch of new liberal arts research and reform practice projects in March 2021. The Outline of the Development Plan for the Guangdong-Hong Kong-Macao Greater Bay Area and the South China University of Technology will take the implementation of the new liberal Arts research and reform practice project as an opportunity to promote the realization of true reform, real reform, new reform and deep reform of liberal arts education, accelerate the construction of new liberal arts, and vigorously train the "three creative types" (innovation, creation, and entrepreneurship) of the first class liberal arts talents, and so on. This paper puts forward the theory of teaching method innovation and practice of information and interactive design under the background of new liberal arts and the practice of application countermeasures.

Acknowledgments. This research was funded by "2022 Constructing Project of Teaching Quality and Teaching Reform Project for Undergraduate Universities in Guangdong Province" Higher Education Teaching Reform Project (project No. 386), 'Innovation and practice of teaching methods for information and interaction design in the context of new liberal arts' (project grant number x2sj-C9233001).

References

1. The State Council Approved 'the Implementation Plan of the 14th Five-Year Plan for Promoting High-quality Development of Resource-Based Regions'. http://www.mohrss.gov.cn/SYrlzyhshbzb/dongtaixinwen/shizhengyaowen/202109/t20210924_423714.html. Accessed 30 Dec 2023

2. 2018 National Education Conference. http://www.moe.gov.cn/jyb_xwfb/xw_zt/moe_357/jyzt_2018n/2018_zt18/. Accessed 30 Dec 2023
3. New Liberal Arts Construction Workshop Held at Shandong University. http://www.moe.gov.cn/jyb_xwfb/gzdt_gzdt/s5987/202011/t20201103_498067.html. Accessed 30 Dec 2023
4. General Office of the Ministry of Education on the Announcement of the First Batch of New Liberal Arts Research and Reform Practice Programs. https://hudong.moe.gov.cn/src site/A08/moe_741/202111/t20211110_578852.html. Accessed 30 Dec 2023
5. The New Liberal Arts: A Feast of Disciplinary Integration. http://www.qstheory.cn/science/2019-05/08/c_1124487626.htm. Accessed 30 Dec 2023
6. South China University of Technology Homepage. https://www.scut.edu.cn/new/9015/list.htm. Accessed 30 Dec 2023
7. Guangdong-Hong Kong-Macao Greater Bay Area Portal Homepage. http://www.cnbayarea.org.cn/. Accessed 30 Dec 2023
8. The Ministry of Education to Deepen Undergraduate Education and Teaching Reform 22 Initiatives to Come. https://www.gov.cn/fuwu/2019-10/14/content_5439224.htm. Accessed 30 Dec 2023
9. World-class Cultivation of Excellent Talents "Nanfang Daily" Reports on the University's "Three Creative" Talent Cultivation. https://news.scut.edu.cn/2020/0714/c41a42492/page.htm. Accessed 30 Dec 2023
10. School of Design of South China University of Technology Homepage. http://www2.scut.edu.cn/design/2759/list.htm. Accessed 30 Dec 2023
11. South China University of Technology Adds 16 National First-class Undergraduate Major Construction Sites. https://news.scut.edu.cn/2021/0301/c41a43490/page.htm. Accessed 30 Dec 2023
12. Training plan of School of Design at South China University of Technology. http://www2.scut.edu.cn/design/2767/list.htm. Accessed 30 Dec 2023
13. Liu, Z., Yang, J., Chen, Y., Cui, J.: The 'three creative' talent characteristics model. In: Marcus, A., Rosenzweig, E., Soares, M.M. (eds.) HCII 2023. LNCS, vol. 14031, pp. 514–525. Springer, Cham (2023). https://doi.org/10.1007/978-3-031-35696-4_37
14. Yang, B., Wang, K., Zhan, X., Chen, S., Liu, Z.: Experience economy and green economy research in China: a 30-year bibliometric analysis. In: Marcus, A., Rosenzweig, E., Soares, M.M. (eds.) HCII 2023. LNCS, vol. 14030, pp. 406–424. Springer, Cham (2023). https://doi.org/10.1007/978-3-031-35699-5_30
15. The Double Diamond - Design Council Homepage. https://www.designcouncil.org.uk/our-resources/the-double-diamond/. Accessed 30 Dec 2023
16. Li, M., Qiao, T.: Characteristics and guidance of the network communication of neo-confucianism. Inner Mongolia Soc. Sci. 180–186+2 (2020). https://doi.org/10.14137/j.cnki.issn1003-5281.2020.05.025
17. 2022 the 14th UXDA Competition to Advance to the National Finals List, Here. https://mp.weixin.qq.com/s/wMxY-6gCEskgvmrsK929dw. Accessed 30 Dec 2023
18. 2023 the 15th UXDA Competition Preliminary Round Advancement List is Freshly Released. https://mp.weixin.qq.com/s/tBy4yEnX_tPp74oEhiLduA. Accessed 30 Dec 2023
19. 2023 the 15th UXDA International UX Innovation Competition National Finals and Award Ceremony Wrapped Up Successfully. https://mp.weixin.qq.com/s/b0HXZgaG4GbUSW2 5mvxFtQ. Accessed 8 Jan 2023
20. Gong, S., Liu, Z., Tan, Z.: A new transmission mode of Chinese neo-confucianism combined with digital technology: a case of Guanhai Lou. In: Marcus, A., Rosenzweig, E., Soares, M.M. (eds.) HCII 2023. LNCS, vol. 14034, pp. 58–73. Springer, Cham (2023). https://doi.org/10.1007/978-3-031-35705-3_5

21. Tan, Z., Liu, Z., Guo, Z., Gong, S.: Designing a robot for enhancing attention of office workers with the heavily use of screen. In: Marcus, A., Rosenzweig, E., Soares, M.M. (eds.) HCII 2023. LNCS, vol. 14031, pp. 246–261. Springer, Cham (2023). https://doi.org/10.1007/978-3-031-35696-4_18

Becoming More Curious About the Future: ReadySetFuture_

Cassini Nazir[1]([✉]) [iD], Mike Courtney[2], and Kuo Wei Lee[3] [iD]

[1] University of North Texas, Denton, TX, USA
cassini.nazir@unt.edu
[2] Aperio Insights, Dallas, TX, USA
mike@aperionsights.com
[3] Georgia Institute of Technology, Atlanta, GA, USA
klee934@gatech.edu

Abstract. This paper shows how a tool that explore future possibilities, ReadySet-Future_, helped a major automotive maker understand how shifts in consumer values may impact the features and use cases that surprise and delight future vehicle consumers in the year 2033. It contrasts two common mindsets when thinking about the future: a there is no alternative (TINA) mindset and a there are many alternatives (TAMA) mindset. The future contains numerous alternatives and possibilities, ripe for exploration and proactive planning. ReadySetFuture_ was included in a series of workshops to cultivate a heightened sense of curiosity about future possibilities. The paper examines the planning and development stages of ReadySetFuture_ and highlights key findings that demonstrates how the tool enhances users' curiosity. The paper details the design, development, and testing processes, emphasizing its approaches to evoke curiosity. Additionally, it discusses the strategic integration of various curiosity-invoking techniques, which contributes to a more extensive approach to futures thinking. The game's success in generating over 100 scenarios across workshops highlights its effectiveness in encouraging participants to explore diverse perspectives on potential futures.

Keywords: Curiosity · Futures thinking · Alternative futures · Co-creation · Design tools · Card decks

1 Introduction

All design work negotiates with the future. A present-day plan is executed over time, ultimately realizing an outcome in some near or distant future. If the often-quoted definition of design from Herbert Simon is correct—that design is devising "courses of action aimed at changing existing situations into preferred ones" [1]—Ramia Mazé reminds us that this preferred future is not empty. It is "loaded with our fantasies, aspirations and fears" [2]. Long-held beliefs and assumptions about a future that looks all too similar to the present block new ways of perceiving the future. The past inexorably pushes its way into the future. These intense emotions and deeply entrenched beliefs can sometimes overshadow or suppress curiosity about the future.

A. Marcus et al. (Eds.): HCII 2024, LNCS 14713, pp. 336–352, 2024.
https://doi.org/10.1007/978-3-031-61353-1_23

Inayatullah [3] triangulates this tension, distributing the weight of the past, the present's push, and the future's pull against each other. The inertia of the present is exemplified in four words frequently employed by former British Prime Minister Margaret Thatcher in speeches on the market economy: there is no alternative [4]. Those words, eventually shortened to TINA, convey an entrenched belief in a near-unstoppable flow of the present trajectory and suggest an inability to forge new paths or insurmountable difficulties in clearing the way.

The acronym made famous by Thatcher has its limits: Resisting the push of the present and the weight of the past is possible. Tony Fry called such a resistance *defuturing* [5]. When current unsustainable practices and lifestyles shape an undesirable or unsustainable future, they must be critically examined, challenging the prevailing assumptions and trajectories that lead to those futures. The future contains numerous alternatives and possibilities, ripe for exploration and proactive planning. The idea that *there are many alternatives*, or TAMA—a much less pleasant-sounding acronym but still better than Susan George's slogan *another world is possible* or AWIP [6]—is deceivingly simple. Understanding the idea is easy enough. Visualizing those alternatives can be incredibly challenging. Additionally, we often confuse which situations are TINA and which are TAMA. Starting from the TAMA mindset—where alternatives abound, if we can find them—forces us into the hard work of discovery.

As important as the future is, organizations struggle to utilize frameworks and exercises that help them systematically plan and prepare for future possibilities. This paper introduces an online futures game called ReadySetFuture_ that invites the exploration of useful and relevant future possibilities. It will show the context of how this custom-built card game came to be, its inspiration, how the game is played, and approaches used to invite curiosity in participants.

2 Workshop Background

2.1 Workshop Goals

A major automotive maker invited Aperio Insights [7], a Dallas-based research and strategic foresight agency, to conduct four two-day workshops from May through September 2023. The workshop was designed to help a major automotive maker understand how shifts in consumer values may impact the features and use cases that surprise and delight future vehicle consumers in the year 2033.

Aperio Insights (from this point forward referred to as the design team) developed a foresight toolkit that includes workshop exercises to help the engineering group imagine scenarios of the 10 or more years into the future and explore how these changes will influence traditional mobility solutions. The design team conducted these workshops with cross-functional teams across the automaker's organization to identify potential unmet consumer needs in 2033. The sessions had three overarching goals:

1. Teach workshop participants how to utilize basic foresight methods.
2. Create future scenarios and stories on appropriate time horizons.
3. Challenge present assumptions and identify both possibilities and problems.

The parameters of the workshop, as defined by the client, did not require the use of a game or cards. The design team decided that creating an interactive card game would help the automotive maker's employees better retain the information presented during the workshop, enable the teams to better explore unforeseen or difficult-to-imagine combinations of potential scenarios, and enable anyone in the organization—even those who did not attend the workshop—to use the card game.

Each of the four workshops had 15 to 50 participants. The ReadySetFuture_ game was conducted in the second, third, and fourth workshops. The game's adaptability across various levels of expertise and backgrounds was showcased by participants ranging from subject matter experts (SMEs) to executive/administration teams. Participants were gathered in circular tables, each holding eight people. Teams were divided by tables. The workshop with the largest number of participants had eight teams, each with no more than eight people. Throughout the workshop, the design team roved around the tables and assisted each team as needed. ReadySetFuture_ was only one of a series of activities held during the two days allotted for the workshop.

Three important questions permeated the creation of activities for the workshop in general and ReadySetFuture_ in particular.

2.2   Whose Job is It to Think About the Future?

Some organizations commonly relegate the task of envisioning the future to a small handful of leaders, a specialized department, or external consultants. Although research and development teams often handle this vital task, it is critical that all business units understand potential future scenarios and cultivate the ability to respond quickly and efficiently to change. Encouraging thinking about the future more broadly throughout the organization not only increases the surface area of ideas explored (see Fig. 1) but also can create a culture of futures literacy [8] throughout various business units. For example, the design team proposed "Foresight Fridays": a weekly or bi-weekly half-hour event at the end of the week where business units throughout the organization use ReadySetFuture_ and strengthen the future-thinking capabilities of their employees.

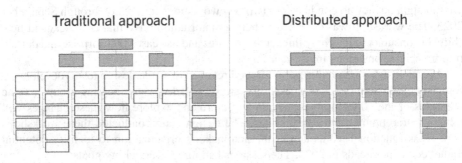

Fig. 1. Comparison of surface area explored when thinking about the future is prioritized by research and development teams versus a distributed approach across the entire organization.

2.3 What Role Does Artificial Intelligence Play?

Global management consulting firm McKinsey named 2023 as the "breakout year" for generative AI [9]. In that year, generative AI tools sparked broad interest across various business sectors, with more companies finally experimenting with the tools and discovering new purposes they might serve in their organization. One-third of respondents in the McKinsey survey reported their organization's use of generative AI [9]. During development, we viewed future thinking as being enhanced by generative AI tools, with ReadySetFuture_ acting as a complementary counterpart.

2.4 How Might We Surface Grand Challenges?

Grand challenges are complex issues that transcend national borders and pose significant hurdles to humanity. The 17 Sustainable Development Goals identified by the United Nations are one example of grand challenges. Because "the fundamental principles underlying a grand challenge are the pursuit of bold ideas and the adoption of less conventional approaches to tackling large, unresolved problems," [10] we framed the workshops as not just uncovering scenarios, problems, and possibilities that might affect business units but also an opportunity the surface large, overarching challenges the organization will likely face. Addressing grand challenges requires collaboration among various stakeholders: governments, communities, businesses, non-profit organizations, and academia. Similarly, the design team felt that if the organization could identify a limited number of grand challenges from this workshop, addressing these challenges would require collaboration among business units in cross-functional teams. At the end of the fourth and final workshop, nine grand challenges that the organization will inevitably confront in the near or far future were identified.

3 Inspiration for ReadySetFuture_

3.1 Cards: Tools for Future Thinking

Cards are practical, tactile ideation tools. Wölfel & Merritt [11] surveyed 18 physical card-based design tools, identifying three archetypes of cards: (i) general purpose/repository cards, (ii) customizable cards, and (iii) context-specific cards. While their work delves into tools used in design, an inherently future-oriented domain, it notably lacks cards commonly used by futurists or in strategic foresight settings. While Wölfel & Merritt place general purpose and customizable cards into discrete categories, we feel this categorization need not be separate, which we will demonstrate later in this paper. Roy and Warren reviewed 155 card-based design tools in a more comprehensive analysis [12]. Their classification system identified the specific domains of use rather than the type of usage, providing a more nuanced landscape of card-based tools. The six categories Roy and Warren identify are:

- Creative thinking and problem-solving
- Domain-specific design
- Human-centered design

- Systematic design methods and procedures
- Team building and collaborative working
- Futures thinking

   The existence of more than 150 card-based design tools calls to mind John Zimmerman's observation that "design methods are like toothbrushes. Everyone uses them, but no one likes to use someone else's." [13]. The diversity of card-based tools reminds us that there are many alternatives (TAMA), each offering tailored approaches and unique functionalities to apprehend uncertain futures.

3.2   Card Inspiration

The design team drew inspiration from a small subset of these 155 cards. Below, we offer concise descriptions of four tools and outline the specific characteristics that inspired the development of ReadySetFuture_.

The Thing from the Future (2015). In Other Prior Projects, the Design Team Used Stewart Candy and Jeff Watson's the Thing from the Future (TTFTF). TTFTF Uses Four Suits: Arc, Terrain, Object, and Mood (Fig. 2). in This Game, Four Cards Are Selected from the Deck. All Participants Craft a Scenario that Incorporates All Four Cards. Participants then Vote to Identify the Most Interesting, Provocative, or Funny Scenario. The Winner Retains the Cards for that Round, and the Participant Who Accumulates the Most Cards is the Overall Winner of the Game.

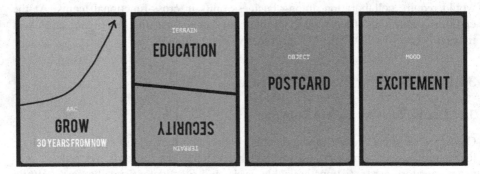

Fig. 2. Example of suits in the futures card game The Thing From The Future.

   The four types of cards in The Thing From The Future [14] include:

- **Arc**, the type of future, based on Dator's four futures archetypes [15] and the applicable time horizon. Dator's archetypes include Continued Growth, Collapse, Disciplined Society, and Transformational Society. The example in Fig. 2 shows *growth 30 years from now*.
- **Terrain**, the context for the object, either a physical location (*education*) or domain of human activity (*security*).
- **Object**, a category of the hypothetical future thing (*postcard*).

- **Mood**, the feeling when interacting with the hypothetical thing (*excitement*).

The accessibility, collaborative nature, and simplicity of Candy's TTFTF inspired the design team significantly. The gameplay inherently affords multiple alternatives and varied viewpoints about the future.

Near Future Laboratory Work Kit (2022). As a Companion to His 2022 Book the Manual of Design Fiction [16], Julian Bleeker Introduced a Work Kit Featuring 102 Cards. Like TTFTF, There Are Four Categories of cards—archetype, Object, Attribute, and action—collectively Offering "916,038 Unique Possible Future Products, Services, Experiences, Scenarios and Situations." [17].

Fabien Girardin, a Bleeker's Near Future Laboratory member, encourages finding a way to "balance optimism, pragmatism, and critics from multiple perspectives" when crafting design fiction [18]. To that end, the Design Fiction cards recommend a 70/20/10 ratio for balancing these components: 70% of ideas focus on desirable outcomes, 20% on open questions, and 10% on critical viewpoints. The notion of identifying desirable outcomes while also actively considering plausible but less desirable scenarios was significant for the design team.

First Five Minutes of the Future (2020). Much like Dante's Inferno, Jane McGonigal's First Five Minutes of the Future (FFMF) Immerses Participants in Medias Res of an Awkward or Unfamiliar Future Scenario, Challenging Them to Navigate Through the Initial Five Minutes of that Future. Unlike Candy's TTFTF and Bleeker's Work Kit, FFMF is Purely Prompt-Based, Without Any Cards. For Example, McGonigal Crafted the Following Prompt for Participants of the Institute for the Future's Ten-Year Forecast Event in September 2020:

"Your workplace sends you a pair of smart shoes it would like you to wear as a condition of employment. Each shoe has sensors in it that track your location, activity, weight, and social proximity (who you are standing near or walking by). It also detects air quality and viruses like SARS-CoV-2." [19].

McGonigal asks participants to "freewrite": describe whatever comes to mind without editing, removing, or recrafting sentences. The sequence of these questions is essential. Participants first explore the emotional landscape of this potential future before delving into questions that focus on strategic planning and preparation:

- What actions do you take in the first 5 min after being informed of the new "Smart shoe" policy?
- How do you feel?
- What do you think others might do?
- What is one real action you could take in the next few days or weeks to feel more prepared for the first 5 min of this scenario if it were really to happen?

The design team valued FFMF for quickly submerging participants into an uncomfortably plausible future and the ways it encourages exploration of both emotional responses and necessary actions in the unfamiliar context. By allowing fears about the future to be felt and named before exploring rational options, FFMF provides a comprehensive engagement with future scenarios.

Teach the Future (2013). Futurist Peter Bishop Established the International Non-Profit Organization Teach the Future to Promote Futures Literacy as an Essential Life Skill [20]. Because Bishop Felt that Futures Literacy Should not Only Be Taught in Universities but also Available to Everyone at an Early Age, He Developed the Teach the Future Website as a Comprehensive Platform that Includes Resources, Events, Profiles, and Tools Tailored for Teachers. World Futures Day, an Annual Event Instituted in 2013, Invites a 24-H Global Conversation Aimed at Building a Better Future for All. Foregrounding the Concept of Futures Literacy for All Was a Significant Idea for the Design Team. This also Meant Eliminating Barriers to Entry for the Client's Business Units and Fostering an Environment Where the Only Limitation is One's Imagination.

The design team drew additional inspiration for what ReadySetFuture_ might become from other sources, such as the online game Cards of Hope from the Finnish Innovation Fund Sitra [21] and the playful The Niche from the Future from Deep Transitions Lab [22]. One overarching goal remained throughout this research and exploration: create situations to cultivate participants' curiosity, rendering them more open to multiple alternatives and possibilities of the future.

4 ReadySetFuture_

This section of the paper will describe suits used in the game, gameplay, the development and refinement of ReadySetFuture, and ways it invites curiosity in participants.

4.1 Suits in the Card Deck

Cards, by necessity, borrow from the world from which they were created. Suits in early Medieval playing cards reflected the social structure of the courts: cups and chalices (now hearts) symbolized the clergy; swords (spades) represented the military; coins (diamonds) signified merchants; and batons (clubs) were associated with peasants [23–25]. In a contemporary context, the five distinctive suits of ReadySetFuture_ encapsulate aspects of modern life that have long arcs into the future and resonate with enduring societal dynamics. The ReadySetFuture_ deck comprises five suits:

- Consumer Segments
- Driving Forces
- Timeless Needs
- Emerging Technologies
- Context and Scenarios

Table 1 defines each suit, how the tool that suit is based on is commonly used when envisioning the future, and an example. Figure 3 shows the visual design of each suit. Each card within the five suits is a product of extensive research, encompassing consumer insights, market research, secondary research, and academic sources. The effort was a collaboration between the client and the design team.

To help participants understand how all five suits fit together, the design team diagrammed a sentence with each element (Fig. 4): *Consumer segments* have *timeless needs*, which are affected by *driving forces* and *trends* that can be meaningfully addressed by

Table 1. The Five Suits in ReadySetFuture_

Suit	Definition	How it is used	Example(s)
Consumer Segments 7 total	The client's current consumer segments, identified through market research	Used to gain consumer mindsets: how they think, feel, act and place value	*Adults age 65 +*
Driving Forces 14 total	A fundamental source of change that sends trends into motion. A trend is pattern or a general direction in which something is developing	Because Driving Forces have longer arcs than trends, use to explain current trends and explore possible future changes	*Medical advancements in healthcare enable preventive care for age-related conditions*
Timeless Needs 25 total	Universal needs not rooted in a particular time, location, or context. These are needs that humans have had in the past, present and will very likely appear in the future	Used to explore new ways of satisfying current or future needs using technology. Helps explore how products or services may change over time horizons	*Physical comfort Mobility and independence*
Emerging Technologies 31 total	Technology whose development and application are not yet fully realized	Used to address Timeless Needs and solve problems in new ways	*Generative AI*
Context and Scenarios 49 total	Factors that can affect any of the above in various subtle but important ways	Used to explore how small factors impact customer segment's experiences	*Relaxed vs rushed*

Fig. 3. Examples of playing cards in ReadSetFuture_. Icons by Oleksandr Panasovskyi.

emerging technologies—all happening in unique *contexts and scenarios* that add nuance. The diagram served as a reference for participants during the workshop, helping them unravel how each might shape the future and the relationships among elements.

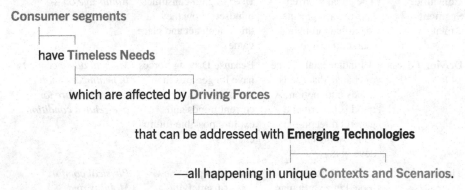

Fig. 4. A diagrammed sentence showing how each ReadySetFuture_ card fits together.

4.2   Timeless Needs

An essential aspect of ReadySetFuture_ is the Timeless Needs suit. Because clients had difficulties imagining future possibilities in radically different ways from the present or with technologies in current use, Mike Courtney introduced the idea of Timeless Needs. He realized that if the current technology layer that services an underlying human need could be stripped away, we could reimagine new ways to serve that need. As outlined in Table 1, Timeless Needs are universal human needs that transcend temporal and geographic boundaries. These needs are deeply ingrained in the context of a domain being explored (e.g., the home, mobility, or indoor climate) and persist across time. They are needs that we have had in the past, currently have in the present, and *will* have in the future. Exploring Timeless Needs creates a foundation for thinking about the future by addressing broad human needs that are not likely to change in a meaningful range of time. Table 2 provides examples of Timeless Needs and a brief synopsis of how those needs were met in the past and are being met in the present. The empty space in the last column opens up possibilities for how that need might be met in the future.

When thinking about Timeless Needs, it is important to keep in mind that they:

- *Are not based on time, technology, or culture.* While values and behaviors may evolve, shaped, and molded by consumer demands and desires, the underlying human needs remain constant.
- *Can be a foundation for personas and products.* Regardless of persona, job-to-be-done, product, or sector, the need propels consumer behavior or human action.
- Free us from thinking in terms of current technology. If we separate the need from the technology, we can be open to new ways of satisfying the need.
- *Require thinking in longer time horizons.* Finding underlying needs can help organizations connect quarterly product roadmaps to longer-term goals (five or more years into the future).

Table 2. Domains, Timeless Needs, and ways the need was/is/will be met

Domain	Timeless Need	How the need was/is/will be met in the...		
		Past	Present	Future
The home	Clean and odor free	We kept the home clean through manual effort and/or hard chemicals	Harsh chemical cleaners give some way to natural cleaners	?
Mobility	Communicate to and from the mobility vehicle	We communicated by honking the horn, flashing lights, or through hand gestures	Vehicles now sync with the phone, allowing calls and other communication	?
Indoor Climate	Maintain a comfortable indoor temperature	We maintained temperature by building fires or using clothing to keep warm or cool	We now use heating, ventilation, and air conditioning units	?

- *Complement Maslow's Hierarchy and Brand's Pace Layers.* Depending on the context, Timeless Needs can be foregrounded (critical or important in that moment) or backgrounded (forgotten, overlooked, or not currently important).
- *Are commonly paired with an Assumption-Reversal activity.* This includes activities that explore alternative ways to service this need except how it is met currently.

Because Timeless Needs help to detach associations built up over time (such as the product, systems, and services presently in place to meet that need), they assist in bringing a TAMA (there are many alternatives) mindset forward.

4.3 Gameplay

Building on the interactive approach from The Thing From the Future, gameplay in ReadySetFuture_ revolves around selecting a set of cards from which all participants at the table then craft scenarios. Three distinct prompts guide participants in capturing possible experiences, identifying consumer needs, and exploring associated emotions related to the hand at play (Fig. 5).

There are 126 cards in the ReadySetFuture_ deck, nearly two and a half times as many as in a standard poker deck. Such a large number of cards can be unmanageable for new players. While the deck features five suits, the gameplay does not require that all suits be played in the game. By making the deck playable with a few suits (a minimum of two), we hoped to undo the tension pair that Wölfel & Merritt [11] identified between general purpose and customizable cards. When ReadySetFuture_ was introduced in workshops, the design team began by using only two suits, Timeless Needs and Driving Forces, to onboard participants in understanding the game mechanics.

To further facilitate initiation into gameplay, AI-generated thought starters accompany each card dealt. These thought starters, generated by OpenAI's ChatGPT 3.5,

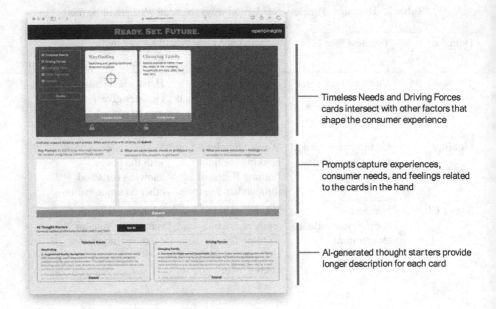

Fig. 5. An overview of the ReadySetFuture_ game

provide extended descriptions for each card, helping participants understand the dense information more quickly and initiate the ideation process. ReadySetFuture_ was completed in time for the second workshop in a series of four. Participants in the second, third, and fourth workshops generated more than 100 scenarios in ReadySetFuture_.

4.4 Design, Development, and Testing

ReadySetFuture_ originated from a physical card-based brainstorming exercise developed by the design team in 2019 that helped participants reimagine possibilities for in-vehicle experiences (Fig. 6). ReadySetFuture_ expanded the 2019 activity into an online card game to ensure the cards could be updated, changed, and adapted over time. Because of the cost of printing multiple deck sets with 126 cards, digital gameplay for ReadySetFuture_ took precedence in the design and development. No physical cards were printed for the workshops.

The name ReadySetFuture_ calls to mind the phrase commonly used to initiate a race or competition: Ready, set, go! The trailing underscore appended to the name is reminiscent of the blinking cursor of a terminal window awaiting input from the user.

The ReadySetFuture_ cards (Fig. 3) were designed to have a variety of visual cues: color and iconography indicate each suit, vibrant colors, and clear iconography, which suggests a category system that aids users in navigation through different themes and exercises. The card layout was crafted with software-development in mind. The visual or information elements on the cards can be managed through external data-management resources such as an Airtable spreadsheet or a JSON file.

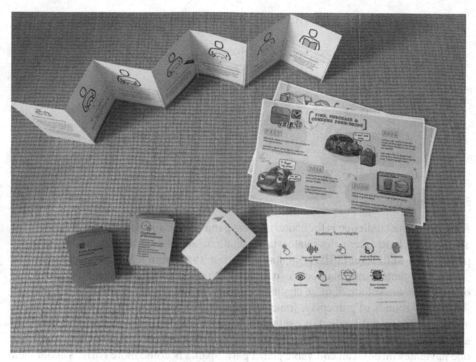

Fig. 6. A 2019 card-based brainstorming exercise and predecessor of ReadySetFuture_. Hand-drawn images by Cyrene Quiamco.

ReadySetFuture was developed using the open-source React-based web framework Next.js and deployed on the Vercel cloud platform. Participant submissions are saved to the cloud-based database Airtable, which also provides a user-friendly interface for the client to organize and download information. Airtable also makes updating the individual cards very easy. Inputs can be stored and retrieved quickly. Two rounds of informal usability testing and targeted focus play-throughs generated several interface improvements before launching to the client.

5 Approaches to Curiosity

The design team strategically incorporated ways to evoke curiosity when designing gameplay interactions. Tieben et al. use the phrase "making people curious" in the title of a 2011 conference paper on curiosity [26]. This paper's authors believe that designers can only invite curiosity [27], creating conditions whereby individuals might be more curious.

The design team employed a subset of 10 common approaches identified by Nazir [28], listed in Table 3, in both ReadySetFuture_ gameplay and overall workshop facilitation. This section will delineate those approaches.

Table 3. A 10 Common Approaches Used to Invite Curiosity (Nazir, 2023)

Approaches, organized alphabetically	
Challenge	Obscure
Delay	Play
Hide	Perceptual
Humor	Sensory
Novelty	Tease

5.1 Challenge

An appropriate challenge is the center of most gameplay. Csikszentmihalyi notes that we are more likely to enter a flow state when a game balances a challenge appropriate to the participant's skill level [29]. As mentioned earlier, the design team introduced only two suits at the game's introduction. As participants gained greater skill and understanding of the game, the source of these challenges turned from external motivations to internal. After early rounds of gameplay, some participants felt the need for a greater challenge, adding in additional cards. For example, of the 96 submissions generated in the third and fourth workshops, about two-thirds (60 submissions) used two or more cards. As one navigates through an enjoyable game, participants become more curious about their abilities to withstand greater and greater challenges.

5.2 Delay

As Nazir notes, the worst thing one can do with a good question is to answer it too quickly [30]. Creating a delay is an overlooked way to develop a TAMA (there are many alternatives) mindset. Workshop participants were actively encouraged to find additional alternatives or ways of seeing the hand. By encouraging moments of delay followed by a brief period of reflection, 165 alternatives were identified from the 96 submissions in the third and fourth workshops. A participant's first response should not be their only response.

Encouraging alternatives was evident in the phrases used in the workshops. Rather than using the question stem "How might we…," commonly employed in design practice, the design team reinforced a TAMA mindset by using the phrase "What are ways…" The difference between the two is more than semantics. While seasoned designers have trained themselves to come up with multiple ideas, workshop participants, primarily composed of non-designers from various business units across the organization, were not. When an answer to a question has been presented, non-designers hold a common sentiment: "We have found an answer to the question. Let us now move on." The phrase "What are ways…" more clearly foregrounds the importance of identifying multiple alternatives in non-designers and invites a spirit of curiosity to seek them out.

5.3 Novelty

In a well-known story by Washington Irving, Rip Van Winkle wakes from a 20-year slumber only to find that the American Revolution has passed and that he now lives in a vastly different world. The future holds many novelties, which can be disorienting and exciting. A rapidly warming climate, ubiquitous surveillance, and social media are novelties of 21st-century life that a person sleeping since the 20th century might find alarming, disorienting, or altogether strange. A fundamental aspect of the gameplay was to look at familiar things in new ways, which Bell et al. [31] describe as making strange or strange-making. Facilitators encouraged participants to follow intuitions or hunches about future experiences that, to present-day eyes, seem strange, unlikely, or even counterintuitive.

5.4 Obscure

William Gibson's often quoted aphorism, "The future is already here – it's just not evenly distributed" serves as the foundation for this approach to curiosity. In the context of ReadySetFuture_, the obscure approach refers to the practice among futurists of scanning the horizon, or simply monitoring current events, trends, and emerging developments in order to identify possibilities. As opposed to the approach of hide, where the entirety of the thing is covered, obscure may show parts of it. In contrast to the tease approach, obscure does not necessarily imply intentionality. Participants were encouraged to explore obscure technologies in order to uncover potential uses.

5.5 Perceptual

At the beginning of each two-day workshop, the organization's market research team presented a short video that showcased how their consumer segments reacted to the current market offerings. They also provided the participants with detailed, up-to-date research materials about each segment. As previously mentioned, the design team found inspiration in Jane McGonigal's First Five Minutes of the Future and how it surfaced feelings about the future. Workshop participants used Timeless Needs as a reference point to identify the emotions that consumer segments might experience during these changes. This approach helped participants to see possibilities through multiple eyes and invited curiosity around actual end-user needs instead of superficial features or technological advancements.

5.6 Additional Futures Tools

While this paper discusses a game played during a two-day workshop and its relationship to arousing curiosity in participants, it is important to briefly note the other future-oriented activities that contributed to this environment.

Futures Wheel. The Futures Wheel is a Visual Tool that Puts a Source of Change at the Center, and Various Spokes Radiate Outward. Each Spoke Explores First-, Second-, and Third-Order Implications of that Change. This Tool Helps Systematically Analyze the Effects of a Decision or Event.

Assumption Reversal. The Assumption Reversal technique challenges conventional assumptions related to a problem or situation. Participants first clearly articulate as many deeply held assumptions about the problem as they can. Then, participants systematically challenge each assumption fundamentally by opposing or reversing it. For example, if the assumption is that "vehicles have four wheels," reversals might include "vehicles have anything but four wheels," "vehicles no longer need wheels," or "vehicles can fly."

Technology Two Ways. The Design Team Adapted Marshall McLuhan's Tetrad [32] to Explore Four Questions About Emerging Technologies. These Four Questions Help Product Development Teams to Think Through Various Alternatives a Technology Might Afford Throughout Its Lifetime.

- Where might this technology first appear in a user's life?
- What tasks are dramatically impacted when this technology has matured?
- How might this technology enhance consumer experiences?
- What problems might arise alongside this technology?

6 Discussion and Conclusion

This paper introduced the concept of design's role in shaping the future, outlined the development and implementation of the game ReadySetFuture_ in a series of workshops, and explored various approaches ReadySetFuture_ and the workshops used to invite curiosity in participants. The workshops and ReadySetFuture_ were designed to encourage participants from various business units in a major automotive organization to think more broadly about the future. It discussed ways to challenge assumptions, explore alternative futures, and engage participants in creative thinking about potential scenarios. Activities were designed to increase the total surface area of ideas and possibilities explored.

Based on the results of these initial workshops, additional factors must be considered. First, the output of these workshops is a function of not just who participates but also how steeped they are in thinking about alternatives and futures and how imaginative they can be. Jerome Glenn, the creator of the Futures Wheel, notes, "The Futures Wheel is no better than the collective judgments of those involved" [33]. This is true not only for the Futures Wheel but also for all workshop activities. This highlights the need for organizations to build a culture of future literacy, a daunting but increasingly necessary task.

Additional improvements are needed to make ReadySetFuture_ ready for broader public use. These include exploring the game's application in diverse fields/areas to foster a broader range of future-ready thinkers, crafting more straightforward instructions for participants, conducting additional gameplay tests, and finding appropriate topics tied to the game. More research needs to be conducted to explore curiosity's relationship to the futures literacy. Zurn and Shankar describe the burgeoning field of curiosity studies [34] as a broad, transdisciplinary effort. Situating futures literacy in curiosity studies may help unravel the pervasive there is no alternative (TINA) mindset and foster greater exploration of additional mindsets. After all, there are many alternatives.

Acknowledgments. Quyen Nguyen, Tom Rau, Rita Gomez-Boren, Meah Lin, Jonathan Tran, Saja Noor, Lydia Bazan, Rebekah Irizarry, Ariana Hill, Duncan Moore, Arianna Michaud, Kennedy-Alexis Staples, Sophia Carswell, Olivia Palomo, Abigail Morales, Michael Gibson, Keith Owens, Omari Souza, Roger Malina, and Johann Schutte.

References

1. Herbert, S.A.: The Sciences of the Artificial. MIT Press, Cambridge, MA (1996)
2. Mazé, R.: Design and the future: temporal politics of 'making a difference.' In: Smith, R.C., Otto, T. (eds.) Design Anthropological Futures, pp. 37–54. Bloomsbury, London (2016)
3. Inayatullah, S.: Alternative futures of genetics and disability. J. Fut. Stud. **7**(4), 67–72 (2003)
4. Berlinski, C.: There is No Alternative: Why Margaret Thatcher Matters. Basic Books, New York (2011)
5. Fry, T.: Design as Politics. Bloomsbury, New York (2010)
6. George, S.: Another World is Possible If. Verso Books, United Kingdom (2004)
7. Aperio Insights. https://www.aperioinsights.com. Accessed 12 Jan 2024
8. Miller, R.: Futures literacy: a hybrid strategic scenario method. Futures **39**(4), 341–362 (2007)
9. McKinsey: The state of AI in 2023: Generative AI's breakout year, 1 August 2023. https://www.mckinsey.com/capabilities/quantumblack/our-insights/the-state-of-ai-in-2023-generative-ais-breakout-year
10. Colquitt, J.A., George, G.: Publishing in AMJ—Part 1: topic choice. Acad. Manag. J. **54**, 432–435 (2011)
11. Wölfel, C., Merritt, T.: Method card design dimensions: a survey of card-based design tools. In: Kotzé, P., et al. (eds.) INTERACT 2013, Part I. LNCS, vol. 8117, pp. 479–486. Springer, Cham (2013). https://doi.org/10.1007/978-3-642-40483-2_34
12. Roy, R., Warren, J.P.: Card-based design tools: a review and analysis of 155 card decks for designers and designing. Des. Stud. **63**, 125–154 (2019). https://doi.org/10.1016/j.destud.2019.04.002
13. Harrison, S., Tatar, D.: On methods. Interactions **18**(2), 10–11 (2011)
14. Candy, S., Watson, J.: The Thing from the Future: Second Edition (Card Game). Situation Lab, Pittsburgh (2018)
15. Dator, J.: Alternative futures at the Manoa School. J. Fut. Stud. **14** (2009)
16. Bleecker, J., Foster, N., Girardin, F., Nova, N., Frey, C., Pittman, P.: The Manual of Design Fiction: A Practical Guide to Exploring the Near Future. Near Future Laboratory, United States (2023)
17. Bleecker, J.: The Work Kit of Design Fiction 2023 MJ Edition. Near Future Laboratory. https://shop.nearfuturelaboratory.com/products/the-work-kit-of-design-fiction-2023-mj-edition
18. Girardin, F.: The making of things for decision making. https://medium.com/design-fictions/the-making-of-things-before-taking-decisions-fb2145564e68
19. McGonigal, J.: The first five minutes of the future. https://medium.com/institute-for-the-future/the-first-five-minutes-of-the-future-b7e8e275aa8f
20. Bishop, P.: Teach the Future. https://www.teachthefuture.org
21. Sitra: Digital cards of hope. https://www.sitra.fi/en/digital-cards-of-hope/
22. Deep Transitions, "The Niche from the Future" – A card game for investments in transformation. https://deeptransitions.net/2022/04/29/the-niche-from-the-future-a-card-game-to-imagine-a-sustainable-tomorrow/
23. Husband, T.B.: The World in Play: Luxury Cards 1430–1540. Metropolitan Museum of Art (2016)

24. Leonhard, K.: Game of thrones: early modern playing cards and portrait miniature painting. Br. Art Stud. (17) (2020)
25. Bernhard, A.: The Lost Origins of Playing-Card Symbols. The Atlantic. https://www.the atlantic.com/technology/archive/2017/08/the-lost-origins-of-playing-card-symbols/537786/ (2017)
26. Tieben, R., Bekker, T., Schouten, B.: Curiosity and Interaction: making people curious through interactive systems. In: Proceedings of the Conference on Human-Computer Interaction (HCI), pp. 361–370 (2011). https://doi.org/10.14236/ewic/HCI2011.66
27. Nazir, C., Wang, J.: Designing Curiosity: A Beginner's Guide. User Experience Magazine: The Magazine of the User Experience Professionals Association (online magazine) (2022). https://uxpamagazine.org/designing-curiosity-a-beginners-guide. Accessed 1 June 2023
28. Nazir, C., Farrar, E.: Curious gestures: inviting curiosity in and out of the classroom. In: Motion Design Education Summit 2023 Edited Conference Proceedings. Focal Press, MA (2023)
29. Csikszentmihalyi, M.: Flow: The Psychology of Optimal Experience. Harper & Row (1990)
30. World Information Architecture Day 21 Designing Curiosity | Cassini Nazir. https://youtu.be/JKShjK4Ywfs. Accessed 12 Jan 2024
31. Bell, G., Blythe, M., Sengers, P.: Making by making strange. ACM Trans. Comput.-Hum. Interact. **12**, 149–173 (2005). https://doi.org/10.1145/1067860.1067862
32. McLuhan, M.: McLuhan's laws of the media. Technol. Cult. (1975)
33. Glenn, J.C., Gordon, T.J.: The futures wheel. In: Futures Research Methodology–V3.0, The Millennium Project (2009). https://jeasprc.org/wp-content/uploads/2020/08/06-Futures-Wheel.pdf
34. Zurn, P., Shankar, A.: Curiosity studies: A New Ecology of Knowledge. U of Minnesota Press (2020)

"Let's Fashion Fiction!" Fashion Designers as Speculators, Alternative Present and Possible Future with Speculative Design

Chen Siyin(✉)

Future Study and Fashion Design Studio, Zhanjiang 524000, China
chensiyin369@gmail.com

Abstract. This research explores the transformative potential of speculative design in shaping the future of fashion, with a specific focus on the concept of fashion fiction. The article analyses two case studies from Demna Gvasalia's Balenciaga fashion collections, the 2021Fall - Afterworld game film and the 2022 Spring - Clones fashion show, to demonstrate how different ways of combining narrative building, scenario design, and parallel worldviews of fashion fiction stimulate audience imagination and discussion. It also presents a comprehensive analysis of the aesthetic system and worldview of fashion design cases, shedding light on their pivotal role in envisioning and shaping the future of fashion. Furthermore, the evolving significance of clothing in fashion shows is examined, highlighting the profound influence of fashion fiction in reshaping the experiential and conceptual dimensions of fashion presentations. By delving into the role of fashion designers as visionary speculators, the study investigates their capacity to craft alternative presents and possible futures through the creative lens of fashion fiction.

Keywords: Speculative Design · Fashion Designers · Alternative Present · Possible Future · Fashion Fiction

1 Introduction

The fashion business currently confronts several issues in terms of sustainability, ethics, and social responsibility. Current industry methods frequently involve overproduction, overconsumption, and waste, all of which have significant environmental and social consequences [1]. The giants of the fashion industry, such as LVMH, have made sustainable fashion their main strategy for the present and the future, and are developing environmentally friendly production models and fashion products [2]. But even so, the giants' sustainability mantra and strategic pivot have not prevented many brands from unavoidably ignoring sustainability and prioritising economic benefits in their quest to innovate and attract customer attention. The fashion design sector's future relies on striking a balance between innovation and sustainability. Twigger [3] has argued that integrating the fashion fiction approach into the fashion sector for visioning the alternative fashion world can improve the industry's creativity, ethics, engagement, and sustainability.

A. Marcus et al. (Eds.): HCII 2024, LNCS 14713, pp. 353–368, 2024.
https://doi.org/10.1007/978-3-031-61353-1_24

Although design methods related to fashion fiction, such as speculative design [4] and design fiction [5], are widely used in interaction design and conceptual design, there is a lack of theoretical and practical exploration and research in the fashion field. Moreover, fashion fiction is also in the dilemma of being vaguely defined, underexposed, methodologically imperfect, and unrecognized by the fashion field. This novel approach allows fashion designers to imagine and create fictional worlds and futures, challenging the status quo and offering fresh perspectives on "wicked problems" for our reality.

This study aims to improve part of the missing methodological aspects of fashion fiction by incorporating speculative design theory to identify two valid cases from the Georgian fashion designer Demna Gvasalia's works, to demonstrate how different ways of combining narrative building, scenarios design, and parallel worldviews of fashion designers with the paradigms of speculative design can build the fashion fiction works. These two representative fashion case studies summarise two subsets in fashion fiction that split from the main methods of fictionalizing parallel world-views: alternative present and possible future. The Possible future case includes a representative case study that contains a feedback case, meaning it includes both the case itself and a feedback study about the case. Alternative present cases offer specific fashion design languages and methods in fashion fiction. This article provides reference material for fashion designers interested in experimenting with fashion fiction. At the same time, it provides specific design paths and steps for fashion fiction towards fashion performance design and practice.

2   Relevant Literature

2.1   Narrative Building and Scenario Design in Speculative Design

Speculative design is a design approach that involves the creation of speculative scenarios, objects, narratives, and systems that explore alternative possibilities for the future [4]. It is also a cross-media practice that uses the 'What-If' thought experiment to explore the potential side effects of emerging technologies through the use of props and fictional aesthetics [6]. Dunne and Raby [4] aim to rekindle social dreaming by incorporating narrative qualities of science fiction into design and envisioning both utopian and dystopian scenarios. The goal is to stimulate public debate on societal issues by 'expressing the unthinkable' through design language [7]. They propose that designers can employ speculative design and design fiction [5] to investigate alternative presents and possible futures, creating physical artefacts that question preconceptions and offer fresh perspectives on what are frequently dubbed "wicked problems" [4].

Narrative building is the process of creating a cohesive and interesting story or series of events that could be applied to many aspects of design, which entails developing a tale or framework to provide depth, meaning, and emotional resonance to the designed product or experience. It aims to create a cohesive and impactful narrative that resonates with users, adds value to the designed object, and enriches the overall user experience [8]. Narrative building is essential for producing convincing speculative design projects because it helps designers place their ideas within familiar surroundings and complex human needs or anxieties. By creating captivating narratives, designers may engage their audience and empower them to transfer the designed artefacts into their own lives, thereby making them protagonists in the story [9].

Scenario design is the process of creating hypothetical events or stories that show how people may interact with a product, service, or environment. It is also an important tool in the design process since it enables designers to predict user demands, behaviours, and reactions in a variety of situations [8]. It involves creating a series of narratives that depict various potential future states of the world [10]. Scenario design is used in speculative design to imagine and analyse alternative present and possible futures, allowing designers to investigate the repercussions of various decisions and advancements. This process aids in comprehending the complexities of future issues and opportunities in a variety of sectors, including social, economic, environmental, and technological factors, and it can guide decision-making and innovation in anticipating and preparing for probable changes and disruptions [4, 7, 10].

In the framework of speculative design, Narrative building and scenario design collaborate to produce immersive and thought-provoking experiences. The narratives give context to the speculative designs, but the scenarios assist in rooting them in credible and logical future situations. Together, they allow designers to successfully express and explore alternate ideas of the present and future, challenging preconceptions and opening up new possibilities [4].

2.2 Fashion Fiction and Digital Fashion Towards Future Fashion

Goggans [13] defines "Fashion in Fiction" examines the role of fashion within literature, while "Fiction in Fashion" explores the impact of literature on the world of fashion. Both concepts offer valuable insights into the interconnectedness of fashion and storytelling. According to Twigger [3, 11, 12], fashion fiction is a new sort of design practice or research project that aims to imagine, prototype, and analyze attractive alternate fashion worlds through a co-creation design process with a participatory approach in which designers and participants become co-researchers that is both enjoyable and educational. It is also an emerging area that takes design out of its commercial framework and investigates political, social, and cultural themes via speculative design's 'what-if' scenarios [4], promoting critical thinking about fashion's future [3] towards real-world change [11, 12].

Digital fashion is the junction of fashion and technology, covering elements like digital design, virtual try-ons, augmented reality experiences, e-commerce platforms, virtual fashion shows, digital garment design, and social media marketing in the fashion industry [14, 15]. It has become increasingly essential in the current fashion environment and influences how fashion is developed, exhibited, and consumed in this digital era [14]. Some scholars explore the intersection of fashion and digital game design, emphasizing the need for fashion designers to understand the technical and socio-dynamic peculiarities of digital worlds to create meaningful fashion-related outcomes [16, 17]. These digital fashion items are created to be worn by avatars in virtual worlds or online games, blurring the lines between real and virtual fashion experiences [17]. Incorporating co-creation processes and digital tools in fashion education can prepare future fashion designers to navigate hybrid practices and contribute to the development of digital fashion in multiple environments [18].

3 Methods

This study utilizes a qualitative case study strategy to explore real-world fashion design cases closely related to speculative fashion. Case study research can give thorough and contextualized insights into complicated phenomena in their real-world contexts [19]. The analysis involves delving into the characteristics and mechanisms of representative fashion design works, particularly focusing on the case studies of two fashion shows from Demna Gvasalia's Balenciaga. As research material, Demna Gvasalia's Balenciaga case data were collected from a variety of media sources, official fashion shows, websites, fashion magazine reviews, designer's own words, previous public interviews, press releases, fashion blog postings, fashion YouTuber videos, Chinese Bilibili video platform, social media, and streaming design conferences. Data collection followed academic ethical guidelines. Through qualitative analysis, the study aims to understand how these designers are shaping the future of fashion through narrative building and fictional scenarios. The qualitative case study strategy allows for an in-depth exploration of the specific niche cases, providing rich insights into the world of fashion fiction.

4 Demna Gvasalia's Balenciaga Case Study

The case of Demna Gvasalia's Balenciaga contributes to the field of speculative design methods for fashion collection design, i.e. a parallel world-view approach in which the fashion designer builds on possible future and alternative present [3, 10]. Demna Gvasalia is a fashion designer from Georgia, currently serving as the creative director of Balenciaga and co-founding Vetements. Balenciaga is a French luxury fashion house that was founded in 1919. Since 2015, it has experienced meteoric growth due to Gvasalia's successful designs and innovative approach. In 2019, the brand surpassed the billion-dollar sales mark, doubling its size in just three years [20]. In January 2020, he announced the reopening of the Haute Couture collection to bring Balenciaga back to"its sources of origin" and create"an unexplored mode of creative freedom and a platform for innovation" [21]. Balenciaga's CEO, Cédric Charbit, who led the expansion of the house, said, "Thanks to the success and magnitude of Demna's creative vision, we now have the resources and the platform.". Over the past few years, Gvasalia has transformed Balenciaga from one of many fashion houses into a mesmerising and uniquely shaped gem. The house has taken a path that is unique in the industry, and the future is full of possibilities and speculation [22].

Demna Gvasalia's design approach and creative vision have been key to Balenciaga's success in recent years. Even though they experienced their communication crisis on social media in 2022 [23], there is still no denying the creativity and unique design thinking that set Gvasalia apart from his peers today. He has also attracted a millennial clientele with his critical thinking, rebellious spirit, and alternative designs. Charbit claims that 65 per cent of Balenciaga's customers are millennials, accounting for over 50 per cent of sales [24]. Gvasalia has said that Balenciaga's true fans relate to the "more conceptual and intellectual part of fashion. They always react to an authentic idea. And this authentic idea never comes from the commercial list." [25].

Balenciaga has had such a strong young consumer base in recent years because the current younger generation is more willing to pay for concepts and symbolism rather than just tangible products which is Gvasalia's strength. He is one of the most skilled storytellers in the fashion area. He has developed some fashion fiction about Balenciaga's new fashion universe by using the method of creating parallel universes in speculative design. This has resulted in an iconic fashion narrative that explores possible futures and alternative presents.

4.1   Possible Future with Fashion Games: 2021 Fall - Afterworld: The Age of Tomorrow Case

"Today's customer does gaming. It's an important luxury customer base. They project so much onto their character. It's a parallel world."-Demna Gvasalia [28].

Balenciaga envisioned the next generation of virtual fashion shows as Fashion Weeks around the world were forced to go online during the pandemic. Afterworld: The Age of Tomorrow is a 3D online game that takes players on an interactive trip through "mythological pasts and projected futures". VOGUE magazine described this show as a "Quantum Leap" for the fashion industry [26].

Balenciaga's Afterworld is both an innovative vehicle for combining fashion design with virtual technology and an innovative model for fashion design with speculative design, as it creates a virtual parallel world, explores a possible future and stimulates the audience's imagination and debates [4]. Gvasalia has a history of using his runway presentations to comment on the environment and political instability. Afterworld is no exception, as he visualizes a dystopian future society. This message is now accessible to the masses, allowing everyone to experience a possible future that could become our reality without systemic change [27]. Moreover, this futuristic blend of volumetric capture and video games has opened the industry's eyes to the endless possibilities of using realistic avatars and game engines like Unreal Engine [28].

The audience has two ways to experience this 2021 Fall show: one is to play this open-source game Afterworld: The Age of Tomorrow, but only the brand's VIP customers received their VR gaming devices with a better sense of immersion, and the other is to watch a fashion film from the set of this game. Even if Gvasalia once said, "I hate the idea of fashion film. I find it very dated." But this edited video from in-game set footage with hidden allegories from the designers still falls under the category of a fashion film, but what sets it apart from a traditional fashion film is that it's an interactive immersive fashion sci-fi film that's as much a game as it is a film, it blurred the boundaries between games and films, opening up a whole new avenue for fashion films. To be precise, he doesn't replace fashion films but rather widens fashion films and fashion narratives, and the path he widens is fashion fiction.

Scenario Design: "Afterworld" Fashion Game Film.   Demna Gvasalia has envisioned this adventure game set in 2031, in which players can explore five chapters, from the brand's virtual shop to picturesque mountaintops at sunrise on the horizon. The official "Afterworld" game film is an iconic piece of fashion fiction, divided into 5 chapters corresponding to the 5 zones of the game. And the clothes of the Fall 2021 collection are all displayed on the game's characters. Players can choose their preferred character to experience the game. But no matter what choice they start with, there is only one way they will end up: they will become a knight in silver armour, stick down the sword of Balenciaga, and the sun will rise.

Beginning: Burying Metaphors and Hinting at Where the Story is Going. At the Start of the Film, the Sound of Breathing and Heartbeats is Heard, Followed by the Sensation of Being Shaken Awake in an Empty Room by a Non-Playable Character (NPC) Dressed in a Balenciaga 2021 Fall Outfit and Silver Shoes. This Initiates a First-Person Immersion Mode. The View then Shifts to a Holographic Projection Map that is Divided into 3 Blocks. At the Same Time, a Band of Light Travels from the City Through Nature to Reach the Mountains (Which Contain Pyramid-Like Objects), Here Foreshadowing the Direction of the Story with the Story Framework of This Parallel World (See Fig. 1).

Fig. 1. A holographic projection map at the beginning of the "Afterworld" game film [33].

Chapter 1-Zone 1: Balenciaga's Store. The scene switches to a Balenciaga's shop displaying the latest season's clothing with the brand's aesthetic décor, and the shop seems to be a gateway to the outside world, where the future elements of facial recognition are also mentioned. A woman who appears in the last scene in Zone 1 is wearing a black coat with silver shoes.

Chapter 2-Zone 2: Urban District. The scene is set in a bustling urban environment, with people of diverse identities traversing busy streets. The billboard reveals the planet's ecological problems, such as the depletion of resources and endangerment of species, faced by mankind in this world. The camera focuses on a young man holding a flower and another young man with silver knee pads and silver shoes who appears to breathe fire by hand. There is a speeding #7 Afterworld bus that disappears into space.

Chapter 3-Zone 3: Rainy Night Dark Zone. Arriving at a dim and decaying underground or slum-like area where weeds grow in certain corners, the point man with silver gloves and shorts underneath full of silver elements points to a poster with a drawing of a rabbit, and a rabbit hops by. Another NPC in silver heels opens the holographic projection map again, and the location showing the T-party lights up red, suggesting that this is the place to be.

Chapter 4-Zone 4: Psychedelic Forest. The scene comes to the forest, with the rabbit leading the way and a group of people dancing freely and revelling in the psychedelic forest, with close-ups of a lady in silver armour's thigh-high boots, and shaking nature's flora and fauna. The scene skims over many people, and it's clear that the further down the path you go, there are more and more people wearing silver armour fittings, and the silver part of their clothing is constantly expanding.

Chapter 5-Zone 5: Rocky Mountain. Coming to a dark mountain path and climbing upwards, a light shone on a silver sword stuck on the ground, A human in full armour drew the sword, the wall at the end fell and a new passage appeared, and more lights shone in. Then the knight travelled through the cave up to the true end. In front of the endless vastness of the mountains and the sky, this human being inserted the sword in hand at the true end, the sword engraved with the font of Balenciaga.The sun then rose from the sky. In the view of some commentators, this scene is borrowed from a legend about pulling a sword out of a stone from the medieval period in Europe. King Arthur, the King of England, in a battle to defeat the invasion of the Germanic peoples, became a hero to protect the country. The "sword in the stone" is also a symbol of the power of the king.

The film starts with four grey and grotesque scenes before suddenly brightening up in the fifth scene. Balenciaga draws inspiration from the legend of King Arthur, using the darkness of the Middle Ages and the spread of the plague to allude to the current world at that time, which is also shrouded by an epidemic. The light of King Arthur's triumph is used to foreshadow mankind's ability to overcome difficulties and to inspire hope for the future of the world.

The scenario design of this film has a strong futuristic style and narrative, with various metaphors and elements that convey the author's imagination of the future and the design concept of this fashion collection. The story, scenes, characters, fashions, and gameplay segments come together to form this fashion game film. Instead of releasing a full story description and explanation, the brand invites viewers to experience this possible future in two ways (either by watching the film directly or by playing the game themselves) through the film's open-ended storyline and the game's interactive experience. It welcomes any understanding and interpretations of this fictional future story (see Fig. 2).

A Possible Future towards More Possible Futures: A Reaction Case from Chinese Fashion KOL. Aha, and Lolo are two Chinese fashion critics and key opinion leaders who co-founded the fashion channel AHALOLO, which has 1.26 million followers so far on the Bilibili video platform. They created a feedback video about Balenciaga's Afterworld, explaining this fictional future as they understood it. This video has so far received 205,000 views, 31,000 likes, and over 1,000 comments. This meant that their commentary on the show gained a lot of attention and stimulated discussion among the audience. In their commentary, they relate and analogize the show to the sci-fi film "The Matrix", in that the rabbit element in the game and the sun rising at the end of the film are similar to "The Matrix". After viewing the possible future scenarios in the show, they extended two possible futures in their understanding of Gvasalia's new design worldview [30]:

Fig. 2. Some scenes in the "Afterworld" game film [33].

- Possible future 1 - Being in reality but living in a virtual network (as humans know it): In the future, with the plethora of social media and gaming, the human presence will appear as a cyber image. Gradually, online images of humans are replacing real-world roles.
- Possible future 2 - Living in a virtual network but in a cage (unbeknownst to humans): In the future, like the world fictionalised by "The Matrix", a person may not be able to realise they are a code. Possibly due to environmental degradation, resource scarcity, or world wars, humans have to hide in a small space to survive. The rulers will create an illusion so that one never knows that he or she is just a standalone code brain implanted with a microchip, like an animal on a farm that has never seen the real world.

As seen in this reaction case, a fashion fiction piece with speculative thinking exploring possible futures can catalyse imaginings and debates about more possible futures. As Marshall McLuhan said, "Art at its most significant is a distant early warning system that can always be relied on to tell the old culture what is beginning to happen." While fashion design is not exclusively an art form, it cannot be ignored that fashion design has many of the characteristics of and interactions with art, which means that fashion designers can think more about "What is beginning to happen?", "What is possible?" and

"What if?" [4]. In other words, the fashion designer can act as a speculator and catalyse more thinking about the future by using the fashion infrastructure [35] to design possible future scenarios in a fictional parallel worldview.

The Role of Fashion Design in the Narrative of Possible Futures

- Metaphor and story advancement: the silver and armour elements accompany the storyline. The combination of the film images, the author's words, and the fashion critics' explanations suggest that this is a reference to medieval chivalry, which at its core represents the human spirit of discovery [4], as well as to the awakening and courage of mankind and heralds hope.
- Characterization and Design Philosophy: The film depicts NPCs wearing clothing from the latest season, which reflects their social status and group affiliations. The portrayal of fashion in the film suggests that it is not limited to the upper class but is accessible to people of all classes. A near future is envisaged in which clothing will change over the years. The treatment combs through the ageing process of the material, emphasising the idea that it can be worn for decades or repurposed forever. Certain garments may have multiple functions as materials are reinterpreted for new uses. For example, satin trench coats can also be worn as party dresses. Similarly, jeans layered over trousers and sweatshirts with a short waistband for boxer shorts are a single item. As animal furs are no longer considered ethical, duvets have been created using laser-cut recycled fabric to imitate the look and feel of a fur jacket. Many products can be repurposed to serve new functions. For instance, blankets can be transformed into jackets or hooded cloaks. Transformer parkas with large external pockets can also double as practical duffel bags. Scooter aprons can be repurposed into warm jackets. Military jumpsuits can be transformed into evening dresses. The discreet black jacket can be worn on both sides, one for danger and the other for high visibility.
- Designer's worldview and aesthetic system: "There was a whole study of authentic ageing treatments for most of the garments," Gvasalia told WWD. "I believe the sustainable and smart consumption in the future will encourage us to wear our clothes until they fall apart and decay, so this collection is full of clothes that look old, somewhat worn in and pretty destroyed." According to Aha & Lolo's comments, this is a way for designers to show their worldview and aesthetic system through their clothes, not just the preciousness of the cuts and fabrics. They propose three keywords to define a designer's design worldview: "Pioneer, game changer, and innovation leader." And the film shows that many of this season's garments have holes and ruffles. This is in line with Gvasalia's anti-conformist fashion preference of "Ironing is not fashion. In his aesthetic system, ugliness is not the opposite of beauty, but a subset of it.

4.2 Alternative Present with Fashion Shows: 2022 Spring - Clones Case

Demna Gvasalia delivers a deep-fake runway for Balenciaga's Spring 22 collection in collaboration with French art director Quentin Deronzier [31]. This fashion show examines our changing sense of reality and an alternative present via the lens of technology.

Wrote at the beginning of the show: "We see our world through a filter—perfected, polished, conformed, photoshopped. We no longer decipher between unedited and altered, genuine and counterfeit, tangible and conceptual, fact and fiction, fake and deepfake. Technology creates alternate realities and identities, a world of digital clones.".

The show is themed around the digitised world of the Clones and explores the unsettling nature of technological lenses on reality through the use of clothing. It prompts viewers to consider what is real and what is not. Gvasalia uses cloning technology as a critical tool to explore the issues of truth and falsehood. The current world has become accustomed to seeing things through a filter, with many aspects being polished, embellished, retouched, homogenised, and photoshopped. As a result, it is difficult to judge the same thing in both unedited and altered forms. Both human beings and lifestyles have been improved and affected by technology. The reality we live in may not always be truthful. Gvasalia explores the current issue through the language of clothing design and alternative interpretations. He claimed that it is a show that"never happened…no one was there and no one is 'real', only the clothes are".

Gvasalia utilises an exaggerated or distorted design technique, enabling fashion to represent an alternative present. This prompts the viewer to contemplate the current state of affairs, which in turn stimulates thoughts about the future. According to WWD, Gvasalia believes that Douglas' clones are a reflection of the homogeneity of trends and the loss of originality. At the same time, the video presentation as a whole is intended to urge viewers to consider society's fixation with screens. Technology brings us to progress as well as falsehood. Critical thinking and irony are the core design ideas of this show. Speculative design is a subset and future extension of critical design [6], and this show is also characterised by speculative design because it uses alternative design techniques to artistically amplify the current status quo, thus generating thoughts on technology and the future and looking at technology and development from a different perspective.

Alternative Present Design Methods in Clones Fashion Show. See Fig. 3.

- Contrasts - Truth and Falsehood: The hoodies in this collection are designed to express individuality and authenticity. For example, one hoodie has the phrase 'No Comment' printed on it, while another features a blank square with the words 'Your Ad Here'. The collection includes shapes that serve as props to depict human manipulation. For instance, there is a chainmail headdress made of silver, gold, chrome, and rusted metal chains that cover the model's face. This conveys the idea of artificially concealing the truth. However, the face beneath the cover could be cloned, suggesting that beneath the falsehood, there may be an even deeper falsehood.
- Repetition - Exaggeration and Irony: Although "cloning" was the theme of the collection, it was not an object but a tool of satire. The designer embodied the concept of "cloning" in the use of face-copying technology in the fashion show and each look released in the collection shared the same face. Eliza appeared in a series of digitized clones, some of which used face-swapping technology, while others captured Eliza's face image and digitally grafted it through CG scanning, like countless Eliza's clones walking the runway, in a satirical attempt to say, "What is the real thing?".
- Exchange - Identity Displacement: Instead of walking on the catwalk, Balenciaga's usual models sat expressionlessly in black uniforms as spectators, picking up their

Fig. 3. Parts of fashion design and performance in clones show [34].

mobile phones to film Eliza's clone catwalk show, a dislocation of identities that gave the viewer a sense of otherness, a subversion of the ordinary.

- Distort - counterfeiting and appropriation: "The Hacker Project" in this Balenciaga's collection is a conceptual interpretation of Gucci's iconic motifs, with the iconic combination of the letters GG transformed into a double B motif, embellished with classic Gucci designs using Gucci's signature colour palette across a wide range of leathers and vintage accessories, and emblazoned with the "This Is Not a Gucci Bag", exploring and questioning the status quo of fashion about originality, forgery, and appropriation, while the design became a marketing hit [32].
- Splicing - Future and Classic: BFRND's re-created sci-fi-style fashion show sound-track also included a futuristic AI chant paired with the French classic La Vie En Rose, which is a surreal collage of different time and space elements.

The Role of Fashion Design in the Alternative Present's Narrative

The Fashion Show is the Vehicle, and the Models are the Performers. The Clothes are the Mainstay Matter that Together Form the Narrative of the Alternative Present. The 2022 Spring Clones show, which featured a pure white minimalist spatial design as the vehicle for the performance, paired with the AI-covered song 'La Vie En Rose' to create a surreal atmosphere. All models on the runway with the same face act as main performers to convey the theme of cloning. and other normal-faced, all-black-clad audience members as supporting performers to create an alternative atmosphere. The clothes de-tails and stylist are the mainstay of the narrative, as the designers communicate concepts, discourses, and worldviews to the audience through the language of clothing de-sign. These elements come together to create an environment that blurs the line between reality and artifice which is an alternative present world. Alternatively, the narrative is also conveyed through scenic design and atmospheric shaping.

Fashion Fiction as a Distorting Mirror of Reality: In Fashion Fiction, the Ordinary World is Distorted and Presented as an Alternative Reality. Certain aspects are magnified to the point of causing discomfort, which can prompt viewers to contemplate and discuss is-sues of reality. For instance, Gvasalia used cloning technology as a theme to construct a fictional parallel world that shares similarities with our own but is not identical. By immersing the audience in this fictional narrative world, they experience a sense of a fait accompli, akin to the feeling of being in a dream or looking into a distorted mirror that presents an alternative reality. This experience is the catalytic power of discursive fashion fiction, where designers ask 'what if...?' questions [4] about the present. They question the status quo and use fashion infrastructure with narrative building to con-struct an alternative world that prompts viewers to think and worry about the current situation, ultimately inspiring debate and imagination about the future.

5   Fashion Fiction

5.1   Possible future and Alternative Present

The primary design method of fashion fiction involves creating parallel worlds, con-sisting of two subsets: the possible future and the alternative present. The difference between the two is that while the possible future is more conducive to future imag-ination, the alternative present is more reflective of the present due to the difference in their spatial and temporal perspectives. The former is grounded in the future, while the latter is grounded in the present. However, the alternative present also serves the purpose of envisioning the future. As the viewer observes the magnified present, they may contemplate the possibility of an unexpected future if the current situation remains unchanged. Possible futures serve the purpose of responding to the present because in experiencing the narratives and scenarios of possible futures, the audience also thinks about whether action should be taken in the present if such a future might (for better or worse) happen. These two approaches represent two different perspectives and direc-tions of the parallel-world-building approach, but they share the same essence. Both aim to stimulate the human imagination of the future and reflect on the present, by asking 'What if?' to start the design and fictionalizing a parallel world through speculation [4, 6, 7].

However, in terms of the catalytic effect of imagining the future and stimulating audience discussion, using the two Balenciaga shows as case studies demonstrate that possible futures have a stronger impact than the alternative present. Based on the discussions and feedback stimulated by the two shows, it is easier to obtain the representative feedback case about 2021 Fall - Afterworld, while 2022 Spring - Clones can only be analysed from the point of view of the show itself, and the discussion about this show is hardly an effective feedback case. Effective cases are evaluated and selected based on three factors: the completeness of the direct feedback on the show, the audience's attention, and the discussion of the topic, whereas piecemeal show evaluations and magazine reports are not enough to be effective feedback cases. The result of the screening is that only 2021 Fall - Afterworld has a feedback case with this condition, while 2022 Spring - Clones does not. One potential factor is that possible futures are closely related to the future. The scenes and narratives of a possible future can be very immersive for the viewer, fueling future discussion and imagination. However, the scenes and narratives of an alternative present require the audience to first experience a deformed critical present event or topic before relating to the future through their discursive ability. Some viewers may only explore the present without extending their imagination to future scenes. Even so, the future discourse of the alternative present cannot be ignored.

5.2 How to Fashion Fiction

Dr Twigger is an important researcher in the field of fashion fiction, which is a narrow and still-defined field under the influence of speculative design and design fiction. She has created a website [12] dedicated to a diverse collection of fashion fiction ideas and cases, intending to use fashion fiction as a tool to invite people to co-create, experience, and reflect on alternative fashion universes through a fictionalised vision, and it involves several key steps:1. Imagining Alternative Worlds; 2. Prototyping; 3. Co-creation and Participation [3]. However, this project is currently in the experimental stage as an educational workshop. Therefore, it is more appropriate for the development of fashion fiction as a case study related to the advancement of a new type of fashion design education.

Furthermore, through the case study of fashion design works closely related to fashion fiction in the real fashion industry, this study found that some core fashion designers already used fashion fiction methods on a small scale without explicitly identifying them as such. These fashion fiction works have also garnered attention and discussion from fashion audiences. Although not explicitly identified as such, fashion fiction influenced the content of fashion works through the inclusion of fiction, stories, criticism, and debate, thus stimulating audience discussion and contemplation.

Based on the research of two fashion cases and a literature review, the process steps of fashion fiction in the field of actual fashion design, particularly fashion performance design:

1. Construction of parallel worldview: fictionalize a parallel world through the "what if?" thought experiments [4];
2. Select the time and space background for the story scene: Possible Future or Alternative Present. Determine the time and space context for the parallel universe. Catalytic effects vary over time and space, but they also rely on the target of criticism [7];

3. Scenario Design and Narrative building: Combine scenes and narrative using various performance media, such as fashion movies, fashion shows, and fashion games, to create a cohesive experience;
4. Integrating Fashion and Rendering: Utilize fashion infrastructure and design language, including clothing design details, fabric selection, design techniques, fashion stylist, craftsmanship, and business strategies, to fully implement fashion products.

6 Conclusion and Further Research

This study examines the methodological deficiencies of fashion fiction, an emerging design method that remains undefined. By integrating the theories of speculative design and design fiction and using case study strategies, it classifies and analyses fashion fiction in the real fashion industries. The characteristics and mechanisms of representative fashion works were discovered, and the two subset design methods from parallel world construction as main methods in fashion fiction were proposed: Possible futures and Alternative presents. Central to this exploration is an in-depth analysis of the aesthetic system and worldview of designers, illuminating their pivotal role in redefining the narrative and impact of fashion collections. Furthermore, by a comparative examination of the link and role of these two subset methods, our research findings reveal that fashion fiction offers a potential new design path for future fashion designers and the fashion industry to consider. The details, descriptions and explanations of the scenario design and narrative building in the analysis of the two main cases have shaped part of the design mechanism and process of fashion fiction in the real fashion industry. With the findings, our study makes several theoretical and practical contributions to fashion fiction.

Due to the vague definition of fashion fiction and its low exposure in the fashion world, it is difficult to find a large number of cases of fashion fiction. This research is also limited to qualitative analysis and two specific niche cases under a single fashion designer, indicating the need for further research to explore a larger number of speculative fashion cases and to consider quantitative research methods, such as surveying audience feedback. This requires a comprehensive understanding and definition of the concept of fashion fiction, as well as further exploration of undiscovered fashion designers, their design mechanisms, and fashion design works. This will enrich the theoretical framework and methodology of fashion fiction. Therefore, on a larger scale, other types of fashion fiction practitioners, designers, and design works still need to be searched, defined, discussed, and analyzed in future studies. Who is the most iconic fashion fiction designer? What are the hidden design mechanisms and processes of fashion fiction? Does fashion fiction influence and change the fashion world? Can the fashion industry catalyze the future through fashion fiction? This scholarly pursuit aims to enrich the theoretical framework and methodology of fashion fiction, ultimately contributing to the advancement of the fashion industry towards a more visionary, sustainable, and ethically conscious future.

Acknowledgements. I want to thank the case's designer Demna Gvasalia and the fashion industry practitioners and researchers who have been cited in this article. I am also grateful to my funder ChenSiyin Future Study and Fashion Design Studio and my advisor Dr. Miao Qiao and Associate Professor Xu DongLiang.

Disclosure of Interests. The authors have no competing interests to declare that are relevant to the content of this article.

References

1. Mandarić, D., Hunjet, A., Vuković, D.: The impact of fashion brand sustainability on consumer purchasing decisions. J. Risk Financ. Manag. **15**(4), Article 4 (2022)
2. Rambourg, E.: Luxury back in Vogue. Asian Manag. Insights (Singapore Manag. Univ.) **8**(2), 74–79 (2021)
3. Twigger Holroyd, A.: Designing fashion fictions: speculative scenarios for sustainable fashion worlds. In: The Design After: Cumulus Conference proceedings, pp. 341–351. Universidad de los Andes, Bogota (2019)
4. Dunne, A., Raby, F.: Speculative Everything: Design, Fiction, and Social Dreaming. The MIT Press, Cambridge (2013)
5. Sterling, B.: Patently untrue: fleshy defibrillators and synchronised baseball are changing the future. Wired UK (2013)
6. Zhang, L.: The value of fiction: the aesthetic politics and future poetics of speculative design. Theor. Stud. Lit. Art **39**(6), 152–160 (2019)
7. Johannessen, L.K., Keitsch, M.M., Pettersen, I.N.: Speculative and critical design—features, methods, and practices. In: Proceedings of the Design Society: International Conference on Engineering Design, vol. 1, no. 1, pp. 1623–1632 (2019)
8. Grimaldi, S., Fokkinga, S., Ocnarescu, I.: Narratives in design: a study of the types, applications and functions of narratives in design practice. In: Proceedings of the 6th International Conference on Designing Pleasurable Products and Interfaces, pp. 201–210. New York (2013)
9. Auger, J.: Speculative design: crafting the speculation. Digit. Creat. **24**(1), 11–35 (2013)
10. Mitrovic, I.: Introduction to Speculative Design Practice – Eutropia, a Case Study. Arts Academy/University of Split, Croatian Designers Association (2015)
11. Twigger Holroyd, A.: Fashion Fictions: Unreasonable Dreaming—YouTube. https://www.youtube.com/watch?v=VBbFwiZHzk0. Accessed 30 Jan 2024
12. Fashion Fictions Homepage. https://fashionfictions.org/. Accessed 30 Jan 2024
13. Goggans, J.: Fashion in Fiction, Fiction in Fashion. Make It Work, pp. 15–26 (2019)
14. Noris, A., Nobile, T. H., Kalbaska, N., Cantoni, L.: Digital fashion: a systematic literature review. A perspective on marketing and communication. J. Glob. Fashion Mark. **12**(1), 32–46 (2021)
15. Sabatini, N., Sádaba, T., Tosi, A., Cantoni, L. (eds.): Fashion Communication in the Digital Age: Proceedings of the FACTUM 23 Conference. Springer, Cham (2023). https://doi.org/10.1007/978-3-031-38541-4
16. Gibson, J.: When games are the only fashion in town: Covid-19, animal crossing, and the future of fashion. Queen Mary J. Intellect. Property **11**(2), 117–123 (2021)
17. Milanesi, M., Guercini, S., Runfola, A.: Let's play! Gamification as a marketing tool to deliver a digital luxury experience. Electron. Commer. Res. **23**(4), 2135–2152 (2023)
18. Tepe, J., Koohnavard, S.: Fashion and game design as hybrid practices: approaches in education to creating fashion-related experiences in digital worlds. Int. J. Fashion Des. Technol. Educ. **16**(1), 37–45 (2023)
19. Hollweck, T., Robert, K.Y.: Case study research design and methods (5th ed.). Can. J. Program Eval. **30**(1), 108–110 (2015) (2014)
20. Demna Gvasalia, creative Director of Balenciaga | Kering homepage. https://web.archive.org/web/20211004230750/, https://www.kering.com/en/houses/couture-and-leather-goods/balenciaga/demna-gvasalia/. Accessed 18 Jan 2024

21. Why Balenciaga's Next Big Drop Is Haute Couture. The Business of Fashion. https://www.businessoffashion.com/articles/luxury/balenciaga-goes-back-to-haute-couture-demna-gvasalia/. Accessed 10 Jan 2024

22. Heller, N.: Demna Gvasalia on Balenciaga, Haute Couture, and Why He's Staying Put in Zurich. https://www.vogue.com/article/demna-gvasalia-on-balenciaga-and-haute-couture, Vogue (2020)

23. Gárgoles, P., Ambás, G.: The Power of Consumers on Social Media: A Case Study of Balenciaga's Crisis Communication. FACTUM2023, SPBE, pp. 3–13 (2023)

24. Ellison, J.: Balenciaga's billion-euro plan (2018). https://www.ft.com/content/b8da67b2-f09b-11e7-b220-857e26d1aca4

25. Socha M.: EXCLUSIVE: Demna Gvasalia Thinks Couture Can Change Fashion. https://wwd.com/fashion-news/designer-luxury/demna-gvasalia-balenciaga-interview-couture-men-1234584700/, WWD (2020)

26. Nower S.: Balenciaga Fall 2021 Menswear Collection. https://www.vogue.com/fashion-shows/fall-2021-menswear/balenciaga, Vogue (2020)

27. Samaha B.: Balenciaga Launches a Video Game for Its Fall 2021 Collection. https://www.harpersbazaar.com/fashion/fashion-week/a34892239/baleciaga-video-game-fall-2021-collection/, Harper's BAZAAR (2020)

28. Balenciaga's Afterworld: The Age of Tomorrow | Dimension, https://dimensionstudio.co/work/balenciaga-afterworld-age-tomorrow-volumetric. Accessed 02 Jan 2024

29. Vogue Runway. https://www.vogue.com/fashion-shows/fall-2021-ready-to-wear/balenciaga. Accessed 15 Dec 2023

30. Aha and Lolo. https://www.bilibili.com/video/BV17i4y157Bg/?spm_id_from=333.999.0.0. Accessed 20 Jan 2024

31. Noel K.: Living in a deep-fake reality: Balenciaga Clones Spring 22 show. L'Officiel Malaysia | Fashion, Beauty, Lifestyle, Arts & Culture. https://www.lofficielmalaysia.com/fashion-week/a-deep-fake-reality-balenciaga-clones-spring-22-show. Accessed 23 Jan 2024

32. Au S.: Vogue Hong Kong. https://www.voguehk.com/zh/article/runway/balenciaga-spring-2022/. Accessed 23 Jan 2024

33. "Afterworld" game film. https://www.balenciaga.com/en-us/fall-21. Accessed 29 Jan 2024

34. "Clone" fashion show. https://www.balenciaga.com/en-us/spring-22. Accessed 29 Jan 2024

35. Särmäkari, N., Vänskä, A.: 'Just hit a button!' – fashion 4.0 designers as cyborgs, experimenting and designing with generative algorithms. Int. J. Fashion Des. Technol. Educ. 15(2), 211–220 (2022)

Creating an Online Exhibition About Shoe Heritage

A Story on Swiss Footwear on Google Arts & Culture

Charlotte Stachel$^{(\boxtimes)}$ ⓘ and Lorenzo Cantoni ⓘ

USI – Università della Svizzera italiana, Lugano, Switzerland
{charlotte.stachel,lorenzo.cantoni}@usi.ch

Abstract. The paper documents the full process of creating the *story* "Climbing the highest point on earth – How Swiss footwear contributed to the first ascent of Mount Everest in 1953" on Google Arts & Culture (GAC). To the authors' best knowledge, this paper is the first of its kind dedicated to the design, development, promotion, and evaluation of an online exhibition in the form of a story on GAC from a digital fashion communication perspective. Starting from the historical archive of Swiss fashion brand Bally, the paper follows the steps proposed by the ADDIE Model of Instructional Design and outlines how storytelling with heritage narratives and multimedia can be used to create a didactic and entertaining online exhibition while adhering to the best practices of the platform. The main challenges that arise throughout the different phases are demonstrated.

Keywords: Shoes · Google Arts & Culture · Online Exhibition Design · User Experience · Digital Fashion

1 Introduction

For luxury fashion companies, museum exhibitions are among the most effective and popular means to leverage their history and heritage [26]. Information and communication technologies (ICTs) have catalyzed the entertainment potential of such exhibitions, by enhancing physical spaces with digital tools and thus providing phygital experiences [1]. Furthermore, online exhibitions, due to their independence of the visitors' location and their potential to provide a much more enhanced view of fragile clothing items [27, 33], have proven to be especially successful [1]. Digital technologies have also found their way into the backstage of such fashion exhibitions, which means the storage spaces and archives. These spaces have originally been at the forefront of applying digital technologies to organize fashion objects and associate knowledge in databases, which served internal staff or researchers. However, archives are increasingly adapting to the new realities of preserving and curating fashion and its manifold related material [27]. These former enclosed spaces, dedicated to experts, nowadays move between secrecy and display, in the same way that traditional fashion brands move between heritage and innovation. With Google, a big tech company has filled this space, by offering technological solutions that serve both, institutions and visitors, to communicate and experience fashion heritage on a large scale [5]. Steele [41: 14] is convinced that "there is no reason why exhibitions cannot be both beautiful and intelligent, entertaining and educational". Google lives up to this claim through its platform Google Arts & Culture (GAC), which provides technological tools for cultural institutions to activate, disseminate, and appealingly communicate their content to a large audience [37]. Given the aesthetic dimension inherent to the fashion domain, the platform and especially its visual story format of online exhibitions have gained great popularity among institutions with collections of fashion items. GAC's interface and software therewith contribute to shaping how the visitors perceive the digital content and how they experience fashion and its connection to broader cultural heritage online [21, 33].

Despite the great potential of fashion exhibitions for museums, fashion brands, and visitors alike, academic research on online exhibitions, as well as on the relationship between fashion and archives, which build the basis for successful exhibitions, is still in its early stages [23, 34]. A Digital Fashion Communication approach can contribute to understanding these "tentacular" [12: 86] interlinkages by drawing from different disciplines and points of view, such as human–computer interaction (HCI), as visitors of online exhibitions are at the same time users [23, 42]. This paper documents the full process of creating the geographical exploration story *"Climbing the highest point on earth* – How Swiss footwear contributed to the first ascent of Mount Everest in 1953" on GAC.[1] The exhibition was established as part of a larger project on digital archives and done as a collaboration between USI and the historical archive of the Swiss fashion brand Bally, whose shoes are involved in the story.

The paper is organized according to the educational model ADDIE Model of Instructional Design and describes the design, development, promotion, and evaluation of such an online exhibition in the form of a story. It outlines how storytelling with heritage narratives and multimedia is used while adhering to the best practices of the platform. It aims to answer the following research questions:

1. What does the process of creating a story on shoe heritage on Google Arts & Culture look like?
2. What are the main challenges that arise?

2   Literature Review

2.1   Digital Fashion Archives and Fashion Exhibitions

In the past years, fashion brands have increasingly recognized their history and corporate heritage as a valuable resource and unique asset [19]. Drawing upon the major potential of corporate archives, many fashion brands have begun to (partially) open them and transform the formerly dusty storage spaces that were highly protected into shiny innovation hubs, offering full brand experiences and self-staged exhibitions, uniting heritage and innovation [27, 36]. This brings with it two at-first-glance paradoxical demands: On the one hand, historical artifacts must be better preserved from excessive physical contact, light exposure, and fluctuating temperatures, to survive the test of time. On the other hand, they should be made accessible to an ever-larger group of internal and

---

[1] https://artsandculture.google.com/story/MgVBJ4NRD-ljSw.

external stakeholders, and in a better way than would be possible in a display case. This has raised the need to introduce digital technologies into fashion archives, which mainly bring four advantages: (i) *conservation*, by reducing the need to handle fragile items, hence protecting them from the elements; (ii) *accessibility*, by minimizing the necessity to travel to a physical space; (iii) *comprehensibility*, by creating networks between the fashion objects and related materials; and (iv) *enhancement*, by the possibility to create augmented digital experiences for external audiences [27, 33, 36, 37, 43].

Fashion exhibitions worldwide have proved to be crowd-pleasers and money-makers [30, 36]. For the public, such exhibitions "have become an important space for learning and exchange about the history, cultural relevance and artistic importance of fashion" [27: 3]. Since the 2000s, fashion exhibitions have progressively become digital [37]. Four different ways in which museums offer online access to their collections can be generally observed: *virtual tours* (digitized physical exhibition spaces); *online exhibitions* (thematically curated items with further information); *online collections* (selection of items from the collection); and *online archives/inventories* (databases with metadata and search/classification options) [40]. What distinguishes these four ways of providing online access to collections is the level of curation involved. Granting a glimpse of what the collection looks like and uploading object-oriented databases that are already used internally requires minor effort for curators. However, in order to deliver a message effectively and to reach a rather heterogeneous audience aside from researchers and experts, it is not enough to make information simply available, but it needs to be intellectually accessible and culturally mediated. Isolated information pieces fail to do so, as they do not create a flow and enjoyable experience and do not foster learning [9, 27, 38].

An ideal setting for virtual exhibitions should consist of "free navigation, a playful immersive environment, shared multi-user experience, high-quality representation of artifacts and usable tools for zooming-in and examining" [44: 26]. Although the web and thus online exhibitions offer almost endless space for information provision and the employment of multimedia, effective communication between the exhibition providers and the visitors can only be achieved through adequate information in terms of quality and depth, which is in balance with the chosen presentation mode [23]. In this sense, it is also important to reflect on the effect an online exhibition aims to promote. Apart from the fact that in most cases well-made exhibitions entertain to some degree, lead to the elicitation of certain emotions, and desirably lead to a learning outcome for the viewers, it is advised to cover one (or more) of the following exhibition effects during the design phase, after Kalfatovic [22]: *aesthetic* (beauty of the objects); *emotive* (emotions); *evocative* (atmosphere); *didactic* (teaching about a topic); and *entertaining* (fun).

2.2 Google Arts & Culture (GAC)

Digital projects and platforms like Google's *We Wear Culture*, the European project *Europeana Fashion*, and the FIT's *Fashion History Timeline* are offering "extensive online data collections [and are] providing rich user experiences" [23: 243], and have successfully addressed the broader public's growing interest in fashion history [27]. Since its initiation as *Google Art Project* in the 2000s, the heritage digitalization project *Google Arts & Culture* has become one of the major providers of online exhibitions.

On the platform and corresponding mobile application, the more than 2000 participating partners, which are usually museums, galleries, archives, and other cultural and/or non-profit institutions, can share their digitized heritage and knowledge with a broad and international audience [17, 37]. Due to its popularity in the fashion realm [30], GAC contributes also to popularizing the exclusive resources held by corporate fashion archives [27]. The resources provided by Google range from tools like *Google Street View* that enable virtual tours based on physical exhibition spaces, to high-resolution photography for *Guided Zoom* features [17]. These technological possibilities serve the main purpose of activating, disseminating, and communicating stories [37]. Even though it is possible to create an online exhibition on GAC from scratch, Google suggests choosing from its six templates. Whereas four of them are a *Virtual Tour*, a *Listicle*, an *In-Painting Tour*, and a *3D Tour*, the remaining two templates are more suited for a story in the classical sense: *One topic in focus* (longer stories) and *STAMP* (short story with max. 5 slides) [14]. Because all stories on GAC are created within the framework of the platform's *Story Editor*, Riegels Melchior [37: 64] notes that they are "not only visually homogeneous but also similar in linguistic tone and readability", which ultimately leads to "make them more inviting to potential users", who might get a consistent user experience across different themes.

On its help platform for GAC, Google does not only give an instruction manual on how to "create immersive, mobile-friendly stories to showcase your collection", but also has a paragraph on best practices. It suggests:

- "Starting stories with full screen or half screen (…)
- keeping the character limit of 280 characters per slide (…)
- [adding] immersive components (…)
- [using] short, engaging, and easy to understand text (…)
- [keeping] a maximum of 10–15 [slides] per story" [14].

Additionally, it points to the positive effects of "chang[ing] the transition between slides (…) to make your story more impactful" and "stack[ing] two (…) [half screen sections] together with the text and image on alternating sides for a fun effect". Further, it recommends "using video clips no longer than 90 s" and adding "hyperlinks to relevant additional content" at the end of the story [14]. These recommendations are not binding, as "Google does not edit or validate the stories before publishing" [37: 58].

While its content guidelines state that "the platform should not be used for any commercial activity" [16], that does not exclude being used by companies to present their heritage. An example of the activities of a fashion brand's museum on GAC is provided by Candeloro [5], who studied the presence of the Salvatore Ferragamo Museum. Besides a virtual tour through the physical museum in Florence, Italy, the institution mainly relies on GAC's story format. The eight stories are characterized by a thematic organization and focus on visual elements through their use of photos that convey aesthetic elements, which is in line with Ferragamo's values and heritage such as design and beauty. At the same time, the stories fulfill a didactic purpose, by transmitting cultural knowledge connected to the brand. The author notes that concise descriptions of photos and items, which use a non-specialist vocabulary, are fundamental to guarantee a successful dissemination of knowledge. The objects of the Salvatore Ferragamo Museum's collection can not only be viewed in the stories, but also through augmented- and virtual reality, and

3D visualization. These digital technologies offered by GAC make the analyzed digital fashion exhibitions more attractive, vivid, and immersive, which decisively shapes the visitor's journey into a more engaging, interactive, and empowering experience [5].

2.3 Storytelling in Exhibitions

A story is a decisive element that distinguishes an exhibition from a mere collection of items [28]. Storytelling in digital spaces can be especially effective and memorable by creating entertaining and engaging surroundings and using "multimedia tools that can amplify the effects of narration" [38: 6]. Objects are often the starting point of stories, which are enriched by context and woven through narratives that convey the meaning of these objects and how they might have changed over time [4, 9, 12, 38]. Instead of putting a single object in the center of attention, it is recommended to "lead with (...) historical context, important people and places" [9] and tell how they are interrelated [7]. Narratives around historical contexts that are related to specific events are especially effective for learning because the visitor is immersed more deeply into the narrative when he or she knows that the story is based on real incidents [32]. This plays into the hands of fashion archives, as they usually do not only hold "individual stories related to a single product, brand or designer but also collective stories related to the culture of a specific time or place" [26: 5903]. As storytelling usually also includes cultural values besides factual knowledge, it is a popular means for luxury fashion brands to convey elements of brand heritage, including know-how, craftsmanship, as well as iconic products [4, 11, 38]. By communicating such elements through storytelling, the brands imply values such as authenticity, exclusivity, and quality. In the European luxury fashion industry, such traits and "intangible, cultural constructions" [24: 156] are often linked to the national identity and lifestyle of the territorial area the brand is based in [10, 11, 27, 29, 31].

The literature describes different ways to create a consistent storyline or narrative [e.g., 24, 32]. Collins et al. [8] propose the following aspects for the conceptual structure of curatorial narratives:

- "A **story** (i.e. what can be told) is conceptualized as
- a set of **events** that can be described according to
- **facets** such as time, location, and theme.
- A **plot** (i.e. an interpretation of the story) is then represented as the specification of a network of significant relationships between the events of the story, thereby, imposing a particular interpretation on the story.
- Finally, the **narrative discourse** (i.e., its presentational form) refers to the structure of the presentation that could be, for example, a physical or hypermedia space" [8: 2].

The same story can be told in various ways by combining different narratives and plots. In doing so, a storyline may be formed that is adapted to a specific medium or emphasizes certain aspects, rather than simply following a chronological sequence of occurrences to describe a story [8].

3 The Case

3.1 Bally and Its Historical Archive

Bally is a Swiss luxury fashion brand, founded in 1851 in Schoenenwerd (Switzerland). The company has specialized in producing footwear since its beginnings. Over the years, Bally has extended its product range, which nowadays encompasses shoes, bags, and accessories as well as ready-to-wear clothing (the latter has been produced since 2013). With an age of more than 170 years, Bally is among the oldest luxury fashion brands in the world still in operation. Thanks to the continual meticulous collection of various objects relevant to the company, Bally now possesses both an extensive business archive and a rich historical archive. With a collection of about 35,000 pairs of shoes (45% men's, 55% women's) – produced themselves and collected from other manufacturers and brands – the Bally Historical Archive is considered one of the largest shoe archives worldwide.

3.2 Bally's Reindeer Fur Boots

One of the company's most iconic artifacts is a pair of high reindeer fur boots; a "monster-piece" [translated from German], characterized by its distinctive greyish-brownish furry exterior [13: 34]. Tenzing Norgay, Head of the Sherpas, wore these reindeer fur boots when he was a full member of the 1952 Swiss post-monsoon expedition, which narrowly missed reaching the summit of Mt. Everest. When the British Everest expedition 1953 made a successful attempt to climb Mt. Everest for the first time in history, Sherpa Tenzing wore the same pair of reindeer fur boots again, in contrast to the other crew members who bet on British shoes. Over the past 70 years, Bally has celebrated summitting Mt. Everest by producing a few special anniversary collections. For example, a fashionable re-edition of Sherpa Tenzing's reindeer fur boots was the centerpiece in the 'Bally Everest collection AW 2013' [6].

The story is emblematic of some of the company's core values: *craftsmanship* (the boots were handmade by artisans), *innovation* (through research and new technology), *collaboration* (such as with the Swiss Foundation for Alpine Research), *community* (the relationship to the Sherpas in the Himalayas), *environment* (by conducting mountain preservation programs through the 2020 established Bally Peak Outlook Foundation), and its *Swiss heritage* (with parallels to mountaineering in the Swiss Alps) [3].

4 Research Design

This paper aims to answer the following research questions:

1. What does the process of creating a story on shoe heritage on Google Arts & Culture look like?
2. What are the main challenges that arise?

In the existing literature, no model or step-by-step guidance has been found for the creation of an online exhibition or story on GAC. Most studies are devoted to the technological-, usability-, and thus interface aspects of designing an online exhibition [e.g., 2, 39]. However, these requirements, which generally call for considerable time, resources, and skills, are already largely covered by the platform of choice, GAC. For the design and development of the story *Climbing the highest point on earth* we will thus allow for HCI considerations in the given ADDIE framework.

5 Methodology: ADDIE Model of Instructional Design

Alwi and McKay [1: 12] state that the use of ICT tools in online exhibitions "needs to align with appropriate instructional strategies to ensure the effectiveness of their visitors' learning experiences". Therefore, we use the ADDIE Model of Instructional Design as guiding steps. Its framework consists of the following five phases, which run cyclically: *Analysis*, *Design*, *Development*, *Implementation*, and *Evaluation*. Because its structure is systematic and generic, the ADDIE model is applicable in various settings, beyond the classical educational context [35]. The following is a condensed and simplified summary of the content of each phase, applied to the context of this paper.

- **Analysis**: In the first phase designers identify the audience, topic, and content, as well as learning objectives [35]. The analysis of other online exhibitions in the relevant field belongs also to a common practice in the preparatory phase [25].
- **Design**: The second phase consists mainly of planning the setup and conducting research on the topic. The designers determine with which methods and media they intend to reach the defined objectives [35].
- **Development**: The third phase "transforms the designer's role from research and planning to a production mode" [35: 231]. He or she selects materials, creates a prototype, and conducts first evaluations to improve the learning outcomes [35].
- **Implementation**: In the fourth phase the designer delivers the product to the audience and performs assessments "to ensure that learning has occurred" [35: 234].
- **Evaluation**: The fifth phase is dedicated to evaluating what the product's impact was, if the learning objectives have been met, and what future changes are necessary [35]. As regards the success of online exhibitions, web usage statistics are the most common evaluation means [25].

The authors are aware of the fact that the ADDIE Model of Instructional Design suggests a linear process for creating the story. However, especially the steps *analysis*, *design*, and *development* are going to be run iteratively, to continuously assess emerging new materials, meet unexpected challenges, and ultimately enhance the final product [35: 231].

6 Results and Discussion

6.1 Analysis

Preparatory Work. The process of creating the story Climbing the highest point on earth began in March 2023, with a timeframe of four months until going live. The choice for GAC was made for several reasons: The platform is impactful in terms of audience, not least because it is open access. From an institutional point of view, it has the advantage that it is free of charge and the content ownership stays within the providing organization. USI already had a profile on GAC and had positive experiences with six other stories. Due to the Story Editor, almost no prior (technological) knowledge of interface design is required, which makes setting up new online exhibitions on GAC comparatively easy as well as efficient and thus keeps the development costs low [5]. To have an overview of how other museums and cultural institutions engage with the topics of shoes (heritage) and mountaineering, the design and contents of such stories on GAC were examined. This allowed the authors to get familiar with the different possibilities of the platform, and ascertain which features they perceived as informative, enriching, immersive, or pleasant, in addition to the best practices defined by Google.

Choice of Topic. The topic, Swiss footwear on the first ascent of Mt. Everest, was chosen in coordination with Bally, and favored among others for three reasons: Firstly, 2023 constituted the 70th anniversary of the event and there were other activities planned by the brand. Secondly, because of the topic's previous and current use for communicational purposes [e.g., 3], the bulk of the work of gathering dispersed material at the archive had been already done, which was conducive to meeting the timeframe. Thirdly, the topic allowed to use synergies with a physical exhibition on Fashion, Sport, and Tourism, which was equally planned for the summer of 2023 [6]. Once agreed with the company on a general framework and the major parameters of the story, the authors were free to proceed in creating the story independently.

Requirements and Goals. The story was primarily conceived as a *didactic exhibition*, in which "the curator aims to teach the viewer about a specific topic" [22: 5], but it should provide some entertainment and a suitable atmosphere. The intended audience was defined as adults of various ages and geographical backgrounds, interested in the following topics: mountaineering, hiking, history of climbing, and footwear, with or without a specific interest in the Bally company. An attention span of roughly 5 to 10 min was assumed.

Review of Materials. In April 2023, the authors began examining the material at disposal at the Bally Historical Archive in Schoenenwerd (Switzerland). For previous occasions, two PDF documents on Bally and Mt. Everest expeditions were already compiled (July 2012, 75 pages; and 2013, 31 pages) [13]. Those documents contained photos of expeditions, articles from internal company magazines and newspapers, posters, promotional material such as advertising campaigns and press kits, letters, bills, URLs, and book recommendations, as well as further paper documents, mainly from the 1950s and the 2010s. Additionally, three digitized historical films were provided. To gain a deeper understanding of the topic, the research was extended beyond the archive, around the topic of the first ascent of Mt. Everest, the Swiss Himalaya expeditions from 1952, and the used footwear, consulting websites, online blogs, and newspaper articles, YouTube films, and online encyclopedias. Advantageously, some articles had already been published in the course of the 70th anniversary of the ascent of Mt. Everest, which provided not only insights but also gave hints to further references.

6.2 Design

Storyline. In April 2023, the authors started creating the storyline. To compose a coherent narrative, the approach outlined by Collins et al. [8] was employed. The story *Climbing the highest point on earth* has a curatorial narrative: it "weaves threads across events (…) [and] makes relationships across a set of exhibits" [8: 2]. The story is composed of three events (*Mt. Everest, Boots,* and *Bally*), each with three facets, and related through three plots, which are all connected to footwear (cf. Fig. 1). Whereas the term *topic* would be more appropriate than *event* to describe the story's components, the terminology proposed by Collins et al. [8] was adhered to. The story's main protagonists are mountaineers (people) and mountains (places), while boots (objects) appear throughout the story in text and visuals. The title, which together with the front image is the most noticeable feature for potential visitors, includes a notion of space (highest point on earth) and time (1953) [37]. The introduction provides context for the audience by bringing up a fundamental human desire, which is not exclusive to a specific culture but can be seen around the world: climbing mountains through hiking. With the use of Google's 360° view from the top of Mt. Everest as well as the quote from the film *Ruf der Berge* (1955), the authors wanted to obtain a certain immersion and evoke emotions.

Structure. Although classical exhibitions are oftentimes not experienced linearly but more as experiential spaces, GAC's story layout with a scroll implies a unidimensional course [18]. However, both types of visitor behavior were taken into account; people who roam around freely should also be able to find a connecting point easily, without the need to trace back the whole storyline to comprehend it. Therefore, the authors interchanged the order of the different elements. Each of the versions resulted in a consistent storyline, which confirmed that the single events, their facets, and the connecting plots were self-explanatory. From a company viewpoint, the following elements have been considered: different values that Bally attributes to itself as a brand, such as craftsmanship, innovation, and collaboration were placed throughout the events and plots; the reindeer fur boots as one of the company's iconic products were given a prominent space; and reference to the company's Swiss origins, as well as its lifestyle, hiking and mountaineering, was made [3]. Once all components were defined, a storyboard was sketched out on Microsoft PowerPoint with screenshots of the archive material, and the texts were written, whose final versions were fact-checked by Bally when needed.

Components and Assets. For the setup of the story in the Story Editor, the *One topic in focus* template was selected, because this format allowed the authors to make the best use of the diverse material to tell a compelling story. All points and suggestions from Google's best practices and further advice were followed, except for three recommendations concerning text length, number of slides, and transition between slides [14]. First, the length of one citation out of a letter is almost double as long as recommended, because the provided context was considered an added value. Second, the maximum of 15 slides "for the best reading experience" [14] is exceeded with 39 total slides: to go through the whole story, visitors must click 38 times. Given the target timing of about 10 min in total, this would mean about 15 s per slide, which is rather short. Two notifications appeared in the header of the Story Editor: "Your story contains a lot of text. Could you perhaps make it simpler and more vivid by using fewer text elements?" and "Your story contains

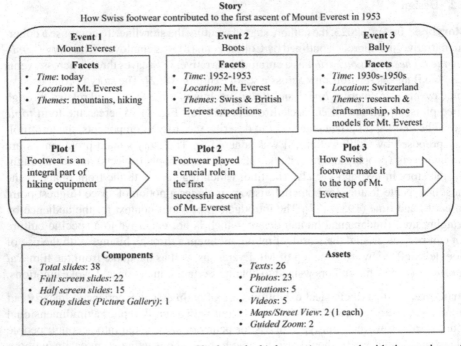

Story
How Swiss footwear contributed to the first ascent of Mount Everest in 1953

| **Event 1** | **Event 2** | **Event 3** |
| Mount Everest | Boots | Bally |

Facets
- *Time*: today
- *Location*: Mt. Everest
- *Themes*: mountains, hiking

Facets
- *Time*: 1952-1953
- *Location*: Mt. Everest
- *Themes*: Swiss & British Everest expeditions

Facets
- *Time*: 1930s-1950s
- *Location*: Switzerland
- *Themes*: research & craftsmanship, shoe models for Mt. Everest

Plot 1
Footwear is an integral part of hiking equipment

Plot 2
Footwear played a crucial role in the first successful ascent of Mt. Everest

Plot 3
How Swiss footwear made it to the top of Mt. Everest

Components
- *Total slides*: 38
- *Full screen slides*: 22
- *Half screen slides*: 15
- *Group slides (Picture Gallery)*: 1

Assets
- *Texts*: 26
- *Photos*: 23
- *Citations*: 5
- *Videos*: 5
- *Maps/Street View*: 2 (1 each)
- *Guided Zoom*: 2

Fig. 1. Composition of the GAC story *Climbing the highest point on earth* with the numbers of used components and assets

many different components. Can you perhaps make it simpler and more descriptive if you use fewer components?" (authors' translation from German). It is assumed that the two notifications were related to the insertion of the Guided Zoom slides, which are a total of nine slides, whereas *classical* text slides (half-screen slides with photo) make up 15 slides. Due to the positive feedback of the test users on the Guided Zoom, which will be introduced below, the length of the story was anyway maintained. Third, the default settings for the transitions between the slides were kept, because one of the authors felt a certain dizziness by scrolling through other stories which applied – as suggested by GAC – more noticeable changes when scrolling.

For all regular text, half-screen components were used, which divide the screen into a side with text and another side with a photo. Full-screen components were used if other assets than photos were involved. These assets were considered to add additional benefit to the storyline, but it was intended that visitors were also able to understand the story without these citations, videos, etc.

Visuals. As the story mainly focuses on providing educational content, the authors avoided every representation that could be considered a marketing initiative or advertisement for the company. Creating a narrative in a broader cultural heritage context instead of laying the focus on the brand supported this endeavor. Therefore, mostly historical photos of the different ascents were selected, featuring mountain landscapes, illustrating footwear in the broader context of its wear, and presented in full looks.

6.3 Development

In June 2023, the production of the story in the Story Editor was tackled. Whereas the integration of the material itself, such as photos, illustrations, and videos worked quite well thanks to the Story Editor's interface, uploading the material on USI's object repository on GAC and compiling the required and recommended metadata posed difficulties [15]. Various questions had to be solved in e-mail exchanges with Google's point of contact on GAC for USI, and some bugs remain to this day. Instead of going into platform-specific struggles, which may be perceived differently by different users, more general points that were encountered and need to be considered are pointed out.

Copyrights and Metadata. After a first choice of footage was made based on the two documents by Bally, it quickly became evident that various copyrights as well as much of the required and recommended metadata could no longer be located. For multiple photos, it was unclear by what means Bally had acquired them back in the early 1950s, who was the intellectual property holder, and which were the underlying rights for future usage. Hence, it was decided to directly contact the rightful owners of the photos, where known, such as the Royal Geographical Society (RGS). Despite Bally owning some original prints of the RGS's photos, a fee had to be paid for the supply of the files and the clearance for their use in the story. Another detour that had to be made was for the film *Ruf der Berge* from 1955. No ownership was registered in the archive, but the opening credits mentioned the Swiss Alpine Museum. However, neither this institution nor the alleged production company was aware of the film's existence and thus they did not claim any rights. Therefore, it was decided to use the general wording "All rights reserved" for the copyright information, and the film was uploaded onto the YouTube channel of the USI UNESCO Chair, without publicly listing it. Google [14] states that the "best practice is to use videos from your own channel". Yet, the rules had to be softened another time: a scene from the film *The Race for Everest*, produced in 2003 by the BBC, was fitting the story's topic and created added value to it. As no official version published by the BBC itself could be found online and the broadcaster did not respond to any contacting from the authors, it was decided to embed a version on YouTube uploaded by a private person (7 years ago, with 1.9 million views). Unfortunately, it exposes the visitors of the story to an advertisement before the video is shown and bears the possible risk of the video being taken down without further notice. Because of the aforementioned challenges concerning the provenance of archival footage, most of the photos used in the story were provided by the Swiss Foundation for Alpine Research, which was able to deliver their original files and compile almost all the required metadata. This finally allowed us to set meaningful picture titles and descriptions for interested visitors.

3D Model. As one of the most iconic Bally shoes, the reindeer fur boot worn by Sherpa Tenzing on the first ascent of Mt. Everest had been digitized through photogrammetry. It was originally planned to make use of GAC's possibility to embed a 3D model into the story, but due to missing photos of the boot's upper view and sole, this was not available. Instead, it was decided to combine the existing photos of the boot into an animated video of a 360° view. As some glitch still occurs in the video, this is seen as a temporary solution, and it is planned to add a 3D model at a later time.

First Usability Testing. The first usability testing with an alpha version of the story was conducted in June 2023. After a short introduction by a researcher, two researchers in Digital Fashion Communication at USI and two employees from the university's eLearning Lab viewed the story's preview version, one half on a laptop and the other half on a smartphone. Their feedback yielded insights into their perception of the storyline's logic and the different assets. The test users evaluated the two Guided Zoom features as particularly engaging and helpful in improving their memorability. Additionally, it was decided to keep two anecdotes, because they were considered entertaining and adding value to the storyline, although the authors estimated them to be rather nice to have than an integral part of the story.

6.4 Implementation

Following major fine-tuning, Bally was provided access to the preview mode of the story for a last check before it went live on 28 July 2023. To reach the intended public, the original English version was translated into Italian, German, and French, followed by offline- and online promotion.

Physical Exhibition. The first announcement of the upcoming story was made on the evening of 4 July. As part of the opening of the physical exhibition *Fashion, Sport, Tourism* at the Museo della Grafica in Pisa, Italy, a preview version was introduced to the audience. A copy of the reindeer fur boot was exhibited in one room of the exhibition, which was dedicated to Bally's longstanding history in producing sports shoes. After the story was published, a QR code was prepared to be installed next to the boot at the exhibition in Pisa, which invited visitors to discover how it became the first shoe on the summit of Mt. Everest. At the beginning of October 2023, the exhibition catalog was published, which did not directly mention the story on GAC, but included the chapter *Fashion, Sport and Tourism. An itinerary in their shoes* with a paragraph on the history of the reindeer fur boot [6].

Social Media. The first social media publication was a LinkedIn post by Bally on 31 July 2023. This post has been shared, among others, by Bally's CEO, Global Head of Men's Merchandising, and Head of Cultural Engagement. On 6 August 2023, a post on X has been made, which was shared by 16 persons. Through personal contacts, About Switzerland, an account managed by the Federal Department of Foreign Affairs FDFA, made an Instagram post about the story on 17 August 2023. Finally, everyone involved in the making of the story as well as people and institutions with affiliations to the project or the topic had been informed personally by the authors or through newsletters about its publication.

6.5 Evaluation

Google Analytics. To quantitatively evaluate the story, the page view analytics provided by Google for the first six months (July-December 2023) were used. The total number of views is 854. The story was viewed from 51 different countries on all continents, with the highest share coming from Switzerland. The average time spent on the story page is 216 s (i.e., 3.6 min). It is important to note that further numbers provided by Google Analytics are not fully clear and leave room for interpretation. The most clicked-on assets were color photos by the Royal Geographical Society, which depict Sherpa Tenzing Norgay on the summit of Mt. Everest, Sherpa Tenzing Norgay and Edmund Hillary drinking tea in the Western Cwm, as well as Edmund Hillary and Sherpa Tenzing Norgay on the South-East ridge below Mt. Everest.

Social Media Analytics. Further, the analytics from Bally's LinkedIn post (119.623 followers), Prof. Cantoni's post on X (2.797 followers), and About Switzerland's Instagram post (37.000 followers), as of 15 September 2023 were collected, one and a half months after the publication of the story. In total, the posts have reached 13,365 impressions, 286 engagements, 289 likes, and were reposted 29 times, as well as commented on 9 times.

Exploratory Usability Testing. In November 2023, a pre-, post-, and short-term memorability test of the story was conducted with a class of 18 international students of the MSc in Digital Fashion Communication at USI. This prototype usability test served to understand if the questions were clear, led to meaningful results, and if the designated timing was reasonable. The first results indicate that the story achieves a high level of approval regarding its visuals, content, structure, and length. Concerning the interface, the students were mostly intrigued by the Guided Zoom feature and the flow of the navigation. Finally, the results suggest that the students' perceptions about Bally have improved after having viewed the story, especially when it comes to the following dimensions: brand innovativeness, its environmental and social attention, as well as its rich heritage. This exploratory usability testing allowed to develop a user testing protocol, which will be applied to a larger test group.

7 Conclusions

This paper aimed to answer the following research questions:

1. What does the process of creating a story on shoe heritage on Google Arts & Culture look like?
2. What are the main challenges that arise?

To create the story *Climbing the highest point on earth* on GAC, the ADDIE Model of Instructional Design was used as guiding steps. Although originally intended for educators to develop courses and didactic programs, the single phases provided orientation for non-professional exhibition curators in designing, developing, and implementing the story in a structured way [35]. Nevertheless, the authors took the freedom to apply the model in a non-linear way, by revisiting certain phases iteratively. This was necessary, especially because of the duration of the whole process, spanning over four months, and certain challenges that were encountered. The creation of storytelling was imperative to obtain a cohesive narrative, that follows pre-defined educational goals as well as a balanced storyline that covers diverse topics. GAC has demonstrated its design-wise user-friendly interface, both for the students who viewed the story and the authors who used the Story Editor. However, technology-wise, there were and are still shortcomings that are yet to be resolved.

This leads to the challenges that arose. By uploading their content on GAC, institutions assume responsibility in terms of correctness, authenticity, and copyright clearance [45]. The fact that a historical archive physically possesses an item, does not mean that it is allowed to use it for external (communication) purposes. Ownership and copyrights are ideally to be cleared already at the time of acquisition or inventorying of materials [20]. If not done beforehand, sources should whenever possible be double-checked and verified before information and/or visuals are published, to live up to the notions of authority and legitimacy conferred through the platform [37]. The not fully clarified provenance of certain items in the archive often came along with gaps in the metadata, such as missing creators, dates, locations, and descriptions. This information is classified as *recommended fields* by GAC. As such, they are not binding as the *required fields*, however, it does make sense to fill them in [15]: using AI, which is supposedly based on the items' metadata, GAC clusters objects with semantic connections, sorts them by popularity, arranges them on a time bar, or allows visitors to discover similar contents. If cultural institutions aim to capitalize on the platform's possibilities for users to individually organize, share, and redefine an endless amount of cultural heritage, then providing expressive metadata is crucial.

Speaking of it, connecting fashion (heritage) to an event of broader cultural heritage has not only served to address a larger audience regarding interest in the chosen topic, geography, and possibly demography, but it has also contributed to drawing a clearer line between education on footwear as such, and advertisement for a specific footwear company. Given that the story was published on USI's GAC account, it had largely to be limited to intangible brand constructs [24]. This decision also meant that compromises had to be made in terms of the visual appeal of the story. Bally's promotional material would probably have contributed more to the visitors' entertainment, as the first test with an alpha version showed, than the generic black-and-white photos.

The Bally Historical Archive formed a rich and meaningful basis for the creation of this online exhibition and constituted the starting point to tell a new and balanced story, which does not end here. The authors will conduct further user testing, involving a larger group of visitors, to assess the parameters that have been defined in the protocol of the exploratory usability testing. Eventually, Bally's historical archive holds many more stories that are waiting to be told – or better: experienced, enjoyed, and interacted with in a multimedia way.

Acknowledgements. This research has been conducted within the framework of the Lifestyle Tech Competence Center in Lugano, Switzerland.

References

1. Alwi, A., McKay, E.: Investigating an online museum's information system: Instructional design for effective human-computer interaction. In: Ifenthaler, D., Spector, J.M., Kinshuk, P.I., Sampson, D. (eds.) Multiple Perspectives on Problem Solving and Learning in the Digital Age, pp. 11–22. Springer, New York (2011). https://doi.org/10.1007/978-1-4419-7612-3_2

2. Antoniou, A., Lepouras, G., Vassilakis, C.: Methodology for design of online exhibitions. DESIDOC J. Libr. Inf. Technol. **33**(3), 158–167 (2013). https://doi.org/10.14429/djlit.33.4615
3. Bally Schuhfabriken AG: A journey in the making since 1851. https://www.bally.ch/en/editorial/about-us/. Accessed 18 Dec 2023
4. Cabigiosu, A.: Digitalization in the Luxury Fashion Industry. Strategic Branding for Millennial Consumers. Palgrave Macmillan, Cham (2020). https://doi.org/10.1007/978-3-030-48810-9
5. Candeloro, D.: Digital fashion exhibition: Salvatore Ferragamo Museum and Google Arts & Culture. In: Sádaba, T., Kalbaska, N., Cominelli, F., Cantoni, L., Torregrosa Puig, M. (eds.) Fashion Communication, FACTUM 2021, pp. 129–142. Springer, Cham (2021). https://doi.org/10.1007/978-3-030-81321-5_11
6. Cantoni, L., Stachel, C., Sabatini, N.: Fashion, sport and tourism. An itinerary in their shoes. In: Tosi, A., Cantoni, L. (eds.) Fashion, Sport, Tourism, pp. 66–76. Edizioni ETS, Pisa (2023)
7. Caspani, S., Brumana, R., Oreni, D., Previtali, M.: Virtual museums as digital storytellers for dissemination of built environment: possible narratives and outlooks for appealing and rich encounters with the past. Int. Arch. Photogram. Remote Sens. Spatial Inf. Sci. **XLII-2W5**, 113–119 (2017). https://doi.org/10.5194/isprs-archives-XLII-2-W5-113-2017
8. Collins, T., Mulholland, P., Wolff, A.: Web-supported emplotment: using object and event descriptions to facilitate storytelling online and in galleries. In: WebSci 2012, Evanston, IL, USA, pp. 104–107 (2012). https://doi.org/10.1145/2380718.2380728
9. Donovan, K.: The Best of Intentions: Public Access, the Web & the Evolution of Museum Automation. https://www.archimuse.com/mw97/speak/donovan.htm. Accessed 05 Aug 2023
10. Donzé, P.Y., Wubs, B.: Storytelling and the making of a global luxury fashion brand: Christian Dior. Int. J. Fashion Stud. **6**(1), 83–102 (2019). https://doi.org/10.1386/infs.6.1.83_1
11. Fionda, A.M., Moore, C.M.: The anatomy of the luxury fashion brand. J. Brand Manag. **16**(5/6), 347–363 (2009). https://doi.org/10.1057/bm.2008.45
12. Franceschini, M.: Navigating fashion: on the role of digital fashion archives in the preservation, classification and dissemination of fashion heritage. Critical Stud. Fashion Beauty **10**(1), 69–90 (2019). https://doi.org/10.1386/csfb.10.1.69_1
13. Gerber, R., Gut, U.: Bally shoes 8840 m a.s.l. Mount Everest expeditions 1952–1956. Research July 2012. Unpublished internal report (2012)
14. Google: Create an exhibit in the new Story Editor. https://support.google.com/culturalinstitute/partners/answer/10460872. Accessed 05 Oct 2023
15. Google: Metadata fields. https://support.google.com/culturalinstitute/partners/answer/7574684. Accessed 17 Oct 2023/10/17
16. Google: Content guidelines. https://support.google.com/culturalinstitute/partners/answer/6190689. Accessed 05 Dec 2023
17. Google: A new way of experiencing art and culture. https://about.artsandculture.google.com/experience/. Accessed 21 Oct 2023
18. Hughes, P.: Storytelling Exhibitions. Identity, Truth and Wonder. Bloomsbury Publishing, London (2021)
19. Hull, A., Scott, P.: The 'value' of business archives: assessing the academic importance of corporate archival collections. Manag. Organ. Hist. **15**(1), 1–21 (2020). https://doi.org/10.1080/17449359.2020.1769676
20. Hylland, O.M.: Even better than the real thing? Digital copies and digital museums in a digital cultural policy. Cult. Unbound **9**(1), 62–84 (2017). https://doi.org/10.3384/cu.2000.1525.179162
21. Kalbaska, N., Sadaba, T., Cantoni, L.: Fashion communication: between tradition and digital transformation. SComS – Stud. Commun. Sci. J. **18**(2), 269–285 (2018). https://doi.org/10.24434/j.scoms.2018.02.005

22. Kalfatovic, M.R.: Creating a Winning Online Exhibition. A Guide for Libraries, Archives, and Museums. ALA Editions, Berkeley (2002)

23. Kim, S.: Virtual exhibitions and communication factors. Museum Manag. Curatorsh. **33**(3), 243–260 (2018). https://doi.org/10.1080/09647775.2018.1466190

24. Lascity, M.E.: Communicating Fashion. Clothing, Culture and Media. Bloomsbury Publishing, London (2021)

25. Liew, C.L.: Online cultural heritage exhibitions: a survey of strategic issues. Program: Electron. Libr. Inf. Syst. **40**(4), 372–388 (2021). https://doi.org/10.1108/00330330610707944

26. Linfante, V., Pompa, C.: Learning by archives. The role of fashion exhibitions and fashion archives to defining (and stimulating) possible new educational paths. In: Proceedings of EDULEARN21 Conference, pp. 5903–5909 (2021). https://doi.org/10.21125/edulearn.2021.1196

27. Martin, M., Vacca, F.: Heritage narratives in the digital era: How digital technologies have improved approaches and tools for fashion know-how, traditions, and memories. Res. J. Text. Appar. **22**(4), 335–351 (2018). https://doi.org/10.1108/RJTA-02-2018-0015

28. Minelli, S.H., Natale, M.T., Ongaro, P., Piccininno, M., Saccoccio, R., Ugoletti, D.: MOVIO: a toolkit for creating curated digital exhibitions. Procedia Comput. Sci. **38**, 28–33 (2014). https://doi.org/10.1016/j.procs.2014.10.006

29. Muñoz Domínguez, G., Díaz Soloaga, P.: The revival of heritage fashion houses: brand identity in the digital era. In: Sádaba, T., Kalbaska, N., Cominelli, F., Cantoni, L., Torregrosa Puig, M. (eds.) Fashion Communication, FACTUM 2021, pp. 129–142. Springer, Cham (2021). https://doi.org/10.1007/978-3-030-81321-5_22

30. Noris, A., Cantoni, L.: Digital Fashion Communication. An (Inter)cultural Perspective. Brill, Leiden (2022). https://doi.org/10.1163/9789004523555

31. Ok, P.: European luxury fashion brand advertising and marketing relating to nostalgia. Stud. Commun. Sci. **18**(2), 307–324 (2018). https://doi.org/ https://doi.org/10.24434/j.scoms.2018.02.007

32. Palombini, A.: Storytelling and telling history. Towards a grammar of narratives for cultural heritage dissemination in the digital era. J. Cult. Herit. **24**, 134–139 (2017). https://doi.org/10.1016/j.culher.2016.10.017

33. Pecorari, M.: Fashion archives, museums and collections in the age of the digital. Critical Stud. Fashion Beauty **10**(1), 3–29 (2019). https://doi.org/10.1386/csfb.10.1.3_7

34. Peirson-Smith, A., Peirson-Smith, B.: Fashion archive fervour: the critical role of fashion archives in preserving, curating, and narrating fashion. Arch. Rec. **41**(3), 274–298 (2021). https://doi.org/10.1080/23257962.2020.1813556

35. Peterson, C.: Bringing ADDIE to life: instructional design at its best. J. Educ. Multimedia Hypermedia **12**(3), 227–241 (2003)

36. Petrov, J.: Fashion, History, Museums. Inventing the Display of Dress. Bloomsbury Academic, London (2019). https://doi.org/10.5040/9781350049024

37. Riegels Melchior, M.: Digital fashion heritage: understanding europeanafashion.eu and the Google Cultural Institute's We Wear Culture. Critical Stud. Fashion Beauty **10**(1), 49–68 (2019). https://doi.org/10.1386/csfb.10.1.49_1

38. Schweibenz, W.: How to create the worst online exhibition possible - in the best of intention. https://swop.bsz-bw.de/frontdoor/deliver/index/docId/908/file/online_exhibition_2012_schweibenz.pdf. Accessed 05 Aug 2023

39. Shimray, S.R., Ramaiah, C.K.: Design and development of an online exhibition on the Tangkhul tribe festivals. DESIDOC J. Libr. Inf. Technol. **35**(2), 124–131 (2015). https://doi.org/10.14429/djlit.35.2.8396

40. Stachel, C., Cantoni, L.: When shoe heritage is on display: a digital fashion communication approach. In: Sabatini, N., Sádaba, T., Tosi, A., Neri, V., Cantoni, L. (eds.) Fashion Communication in the Digital Age, FACTUM 2023, pp. 290–303. Springer, Cham (2023). https://doi.org/10.1007/978-3-031-38541-4_27

41. Steele, V.: Museum quality: the rise of the fashion exhibition. Fashion Theory: J. Dress Body Cult. **12**(1), 7–30 (2008). https://doi.org/10.2752/175174108X268127

42. Sylaiou, S., Mania, K., Paliokas, I., Pujol-Tost, L., Killintzis, V., Liarokapis, F.: Exploring the educational impact of diverse technologies in online virtual museums. Int. J. Arts Technol. **10**(1), 58–84 (2017). https://doi.org/10.1504/IJART.2017.083907

43. Vacca, F.: Knowledge in memory: corporate and museum archives. Fash. Pract. **6**(2), 273–288 (2014). https://doi.org/10.2752/175693814X14035303880830

44. Vosinakis, S., Tsakonas, Y.: Visitor experience in Google art project and in second life-based virtual museums: a comparative study. Mediter. Archaeol. Archaeom. **16**(5), 19–27 (2016)

45. Zucconi, F.: Heritage and digital technology: Google Arts and Culture. https://culture360.asef.org/news-events/cartaditalia-special-issue-on-the-2018-european-year-of-cultural-heritage/. Accessed 05 Oct 2023

Author Index

rinted in the United States
Baker & Taylor Publisher Services